Advanced Precalculus

Daniel Kim

Contents

Preface   vii

To the Reader   ix

1 Logic   **1**
    1.1 Logical Operators 1
    1.2 Logical Arguments 8
    1.3 Quantified Statements 12

2 Set Theory   **19**
    2.1 Introduction 19
    2.2 Operations on Sets 21

3 Fields   **29**
    3.1 Field Axioms 29
    3.2 Subtraction, Division 35

4 Sequences and Series   **39**
    4.1 Sequences 39
    4.2 Series 42
    4.3 Limits of Sequences 49
    4.4 Summation and Product Notation 59

5 Mathematical Induction   **65**
    5.1 Standard Applications 65
    5.2 The Binomial Theorem 78

6 Basic Trigonometry — 87

- 6.1 Review . . . 87
- 6.2 The Unit Circle . . . 91
- 6.3 Graphing . . . 105
- 6.4 Inverse Trigonometric Functions . . . 117
- 6.5 More Trigonometric Identities . . . 124
- 6.6 Areas, Law of Sines, Law of Cosines . . . 139

7 Advanced Trigonometry — 149

- 7.1 Polar Coordinates . . . 149
- 7.2 Parametric Equations . . . 158
- 7.3 Complex Numbers . . . 167
  - 7.3.1 Review . . . 167
  - 7.3.2 The Complex Plane . . . 170
  - 7.3.3 Rotation . . . 181

8 Linear Algebra — 189

- 8.1 Vectors . . . 189
- 8.2 Linear Transformations and Matrices . . . 198
- 8.3 3-D Geometry . . . 237

9 Limits — 249

- 9.1 Linear Functions . . . 250
- 9.2 Non-linear Functions . . . 254
- 9.3 Limit Properties . . . 260
- 9.4 Other Limits . . . 267
- 9.5 Trigonometric Limits . . . 272
- 9.6 Advanced Concepts . . . 277
- 9.7 Continuity . . . 282

10 Derivatives — 287

- 10.1 Introduction . . . 287
- 10.2 Implicit Differentiation . . . 306
- 10.3 Related Rates . . . 311
- 10.4 Significance of the Derivative . . . 318
- 10.5 Optimization . . . 332

10.6 L'Hôpital's Rule	335
10.7 Inverses	337
10.8 Parametric and Polar Equations	339
10.9 Review	340

Preface

This textbook was the result of consolidating my typed notes for Advanced Precalculus, a math class instructed by Dr. Michael Abramson and offered at my magnet high school, Bergen County Academies, to a select group of sophomores and freshmen learning an accelerated math curriculum. This class is quite unlike standard math classes in most American high schools because it focuses on developing the students' aptitude in precalculus concepts using a more theoretical and abstract perspective with emphasis on formulating mathematically precise definitions and rigorous proofs. I initially took notes to organize and properly document the material covered in this fast-paced class, but I soon realized that my notes could also be used to assist my classmates in acclimating to this new emphasis on theory rather than straightforward application. As such, I have written this textbook to introduce and guide readers through various topics in a perspective that other precalculus textbooks fail to provide.

A student enrolled in a standard high school curriculum will observe that the majority of math classes today involve the mechanical process of introducing a formula for memorization, followed by a series of exercises that repeat the application of the same formula. Often, each formula is presented with a brief explanation of its origin and an abundance of related problems.

However, this book will incorporate problems using *proof*: the formal, mathematical way of arguing that an assertion, such as the formulas or identities that we take for granted in school, is definitely and irrevocably true. Although studying proofs are often overlooked, they are often the key to understanding how the subject was developed after centuries' worth of contributions. How can we be sure that applying the formula correctly lends itself to the correct answer? Can we guarantee that the formulas and relationships we learn are even valid in the first place? After all, mathematics is all about building on top of previously established concepts and finding (and proving) new, fascinating results. This textbook will highlight the journey of developing these concepts from scratch rather than provide routine drill exercises.

"Advanced Precalculus" reviews traditional precalculus topics such as trigonometry, polar coordinates, complex numbers, sequences and series, vectors, and matrices, and also explores more advanced topics beyond the standard curriculum, such as logic, set theory, fields, induction, and up to the introductory calculus topics of limits and derivatives.

Reflecting the ideology of my math class, this textbook will take the reader on a journey through these topics on a profound level. We will start with basic symbolic logic and set theory to prepare for interpretations of mathematical statements and properly tackle proof questions. A brief segue in fields will demonstrate how even the most trivial results like $0 \cdot x = 0$ must be proved solely with a set list of initial mathematical assumptions. Our discussion on the limit of a sequence will demonstrate that hand-waving statements such as "$\frac{1}{n}$ will be a very small number as n gets larger" are no longer acceptable without proper proof according to established definitions. Mathematical induction is such a distinct and useful method of proving certain statements that another chapter will be dedicated to it. The trigonometry chapters will document the process of going from the basic right-triangle definitions to the careful derivations of various identities and formulas that we often use in regular math classes. This will lend itself to polar coordinates, parametric equations, and complex numbers. Then, an introductory review in linear algebra will reveal how vectors and matrices are applicable in two- and three-dimensional geometry as well as the underlying abstract ideas motivating the formation of matrices in the first place. Lastly, we will exit with a brief introduction to calculus, particularly limits and derivatives, while building on top of basic, precise definitions.

You may wonder, "What is the point of learning proofs?" Training yourself in the art of mathematical proof will develop your everyday critical thinking and writing skills. You will find that writing out formal proofs clears the clutter in your mind and allows you to focus only on the essentials; such skills can facilitate in communicating your ideas, such as in essays, more efficiently. Practicing proofs will also train you to read other documents with precision: every word must be accounted for in proving a theorem. Thus, your reading skills will inevitably develop from learning to pay closer attention to detail. More importantly, proofs will direct you to think more logically and creatively, since formulating a proof requires using previously established ideas to achieve the desired result. In short, learning proofs highly increases your skills at deduction.

Lastly, as I stated before, higher fields of mathematics will primarily involve proof-based problems. Those who are seeking a glimpse of higher mathematics will be delighted to find that this textbook is neatly structured in a "definition-proof-theorem-problem" format, which is straightforward and aids in approaching math sequentially through a dual emphasis on theory and application. My approach is systematic and demonstrates the relationship between establishing a definition and applying that definition to problems. Furthermore, I have written out solutions to problems in great detail without skipping any steps. I hope that this attention to detail assists other students in understanding abstract concepts.

I also recommend this book as a supplement to students who are currently taking precalculus and want to acclimate to an emphasis on theory. Even those who are merely intrigued by the infallibility of math will find this textbook engaging.

I would first like to thank Dr. Abramson for his instruction, which was crucial in helping me understand mathematics on a deeper level and ultimately write this textbook. I also thank my classmates for their positive response to my notes and for encouraging me to expand upon them. They have contributed to answering numerous questions and improving upon many of the explanations supplied in this book.

- Daniel Kim

To the Reader

As you peruse this book, you may find the format slightly unfamiliar. However, do not fret, as the book is meant to introduce the material in a direct and straightforward fashion. First, a **Definition** will introduce a new idea, concept, or vocabulary word, and usually this definition is necessary to proceed with the discussion of the current topic. To maximize your benefit from working through this book, it is strongly encouraged that you attempt any **Example** or **Problem** before looking at the provided solution. Nonetheless, reviewing the solutions will also be rewarding. While an **Example** is meant to demonstrate how to approach a particular kind of problem, the **Problem**s will be largely responsible for reinforcing your grasp on the subject. A **Theorem** is simply a mathematical assertion or statement that can be shown to be irrevocably true using standard mathematical tools. Most of the time, I will introduce a **Theorem** for a major result, and leave other results as **Problem**s. The practice of using these various labels is meant to highlight how learning mathematics is a process of accruing experience in comprehending abstract concepts and solving difficult problems in an accumulative manner.

As a result of the book's tendency to cut to the chase, the content may appear rather dense at times. Do not be afraid to dedicate sufficient time to ponder each newly introduced equation, identity, proof, or solution – perhaps over the course of several hours, days, or weeks if necessary. Building a strong foundation for each topic before proceeding to the next one is imperative; for instance, one should master basic right triangle trigonometry before even beginning complex numbers. For the most part, it is heavily recommended that you go through the book's topics in the given order, as later chapters will assume that you have a firm grasp on the material in earlier chapters.

Keep in mind that this is definitely not an easy book, and you will discover that your mathematical understanding and hopefully, your appreciation of mathematics, will have significantly grown after persevering through these problems.

Chapter 1

Logic

To understand how proofs work, it is essential to understand the underlying mathematical logic involved. In this chapter, we will only provide a relatively brief overview of how logic works. It will also cover mathematical notation that is universally acknowledged, which will then develop your ability to read outside mathematical content.

1.1 Logical Operators

The **Law of Excluded Middle** states that every statement is always either **true** or **false**. We usually use variables p, q, r, etc. to denote such a statement.

Definition 1.1.1. The **negation** of a statement p reverses the original truth value, and is denoted as $\sim p$. This is read as "not p."

For instance, if p was true, then $\sim p$ is false, and vice-versa.

Definition 1.1.2. The **disjunction** of statements p and q is denoted as $p \vee q$, and it is read as "p or q." This new statement is true if *either* or *both* of p or q are true.

In other words, as long as at least one of p or q is true, then $p \vee q$ is true. Otherwise, it is false. As such, it is also known as "inclusive-or."

This relationship can be depicted in a **truth table**, where all possible combinations of truth values for the considered statements are enumerated in an organized table form. For brevity, the values of true and false will respectively be denoted as **T** and **F**.

Here is the truth table for $p \vee q$:

p	q	$p \vee q$
T	T	T
T	F	T
F	T	T
F	F	F

For each pair of truth values for p and q, we read the truth table by horizontal rows. For example, the first row of this table would indicate, "if p is true and q is true, then $p \vee q$ is true."

Review the table and confirm that it matches with your understanding of disjunction.

Since there are two initial statements that we consider (p and q) with two possible truth values for each (true or false), there are $2^2 = 4$ rows in the truth table.

For a truth table demonstrating negation, we only have to consider the initial statement p, there would only be two rows:

p	$\sim p$
T	F
F	T

Definition 1.1.3. The **conjunction** of statements p and q is denoted as $p \wedge q$, and read as "p and q." This new statement is true if *both* of p and q are true.

In other words, if at least one of the statements p and q is false, then $p \wedge q$ will necessarily be false. Here is the truth table representing conjunction:

p	q	$p \wedge q$
T	T	T
T	F	F
F	T	F
F	F	F

Again, convince yourself that this truth table is valid.

Negation, disjunction, and conjunction are the most basic logical operators from which all other aspects of mathematical logic will be based on.

> **Example 1.1.4**
> Construct a truth table for $\sim p \wedge q$.

Solution. When we break down this statement, notice that we will have to evaluate the possible truth values of p, q, $\sim p$, and lastly, $\sim p \wedge q$. The truth table illustrates this process:

p	q	$\sim p$	$\sim p \wedge q$
T	T	F	F
T	F	F	F
F	T	T	T
F	F	T	F

Once we get the truth values for $\sim p$, we perform the conjunction on the $\sim p$ column and the q column to get our result. □

Definition 1.1.5. The operation **exclusive-or**, shortened to "XOR," is denoted as $p \oplus q$. This new statement is true as long as p and q have different truth values.

In short, we would expect the truth table to look like:

p	q	$p \oplus q$
T	T	F
T	F	T
F	T	T
F	F	F

But in fact, it is possible to express $p \oplus q$ in terms of the basic logical operators! We need to find a statement that only uses negation, disjunction, and conjunction operators which fulfills the same purpose as $p \oplus q$.

Definition 1.1.6. Two statements are **logically equivalent** if they have corresponding equal possible truth values. If p and q are two such statements, then their equivalence is represented by $p \equiv q$.

In other words, their columns must be identical in a truth table.

Problem 1.1.7. Prove that $p \oplus q \equiv (p \vee q) \wedge \sim(p \wedge q)$.

Proof. We end up with a large truth table since we have to break up that unwieldly statement.

p	q	$p \vee q$	$p \wedge q$	$\sim(p \wedge q)$	$(p \vee q) \wedge \sim(p \wedge q)$	$p \oplus q$
T	T	T	T	F	F	F
T	F	T	F	T	T	T
F	T	T	F	T	T	T
F	F	F	F	T	F	F

It can then be confirmed that the columns for $(p \vee q) \wedge \sim(p \wedge q)$ and $p \oplus q$ have the same values. Note that they must be the same for each row (i.e. when viewing the two columns top-to-bottom or vice versa, the order of the truth values must match). □

Problem 1.1.8. Prove that $p \wedge (q \vee r) \equiv (p \wedge q) \vee (p \wedge r)$.

Proof. Since we have three initial statements to consider (p, q, and r), our truth table will have

$2^3 = 8$ rows.

p	q	r	$q \vee r$	$p \wedge q$	$p \wedge r$	$p \wedge (q \vee r)$	$(p \wedge q) \vee (p \wedge r)$
T	T	T	T	T	T	T	T
T	T	F	T	T	F	T	T
T	F	T	T	F	T	T	T
T	F	F	F	F	F	F	F
F	T	T	T	F	F	F	F
F	T	F	T	F	F	F	F
F	F	T	T	F	F	F	F
F	F	F	F	F	F	F	F

Note that this equivalence resembles the *distributive property* from algebra. □

Problem 1.1.9. Is this equivalence true or false?

$$(p \wedge q) \vee r \equiv p \wedge (q \vee r)$$

Proof. This equivalence is false. It suffices to supply one counterexample, since a logical equivalence must hold for *all* possible truth value combinations for the initial statements (which would be p, q, and r in this problem).

Consider $p = \mathbf{F}, q = \mathbf{F}$, and $r = \mathbf{T}$. These truth values lead to the following equivalences:

$$(p \wedge q) \vee r \equiv \mathbf{T},$$
$$p \wedge (q \vee r) \equiv \mathbf{F}.$$
□

In fact, there is an abundance of logical equivalences, and the most important laws are listed in the table below.

Logical Equivalences		
Commutative laws	$p \wedge q \equiv q \wedge p$	$p \vee q \equiv q \vee p$
Associative laws	$p \wedge (q \wedge r) \equiv (p \wedge q) \wedge r$	$p \vee (q \vee r) \equiv (p \vee q) \vee r$
Distributive laws	$p \wedge (q \vee r) \equiv (p \wedge q) \vee (p \wedge r)$	$p \vee (q \wedge r) \equiv (p \vee q) \wedge (p \vee r)$
Identity laws	$p \wedge t \equiv p$	$p \vee c \equiv p$
Negation laws	$p \wedge {\sim}p \equiv c$	$p \vee {\sim}p \equiv t$
Double negation law	${\sim}({\sim}p)) \equiv p$	
Idempotent laws	$p \wedge p \equiv p$	$p \vee p \equiv p$
DeMorgan's laws	${\sim}(p \wedge q) \equiv {\sim}p \vee {\sim}q$	${\sim}(p \vee q) \equiv {\sim}p \wedge {\sim}q$
Universal bound laws	$p \vee t \equiv t$	$p \wedge c \equiv c$
Absorption laws	$p \vee (p \wedge q) \equiv p$	$p \wedge (p \vee q) \equiv p$
Dichotomies	${\sim}t \equiv c$	${\sim}c \equiv t$

In this table, we use t and c to denote **tautology** and **contradiction** respectively. These are interchangeable with **T** and **F**.

Exercise 1.1.10. Go through each equivalence listed here and develop a truth table to prove it, until you are familiar with the proof-by-truth-table method.

It is recommended that you familiarize yourself with these rules, as invoking them tremendously simplifies proofs later on.

> **Example 1.1.11**
> Simplify $((q \vee p) \wedge q) \vee (r \wedge ({\sim}r \wedge {\sim}q))$.

Solution. To keep it brief and simple, we will glance over steps using the Commutative laws.

$$\begin{aligned}
((q \vee p) \wedge q) \vee (r \wedge ({\sim}r \wedge {\sim}q)) &\equiv q \vee (r \wedge ({\sim}r \wedge {\sim}q)) & \text{(Absorption)} \\
&\equiv q \vee ((r \wedge {\sim}r) \wedge {\sim}q) & \text{(Associative)} \\
&\equiv q \vee (c \wedge {\sim}q) & \text{(Negation)} \\
&\equiv (q \vee {\sim}q) \wedge (q \vee c) & \text{(Distributive)} \\
&\equiv t \wedge (q \vee c) & \text{(Negation)} \\
&\equiv t \wedge q & \text{(Identity)} \\
&\equiv q. & \text{(Identity)}
\end{aligned}$$

This method is much easier and less tedious than using a truth table, as long as the laws are invoked correctly. □

Often in life, things happen as a result of other things. In fact, there is a special operation in logic that illustrates this cause-and-effect dynamic.

Definition 1.1.12. The **conditional** of two statements p and q is denoted as $p \to q$. This is pronounced "if p, then q." It could also be read as "p implies q." This new statement is only false when p is true but q is false.

Consider the situation in which p is false. Regardless of what truth value q is, $p \to q$ will automatically be true. In this case, $p \to q$ is **vacuously true**, since the conditional is irrelevant in the first place.

Otherwise, consider p to be true. If q is true, then $p \to q$ will be true, since our "if-then" relationship is satisfied. However, if q is false, then this fails our notion of "if p, then q" so $p \to q$ would be considered false in this case.

These observations can be illustrated in the following truth table.

p	q	$p \to q$
T	T	T
T	F	F
F	T	T
F	F	T

For future reference, whenever we are given a statement of the form $p \to q$ to prove, then we should assume p to be true in our proof, because the statement is meaningless when p is false.

Problem 1.1.13. Is this equivalence true or false?
$$p \to (q \to r) \equiv (p \to q) \to r.$$

Solution. This equivalence is false. Let $p = \mathbf{F}$, $q = \mathbf{F}$, and $r = \mathbf{F}$. Then,
$$p \to (q \to r) \equiv \mathbf{T},$$
$$(p \to q) \to r \equiv \mathbf{F}.$$
$\square$

Problem 1.1.14. Is this equivalence true or false?
$$(p \to r) \land (q \to r) \to ((p \land q) \to r)$$

Solution. This equivalence is true. We can construct a truth table and then analyze the truth values.

p	q	r	$p \to r$	$q \to r$	$p \land q$	$(p \to r) \land (q \to r)$	$(p \land q) \to r$	$(p \to r) \land (q \to r) \to ((p \land q) \to r)$
T	T	T	T	T	T	T	T	T
T	T	F	F	F	T	F	F	T
T	F	T	T	T	F	T	T	T
T	F	F	F	T	F	F	T	T
F	T	T	T	T	F	T	T	T
F	T	F	T	F	F	F	T	T
F	F	T	T	T	F	T	T	T
F	F	F	T	T	F	T	T	T

The last column (which represents the possible truth values of the given equivalence) only has **T** as a value, so the equivalence must overall be true. □

How do we represent the conditional in terms of the basic logical operators? Note that $p \to q$ is guaranteed to be true when p is false, i.e. $\sim p$ is true. The only other case in which $p \to q$ is true is when both p and q are true. Ultimately, we either want $\sim p$ to be true or q to be true. Thus, we would expect that
$$p \to q \equiv \sim p \vee q.$$

Exercise 1.1.15. Use a truth table to demonstrate $p \to q \equiv \sim p \vee q$.

Definition 1.1.16. Given the conditional $p \to q$, there are three variations:

1. The **inverse** is $\sim p \to \sim q$.

2. The **converse** is $q \to p$.

3. The **contrapositive** is $\sim q \to \sim p$.

Are these variations necessarily logically equivalent to $p \to q$? It turns out that the original conditional and its contrapositive are logically equivalent, and so are the converse and inverse.

In some cases, we may find it easier to prove the contrapositive of some theorem statement, rather than prove the given implication.

Given the original conditional, directly assuming that the converse is true is called the **converse error**, and likewise for the inverse it is called the **inverse error**.

Definition 1.1.17. The **biconditional** of statements p and q is denoted as $p \leftrightarrow q$. We read this as "p if and only if q." This is only true when p and q have the same truth value.

Some mathematical texts will abbreviate "if and only if" to simply "iff."

Exercise 1.1.18. Prove that $p \leftrightarrow q \equiv (p \to q) \wedge (q \to p)$.

Notice that $p \leftrightarrow q$ when $p \to q$ and its converse are both true. Usually, for mathematical theorems, when we want to show that both the initial implication and its converse are both true, we use $\leftrightarrow$ to emphasize both directions. When we need to prove such theorems, it is often the case that we prove $p \to q$ and $q \to p$ separately. They are respectively referred to as the 'right direction' and 'left direction.'

Notice that the conditions needed for $p \leftrightarrow q$ to be true are the opposite of those for $p \oplus q$. Indeed, the following equivalence also holds true.

Exercise 1.1.19. Prove that $p \leftrightarrow q \equiv \sim(p \oplus q)$.

Problem 1.1.20. Express the disjunction, conditional, biconditional, and exclusive-or only in terms of conjunction and negation.

Solution. We take previous results and apply DeMorgan's laws when needed.

$$p \vee q \equiv \sim(\sim p \wedge \sim q)$$
$$p \rightarrow q \equiv \sim p \vee q$$
$$\equiv \sim(p \wedge \sim q)$$
$$p \leftrightarrow q \equiv (p \rightarrow q) \wedge (q \rightarrow p)$$
$$\equiv \sim(p \wedge \sim q) \wedge \sim(q \wedge \sim p)$$
$$p \oplus q \equiv \sim(p \leftrightarrow q)$$
$$\equiv \sim(\sim(p \wedge \sim q) \wedge \sim(q \wedge \sim p))$$

□

1.2 Logical Arguments

Again consider the conditional $p \rightarrow q$. Given that p is true and the implication holds, it is clear that q must be true as a result. This reasoning can be organized in an argument form:

$$p \rightarrow q$$
$$p$$
$$\therefore q$$

This form is known as **modus ponens**, and it is the most basic rule of inference in logic. The statements $p \rightarrow q$ and p are called **premises**, while q is the **conclusion**.

Consider another valid argument form,

$$p \rightarrow q$$
$$\sim q$$
$$\therefore \sim p$$

and this is called **modus tollens**. By considering the contrapositive, it should be clear why this is true.

An argument is valid if at any time all the premises are true, then the conclusion is also true.

> **Example 1.2.1**
> Prove that modus pollens is valid.

Proof. Once again, we use the truth table.

		Premises		Conclusion
p	q	$p \rightarrow q$	p	q
T	T	T	T	T
T	F	F	T	F
F	T	T	F	T
F	F	T	F	F

We only consider the row(s) in which all of the premises are true. A row which satisfies this is called a **critical row**. The argument is valid if for each critical row, the conclusion(s) is also true. In this example, we see that the only critical row is the first row, and q is true in that row, so the argument is valid. $\square$

Of course, argument forms can be much more complex, rendering the truth-table method tedious and time-inefficient. Like before, we have a set of tools at our disposal, called the **rules of inference**:

Modus Ponens	Modus Tollens
$p \to q$	$p \to q$
p	$\sim q$
$\therefore q$	$\therefore \sim p$
Disjunctive Syllogism	**Disjunctive Addition**
$p \vee q$	p
$\sim p$	$\therefore p \vee q$
$\therefore q$	
Conjunctive Simplification	**Conjunctive Addition**
$p \wedge q$	p
$\therefore p$	q
	$\therefore p \wedge q$
Hypothetical Syllogism	**Dilemma: Proof by Cases**
$p \to q$	$p \vee q$
$q \to r$	$p \to r$
$\therefore p \to r$	$q \to r$
	$\therefore r$

It can be verified using the truth table that all of these are valid.

Lastly, there is another important argument form called the **rule of contradiction**:

$$\sim p \to \mathbf{F}$$
$$\therefore p$$

This is the essence of the popular "proof by contradiction" — if the negation of a given statement leads to a false conclusion, then the statement has to be true. Proof by contradiction will become a very useful tool for proofs in the future.

Example 1.2.2
Demonstrate the following argument's validity or invalidity.

$$p \vee q \tag{1}$$
$$q \to r \tag{2}$$
$$(p \wedge s) \to t \tag{3}$$
$$\sim r \tag{4}$$
$$\sim q \to (u \wedge s) \tag{5}$$
$$\therefore t$$

Note that the variable t here represents a statement rather than a tautology.

Proof. We will show that this is valid, through a proof with multiple steps.

Step 1:

$$q \to r \qquad \text{(by 2)}$$
$$\sim r \qquad \text{(by 4)}$$
$$\therefore \sim q \qquad \text{(modus tollens)}$$

Step 2:

$$p \vee q \qquad \text{(by 1)}$$
$$\sim q \qquad \text{(by step 1)}$$
$$\therefore p \qquad \text{(disjunctive syllogism)}$$

Step 3:

$$\sim q \to (u \wedge s) \qquad \text{(by 5)}$$
$$\sim q \qquad \text{(by step 1)}$$
$$\therefore u \wedge s \qquad \text{(modus ponens)}$$

Step 4:

$$u \wedge s \qquad \text{(by step 3)}$$

$$\therefore s \qquad \text{(conjunctive simplification)}$$

Step 5:
$$p \qquad \text{(by step 2)}$$
$$s \qquad \text{(by step 4)}$$
$$\therefore p \wedge s \qquad \text{(conjunctive addition)}$$

Step 6:
$$(p \wedge s) \to t \qquad \text{(by 3)}$$
$$p \wedge s \qquad \text{(by step 5)}$$
$$\therefore t \qquad \text{(modus ponens)}$$

$\square$

Problem 1.2.3. Prove that this argument is valid.
$$p \to q \wedge r \qquad (1)$$
$$\sim q \qquad (2)$$
$$\therefore \sim p$$

Proof. You may use a truth table and examine the truth values of the critical rows, but rules of inference are still applicable:

Step 1:
$$\sim q \qquad \text{(by 2)}$$
$$\therefore \sim q \vee \sim r \qquad \text{(disjunctive addition)}$$

Step 2:
$$\sim q \vee \sim r \qquad \text{(by step 1)}$$
$$\therefore \sim(q \wedge r) \qquad \text{(DeMorgan's laws)}$$

Step 3:
$$p \to q \wedge r \qquad \text{(by 1)}$$
$$\sim(q \wedge r) \qquad \text{(by step 2)}$$
$$\therefore \sim p \qquad \text{(modus tollens)}$$

$\square$

Alternative Proof. The argument is only valid when if the premises are all true, then the conclusion must be true. Thus, assume that the premises are true.

If $\sim q$ is true, then q must be false. This then implies that $q \wedge r$ is also false, by universal bound laws. By modus tollens, p must be false, i.e. $\sim p$ is true, and we are done. $\square$

1.3 Quantified Statements

A **predicate** is a declaration involving unknown variables, and if values were assigned to these variables, the predicate would become a *statement* with a truth value. For example:

$$P(x): \ x > 3 \quad \leftarrow \text{Predicate}$$
$$P(7): \ 7 > 3 \quad \leftarrow \text{Statement (Truth value: } \mathbf{T})$$

The **domain** is the set of all values that can be assigned to the predicate variables.

Quantifiers serve to specify how many elements are able to be substituted into the predicate and resulting in a true statement. There are two types:

Definition 1.3.1. The **universal quantifier**, denoted by $\forall$, indicates that *all* elements in the domain result in a true statement when substituted into the predicate.

For instance, $\forall x \in D, P(x)$ is read as "for all x in D, $P(x)$ is true." Thus, this **quantified statement** is true precisely when $P(x)$ is true for *every* x in D.

The symbol $\in$ when we have $x \in D$ indicates that x is an element of set D, where a set is a collection of elements (refer to Definition 2.1.1). For example, $1 \in \mathbb{Z}$ is true, but $\pi \in \mathbb{Q}$ is false.

We will go over sets in greater detail in the next chapter.

Definition 1.3.2. The **existential quantifier**, denoted by $\exists$, indicates that there is *some* element in the domain that results in a true statement when substituted into the predicate.

For example, $\exists x \in D, P(x)$ is read as "there exists an x in D such that $P(x)$ is true." Thus, this quantified statement is true precisely when $P(x)$ is true for *some* x in D.

Often, in math, we use quantified statements with respect to sets of numbers. Here is a list of the generally accepted symbols for well-known sets.

$$\mathbb{R} - \text{Real numbers}$$
$$\mathbb{Q} - \text{Rational numbers}$$
$$\mathbb{Z} - \text{Integers}$$
$$\mathbb{W} - \text{Whole numbers}$$
$$\mathbb{N} - \text{Natural numbers}$$
$$\mathbb{C} - \text{Complex numbers}$$
$$\mathbb{H} - \text{Quaternions}$$

In particular, you should be able to distinguish and understand the first five sets. As a note, the natural numbers are defined starting from 1, while the whole numbers are the natural numbers including 0.

Lastly, before proceeding further, it will be assumed that you are familiar with interval notation from previous experience with algebra.

Problem 1.3.3. For each quantified statement, determine if it is true or false.

1. $\forall x \in \mathbb{R}, x^2 \geq 0$

2. $\exists x \in \mathbb{Z}, x^2 < 1$

3. $\forall x \in \mathbb{R}, x \in \mathbb{Q}$

4. $\forall x \in \mathbb{Z}, x \in \mathbb{Q} \to x \in \mathbb{R}$

Solution. The quantifier can change the whole meaning of the statement, so be sure not to get confused.

1. **True.** This is the statement of the *Trivial Inequality*.

2. **True.** There is an existential quantifier, so the statement will be true provided that we can give at least one example: note that $x = 0$ satisfies $x^2 < 1$.

3. **False.** Analogously, for a universal quantifier, we can provide at least one counterexample to disprove the statement: note that $x = \pi$ is a real but not rational number.

4. **True.** All integers are rational numbers, and all rational numbers are real numbers. $\square$

Problem 1.3.4. For each quantified statement, determine if it is true or false.

1. $\forall n \in \mathbb{Z}, 2 \mid n \to 4 \mid n$

2. $\forall n \in \mathbb{Z}, 4 \mid n \to 2 \mid n$

3. $\exists n \in \mathbb{Z}, 2 \mid n \to 4 \mid n$

4. $\forall x \in \mathbb{R}, x^2 > 0$

5. $\exists x \in \mathbb{R}, x^3 - x^2 + 4972x - 11.62\pi = 0$

6. $\exists x \in (0, 2\pi), \sec x = 29$

Note: the notation "$a \mid b$" indicates that a divides b, i.e. a is a factor of b.

Solution. You may not have encountered some of the math used here, and that is alright. We will eventually examine some of these closely in later chapters.

1. **False.** Counterexample: $n = 6$.

2. **True.** Let $n = 4k$ for some $k \in \mathbb{Z}$. Then $n = 4k \implies n = 2(2k)$, and since $2k \in \mathbb{Z}$, we must have $2 \mid n$.

3. **True.** Example: $n = 8$.

4. **False.** Counterexample: $x = 0$.

5. **True.** By the Intermediate Value Theorem, all cubics have at least one real root.

6. **True.** The range of $\sec x$ is $(-\infty, -1] \cup [1, +\infty)$, which contains 29. Therefore there must be some x which yields this number. $\square$

Problem 1.3.5. Let $L(x,y)$ denote "x likes y." For each of the following statements with double quantifiers,

$$\forall x \, \forall y \, L(x,y),$$
$$\forall x \, \exists y \, L(x,y),$$
$$\exists x \, \forall y \, L(x,y),$$
$$\exists x \, \exists y \, L(x,y),$$
$$\exists x \, \forall y \, L(y,x),$$

find a brief sentence in words that is equivalent to each statement.

Solution. This problem is meant to develop your understanding of universal and existential quantifiers, as well as their relations to each other in a symbolic statement. Notice how switching the order or quantifier can drastically change the meaning of the sentence.

$$\forall x \, \forall y \, L(x,y) \longleftrightarrow \text{Everybody likes everyone.}$$
$$\forall x \, \exists y \, L(x,y) \longleftrightarrow \text{Everybody likes someone.}$$
$$\exists x \, \forall y \, L(x,y) \longleftrightarrow \text{Somebody likes everyone.}$$
$$\exists x \, \exists y \, L(x,y) \longleftrightarrow \text{Somebody likes someone.}$$
$$\exists x \, \forall y \, L(y,x) \longleftrightarrow \text{There's someone whom everybody likes.}$$

To clarify some ambiguity, the statement "everyone likes someone" suggests that each person likes somebody else, but the person who is liked can vary depending on the person who is liking. However, the statement "there's someone whom everybody likes" suggests that everybody likes one particular, common person. □

How would we negate a quantified statement? First, let's consider one with the existential quantifier, $\exists x \in D, \, P(x)$.

There just has to be at least one value of x, when substituted into the predicate, that yields a true statement. Therefore, we can rewrite it as a series of predicates all connected by disjunctions:

$$\exists x \in D, P(x) \equiv P(x_1) \lor P(x_2) \lor P(x_3) \lor \ldots \lor P(x_{n-1}) \lor P(x_n),$$

where $D = \{x_1, x_2, x_3, \ldots, x_n\}$, since a statement with a disjunction only needs at least one of the $P(x_{i \in D})$ to be true.

We wish to find the negation of this. In fact, DeMorgan's laws can be generalized for a series of disjunctions, such that

$$\sim(P(x_1) \lor P(x_2) \lor P(x_3) \lor \ldots P(x_{n-1}) \lor P(x_n)) \equiv$$
$$\sim P(x_1) \land \sim P(x_2) \land \sim P(x_3) \land \ldots \sim P(x_{n-1}) \land \sim P(x_n).$$

But if we have a series of $P(x_{i \in D})$ joined together by conjunctions, then this suggests that the universal quantifier should be applied. It follows that

$$\therefore \sim P(x_1) \land \sim P(x_2) \land \sim P(x_3) \land \ldots \land \sim P(x_{n-1}) \land \sim P(x_n) \equiv \forall x \in D, \sim P(x).$$

Thus, $\sim(\exists x \in D, \, P(x)) \equiv \forall x \in D, \, \sim P(x)$.

Exercise 1.3.6. Use the same reasoning as above to show that $\sim (\forall x \in D, \ P(x)) \equiv \exists x \in D, \ \sim P(x)$.

Problem 1.3.7. Negate the statement: $\exists n \in \mathbb{Z}, \ 2 \mid n \to 4 \mid n$.

Solution. We simply switch the $\exists$ symbol to a $\forall$ symbol, and then negate the remainder of the statement, which is $2 \mid n \to 4 \mid n$. Recall that $p \to q \equiv \sim p \vee q$, so $\sim(2 \mid n \to 4 \mid n) \equiv \sim(2 \nmid n \vee 4 \mid n) \equiv 2 \mid n \wedge 4 \nmid n$ by DeMorgan's law. Thus, we conclude

$$\forall n \in \mathbb{Z}, 2 \mid n \wedge 4 \nmid n. \qquad \square$$

Problem 1.3.8. Negate:

$$\forall \varepsilon > 0 \ \exists \delta > 0 \ \forall x, \ 0 < |x - a| < \delta \to |f(x) - L| < \varepsilon$$

Note: this is the epsilon-delta definition of the limit, and we will go over this extensively in a later chapter.

Solution. This statement has a lot of quantifiers strung together, but we can dissect each part one by one:

$$\sim(\forall \varepsilon > 0 \ \exists \delta > 0 \ \forall x, \ 0 < |x - a| < \delta \to |f(x) - L| < \varepsilon)$$
$$\equiv \exists \varepsilon > 0 \ \sim(\exists \delta > 0 \ \forall x, \ 0 < |x - a| < \delta \to |f(x) - L| < \varepsilon)$$
$$\equiv \exists \varepsilon > 0 \ \forall \delta > 0 \ \sim(\forall x, \ 0 < |x - a| < \delta \to |f(x) - L| < \varepsilon)$$
$$\equiv \exists \varepsilon > 0 \ \forall \delta > 0 \ \exists x, \ \sim(0 < |x - a| < \delta \to |f(x) - L| < \varepsilon)$$
$$\equiv \exists \varepsilon > 0 \ \forall \delta > 0 \ \exists x, \ \sim(\sim(0 < |x - a| < \delta) \vee |f(x) - L| < \varepsilon)$$
$$\equiv \exists \varepsilon > 0 \ \forall \delta > 0 \ \exists x, \ 0 < |x - a| < \delta \wedge |f(x) - L| \geq \varepsilon. \qquad \square$$

Problem 1.3.9. Determine if the following statement is true or false, and explain. Then, find its negation.

$$\forall x \in \mathbb{Q} \ \exists y \in \mathbb{Z}^+, \ xy \in \mathbb{Z}.$$

Solution. The statement is true. By the definition of a rational number, let $x = \dfrac{m}{n}$ such that $m \in \mathbb{Z}, n \in \mathbb{Z}^+$. Let $y = n$ (this choice of y is allowed because the existential quantifier indicates that a certain y can be found based on any given x). Therefore, $xy = \dfrac{m}{n} \cdot n = m$, which has already been established as an integer.

The negation would be $\exists x \in \mathbb{Q} \ \forall y \in \mathbb{Z}^+, \ xy \notin \mathbb{Z}$. $\qquad \square$

Problem 1.3.10. Determine if the following statement is true or false for $\mathbb{U} = \mathbb{R}$ and $\mathbb{U} = \mathbb{Z}$ respectively, and explain. Then, find its negation.

$$\forall x \in \mathbb{U}, \ \forall y \in \mathbb{U}, \ (x > y \to \exists z \in \mathbb{U}, x > z > y).$$

Solution. If $\mathbb{U} = \mathbb{R}$, then the statement is true. To demonstrate this, let $z = \dfrac{x+y}{2}$, i.e. take the average of x and y. Again, as z was defined using an existential quantifier, we should express z in terms of x and y, which represent any real numbers (because of their universal quantifiers). As all are real numbers, $x > \dfrac{x+y}{2} > y$ is clearly satisfied.

If $\mathbb{U} = \mathbb{Z}$, then the statement is false. It suffices to show one counterexample: let $x = 2$, $y = 1$. Then there cannot be any integer z for which $2 > z > 1$.

To find the negation, we dissect the statement similar to before:

$$\sim(\forall x \in \mathbb{U}, \forall y \in \mathbb{U}, (x > y \to \exists z \in \mathbb{U}, x > z > y))$$
$$\equiv \exists x \in \mathbb{U}, \sim(\forall y \in \mathbb{U}, (x > y \to \exists z \in \mathbb{U}, x > z > y))$$
$$\equiv \exists x \in \mathbb{U}, \exists y \in \mathbb{U}, \sim(x > y \to \exists z \in \mathbb{U}, x > z > y)$$
$$\equiv \exists x \in \mathbb{U}, \exists y \in \mathbb{U}, \sim(\sim(x > y) \vee \exists z \in \mathbb{U}, x > z > y)$$
$$\equiv \exists x \in \mathbb{U}, \exists y \in \mathbb{U}, (x > y \wedge \sim(\exists z \in \mathbb{U}, x > z > y))$$
$$\equiv \exists x \in \mathbb{U}, \exists y \in \mathbb{U}, (x > y \wedge \forall z \in \mathbb{U}, \sim(x > z > y)).$$

Remember that $x > z > y$ is actually an "AND" statement: $x > z > y \equiv x > z \wedge z > y$. Therefore its negation would be $x \leq z \vee z \leq y$, so the complete negation would be

$$\exists x \in \mathbb{U}, \exists y \in \mathbb{U}, (x > y \wedge \forall z \in \mathbb{U}, x \leq z \vee z \leq y).$$ □

Problem 1.3.11. Determine for each statement whether it is true or false, and justify.

1. $\forall x \in \mathbb{R}, \exists y \in \mathbb{R}, y^2 = x$

2. $\forall x \in \mathbb{Z}, \exists y \in \mathbb{Q}, xy \in \mathbb{Z}$

3. $\forall x \in \mathbb{Q}, \exists y \in \mathbb{Z}, xy \in \mathbb{Z}$

4. $\exists x \in \mathbb{R}, \exists y \in \mathbb{R}, |x - y| > 7 \wedge x^2 + y^2 = 22$

Solution.

1. **False.** Consider $x < 0$. There is no real number whose square is a negative real number. You could specify a particular negative value of x to be specific in demonstrating the failure.

2. **True.** Some rational numbers are also integers. Then, choose y to be a rational number that is also an integer, such that xy will be an integer. We have freedom in choosing y because of the existential quantifier.

3. **True.** Simply let $y = 0$ for any given rational number x. Clearly $x \cdot 0 = 0 \in \mathbb{Z}$, so we're done.

4. **False.** The condition $|x - y| > 7$ indicates that x and y are more than 7 apart. The minimum value of x^2 is 0, attained when $x = 0$, by the Trivial Inequality. Since y would be more than 7 away from 0, we must have $y^2 > 49$, so $x^2 + y^2 > 49$, which fails $x^2 + y^2 = 22$. Likewise, considering $y = 0$ yields $x^2 > 49$, and we get the same result.

   If we consider any other values of x and y, then the sum $x^2 + y^2$ only increases. Thus, it is impossible to have both $|x - y| > 7$ and $x^2 + y^2 = 22$ for any real numbers x and y. □

Problem 1.3.12. Determine for each statement whether it is true or false, and justify.

1. $\forall x \in \mathbb{Q}, \exists y \in \mathbb{Z}^+, xy \in \mathbb{Z}$

2. $\forall x \in \mathbb{Z}\, \exists y \in \mathbb{Z}\, \forall z \in \mathbb{Z}, x \neq z \longrightarrow |x - y| \leq |x - z|$

3. $\forall x \in \mathbb{R}, \forall y \in \mathbb{R}, \exists z \in \mathbb{R}, xz = y$

Solution.

1. **True.** Let $x = \dfrac{m}{n}$, where $m \in \mathbb{Z}$ and $n \in \mathbb{Z}^+$, and let $y = n$. Then $xy = \dfrac{m}{n} \cdot n = m$, which is in $\mathbb{Z}$, so we're done.

2. **True.** As proof, let $y = x$. Then $|x - y| = 0$. No matter what z is, $|x - z|$ will always be 0 or greater, satisfying the given inequality. Furthermore, $x \neq z$ implies that $x - z \neq 0$. Therefore, $|x - z|$ must be positive. Thus, the implication $x \neq z \longrightarrow |x - y| \leq |x - z|$ is always true when $y = x$.

3. **False.** As a counterexample, let $x = 0$ and $y = 1$. Demonstrate why it fails. $\square$

For a brief interlude, let's see how we can combine quantifiers with argument forms. Consider the following premises:

$$P(1)$$
$$\forall n \in \mathbb{Z}^+, \ P(n) \to P(n+1)$$

What would be the conclusion?

Recall that a statement with a universal quantifier can be rewritten as a series of conjunctions. Given that $\mathbb{Z}^+ = \{1, 2, 3, \ldots\}$, realize that $\forall n \in \mathbb{Z}^+, \ P(n) \to P(n+1)$ implies *infinitely many predicates*:

$$\forall n \in \mathbb{Z}^+, \ P(n) \to P(n+1) \equiv (P(1) \to P(2)) \land (P(2) \to P(3)) \land (P(3) \to P(4)) \land \ldots$$

Given the initial case $P(1)$, we can repeatedly apply *modus ponens*, so the second premise results in *infinitely many conclusions*.

$$\left.\begin{array}{l} P(1) \\ P(1) \to P(2) \end{array}\right\} \left.\begin{array}{l} P(2) \\ \end{array}\right\} \left.\begin{array}{l} P(3) \\ \end{array}\right\} P(4)$$
$$P(2) \to P(3)$$
$$P(3) \to P(4)$$

$$\vdots$$

As shown above: $\forall n \in \mathbb{Z}^+$, statements $P(1), P(2), P(3), P(4), \ldots, P(n)$ are all true. Therefore, the complete argument is expressed as:

$$P(1)$$
$$\forall n \in \mathbb{Z}^+, \ P(n) \to P(n+1)$$
$$\therefore \forall n \in \mathbb{Z}^+, P(n)$$

This argument form is known as **mathematical induction**, with base case $P(1)$ and inductive step $P(n)$. This is a very important technique of proving certain theorems that we will go over closely in a later chapter.

Chapter 2

Set Theory

Every field of mathematics uses or refers to sets in one way or another. As the last chapter may have shown, we need to use sets when dealing with quantified statements. In this chapter, we will review some basic aspects of set theory, building from the background of the last chapter. Not only does it serve as application for previously covered symbolic logic, but it also fulfills the role of a predecessor for future concepts that involve sets.

2.1 Introduction

First we start with a definition that seems general and vague.

Definition 2.1.1. A **set** is a collection of things, called **elements**.

Even then, we should have a basic sense of what sets are. You probably already have encountered sets in your mathematical education so far, including $\mathbb{R}$, $\mathbb{Q}$, $\mathbb{Z}$.

For notation, we will use capital letters to refer to sets and lowercase letters to refer to elements. We state $x \in A$ if x is an element of A.

Definition 2.1.2. The **universal set**, $\mathbb{U}$, is the set that contains all elements.

Definition 2.1.3. The **empty set**, $\emptyset$, is the set that contains no elements.

We now introduce some relations between sets.

Definition 2.1.4. For two sets A and B, A is equal to B when

$$A = B \longleftrightarrow \forall x \in \mathbb{U}, x \in A \leftrightarrow x \in B.$$

Definition 2.1.5. For two sets A and B, A is a **subset** of B when

$$A \subseteq B \longleftrightarrow \forall x \in \mathbb{U}, x \in A \to x \in B.$$

Exercise 2.1.6. Under what condition would $A \nsubseteq B$ (A is not a subset of B)? Hint: negate Definition 2.1.5.

> **Theorem 2.1.7**
> $A = B \longleftrightarrow A \subseteq B \land B \subseteq A.$

Proof. We simply apply standard logical equivalences.

$$A = B \longleftrightarrow \forall x \in \mathbb{U}, x \in A \leftrightarrow x \in B$$
$$A = B \longleftrightarrow \forall x \in \mathbb{U}, (x \in A \to x \in B) \land (x \in B \to x \in A)$$
$$\therefore A = B \longleftrightarrow A \subseteq B \land B \subseteq A \qquad \square$$

> **Theorem 2.1.8**
> $A \subseteq B \land B \subseteq C \longrightarrow A \subseteq C.$

Proof. First, note $A \subseteq B \land B \subseteq C \longrightarrow \forall x \in \mathbb{U}, (x \in A \to x \in B) \land (x \in B \to x \in C)$. We know that both $x \in A \to x \in B$ and $x \in B \to x \in C$ are true by conjunctive simplification, and therefore we must have $x \in A \to x \in C$ by hypothetical syllogism.

As such, we have $A \subseteq B \land B \subseteq C \longrightarrow \forall x \in \mathbb{U}, x \in A \to x \in C$, or $A \subseteq B \land B \subseteq C \longrightarrow A \subseteq C$, and we are done. $\square$

Problem 2.1.9. Prove $A \subseteq \emptyset \longrightarrow A = \emptyset$.

Proof. Consider the definition of $A \subseteq \emptyset$, i.e. $\forall x \in \mathbb{U}, x \in A \to x \in \emptyset$. The empty set contains no elements, so $x \in \emptyset \equiv \mathbf{F}$. Then, we have $\forall x \in \mathbb{U}, x \in A \to \mathbf{F}$. This is a contradiction, and therefore $\forall x \in \mathbb{U}, x \notin A$. But this is just the definition of the empty set, so $A = \emptyset$. $\square$

Definition 2.1.10. Let the set $\overline{A}$ denote the **complement** of set A. Then,

$$x \in \overline{A} \longleftrightarrow x \in \mathbb{U} \land x \notin A.$$

We can alternatively express this as

$$\forall x \in \mathbb{U}, x \in \overline{A} \longleftrightarrow x \notin A \longleftrightarrow \sim(x \in A).$$

Problem 2.1.11. $\overline{\overline{A}} = A$.

Proof. This is a simple application of the double negative law.

$$\forall x \in \mathbb{U}, x \in \overline{\overline{A}} \longleftrightarrow \sim(x \in \overline{A})$$
$$\forall x \in \mathbb{U}, x \in \overline{\overline{A}} \longleftrightarrow \sim(\sim(x \in A))$$
$$\forall x \in \mathbb{U}, x \in \overline{\overline{A}} \longleftrightarrow x \in A$$
$$\therefore \overline{\overline{A}} = A. \qquad \square$$

Problem 2.1.12. $A \subseteq B \longrightarrow \overline{B} \subseteq \overline{A}$.

Proof. This results from the implication being logically equivalent to its contrapositive.

$$A \subseteq B \longrightarrow \forall x \in \mathbb{U}, (x \in A \to x \in B)$$
$$A \subseteq B \longrightarrow \forall x \in \mathbb{U}, (\sim(x \in B) \to \sim(x \in A))$$
$$A \subseteq B \longrightarrow \forall x \in \mathbb{U}, x \in \overline{B} \to x \in \overline{A}$$
$$\therefore A \subseteq B \longrightarrow \overline{B} \subseteq \overline{A}. \qquad \square$$

Problem 2.1.13. Prove $A \subseteq B \longleftrightarrow \overline{B} \subseteq \overline{A}$.

Proof. Problem 2.1.12 gives us the right direction. For the left direction, note that Problem 2.1.12 also tells us that $\overline{B} \subseteq \overline{A} \longrightarrow \overline{\overline{A}} \subseteq \overline{\overline{B}}$. Then by Problem 2.1.11, $\overline{\overline{B}} = B$ and $\overline{\overline{A}} = A$, so thus $\overline{B} \subseteq \overline{A} \longrightarrow A \subseteq B$. It follows that $A \subseteq B \longleftrightarrow \overline{B} \subseteq \overline{A}$. $\qquad \square$

Problem 2.1.14. Prove $\overline{\mathbb{U}} = \emptyset$.

Proof. By our previous results,

$$\forall x \in \mathbb{U}, x \in \overline{\mathbb{U}} \longleftrightarrow x \notin \mathbb{U}$$
$$\longleftrightarrow \sim(x \in \mathbb{U})$$
$$\longleftrightarrow \mathbf{F}$$
$$\longleftrightarrow x \in \emptyset.$$

Thus, $\overline{\mathbb{U}} = \emptyset$. For clarification: x was defined to be an element of $\mathbb{U}$, thus $\sim(x \in \mathbb{U})$ would be **F**. $\qquad \square$

Problem 2.1.15. What is $\overline{\{1, 2, 3\}}$?

Solution. It depends on the universe. Any set that does NOT contain any of $1, 2$, or 3 is an answer.

$\overline{\{1,2,3\}}$	$\mathbb{U}$
$\emptyset$	$\{1,2,3\}$
$\{4,5\}$	$\{1,2,3,4,5\}$
$(-\infty, 1) \cup (1, 2) \cup (2, 3) \cup (3, +\infty)$	$\mathbb{R}$

The last example uses notation that may not be familiar; we will introduce it in detail in the next section. $\qquad \square$

2.2 Operations on Sets

Before we define some common operations on sets, we must first review **set builder notation**. In this fashion, we define the set by specifying the *type of element* and the *conditions* that must be met in order to qualify a thing as an element of the set.

For instance, the set of all real numbers whose squares are less than 7 can be written as:

$$\{x \in \mathbb{Z} \mid x^2 < 7\} = \{-2, -1, 0, 1, 2\}.$$

We can then define two very important operations in this manner:

Definition 2.2.1. The **intersection** of A and B is defined as
$$A \cap B = \{x \in \mathbb{U} \mid x \in A \wedge x \in B\}.$$

Definition 2.2.2. The **union** of A and B is defined as
$$A \cup B = \{x \in \mathbb{U} \mid x \in A \vee x \in B\}.$$

Problem 2.2.3. Given $A = \{1, 2, 3\}$ and $B = \{3, 4, 5\}$, find $A \cap B$ and $A \cup B$.

Solution. Remember that the intersection contains only elements both A and B have in common, while the union contains elements from either A or B.
$$A \cap B = \{3\}.$$
$$A \cup B = \{1, 2, 3, 4, 5\}. \qquad \square$$

Consider the following diagram. This gives a visual representation of the intersection and union of two sets.

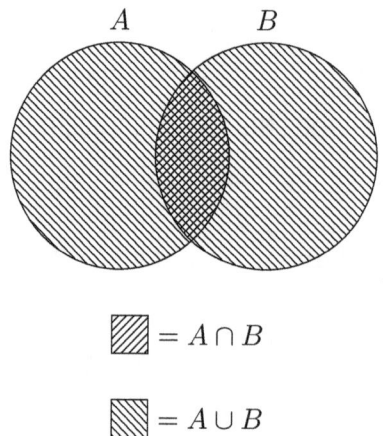

From this, we can quickly deduce two seemingly obvious results:

Problem 2.2.4. Prove $A \subseteq A \cup B$.

Proof. First, note that $A \cap B \longleftrightarrow \forall x \in \mathbb{U}, x \in A \cap B$. But $x \in A \cap B \longleftrightarrow x \in A \wedge x \in B$. By conjunctive simplification, we conclude $x \in A$. Thus, $\forall x \in \mathbb{U}, x \in A \cap B \to x \in A$, which yields $A \cap B \subseteq A$, as desired. $\qquad \square$

Problem 2.2.5. Prove $A \cap B \subseteq A$.

Proof. Given that for a given element $x \in \mathbb{U}$, if we assume that $x \in A$, then by disjunctive addition, $x \in A \vee x \in B$. But this implies that $x \in A \cup B$. Thus, $\forall x \in \mathbb{U}, x \in A \longrightarrow x \in A \vee x \in B$, which gives us $A \subseteq A \cup B$. $\qquad \square$

Exercise 2.2.6. Prove $A \cap B = B \longrightarrow B \subseteq A$.

> **Theorem 2.2.7** (DeMorgan's Laws on Sets)
> For given sets A and B, $\overline{A \cup B} = \overline{A} \cap \overline{B}$ and $\overline{A \cap B} = \overline{A} \cup \overline{B}$.

Proof. The proofs involve direct application of DeMorgan's laws. I encourage you to go through and justify each step of the process.

$$\forall x \in \mathbb{U}, x \in \overline{A \cup B} \longleftrightarrow \sim(x \in A \cup B)$$
$$\forall x \in \mathbb{U}, x \in \overline{A \cup B} \longleftrightarrow \sim(x \in A \vee x \in B)$$
$$\forall x \in \mathbb{U}, x \in \overline{A \cup B} \longleftrightarrow \sim(x \in A) \wedge \sim(x \in B)$$
$$\forall x \in \mathbb{U}, x \in \overline{A \cup B} \longleftrightarrow x \in \overline{A} \wedge x \in \overline{B}$$
$$\forall x \in \mathbb{U}, x \in \overline{A \cup B} \longleftrightarrow x \in \overline{A} \cap \overline{B}$$
$$\therefore \overline{A \cup B} = \overline{A} \cap \overline{B}.$$

The proof for the second result is very similar.

$$\forall x \in \mathbb{U}, x \in \overline{A \cap B} \longleftrightarrow \sim(x \in A \cap B)$$
$$\forall x \in \mathbb{U}, x \in \overline{A \cap B} \longleftrightarrow \sim(x \in A \wedge x \in B)$$
$$\forall x \in \mathbb{U}, x \in \overline{A \cap B} \longleftrightarrow \sim(x \in A) \vee \sim(x \in B)$$
$$\forall x \in \mathbb{U}, x \in \overline{A \cap B} \longleftrightarrow x \in \overline{A} \vee x \in \overline{B}$$
$$\forall x \in \mathbb{U}, x \in \overline{A \cap B} \longleftrightarrow x \in \overline{A} \cup \overline{B}$$
$$\therefore \overline{A \cap B} = \overline{A} \cup \overline{B}. \qquad \square$$

> **Theorem 2.2.8** (Associative Laws on Sets)
> For given sets A and B, $A \cup (B \cup C) = (A \cup B) \cup C$ and $A \cap (B \cap C) = (A \cap B) \cap C$.

Exercise 2.2.9. By directly applying the associative law of logic, prove Theorem 2.2.8.

> **Theorem 2.2.10** (Distributive Laws on Sets)
> For given sets A and B, $A \cup (B \cap C) = (A \cup B) \cap (A \cup C)$ and $A \cap (B \cup C) = (A \cap B) \cup (A \cap C)$.

Exercise 2.2.11. In the same style as the previous theorems, prove Theorem 2.2.10.

> **Example 2.2.12**
> Prove $A \cap B = A \cap C \wedge A \cup B = A \cup C \longrightarrow B = C$.

Proof. By Theorem 2.1.7, it suffices to prove $B \subseteq C$ and $C \subseteq B$. First, we will prove $B \subseteq C$.

To do so, we want to prove that $x \in B \to x \in C$. Assuming $x \in B$, we consider two cases: $x \in A$ or $x \notin A$.

1. If $x \in A$, then by conjunctive addition, $x \in A \wedge x \in B$, or $x \in A \cap B$. However, we are given that $A \cap B = A \cap C$, thus $x \in A \cap C$. But this reduces to $x \in A \wedge x \in C$, from which we invoke conjunctive simplification to conclude $x \in C$, which is what we wanted.

2. If $x \notin A$, then by disjunctive addition, $x \in B \vee x \in A$ (since we have assumed $x \in B$ to be true), or $x \in A \cup B$. We are given that $A \cup B = A \cup C$, so $x \in A \cup C$, from which we get $x \in A \vee x \in C$. However, we know that $x \notin A$, so by disjunctive syllogism, $x \in C$, the same result as the previous case.

Thus, whether $x \in A$ or $x \notin A$, we can conclude that $x \in B \to x \in C$.

The proof of $x \in C \to x \in B$ is very similar, and will be left to the reader. $\square$

Exercise 2.2.13. Finish the proof of Example 2.2.12.

We can alternatively prove Example 2.2.12 using a more logic-based argument.

Alternative Proof. Note that the theorem's statement can be broken down into:

$$((x \in A \vee x \in B) \leftrightarrow (x \in A \vee x \in C)) \wedge ((x \in A \wedge x \in B) \leftrightarrow (x \in A \wedge x \in C)) \longrightarrow x \in B \leftrightarrow x \in C.$$

Let p, q, r denote the statements $x \in A$, $x \in B$, $x \in C$ respectively. Therefore, the logical statement above can be translated into this argument form:

$$p \wedge q \longleftrightarrow p \wedge r$$
$$p \vee q \longleftrightarrow p \vee r$$
$$\therefore q \longleftrightarrow r$$

It is sufficient to prove that this argument form is valid, i.e. *if* the premises are true, then the conclusion must also be true. We can either use a truth table or casework to do so.

Since the truth table method can be time-consuming and tedious, I will proceed by casework on p in particular.

If p is true, then we have

$$\mathbf{T} \wedge q \longleftrightarrow \mathbf{T} \wedge r,$$
$$\mathbf{T} \vee q \longleftrightarrow \mathbf{T} \vee r.$$

By the Negation laws, this simplifies to

$$q \longleftrightarrow r,$$
$$\mathbf{T} \longleftrightarrow \mathbf{T}.$$

Clearly, $\mathbf{T} \longleftrightarrow \mathbf{T}$ is always true, so we can ignore this part. Remember that we want to show that if the premises are true, then the conclusion must also be true. Indeed, if $q \longleftrightarrow r$ is true, then the conclusion must obviously be true since it happens to be the same statement as this premise.

If p is false, then we have

$$\mathbf{F} \wedge q \longleftrightarrow \mathbf{F} \wedge r,$$

$$\mathbf{F} \vee q \longleftrightarrow \mathbf{F} \vee r.$$

By the Identity laws, this simplifies to

$$\mathbf{F} \longleftrightarrow \mathbf{F},$$
$$q \longleftrightarrow r.$$

Obviously $\mathbf{F} \longleftrightarrow \mathbf{F}$ is always true. With the same reasoning as above, if the premise $q \longleftrightarrow r$ is true, then the conclusion is true since it is the same statement.

We have shown that this argument form is valid, thus the theorem itself must be true. $\square$

We now introduce a new class of problems that requires some intuition with sets.

Problem 2.2.14. Prove or disprove the following statements.

1. $A \cap B = A \cap C \longrightarrow B = C$.

2. $A \subseteq B \cup C \longrightarrow A \subseteq B \vee A \subseteq C$.

3. $A \cap (B \cup C) = (A \cap B) \cup C$.

Solution. It is helpful to use Venn Diagrams as a visual aid when thinking about these statements. Then consider counterexamples to disprove them. However, Venn Diagrams are not rigorous enough to prove a true statement. Additionally, when disproving a statement, do not forget to demonstrate how your counterexample actually fails it.

1. **False.** Consider the counterexample: Let $A = \{1, 2\}, B = \{2, 4\}, C = \{2, 3\}$. To demonstrate its failure, we note that $A \cap B = \{2\}$ and $A \cap C = \{2\}$, so the condition that $A \cap B = A \cap C$ is satisfied. However, $B \neq C$, failing the statement.

2. **True.** Here is the proof:

$$A \subseteq B \cup C \longrightarrow \forall x \in \mathbb{U}, x \in A \to x \in B \cup C$$
$$A \subseteq B \cup C \longrightarrow \forall x \in \mathbb{U}, x \in A \to (x \in B \vee x \in C)$$
$$A \subseteq B \cup C \longrightarrow \forall x \in \mathbb{U}, \sim(x \in A) \vee (x \in B \vee x \in C)$$
$$A \subseteq B \cup C \longrightarrow \forall x \in \mathbb{U}, \sim(x \in A) \vee \sim(x \in A) \vee x \in B \vee x \in C$$
$$A \subseteq B \cup C \longrightarrow \forall x \in \mathbb{U}, (\sim(x \in A) \vee x \in B) \vee (\sim(x \in A) \vee x \in C)$$
$$A \subseteq B \cup C \longrightarrow \forall x \in \mathbb{U}, (x \in A \to x \in B) \vee (x \in A \to x \in C)$$
$$\therefore A \subseteq B \cup C \longrightarrow A \subseteq B \vee A \subseteq C.$$

3. **False.** Consider $A = \emptyset, B = \emptyset, C = \{1\}$. Then $A \cap (B \cup C) = \emptyset$, while $(A \cap B) \cup C = \{1\}$. $\square$

Definition 2.2.15. The set that contains all elements in A but not in B is denoted as $A - B$. This is logically represented as

$$A - B = A \cap \overline{B}.$$

For example, $\{1, 2, 3\} - \{1, 2, 4\} = \{3\}$, $\emptyset - A = \emptyset$, and $A - \emptyset = A$.

Problem 2.2.16. Prove or disprove the following statements.

1. $(A - B) \cup (B - C) = (A - C)$.
2. $(A - C) \cup (B - C) = (A \cup B) - C$.
3. $\overline{(A - C)} = C - A$.
4. $(A - B) - C = (A - C) - B$.
5. $A \subseteq C \wedge B \subseteq C \longleftrightarrow (A \cup B) \subseteq C$.
6. $A \subseteq C \longleftrightarrow A - C = \emptyset$.
7. $A \subseteq B \longrightarrow A \cap \overline{(B \cap C)} = \emptyset$.

Solution. Note: we will leave it to the reader to demonstrate how the counterexamples fail their statements.

1. **False.** Counterexample: Let $A = \emptyset, B = \{1\}, C = \emptyset$. Convince yourself why this fails.

2. **True.** *Proof.*
$$(A - C) \cup (B - C) \longleftrightarrow (A \cap \overline{C}) \cup (B \cap \overline{C})$$
$$(A - C) \cup (B - C) \longleftrightarrow \forall x \in \mathbb{U}, (x \in A \wedge x \notin C) \vee (x \in B \wedge x \notin C)$$
$$(A - C) \cup (B - C) \longleftrightarrow \forall x \in \mathbb{U}, x \notin C \wedge (x \in A \vee x \in B)$$
$$\therefore (A - C) \cup (B - C) \longleftrightarrow (A \cup B) - C.$$

3. **False.** Counterexample: Let $A = \{1\}, C = \{1, 2\}$.

4. **True.** *Proof.*
$$(A - B) - C = (A \cap \overline{B}) \cap \overline{C}$$
$$(A - B) - C = \overline{C} \cap (A \cap \overline{B})$$
$$(A - B) - C = (\overline{C} \cap A) \cap \overline{B}$$
$$(A - B) - C = (A \cap \overline{C}) \cap \overline{B}$$
$$\therefore (A - B) - C = (A - C) - B.$$

5. **True.** *Proof.*
$$A \subseteq C \wedge B \subseteq C \longleftrightarrow \forall x \in \mathbb{U}, (x \in A \to x \in C) \wedge (x \in B \to x \in C)$$
$$A \subseteq C \wedge B \subseteq C \longleftrightarrow \forall x \in \mathbb{U}, (x \notin A \vee x \in C) \wedge (x \notin B \vee x \in C)$$
$$A \subseteq C \wedge B \subseteq C \longleftrightarrow \forall x \in \mathbb{U}, (x \in C \vee x \notin A) \wedge (x \in C \vee x \notin B)$$
$$A \subseteq C \wedge B \subseteq C \longleftrightarrow \forall x \in \mathbb{U}, x \in C \vee (x \notin A \wedge x \notin B)$$
$$A \subseteq C \wedge B \subseteq C \longleftrightarrow \forall x \in \mathbb{U}, (x \notin A \wedge x \notin B) \vee x \in C$$
$$A \subseteq C \wedge B \subseteq C \longleftrightarrow \forall x \in \mathbb{U}, \sim(x \in A \vee x \in B) \vee x \in C$$
$$A \subseteq C \wedge B \subseteq C \longleftrightarrow \forall x \in \mathbb{U}, (x \in A \vee x \in B) \to x \in C$$
$$\therefore A \subseteq C \wedge B \subseteq C \longleftrightarrow (A \cup B) \subseteq C.$$

6. **True.** We proceed by proving both directions.

   (a) First, we must prove $A \subseteq C \longrightarrow A - C = \emptyset$.

   Suppose $A \subseteq C$ is true. Therefore, $\forall x \in \mathbb{U}, x \in A \longrightarrow x \in C$, rewritten as $\forall x \in \mathbb{U}, x \notin A \lor x \in C$, is true.

   We must prove: $A - C = \emptyset$, which is $x \in A \land x \notin C \leftrightarrow x \in \emptyset$. However, $x \in A \land x \notin C$ is the negation of $x \notin A \lor x \in C$ (by DeMorgan's Laws), which is true. Therefore, $x \in A \land x \notin C$ is false.

   Furthermore, by definition of an empty set, $x \in \emptyset$ is false.

   Because both sides of the biconditional are false, the biconditional $x \in A \land x \notin C \longleftrightarrow x \in \emptyset$ itself is true. Thus, $A - C = \emptyset$ is true when $A \subseteq C$ is true.

   Therefore, $A \subseteq C \longrightarrow A - C = \emptyset$.

   (b) Now we prove $A - C = \emptyset \longrightarrow A \subseteq C$.

   Suppose $A - C = \emptyset$ is true. Then $\forall x \in \mathbb{U}, x \in A \land x \notin C \longleftrightarrow x \in \emptyset$ is true.

   By definition of an empty set, $x \in \emptyset$ is false.

   A biconditional is true when both sides have the same truth value. Therefore, $x \in A \land x \notin C$ is false.

   Thus, the negation of $x \in A \land x \notin C$, which is $x \notin A \lor x \in C$ (by DeMorgan's Laws) is true.

   Therefore, $x \in A \longrightarrow x \in C$ is true, so $A \subseteq C$ is true.

   Hence, $A - C = \emptyset \longrightarrow A \subseteq C$.

We can now conclude the proof.

7. **False.** Let $A = \{1\}, B = \{1, 2\}$, and $C = \emptyset$. $\square$

To solidify your understanding of sets, here is an assortment of problems.

Exercise 2.2.17. Prove or disprove $(A - B) \cup (A \cap B) = A$.

Exercise 2.2.18. Prove or disprove $A - (B - C) = (A - B) - C$.

Exercise 2.2.19. Prove or disprove $(A - B) \cap (C - B) = (A \cap C) - B$.

Exercise 2.2.20. Prove or disprove $(A - B) \cap (C - B) = A - (B \cup C)$.

Exercise 2.2.21. Prove or disprove $A \subseteq B \longrightarrow A \cap C \subseteq B \cap C$.

Exercise 2.2.22. Prove or disprove $A \cup C = B \cup C \longrightarrow A = B$.

Exercise 2.2.23. Prove or disprove $A \cap C \subseteq B \cap C \land A \cup C \subseteq B \cup C \longrightarrow A = B$.

Exercise 2.2.24. Prove or disprove $(A \cup B) \cap C = A \cup (B \cap C)$.

Exercise 2.2.25. Prove or disprove $A \nsubseteq B \land B \nsubseteq C \longrightarrow A \nsubseteq C$.

Exercise 2.2.26. Prove or disprove $A \subseteq B \land B \nsubseteq C \longrightarrow A \nsubseteq C$.

Exercise 2.2.27. Prove or disprove $A \cap (B - C) = (A \cap B) - (A \cap C)$.

Exercise 2.2.28. Prove or disprove $B \cap C \subseteq A \longrightarrow (A - B) \cap (A - C) = \emptyset$.

Exercise 2.2.29. Prove or disprove $\overline{(A \cup B)} = \overline{A} \cup \overline{B}$.

Exercise 2.2.30. Prove or disprove $A \cap C \subseteq B \cap C \wedge A \cup C \subseteq B \cup C \longrightarrow A \subseteq B$.

Exercise 2.2.31. Prove or disprove $A \subseteq B \cup C \longleftrightarrow A \subseteq B$.

Exercise 2.2.32. Prove or disprove $A \subseteq C \wedge B \subseteq C \longrightarrow A \cap B \subseteq C$.

Exercise 2.2.33. Prove or disprove $A \cap \overline{A} = \emptyset$.

Definition 2.2.34. We denote the **symmetric difference** of sets A and B as $A \star B$. It is symbolically defined as
$$A \star B = (A - B) \cup (B - A).$$

Theorem 2.2.35

$(A \star B) \star C = A \star (B \star C)$.

Proof. First, draw a Venn Diagram to get a sense of this expression. Realize that $A \star B$ is the exclusive-or (XOR) of sets A and B. Then,

$$A \star B \longleftrightarrow \forall x \in \mathbb{U}, x \in A \star B$$
$$A \star B \longleftrightarrow \forall x \in \mathbb{U}, (x \in A \wedge \sim(x \in B)) \vee (x \in B \wedge \sim(x \in A))$$
$$A \star B \longleftrightarrow \forall x \in \mathbb{U}, x \in A \oplus x \in B.$$

Using a truth table, we can show that for any given statements p, q, and r, $(p \oplus q) \oplus r \equiv p \oplus (q \oplus r)$, or in other words, demonstrate that the XOR operation is associative.

p	q	r	$p \oplus q$	$q \oplus r$	$(p \oplus q) \oplus r$	$p \oplus (q \oplus r)$
T	T	T	F	F	T	T
T	T	F	F	T	F	F
T	F	T	T	T	F	F
T	F	F	T	F	T	T
F	T	T	T	F	F	F
F	T	F	T	T	T	T
F	F	T	F	T	T	T
F	F	F	F	F	F	F

The resulting truth values prove their logical equivalence. Therefore, we can conclude:

$$\forall x \in \mathbb{U}, (x \in A \oplus x \in B) \oplus x \in C \longleftrightarrow x \in A \oplus (x \in B \oplus x \in C)$$
$$\forall x \in \mathbb{U}, x \in (A \star B) \star C \longleftrightarrow x \in A \star (B \star C)$$
$$\therefore (A \star B) \star C = A \star (B \star C). \qquad \square$$

Chapter 3

Fields

By middle school, we take many things in mathematics for granted, especially addition, subtraction, multiplication, and division. But where do all of these come from? In this chapter, we discuss why we can use such operations, and establish the foundations from scratch. Hopefully, after finishing this chapter, you should have newfound gratitude for some of the seemingly trivial algebraic manipulations and techniques that we apply subconciously in math problems.

3.1 Field Axioms

An **axiom** is a statement that we assume to be true, from which we develop further mathematical results and consequences. In other words, it is a starting point. Here, we provide a list of field axioms:

Definition 3.1.1. A **field** is a set F with two operations, typically called $+$ and $\times$, satisfying:

a) **Closure**: $\forall a, b \in F, a + b \in F$ and $a \times b \in F$.

b) **Commutative**: $\forall a, b \in F, a + b = b + a$ and $ab = ba$.

c) **Associative**: $\forall a, b, c \in F, a + (b + c) = (a + b) + c$ and $a(bc) = (ab)c$.

d) **Distributive**: $\forall a, b, c \in F, a(b + c) = ab + ac$.

e) **Identities**: $\exists 0, 1 \in F, (0 \neq 1)$ s.t. $\forall a \in F, a + 0 = 0 + a = a$ and $a \cdot 1 = 1 \cdot a = a$.

f) **Inverses**: $\forall a \in F, \exists -a \in F$ s.t. $a + -a = 0$.
$\forall a \in F, a \neq 0, \exists a^{-1} \in F$ s.t. $a(a^{-1}) = 1$.

So first, we start off with addition and multiplication. Notice that subtraction and division can also arise from these properties, and we will get to those operations later.

Some examples of fields would be the sets $\mathbb{Q}, \mathbb{R}, \mathbb{C}$ - take a moment to convince yourself that these properties hold for these sets.

In addition, the set $\mathbb{Z}_p$ (all integers mod p, where p is prime) is a field; it is a well known result in number theory that all integers modulo p do have a multiplicative inverse. However, the set of integers, $\mathbb{Z}$, is not a field because not every integer has an multiplicative inverse that is also an integer.

Remark 3.1.2. When we say "n mod m" or "n modulo m," we are referring to the remainder when n is divided by m. For example, 8 mod 5 is 3, and we write $8 \equiv 3 \pmod{5}$ as shorter notation. Other examples include $33 \equiv 3 \pmod{10}$, $89 \equiv 5 \pmod{7}$, etc. Furthermore, $\mathbb{Z}_n$ refers to the set of integers mod n. For instance, $\mathbb{Z}_3 = \{0, 1, 2\}$.

Considering numbers modulo some other number is part of an entire topic of mathematics called *modular arithmetic*, and this is part of number theory. You are welcome to search for any outside resources pertaining to this topic.

Problem 3.1.3. Do the integers mod 8 form a field? What about the integers mod 27?

Solution. In order for a set of numbers to be a field, all of the properties listed above must be satisfied. Now for $\mathbb{Z}_8$, consider if 4 (which is in this set) has a multiplicative inverse (let this be x). Then we want
$$4x \equiv 1 \pmod{8},$$
and this can be rewritten as $4x = 8k + 1$, where $k \in \mathbb{Z}$. Rearrange this to $4x - 8k = 1$, and clearly the left hand side is even while the right hand side is odd. Thus, there is no x which satisfies this, so 4 does not have a multiplicative inverse. Therefore, $\mathbb{Z}_8$ cannot be a field.

Likewise, for $\mathbb{Z}_{27}$, consider the multiplicative inverse of 3.
$$3x \equiv 1 \pmod{27}.$$

Then we have $3x = 27k + 1$ for $k \in \mathbb{Z}$. Note that the left hand side is divisible by 3, while the right hand side will leave a remainder of 1 when divided by 3, so we cannot find such an x. Thus, 3 does not have a multiplicative inverse, so $\mathbb{Z}_{27}$ is not a field. $\square$

The following proofs of results will seem tedious, but necessary as we are building everything from scratch, using just the field axioms listed above. Be careful not to skip steps, as we cannot assume to apply the usual algebraic techniques we have learned. Make sure you know what property was invoked for each step of a proof.

Theorem 3.1.4 (Cancellation Laws)
For $a, b, c \in F$,

1. $a + b = a + c \rightarrow b = c$

2. $ab = ac \land a \neq 0 \rightarrow b = c$

Proof. For the first part,
$$a + b = a + c$$
$$-a + (a + b) = -a + (a + c)$$
$$(-a + a) + b = (-a + a) + c$$

$$0 + b = 0 + c$$
$$b = c$$

For the second part, we know that a^{-1} exists because we are given that $a \neq 0$. Then,

$$ab = ac$$
$$a^{-1}(ab) = a^{-1}(ac)$$
$$(a^{-1}a)b = (a^{-1}a)c$$
$$1 \cdot b = 1 \cdot c$$
$$b = c$$
□

Henceforth, when invoking either part of this theorem, we will simply refer to it by "Cancellation."

Theorem 3.1.5
The additive and multiplicative identities and inverses are unique.

Proof. Aside from 0, suppose $\widetilde{0}$ is another additive identity. Then we have,

$$0 + \widetilde{0} = 0 \text{ because } \widetilde{0} \text{ is an additive identity.}$$
$$0 + \widetilde{0} = \widetilde{0} \text{ because } 0 \text{ is an additive identity.}$$

Therefore, $0 = \widetilde{0}$, so it is unique.

Aside from $-a$, suppose $-\widetilde{a}$ is another additive inverse for a. Then we have,

$$0 = a + (-a),$$
$$0 = a + (-\widetilde{a}).$$

Therefore, $a + -a = a + -\widetilde{a} \longrightarrow -a = -\widetilde{a}$ by cancellation.

Aside from 1, suppose $\widetilde{1}$ is another multiplicative identity. Then,

$$1 \cdot \widetilde{1} = \widetilde{1} \text{ because } 1 \text{ is a multiplicative identity.}$$
$$1 \cdot \widetilde{1} = 1 \text{ because } \widetilde{1} \text{ is a multiplicative identity.}$$

Therefore $1 = \widetilde{1}$.

Aside from a^{-1}, suppose $\widetilde{a}^{-1}$ is another multiplicative inverse. $\forall a \neq 0$, we have:

$$a \cdot a^{-1} = 1$$
$$a \cdot \widetilde{a}^{-1} = 1$$

Thus, $a \cdot a^{-1} = a \cdot \widetilde{a}^{-1}$. Therefore, $a^{-1} = \widetilde{a}^{-1}$ by cancellation. □

Problem 3.1.6. Prove $-(-a) = a$.

Proof.
$$-a + a = 0$$
$$-a + -(-a) = 0$$
$$\therefore -a + -(-a) = -a + a$$
$$\therefore -(-a) = a.$$
□

Problem 3.1.7. Prove $-(a+b) = -a + -b$.

Proof. Consider the quantity $(-a + -b) + (a + b)$:
$$(-a + -b) + (a + b) = -a + (-b + (a + b))$$
$$= -a + ((-b + b) + a)$$
$$= -a + (0 + a)$$
$$= -a + a$$
$$= 0.$$

Therefore we have $(-a + -b) + (a + b) = 0$. Since $a + b \in F$, it has an additive inverse, so $-(a+b) + (a+b) = 0$.

Then $(-a + -b) + (a + b) = -(a + b) + (a + b)$. By cancellation, we have: $(-a + -b) = -(a+b)$, or $-(a+b) = -a + -b$ by commutativity. □

Problem 3.1.8. Prove $a + (b + c) = c + (a + b)$.

Proof.
$$a + (b + c) = (a + b) + c$$
$$= c + (a + b).$$
□

Problem 3.1.9. Prove $0 \cdot a = 0$.

Proof.
$$0 + 0 = 0$$
$$a(0 + 0) = a \cdot 0$$
$$a \cdot 0 + a \cdot 0 = a \cdot 0$$
$$-a \cdot 0 + (a \cdot 0 + a \cdot 0) = -a \cdot 0 + a \cdot 0$$
$$(-a \cdot 0 + a \cdot 0) + a \cdot 0 = -a \cdot 0 + a \cdot 0$$
$$0 + a \cdot 0 = -a \cdot 0 + a \cdot 0$$
$$a \cdot 0 = -a \cdot 0 + a \cdot 0$$
$$a \cdot 0 = 0$$
$$\therefore 0 \cdot a = 0.$$
□

Problem 3.1.10. Prove $-1 \cdot a = -a$.

Proof. We will have to use the result $0 \cdot a = 0$ from Problem 3.1.9.
$$1 + -1 = 0$$
$$a(1 + -1) = a \cdot 0$$
$$a \cdot 1 + a \cdot -1 = a \cdot 0$$

$$a + a \cdot -1 = a \cdot 0$$
$$a + a \cdot -1 = 0 \cdot a$$
$$a + a \cdot -1 = 0$$
$$-a + (a + a \cdot -1) = -a + 0$$
$$(-a + a) + a \cdot -1 = -a + 0$$
$$0 + a \cdot -1 = -a + 0$$
$$a \cdot -1 = -a + 0$$
$$a \cdot -1 = -a$$
$$\therefore -1 \cdot a = -a. \qquad \square$$

Problem 3.1.11. Prove $ab = 0 \longrightarrow a = 0 \lor b = 0$.

Proof. If $a = 0$, we're done. Suppose $a \neq 0$. Then, a^{-1} exists, so we have

$$ab = 0$$
$$a^{-1} \cdot (ab) = a^{-1} \cdot 0$$
$$(a^{-1} \cdot a)b = a^{-1} \cdot 0$$
$$1 \cdot b = a^{-1} \cdot 0$$
$$1 \cdot b = 0$$
$$\therefore b = 0. \qquad \square$$

Note that the result we just proved helps us deduce roots of a polynomial after factoring.

Problem 3.1.12. Prove that $x^2 = y^2 \to x = y \lor x = -y$.

Proof. First, we rearrange $x^2 = y^2$:

$$x^2 = y^2$$
$$x^2 + -y^2 = y^2 + -y^2$$
$$x^2 + -y^2 = 0.$$

Consider the quantity $(x + y)(x + -y)$.

$$\begin{aligned}
(x + y)(x + -y) &= (x + y)x + (x + y) \cdot -y \\
&= x(x + y) + -y \cdot (x + y) \\
&= (x \cdot x + x \cdot y) + (-y \cdot x + -y \cdot y) \\
&= (x \cdot x + x \cdot y) + ((-1 \cdot y) \cdot x + (-1 \cdot y) \cdot y) \\
&= (x \cdot x + x \cdot y) + (-1 \cdot (y \cdot x) + -1 \cdot (y \cdot y)) \\
&= (x \cdot x + x \cdot y) + (-1 \cdot (x \cdot y) + -1 \cdot (y \cdot y)) \\
&= (x \cdot x + x \cdot y) + (-(x \cdot y) + -(y \cdot y)) \\
&= ((x \cdot x + x \cdot y) + -(x \cdot y)) + -(y \cdot y) \\
&= (x \cdot x + (x \cdot y + -(x \cdot y))) + -(y \cdot y)
\end{aligned}$$

$$\begin{aligned}&= (x \cdot x + 0) + -(y \cdot y)\\&= x \cdot x + -(y \cdot y)\\&= x^2 + -y^2.\end{aligned}$$

Therefore, $(x+y)(x+-y) = 0$. By Problem 3.1.11, $x + y = 0$ or $x + -y = 0$. Consider each case separately:

1. $x + y = 0$

$$\begin{aligned}x + y &= 0\\(x + y) + -y &= 0 + -y\\x + (y + -y) &= 0 + -y\\x + 0 &= 0 + -y\\x &= 0 + -y\\\therefore x &= -y.\end{aligned}$$

2. $x + -y = 0$

$$\begin{aligned}x + -y &= 0\\(x + -y) + y &= 0 + y\\x + (-y + y) &= 0 + y\\x + 0 &= 0 + y\\x &= 0 + y\\\therefore x &= y.\end{aligned}$$

Thus, we have $x = y \lor x = -y$. $\square$

Problem 3.1.13. Prove $(ab)^{-1} = a^{-1}b^{-1}$, provided $b \neq 0$.

Proof. As $b \neq 0$, b^{-1} exists. Then,

$$\begin{aligned}(ab) \cdot (ab)^{-1} &= 1\\a^{-1}((ab) \cdot (ab)^{-1}) &= a^{-1} \cdot 1\\a^{-1}((ab) \cdot (ab)^{-1}) &= a^{-1}\\(a^{-1}(ab)) \cdot (ab)^{-1} &= a^{-1}\\((a^{-1}a)b) \cdot (ab)^{-1} &= a^{-1}\\(1 \cdot b) \cdot (ab)^{-1} &= a^{-1}\\b \cdot (ab)^{-1} &= a^{-1}\\b^{-1}(b \cdot (ab)^{-1}) &= b^{-1}a^{-1}\\(b^{-1}b) \cdot (ab)^{-1} &= b^{-1}a^{-1}\\1 \cdot (ab)^{-1} &= b^{-1}a^{-1}\\(ab)^{-1} &= b^{-1}a^{-1}\\\therefore (ab)^{-1} &= a^{-1}b^{-1}.\end{aligned}$$

$\square$

Alternative Proof. Here is a slightly faster method. First, note that

$$\begin{aligned}
ab(a^{-1}b^{-1}) &= ((ab)a^{-1})b^{-1} \\
&= (a^{-1}(ab))b^{-1} \\
&= ((a^{-1}a)b)b^{-1} \\
&= (a^{-1}a)(bb^{-1}) \\
&= 1 \cdot 1 \\
&= 1.
\end{aligned}$$

We can then conclude:

$$\begin{aligned}
ab(a^{-1}b^{-1}) &= 1 \\
(ab)^{-1}(ab(a^{-1}b^{-1})) &= (ab)^{-1} \cdot 1 \\
(ab)^{-1}(ab(a^{-1}b^{-1})) &= (ab)^{-1} \\
((ab)^{-1}ab)(a^{-1}b^{-1}) &= (ab)^{-1} \\
1 \cdot (a^{-1}b^{-1}) &= (ab)^{-1} \\
a^{-1}b^{-1} &= (ab)^{-1} \\
\therefore (ab)^{-1} &= a^{-1}b^{-1}.
\end{aligned}$$ □

3.2 Subtraction, Division

At this point, we should address the other two operations. We introduced these later because they are, in fact, results from addition and multiplication defined by the field axioms.

Consider the equation $x + b = a$, where a, b are constants. If we solve for x,

$$\begin{aligned}
x + b &= a \\
(x + b) + -b &= a + -b \\
x + (b + -b) &= a + -b \\
x + 0 &= a + -b \\
x &= a + -b
\end{aligned}$$

We now define a new operation to represent the solution to this special equation, $x = a + -b$.

Definition 3.2.1. Subtraction is defined as $a + -b = a - b$.

Likewise, consider $bx = a$. If we solve for x,

$$\begin{aligned}
b \cdot x &= a \\
b^{-1}(b \cdot x) &= b^{-1}(a) \\
(b^{-1}b)x &= b^{-1}(a) \\
1 \cdot x &= b^{-1} \cdot a
\end{aligned}$$

$$x = b^{-1} \cdot a$$
$$x = a \cdot b^{-1}$$

We define another new operation to represent the solution to this special equation, which is $x = ab^{-1}$.

Definition 3.2.2. *Division* is defined as $ab^{-1} = \dfrac{a}{b}$, provided $b \neq 0$.

Problem 3.2.3. Prove $\dfrac{a \cdot d}{b \cdot d} = \dfrac{a}{b}$.

Proof.
$$\begin{aligned}
\frac{a \cdot d}{b \cdot d} &= (a \cdot d)(b \cdot d)^{-1} \\
&= (a \cdot d)(b^{-1} \cdot d^{-1}) \\
&= ((a \cdot d) \cdot b^{-1}) \cdot d^{-1} \\
&= ((d \cdot a) \cdot b^{-1}) \cdot d^{-1} \\
&= (d \cdot (a \cdot b^{-1})) \cdot d^{-1} \\
&= ((a \cdot b^{-1}) \cdot d) \cdot d^{-1} \\
&= (a \cdot b^{-1})(d \cdot d^{-1}) \\
&= (a \cdot b^{-1}) \cdot 1 \\
&= a \cdot b^{-1} \\
&= \frac{a}{b}.
\end{aligned}$$
$\square$

Problem 3.2.4. Prove $\dfrac{a}{b} + \dfrac{c}{d} = \dfrac{a \cdot d + b \cdot c}{b \cdot d}$.

Proof. By Problem 3.2.3, $\dfrac{a}{b} = \dfrac{a \cdot d}{b \cdot d}$ and $\dfrac{c}{d} = \dfrac{c \cdot b}{d \cdot b}$. Then,
$$\begin{aligned}
\frac{a}{b} + \frac{c}{d} &= \frac{a \cdot d}{b \cdot d} + \frac{c \cdot b}{d \cdot b} \\
&= \frac{a \cdot d}{b \cdot d} + \frac{b \cdot c}{b \cdot d} \\
&= (a \cdot d)(b \cdot d)^{-1} + (b \cdot c)(b \cdot d)^{-1} \\
&= (b \cdot d)^{-1}(a \cdot d) + (b \cdot d)^{-1}(b \cdot c) \\
&= (b \cdot d)^{-1}(a \cdot d + b \cdot c) \\
&= (a \cdot d + b \cdot c)(b \cdot d)^{-1} \\
&= \frac{a \cdot d + b \cdot c}{b \cdot d}.
\end{aligned}$$
$\square$

Here are some review problems to help with field proofs. You may use previous results, or, for added difficulty, prove them from scratch (i.e. using only the field axioms in the beginning of this chapter).

Exercise 3.2.5. Prove that $(a + c) - (b + c) = a - b$.

Exercise 3.2.6. Prove $(a+b)(c+d) = (ac+ad) + (bc+bd)$.

Exercise 3.2.7. Prove $\dfrac{a}{b} = \dfrac{c}{d} \longleftrightarrow ad = bc$, provided that $b, d \neq 0$.

Exercise 3.2.8. Prove $(a+b) - (b+c) = a - c$.

Exercise 3.2.9. Prove that $(-a)(-b) = ab$. (Hint: try proving $(-a) \cdot b = -(ab)$ first.)

Exercise 3.2.10. Prove that $-(-a) = a$ and $(a^{-1})^{-1} = a$.

Exercise 3.2.11. Prove that $\left(\dfrac{b}{d}\right)^{-1} = \dfrac{d}{b}$.

Exercise 3.2.12. Prove that $(-1)(-1) = 1$.

Chapter 4

Sequences and Series

Now we move on from the theoretical aspects of math to a relatively more common topic: sequences and series, and their behaviors. What is the difference? How can infinitely many numbers sum to a finite value? What does it mean for a sequence to "approach" a certain value? These are some of the questions that we will explore in this chapter.

4.1 Sequences

Definition 4.1.1. A **sequence** is a list of numbers. It can be represented as

$$\{a_0, a_1, a_2, \ldots\}, \text{ or } \{a_n\}.$$

Sequences can be defined in various ways:

1. Via Formula (Explicit Definition): For example, define the sequence

$$a_n = \frac{n}{n^2 + 1}.$$

   The first 6 terms of the sequence would be: $\frac{1}{2}, \frac{2}{5}, \frac{3}{10}, \frac{4}{17}, \frac{5}{26}, \frac{6}{37}$.

2. Implicitly defined: For example, let $\pi_n = $ the nth digit after the decimal point for π.

3. Recursively defined: Each term is defined in terms of previous terms. We have the famous example, the Fibonacci sequence: Given $f_1 = 1, f_2 = 1, \forall n \geq 1, f_{n+2} = f_{n+1} + f_n$. Then the first few terms are $1, 1, 2, 3, 5, 8, 13, 21, 34, 55, \ldots$

An **arithmetic sequence** is a recursive sequence defined as follows:

$a_1 = a, \forall n \geq 1, a_{n+1} = a_n + d$ where a is the *first term* and d is the *common difference*.

An **geometric sequence** is a recursive sequence defined as follows:

$a_1 = a, \forall n \geq 1, a_{n+1} = r \cdot a_n$ where a is the *first term* and r is the *common ratio*.

From these definitions, we can derive explicit formulas for each type of sequence:

Arithmetic	Geometric
$a_1 = a$	$a_1 = a$
$a_2 = a + d$	$a_2 = ar$
$a_3 = a + 2d$	$a_3 = ar^2$
$a_4 = a + 3d$	$a_4 = ar^3$
$\vdots$	$\vdots$
$a_n = a + (n-1)d$	$a_n = ar^{n-1}$

Check that this matches with the recursive definition.

> **Example 4.1.2**
> Consider a sequence starting with $1, 3, \ldots$ Write the next five terms if the sequence was arithmetic or geometric. Then, find the 100th term of each.

Solution. If the sequence was arithmetic, then note that the common difference is 2 (which can be obtained by subtracting the first term from the second term). Thus, we simply keep adding 2 to get the next five terms: $\boxed{1, 3, 5, 7, 9, 11, 13}$.

If the sequence was geometric, then we can get the common ratio by dividing the second term by the first term to get 3. Then we can simply keep multiplying by the common ratio to get $\boxed{1, 3, 9, 27, 81, 243, 729}$.

Obviously, it would be time-consuming to keep adding on 2 or multiplying by 3 to reach the 100th term, so we find a shorter way. As defined above, in an arithmetic sequence, $a_n = a + (n-1)d$. We know that $a = 1$, $d = 2$, and $n = 100$, so we get $a_{100} = 1 + (100 - 1) \cdot 2 = \boxed{199}$.

Likewise, for a geometric sequence, $a_n = ar^{n-1}$. We know that $a = 1$, $r = 3$, and $n = 100$, so $a_{100} = 1 \cdot 3^{100-1} = \boxed{3^{99}}$. $\square$

Problem 4.1.3. An arithmetic sequence has the fifth term of 19 and 79th term of 22. What is its 2017th term?

Solution. As we have an arithmetic sequence, the fifth term of 19 translates to $a + 4d = 19$ for some first term a and common difference d. Likewise, we have $a + 78d = 22$.

If we subtract the two equations, we get $74d = 3$, which rearranges to $d = \dfrac{3}{74}$.

The 2017th term would be $a + 2016d$. Instead of also solving for a as well, we can just use the given information. Note that $a + 4d = 19$, so $a + 2016d = (a + 4d) + 2012d = 19 + 2012d$. Then we can simply compute to get $19 + 2012 \cdot \dfrac{3}{74} = \boxed{\dfrac{3721}{37}}$. $\square$

Problem 4.1.4. Let a, b, c be three consecutive terms of a sequence. Find

1. c in terms of a, b

2. b in terms of a, c

if the sequence was arithmetic or geometric.

Solution. If the sequence was arithmetic, then using our explicit formulas, we have
$$a = a_0 + (n-1)d,$$
$$b = a_0 + nd,$$
$$c = a_0 + (n+1)d.$$

Notice that a and b are only d apart, so $b - a = d$. We also have that b and c are d apart, so $c - b = d$. We substitute $b - a = d$ into the latter to get $c - b = b - a$, which rearranges to $\boxed{c = 2b - a}$.

Also, b is evenly spaced apart from a and c. This should suggest that b is the average of a and c, i.e. $\boxed{b = \dfrac{a+c}{2}}$. Indeed, we can confirm this using the explicit formulas.

If the sequence was geometric, then our explicit formulas would tell us that
$$a = a_0 r^{n-1},$$
$$b = a_0 r^n,$$
$$c = a_0 r^{n+1}.$$

Likewise, note that $\dfrac{b}{a} = r$ and $\dfrac{c}{b} = r$, so $\dfrac{c}{b} = \dfrac{b}{a}$, which rearranges to $\boxed{c = \dfrac{b^2}{a}}$.

If we multiply a and c together, we get $a_0^2 r^2$, which is just b^2, so $\boxed{b = \pm\sqrt{ac}}$. As we don't know what sign a_0 or r is, we cannot determine what sign b is with certainty. $\square$

Problem 4.1.5. Let $\{a_n\}$ be an arithmetic sequence. Simplify $a_{29} + a_{76} - a_{51}$.

Solution. This is a direct application of the explicit formula for an arithmetic sequence.
$$a + 28d + a + 75d - (a + 50d) = a + 53d$$
$$= \boxed{a_{54}}. \qquad \square$$

Problem 4.1.6. Find all sequences a, b, c such that a, b, c and $a+1, b+1, c+1$ are both geometric.

Solution. If a, b, c is geometric, then we know that $b^2 = ac$. Similarly, $(b+1)^2 = (a+1)(c+1)$.

Note that $(b+1)^2 = (a+1)(c+1)$ simplifies to $b^2 + 2b = ac + a + c$. But we know that $b^2 = ac$, so $b^2 + 2b = b^2 + a + c$, yielding $b = \dfrac{a+b}{2}$.

This implies that a, b, c is an arithmetic sequence. The only possible solution for a sequence that is both geometric and arithmetic is $\boxed{a = b = c}$ (when all terms are equal to each other).

We can also solve this problem by letting $a = b - d$ and $c = b + d$, for some common difference d. Then $b^2 = ac$ becomes $b^2 = (b-d)(b+d)$. From here, we conclude $d = 0$, and this indicates the same result as before. $\square$

4.2 Series

Definition 4.2.1. A **series** is the sum of a sequence.

First, we tackle a problem that gives us a useful formula.

Problem 4.2.2. Find a formula for $1 + 2 + 3 + \ldots + n$.

Solution. Let $S = 1 + 2 + 3 + \ldots + n$. Note that S can also be written backwards: $n + (n-1) + (n-2) + \ldots + 1$. Add these two together:

$$2S = \bigl(1 + 2 + 3 + \ldots + n\bigr) + \bigl(n + (n-1) + (n-2) + \ldots + 1\bigr)$$
$$2S = (1+n) + (2+(n-1)) + (3+(n-2)) + \ldots + (n+1)$$
$$2S = \underbrace{(n+1) + (n+1) + \ldots + (n+1)}_{n \text{ 'copies' of } (n+1)}$$
$$\therefore S = \frac{n(n+1)}{2}.$$

So we have the formula $1 + 2 + 3 + \ldots + n = \boxed{\dfrac{n(n+1)}{2}}$. $\square$

Now, we can discuss notions of an **arithmetic series**, which is simply the sum of all terms of an arithmetic sequence.

Theorem 4.2.3

For some finite arithmetic series $a_1 + a_2 + a_3 + \ldots + a_n$, we have general formulas:

$$a_1 + a_2 + a_3 + \ldots + a_n = na + \frac{n(n-1)}{2}d = \frac{n}{2}(a_1 + a_n).$$

Proof. Keeping in mind that $a_k = a + (k-1)d$, we have

$$a_1 + a_2 + a_3 + \ldots + a_n = a + (a+d) + (a+2d) + \ldots + (a + (n-1)d)$$
$$= (a + a + a + \ldots + a) + (d + 2d + 3d + \ldots + (n-1)d)$$
$$= na + d(1 + 2 + 3 + \ldots + (n-1))$$
$$= na + \frac{n(n-1)}{2}d,$$

using the formula from Problem 4.2.2.

To get the other formula, we perform some clever manipulations:

$$na + \frac{n(n-1)}{2}d = \frac{n}{2}(2a + (n-1)d)$$
$$= \frac{n}{2}(a + (a + (n-1)d))$$
$$= \frac{n}{2}(a_1 + a_n). \quad \square$$

The second formula is much simpler, but can only be used when you know the last term of the arithmetic sequence. Otherwise, use the first formula.

Problem 4.2.4. Find $18 + 19 + 20 + \ldots + 53$.

Solution. Identify the main components of this series: $a = 18$, $d = 1$, and $n = 36$. Then we apply the second formula: $\frac{36}{2}(18+53) = 18 \cdot 71 = \boxed{1278}$. □

Problem 4.2.5. The sum of the first ten terms of an arithmetic series is 10. The sum of the next ten terms is 100. What is the sum of the next ten terms after that?

Solution. This time, the first formula, $na + \frac{n(n-1)}{2}d$, is useful, because we don't know the 10th or 20th term, which is necessary to use the second theorem. We are given the sum of the first ten terms, and the sum of the next ten terms. This indicates that we know the sum of the first twenty terms (just add them together).

We apply the formula on the first ten and the first twenty to get:

$a_1 + a_2 + \ldots + a_{10} = 10$	$a_1 + a_2 + \ldots + a_{20} = 110$
$10a + \frac{10 \cdot 9}{2}d = 10$	$20a + \frac{20 \cdot 19}{2}d = 110$
$\therefore 10a + 45d = 10$	$\therefore 20a + 190d = 110$

We have a system of equations. Multiply the first one by 2 and subtract the two equations to get $100d = 90$. Therefore, we have $d = \frac{9}{10}$ and $a = -\frac{61}{20}$.

Finding the sum of the next ten terms after this 20-term arithmetic sequence is the same thing as finding the sum of the 30-term arithmetic sequence and subtracting the sum of the first 20, which we found to be 110. Thus,

$$a_1 + a_2 + a_3 + \ldots + a_{30} = 30 \cdot -\frac{61}{20} + \frac{30 \cdot 29}{2} \cdot \frac{9}{10}$$
$$= -\frac{183}{2} + \frac{783}{2}$$
$$= \frac{600}{2}$$
$$= 300.$$

Therefore, $a_{21} + a_{22} + \ldots + a_{30} = (a_1 + a_2 + a_3 + \ldots + a_{30}) - (a_1 + a_2 + \ldots + a_{20}) = 300 - 110 = \boxed{190}$. □

Alternative Solution. The previous solution was laborious and inefficient. Let's look for a better way to approach this problem.

The important thing to notice about an arithmetic sequence is that the terms develop linearly. There is a constant, common difference that is added over and over again. Therefore, the difference between the first and last term of each set of 10 terms is constant.

$$a_{21} - a_{11} = a_{11} - a_1$$

$$a_{22} - a_{12} = a_{12} - a_2$$

$$\vdots$$

Therefore, $a_1 + a_2 + a_3 + \ldots + a_{10}$, $a_{11} + a_{12} + a_{13} + \ldots + a_{20}$, and $a_{21} + a_{22} + a_{23} + \ldots + a_{30}$ form an arithmetic sequence. Since $a_1 + a_2 + a_3 + \ldots + a_{10} = 10$ and $a_{11} + a_{12} + a_{13} + \ldots + a_{20} = 100$, there is a common difference of 90, so we get $a_{21} + a_{22} + a_{23} + \ldots + a_{30} = 100 + 90 = \boxed{190}$. This solution was much more elegant! □

Problem 4.2.6. Let $m, n \in \mathbb{Z}$ such that $m \leq n$. Find the sum of all the integers from m through n inclusive.

Solution. Consider the sequence $m, m+1, m+2, \ldots, n$. There are $n - m + 1$ terms in this sequence including m and n. The first and last terms are m and n. We can then apply the second general formula to get $\boxed{\dfrac{(n-m+1)(n+m)}{2}}$. □

Problem 4.2.7. Find all the ways to write 39 as a sum of consecutive integers.

Solution. As the problem suggests, 39 can be represented as $m + (m+1) + (m+2) + \ldots + (n-1) + n$ for arbitrary values of m and n. We apply the formula from Problem 4.2.6 to get

$$(n - m + 1)(n + m) = 78.$$

How are we supposed to find all possible values of m and n? We can take advantage of m and n being integers, and the different parities of $(n - m + 1)$ and $(n + m)$ (i.e. one is odd and one is even). We can enumerate all possibilities below:

$(n - m + 1)$	$(n + m)$	Factorization of 78 into odd and even 'pairs'	Solution (n, m)
$n - m = 1$	$n + m = 39$	$2 \cdot 39$	$(20, 19)$
$n - m = 5$	$n + m = 13$	$6 \cdot 13$	$(9, 4)$
$n - m = 25$	$n + m = 3$	$26 \cdot 3$	$(14, -11)$
$n - m = 77$	$n + m = 1$	$78 \cdot 1$	$(39, -38)$
$n - m = 38$	$n + m = 2$	$39 \cdot 2$	$(20, -18)$
$n - m = 12$	$n + m = 6$	$13 \cdot 6$	$(9, -3)$
$n - m = 2$	$n + m = 26$	$3 \cdot 26$	$(14, 12)$
$n - m = 0$	$n + m = 78$	$1 \cdot 78$	$(39, 39)$

Therefore, 39 can be expressed in the following ways:

$$19 + 20,$$
$$4 + 5 + 6 + \ldots + 8 + 9,$$
$$-11 + -10 + -9 + \ldots + 13 + 14,$$
$$-38 + -37 + \ldots + 39,$$

$$-18 + -17 + \ldots + 20,$$
$$-3 + -2 + \ldots + 9,$$
$$12 + 13 + 14,$$
$$39.$$

□

Likewise, consider the **geometric series**, which is the sum of all the terms of a geometric sequence.

Theorem 4.2.8

For some finite geometric series $a + ar + ar^2 + ar^3 + \ldots + ar^{n-1}$, we have general formulas:

$$a + ar + ar^2 + ar^3 + \ldots + ar^{n-1} = a \cdot \frac{1 - r^n}{1 - r} \text{ if } r \neq 1,$$
$$= na \text{ if } r = 1.$$

Proof. Define $S = a + ar + ar^2 + ar^3 + \ldots + ar^{n-2} + ar^{n-1}$.

First, assume $r \neq 1$. Multiply r on both sides to get $rS = ar + ar^2 + ar^3 + ar^4 + \ldots + ar^{n-1} + ar^n$. Notice that S and rS have terms $ar, ar^2, ar^3, \ldots, ar^{n-1}$ in common. To simplify and eliminate these intermediate terms, subtract rS from S.

$$S - rS = (a + ar + ar^2 + \ldots + ar^{n-2} + ar^{n-1}) - (ar + ar^2 + ar^4 + \ldots + ar^{n-1} + ar^n)$$
$$S - rS = a - ar^n$$
$$S(1 - r) = a(1 - r^n)$$
$$\therefore S = a \cdot \frac{1 - r^n}{1 - r}.$$

□

Otherwise, if $r = 1$, then all the terms are just a. So our sum would be n terms of a added together, which is just na.

Problem 4.2.9. Which expression has a larger value?

$$\underbrace{100 + 200 + 300 + \ldots}_{28 \text{ terms}}$$

$$\underbrace{1 + 2 + 4 + 8 + \ldots}_{28 \text{ terms}}$$

Solution. The first expression is an arithmetic series, which evaluates to $\frac{100 + 2800}{2} \cdot 28 = 40600$. The second expression is a geometric series and it can be computed as $1 \cdot \frac{1 - 2^{28}}{1 - 2} = \boxed{2^{28} - 1}$. It is clear that the latter is much greater (note that $2^{16} = 65536 > 40600$). □

Problem 4.2.10. Evaluate the sum

$$1 - \frac{1}{3} + \frac{1}{9} - \frac{1}{27} + \ldots + \frac{1}{729}.$$

Solution. We start with the first term $\frac{1}{3^0}$ and end with the last term $\frac{1}{3^6}$, so there are 7 terms. The common ratio is $-\frac{1}{3}$, so the sum is

$$1 \cdot \frac{1-\left(-\frac{1}{3}\right)^7}{1-\left(-\frac{1}{3}\right)} = \frac{1+\frac{1}{3^7}}{\frac{4}{3}} = \boxed{\frac{547}{729}}.$$

□

Problem 4.2.11. Let $\{a_n\}$ be a geometric series. If $a_1 + a_2 + a_3 = 10$ and $a_2 + a_3 + a_4 = 20$, what is $a_3 + a_4 + a_5 + a_6 + a_7 + a_8$?

Solution. Using $a_k = ar^{k-1}$, we have the equations

$$a + ar + ar^2 = 10,$$
$$ar + ar^2 + ar^3 = 20.$$

But notice that $ar + ar^2 + ar^3 = r(a + ar + ar^2) = 10r = 20$, so $r = 2$.

We want to compute $a_3 + a_4 + a_5 + a_6 + a_7 + a_8$, which can be rewritten to $ar^2 + ar^3 + \ldots + ar^7$. But this is actually $r^2(a + ar + ar^2) + r^4(ar + ar^2 + ar^3) = 2^2 \cdot 10 + 2^4 \cdot 20 = \boxed{360}$. □

However, for all of the series we have been dealing with so far, we assumed them to be *finite*. What if we had an infinite series? There would be no 'last term' to consider.

Examine the series $\frac{1}{2} + \frac{1}{4} + \frac{1}{8} + \ldots + \frac{1}{2^n}$. The formula gives $\frac{1}{2} \cdot \frac{1-\frac{1}{2^n}}{1-\frac{1}{2}} = 1 - \frac{1}{2^n}$. Let's substitute in some values of n.

$$\frac{1}{2} + \frac{1}{4} + \frac{1}{8} + \frac{1}{16} = \frac{15}{16} = 0.9375.$$
$$\frac{1}{2} + \frac{1}{4} + \frac{1}{8} + \frac{1}{16} + \frac{1}{32} = \frac{31}{32} = 0.96875.$$
$$\frac{1}{2} + \frac{1}{4} + \frac{1}{8} + \ldots + \frac{1}{256} = \frac{255}{256} \approx 0.99609.$$

As n gets larger, we see that the series is getting closer to 1. If we examine the formula $1 - \frac{1}{2^n}$, notice that as n gets large, $\frac{1}{2^n}$ becomes a tremendously small number, so $1 - \frac{1}{2^n}$ approaches 1. To express this notion, we write

$$\lim_{n \to \infty} 1 - \frac{1}{2^n} = 1.$$

Here, we express n getting arbitrarily large as $n \to \infty$. This notation is read as "the limit as n goes to ∞ of $1 - \frac{1}{2^n}$ is 1." Furthermore, we say that the series $\frac{1}{2} + \frac{1}{4} + \frac{1}{8} + \ldots + \frac{1}{2^n}$ **converges** to 1.

Problem 4.2.12. Find the value that this series converges to:

$$\frac{1}{3} + \frac{1}{9} + \frac{1}{27} + \ldots + \frac{1}{3^n}.$$

Solution. First, find the sum in terms of n using the formula $a \cdot \dfrac{1-r^n}{1-r}$:

$$\frac{1}{3} + \frac{1}{9} + \frac{1}{27} + \ldots + \frac{1}{3^n} = \frac{1}{3} \cdot \frac{1-\left(\frac{1}{3}\right)^n}{1-\frac{1}{3}}$$

$$= \frac{1-\left(\frac{1}{3}\right)^n}{2}$$

$$= \frac{1}{2}\left(1 - \frac{1}{3^n}\right).$$

As n gets large, $\dfrac{1}{3^n}$ goes to 0. Then, $1 - \dfrac{1}{3^n}$ goes to 1 and therefore, the entire expression $\dfrac{1}{2}\left(1 - \dfrac{1}{3^n}\right)$ will tend toward $\boxed{\dfrac{1}{2}}$. □

Using this notion of the limit, it is possible to compute certain infinite series. Because some series converge to one value, we can have a finite sum when there are infinitely many terms to add together.

Theorem 4.2.13
For some infinite geometric series $a + ar + ar^2 + \ldots$, if $|r| < 1$, then the sum is $\dfrac{a}{1-r}$.

Proof. Disclaimer: this proof will not be so rigorous as we have not discussed limits in detail yet (in the next section, we will).

Let $S_n = a + ar + ar^2 + \ldots + ar^{n-1} = \dfrac{a(1-r^n)}{1-r}$. Then, we will consider $n \to \infty$, so S_n becomes an infinite geometric series. In the formula $\dfrac{a(1-r^n)}{1-r}$, the only value that is changing because of n is r^n. So, let's analyze r^n as $n \to \infty$.

If we consider all cases of r, we have the following scenarios:

$r > 1$	$r^n \to \infty$ (becomes arbitrarily large)
$r = 1$	$r^n \to 1$ $\quad (S_n = na)$
$0 < r < 1$	$r^n \to 0$
$r = 0$	$r^n \to 0$
$-1 < r < 0$	$r^n \to 0$
$r = -1$	r^n alternates between -1 and 1, so there is no convergence; none
$r < -1$	Similar reason as above; none

In fact, if $r \leq 1$ or $r > 1$, we cannot find a proper formula for such a series, and we have already covered the case when $r = 1$.

Thus, if we restrict r to $-1 < r < 1$, then we know for sure that r^n will go to 0. Then, $\dfrac{a(1-r^n)}{1-r}$ will approach $\dfrac{a}{1-r}$, which is the desired formula. □

Problem 4.2.14. Find the sum of the infinite geometric series

$$1 - \frac{2}{3} + \frac{4}{9} - \frac{8}{27} + \ldots$$

Solution. The common ratio is $-\frac{2}{3}$ and the first term is 1. Using the formula, the sum is simply $\frac{1}{1-(-\frac{2}{3})} = \boxed{\frac{3}{5}}$. □

Problem 4.2.15. Find the following sums:

1. $\frac{9}{10} + \frac{9}{100} + \frac{9}{1000} + \ldots$

2. $0.\overline{23}$

3. $0.1\overline{46}$

Solution.

1. Direct application of the formula gives $\frac{\frac{9}{10}}{1-\frac{1}{10}} = \boxed{1}$. Also notice that $\frac{9}{10} + \frac{9}{100} + \frac{9}{1000} + \ldots$ is equivalent to $0.9999\ldots$, or $0.\overline{9}$, which equals 1.

2. $0.\overline{23} = \frac{23}{100} + \frac{23}{10000} + \ldots = \frac{0.23}{1 - \frac{1}{100}} = \boxed{\frac{23}{99}}$.

3. $0.1\overline{46} = \frac{1}{10} + \frac{46}{1000} + \frac{46}{100000} + \ldots = \frac{1}{10} + \left(\frac{\frac{46}{1000}}{1 - \frac{1}{100}}\right) = \boxed{\frac{29}{198}}$. □

> **Theorem 4.2.16**
>
> A number is rational if and only if it has a decimal expansion that either terminates or repeats.

Proof. First, we prove the right direction: if a number is rational, then it has a decimal expansion that either terminates or repeats.

A rational number can be expressed as $\frac{p}{q}$, where $p, q \in \mathbb{Z}$. If we perform long division with p as the dividend and q as the divisor, then there will only be finitely many possible remainders, namely $0, 1, 2, \ldots, q-1$. Thus, the long division will eventually terminate by a remainder of 0, or it will continue indefinitely due to a cycle of the same non-zero remainders.

For the left direction, if the number has a decimal expansion that either terminates or repeats, then it can be represented as a geometric series or infinite geometric series with common ratio between 0 and 1. In either case, we have an appropriate formula which shows that the sum is a rational number: $\frac{a(1-r^n)}{1-r}$ or $\frac{a}{1-r}$. □

Problem 4.2.17. The sum of an infinite geometric series is 10. The sum of the same series but with each of its terms squared is 12. What is its fifth term?

Solution. We have the equations

$$a + ar + ar^2 + \ldots = \frac{a}{1-r} = 10,$$

$$a^2 + a^2r^2 + a^2r^4 + \ldots = \frac{a^2}{1-r^2} = 12.$$

The first equation gives $a = 10 - 10r$, and the second gives $a^2 = 12 - 12r^2$. Therefore, we can solve for r with the equation

$$12 - 12r^2 = (10 - 10r)^2.$$

We end up with the quadratic $14r^2 - 25r + 11 = 0$, which can be factored into $(r-1)(14r-11) = 0$, giving $r = 1, \frac{11}{14}$. Since it is an infinite geometric sequence, $|r| < 1$, so the common ratio must be $\frac{11}{14}$.

Therefore $a = 10 - 10 \cdot \frac{11}{14} = \frac{15}{7}$, so the fifth term, which is ar^4, would be $\boxed{\frac{15}{7} \cdot \left(\frac{11}{14}\right)^4}$. □

4.3 Limits of Sequences

Earlier, we brought up the concept of the limit as a means to derive our formula for an infinite geometric series. In this section, we will go over them with a very rigorous and technical approach. If you are not yet familiar with quantifiers from the first chapter, make sure you review it, because it is essential to understanding how exactly limits are defined from a theoretical standpoint.

Definition 4.3.1. Let $\{a_n\}$ be an infinite sequence. We define the **limit** of the sequence as follows:

$$\lim_{n \to \infty} a_n = L \longleftrightarrow \forall \varepsilon > 0 \; \exists N > 0 \text{ such that } \forall n > N, \; |a_n - L| < \varepsilon.$$

Now this symbolic definition certainly seems unwieldy, so we will dissect one part at a time.

Often, we use the Greek letter ε, called "epsilon," to represent a preferably small number. Likewise, we are using the capital letter N to represent a preferably large number.

When we start off with $\forall \varepsilon > 0 \; \exists N > 0$, we are saying that for any small positive number ε we choose, we can always find a large positive number N such that the rest of the statement is satisfied. Keep in mind that ε and N are defined to be real numbers in this context.

Namely, the rest of the statement reads $\forall n > N, \; |a_n - L| < \varepsilon$. Remember that $|a_n - L|$ is the distance between a_n and L, which is the value that the infinite sequence converges to. We are saying that all a_n in the infinite sequence whose n is greater than the large number N we found is less than ε away from L.

In other words, a_n can be made *arbitrarily close* to L by making n *sufficiently large*. This should make sense - as we choose a term in the sequence farther down, we should be closer to the limit L than before.

Then ε is our threshold of 'closeness' to L. As we began the statement with $\forall \varepsilon > 0$, this is the 'arbitrarily close' part of the definition. Making ε as small as we want yields terms further down the sequence that are as close to L as we want.

Our choice of N, depending on the given number ε, represents how far we have to go down the sequence in order to find terms that are within ε of L. Thus, N serves to represent the 'make n sufficiently large' part of the definition.

As a last note, I will abbreviate "such that" to "s.t." for concision.

Now we will proceed to prove that some sequences actually have the limit that we suspect it to have.

> **Example 4.3.2**
> Prove $\lim_{n \to \infty} \dfrac{1}{n} = 0$.

Proof. First, write out the symbolic definition:
$$\forall \varepsilon > 0 \; \exists N > 0 \text{ s.t. } \forall n > N, \; \left|\frac{1}{n} - 0\right| < \varepsilon,$$
where $a_n = \dfrac{1}{n}$ and $L = 0$. It is sufficient to find an N in terms of a given ε that satisfies $\forall n > N, \; \left|\dfrac{1}{n}\right| < \varepsilon$. How do we do so?

Usually, we can work backwards. Start from $\left|\dfrac{1}{n}\right| < \varepsilon$. Notice that n is always positive, given the precedent that $N > 0$ and $\forall n > N$. So we can lose the absolute value signs to get $\dfrac{1}{n} < \varepsilon$. As ε is also positive, we can rearrange this to $n > \dfrac{1}{\varepsilon}$.

Recall that we must satisfy $\forall n > N, \; \left|\dfrac{1}{n}\right| < \varepsilon$, and we have just discovered that n must be greater than $\dfrac{1}{\varepsilon}$. In fact, if we let $N = \dfrac{1}{\varepsilon}$, then we have $\forall n > \dfrac{1}{\varepsilon}, \; \left|\dfrac{1}{n}\right| < \varepsilon$, which is true because of the algebraic manipulations we have just done (the steps we have taken are reversible).

Thus, it is sufficient to say that $N = \dfrac{1}{\varepsilon}$ in order to prove the limit.

Unfortunately, the line of reasoning that we've just done cannot be used in a formal proof, because we have worked backwards. To formalize it, we must write the proof *forwards*:

For a given $\varepsilon > 0$, let $N = \dfrac{1}{\varepsilon}$. Then,
$$n > N \implies n > \frac{1}{\varepsilon} \implies n\varepsilon > 1 \implies \frac{1}{n} < \varepsilon \implies \left|\frac{1}{n} - 0\right| < \varepsilon.$$

Therefore, for any given $\varepsilon > 0$, we have found a N which satisfies
$$\forall \varepsilon > 0 \; \exists N > 0 \text{ s.t. } \forall n > N, \; \left|\frac{1}{n} - 0\right| < \varepsilon,$$

and thus we have proven $\lim_{n \to \infty} \frac{1}{n} = 0$. □

For the remainder of the problems, I will write out the steps taken backwards in order to show the motivation behind choosing an N to satisfy the definition. However, I *strongly recommend* that you write formal proofs forward in order to reinforce your understanding of the symbolic definition of the limit. Furthermore, I will glance over some algebraic steps for conciseness, but you should be writing out every step in your proof to be specific.

Problem 4.3.3. Prove $\lim_{n \to \infty} \frac{1}{n^2} = 0$.

Proof. Our symbolic definition is now

$$\forall \varepsilon > 0 \; \exists N > 0 \text{ s.t. } \forall n > N, \; \left|\frac{1}{n^2} - 0\right| < \varepsilon,$$

and now we can work backwards again. We have $\left|\frac{1}{n^2}\right| < \varepsilon$, and again note that n is positive, so $\left|\frac{1}{n^2}\right| = \frac{1}{n^2} < \varepsilon$. We can then rearrange this to $n > \frac{1}{\sqrt{\varepsilon}}$. Then we can let $N = \frac{1}{\sqrt{\varepsilon}}$ to satisfy the definition. □

Problem 4.3.4. Prove $\lim_{n \to \infty} \frac{n}{n+1} = 1$.

Proof. We have the definition,

$$\forall \varepsilon > 0 \; \exists N > 0 \text{ s.t. } \forall n > N, \; \left|\frac{n}{n+1} - 1\right| < \varepsilon.$$

The procedure is similar to that of the previous proofs. To make things easier, condense the absolute value expression: note that $\frac{n}{n+1} - 1 = -\frac{1}{n+1}$, so $\left|-\frac{1}{n+1}\right| = \frac{1}{n+1}$ using that n is positive. Therefore, we have $\frac{1}{n+1} < \varepsilon$, which can be rearranged to $n > \frac{1}{\varepsilon} - 1$.

Thus, given $\varepsilon > 0$, let $N = \frac{1}{\varepsilon} - 1$, and it can be verified that this choice of N satisfies the definition. □

Problem 4.3.5. Prove $\lim_{n \to \infty} \frac{-n+1}{2n+3} = -\frac{1}{2}$.

Proof. Again, write out the definition,

$$\forall \varepsilon > 0 \; \exists N > 0 \text{ s.t. } \forall n > N, \; \left|\frac{-n+1}{2n+3} - \left(-\frac{1}{2}\right)\right| < \varepsilon.$$

We can manipulate the inequality as follows:

$$\left|\frac{-n+1}{2n+3} + \frac{1}{2}\right| < \varepsilon$$

$$\left|\frac{-n+1}{2n+3} + \frac{n+\frac{3}{2}}{2n+3}\right| < \varepsilon$$

$$\left|\frac{\frac{5}{2}}{2n+3}\right| < \varepsilon$$

As n is positive, we have $\frac{\frac{5}{2}}{2n+3} < \varepsilon$. We can rearrange this to get $n > \frac{\frac{5}{2} - 3\varepsilon}{2\varepsilon}$. Thus, for a given $\varepsilon > 0$, let $N = \frac{\frac{5}{2} - 3\varepsilon}{2\varepsilon}$ so the overall symbolic statement is true. □

Problem 4.3.6. Prove $\lim_{n \to \infty} \frac{2n+5}{3n-7} = \frac{2}{3}$.

Proof. Let $N = \frac{29 + 21\varepsilon}{9\varepsilon}$. Note that $n > N$ suggests:

$$3n > 3N$$
$$3n - 7 > 3N - 7$$
$$\frac{1}{3n-7} < \frac{1}{3N-7}$$
$$\therefore \frac{\frac{29}{3}}{3n-7} < \frac{\frac{29}{3}}{3N-7}$$

Then,

$$\left|\frac{2n+5}{3n-7} - \frac{2}{3}\right| = \left|\frac{2n+5}{3n-7} - \frac{2n - \frac{14}{3}}{3n-7}\right| = \left|\frac{2n+5 - \left(2n - \frac{14}{3}\right)}{3n-7}\right| = \left|\frac{\frac{29}{3}}{3n-7}\right| = \frac{\frac{29}{3}}{3n-7}.$$

Thus, if $n > N$, then

$$\left|\frac{2n+5}{3n-7} - \frac{2}{3}\right| = \frac{\frac{29}{3}}{3n-7} < \frac{\frac{29}{3}}{3N-7} = \frac{\frac{29}{3}}{3\left(\frac{29+21\varepsilon}{9\varepsilon}\right) - 7} = \varepsilon.$$

In other words, for a given $\varepsilon > 0$, we have found an N such that for all $n > N$, $\left|\frac{2n+5}{3n-7} - \frac{2}{3}\right| < \varepsilon$. Therefore, $\lim_{n \to \infty} \frac{2n+5}{3n-7} = \frac{2}{3}$. □

Exercise 4.3.7. Let $b_n = c$ for all n, where c is a constant real number. Prove $\lim_{n \to \infty} b_n = c$.

Example 4.3.8

Prove that $\lim_{n \to \infty} (-1)^n$ does not exist.

Proof. Suppose it does exist, such that $\lim_{n\to\infty} (-1)^n = L$. We have its definition,

$$\forall \varepsilon > 0 \ \exists N \text{ s.t. } \forall n > N, \ |(-1)^n - L| < \varepsilon.$$

To prove that there exists no such L, consider the negation,

$$\exists \varepsilon > 0 \ \forall N \text{ s.t. } \exists n > N, \ |(-1)^n - L| \geq \varepsilon.$$

Now, it becomes clear that we simply must find a value for ε such that we arrive at a contradiction for $|(-1)^n - L| < \varepsilon$.

Consider $\varepsilon = \frac{1}{2}$. Then we have $|(-1)^n - L| < \frac{1}{2}$. We break up the absolute signs to get

$$-\frac{1}{2} < (-1)^n - L < \frac{1}{2},$$

which gives us two inequalities,

$$(-1)^n - L > -\frac{1}{2} \text{ and } (-1)^n - L < \frac{1}{2}.$$

Consider each one separately. First, based on the parity of integer n, notice that there are only two possible values of $(-1)^n$: 1 and -1. Now we list all possibilities:

$$(-1)^n - L > -\frac{1}{2} \begin{cases} -1 - L > -\frac{1}{2} \implies L < -\frac{1}{2} \\ 1 - L > -\frac{1}{2} \implies L < \frac{3}{2} \end{cases} \therefore L < -\frac{1}{2}.$$

$$(-1)^n - L < \frac{1}{2} \begin{cases} -1 - L < \frac{1}{2} \implies L > -\frac{3}{2} \\ 1 - L < \frac{1}{2} \implies L > \frac{1}{2} \end{cases} \therefore L > \frac{1}{2}.$$

There is no value of L which satisfies both $L < -\frac{1}{2}$ and $L > \frac{1}{2}$. Therefore, there exists no limit for the sequence $a_n = (-1)^n$. $\square$

Theorem 4.3.9

Let $k \in \mathbb{R}$. If $\lim_{n\to\infty} a_n = L$, then

a) $\lim_{n\to\infty} (a_n + k) = L + k$.

b) $\lim_{n\to\infty} k a_n = kL$.

Proof. The best approach is to rewrite everything in terms of the given definition of a limit. For all parts of the question, keep in mind:

$$\lim_{n\to\infty} a_n = L \longleftrightarrow \forall \varepsilon > 0, \ \exists N \text{ s.t. } \forall n > N, \ |a_n - L| < \varepsilon.$$

a) Regarding this definition, note that
$$\begin{aligned} a_n - L &= a_n - L + (k - k) \\ &= (a_n + k) + (-L - k) \\ &= (a_n + k) - (L + k). \end{aligned}$$

Therefore, we have
$$\forall \varepsilon > 0, \exists N \text{ s.t. } \forall n > N, \ |(a_n + k) - (L + k)| < \varepsilon,$$
which is $\lim_{n \to \infty} (a_n + k) = L + k$.

b) Note that we are able to replace the third quantifier with an implication statement without affecting the original definition, as such:
$$\forall \varepsilon > 0, \exists N \text{ s.t. } n > N \to |a_n - L| < \varepsilon.$$

Consider the definition of $\lim_{n \to \infty} ka_n = kL$, using different variables to avoid confusion:
$$\forall \widetilde{\varepsilon} > 0, \exists \widetilde{N} \text{ s.t. } n > \widetilde{N} \to |ka_n - kL| < \widetilde{\varepsilon}$$
$$\text{i.e. } |k| \, |a_n - L| < \widetilde{\varepsilon}$$
$$\text{i.e. } |a_n - L| < \frac{\widetilde{\varepsilon}}{|k|}.$$

Let $\varepsilon = \frac{\widetilde{\varepsilon}}{|k|}$, which is allowed because ε and $\widetilde{\varepsilon}$ can be any positive real numbers. Then
$$\forall \varepsilon > 0, \exists N \text{ s.t. } n > N \to |a_n - L| < \frac{\widetilde{\varepsilon}}{|k|} \text{ i.e. } |ka_n - kL| < \widetilde{\varepsilon}, \text{ as desired.} \qquad \square$$

A **lemma** is a minor result that we prove in order to help us with a harder proof of a theorem or grander result. Here, we will prove a useful fact relating to absolute value and inequalities that we will use in later proofs of major theorems.

> **Lemma 4.3.10 (Triangle Inequality)**
> For any $a, b \in \mathbb{R}$, $|a + b| \leq |a| + |b|$.

Proof. As the square of any number is nonnegative, it is clear that $|x|^2 = x^2$ for any number x. Then,
$$\begin{aligned} (|a + b|)^2 &= (a + b)^2 \\ &= a^2 + 2ab + b^2 \\ &= |a|^2 + 2ab + |b|^2. \end{aligned}$$

It should also be certain that for any x, $x \leq |x|$ (either $x = |x|$ or $x = -|x|$). Therefore, we must have $ab \leq |ab| = |a| \, |b|$. Using this fact, $|a|^2 + 2ab + |b|^2 \leq |a|^2 + 2|a| \, |b| + |b|^2$, which is equal to $(|a| + |b|)^2$.

Therefore, $(|a + b|)^2 \leq (|a| + |b|)^2$. Since both terms are nonnegative, we can take the square root of both sides to get $|a + b| \leq |a| + |b|$. $\qquad \square$

Theorem 4.3.11 (Sum of Limits)

If $\lim\limits_{n\to\infty} a_n = L$ and $\lim\limits_{n\to\infty} b_n = M$, then $\lim\limits_{n\to\infty} a_n + b_n = L + M$.

Proof. We first write out the definitions of both limits given. For a given $\varepsilon > 0$,

$$\exists N_1 \; \forall n > N_1, \; |a_n - L| < \frac{\varepsilon}{2},$$

$$\exists N_2 \; \forall n > N_2, \; |b_n - M| < \frac{\varepsilon}{2}.$$

Why are we allowed to use $\frac{\varepsilon}{2}$ instead of ε? We can make ε be any positive number we want, so it does not matter.

Let $N = \max\{N_1, N_2\}$, that is to say, the bigger value out of N_1 and N_2. Then conveniently, $\forall n > N, \; n > N_1 \wedge n > N_2$.

Therefore, $\forall n > N$,

$$|a_n - L| < \frac{\varepsilon}{2} \wedge |b_n - M| < \frac{\varepsilon}{2},$$

so by the Triangle Inequality,

$$|(a_n + b_n) - (L + M)| = |(a_n - L) + (b_n - M)| \leq |a_n - L| + |b_n - M| < \frac{\varepsilon}{2} + \frac{\varepsilon}{2} = \varepsilon.$$

Thus, we have found N such that $\forall n > N$,

$$|(a_n + b_n) - (L + M)| < \varepsilon,$$

so $\lim\limits_{n\to\infty} a_n + b_n = L + M$. $\square$

Theorem 4.3.12 (Squeeze Theorem)

If $\lim\limits_{n\to\infty} a_n = 0$ and $0 < b_n < a_n \; \forall n$, then $\lim\limits_{n\to\infty} b_n = 0$.

Proof. Assuming $\lim\limits_{n\to\infty} a_n = 0$, we have

$$\forall \varepsilon > 0, \; \exists N \text{ s.t. } \forall n > N, \; |a_n - 0| < \varepsilon.$$

Since we are given that $0 < a_n$ (in other words, a_n is positive for all n),

$$|a_n - 0| = |a_n| = a_n < \varepsilon.$$

Now, we know that $0 < b_n < a_n < \varepsilon$. This means that $b_n < \varepsilon$, i.e. $|b_n - 0| < \varepsilon$. Therefore, $\forall n > N$, $|b_n - 0| < \varepsilon$, and this statement implies $\lim\limits_{n\to\infty} b_n = 0$. $\square$

Lemma 4.3.13 (Bernoulli's Inequality)
For $h > 0$ and $n \in \mathbb{N}$, $(1+h)^n \geq 1 + hn$.

We don't have the tools required to prove this inequality yet, but it will be available as an exercise in a later chapter when we learn proof by induction.

Theorem 4.3.14
If $0 < a < 1$, then $\lim_{n \to \infty} a^n = 0$.

Proof. If $0 < a < 1$, then $\frac{1}{a} > 1$. Therefore, $\frac{1}{a} = 1 + h$ for some $h > 0$. By Bernoulli's Inequality,

$$\frac{1}{a^n} = \left(\frac{1}{a}\right)^n = (1+h)^n \geq 1 + nh > nh.$$

Thus, $0 < a^n < \frac{1}{nh} = \frac{1}{n} \cdot \frac{1}{h}$. Since $\lim_{n \to \infty} \frac{1}{n} = 0$, by Theorem 4.3.9, $\lim_{n \to \infty} \frac{1}{n} \cdot \frac{1}{h} = 0 \cdot \frac{1}{h}$, which is still 0.

Since $0 < a^n < \frac{1}{nh}$ and $\lim_{n \to \infty} \frac{1}{nh} = 0$, by Theorem 4.3.12, $\lim_{n \to \infty} a^n = 0$. $\square$

Beware that it is quite difficult to grasp the intuition or motivation behind the proofs for the product and reciprocal of limits, so just try your best to understand how they work.

Theorem 4.3.15 (Product of Limits)
If $\lim_{n \to \infty} a_n = L$ and $\lim_{n \to \infty} b_n = M$, then $\lim_{n \to \infty} a_n b_n = LM$.

Proof. Given $\varepsilon > 0$, we know that, by the definition of a limit, we can find N_1, N_2, N_3 such that

$$\forall n > N_1, |a_n - L| < \frac{\varepsilon}{2|M+1|},$$

$$\forall n > N_2, |b_n - M| < \frac{\varepsilon}{2|L+1|},$$

$$\forall n > N_3, |b_n - M| < 1.$$

That third condition implies that, if $n > N_3$,

$$|b_n| = |b_n - M + M| \leq |b_n - M| + |M| < 1 + |M|,$$

where we split the absolute value using the Triangle Inequality. Let $N = \max\{N_1, N_2, N_3\}$. Note that $n > N \to n > N_1 \wedge n > N_2 \wedge n > N_3$. Then if $n > N$,

$$|a_n b_n - LM| = |a_n b_n - b_n L + b_n L - LM| \leq |a_n b_n - b_n L| + |b_n L - LM|$$

$$= |b_n(a_n - L)| + |L(b_n - M)| = |b_n||a_n - L| + |L||b_n - M|.$$

Now, we can substitute in the inequalities we derived earlier (and using the obvious fact that $|L| < |L| + 1$), to get that

$$|b_n| \, |a_n - L| + |L| \, |b_n - M| < (|M|+1)\frac{\varepsilon}{2(|M|+1)} + (|L|+1)\frac{\varepsilon}{2(|L|+1)} = \frac{\varepsilon}{2} + \frac{\varepsilon}{2} = \varepsilon.$$

Thus, given an $\varepsilon > 0$, we have found an N such that $|a_n b_n - LM| < \varepsilon$ for all $n > N$. Therefore, $\lim_{n \to \infty} a_n b_n = LM$. □

Theorem 4.3.16 (Reciprocal of Limits)
If $\lim_{n \to \infty} a_n = L$ and $L \neq 0$, then $\lim_{n \to \infty} \frac{1}{a_n} = \frac{1}{L}$.

Proof. Given $\varepsilon > 0$, we can find N_1, N_2, such that

$$\forall n > N_1, \ |a_n - L| < \frac{|L|}{2},$$

$$\forall n > N_2, \ |a_n - L| < \frac{\varepsilon |L|^2}{2}.$$

Let $N = \max\{N_1, N_2\}$, such that

$$\forall n > N, \ |a_n - L| < \frac{|L|}{2} \wedge |a_n - L| < \frac{\varepsilon |L|^2}{2}.$$

By the Triangle Inequality, we have

$$|L| = |L - a_n + a_n| \leq |L - a_n| + |a_n| = |a_n - L| + |a_n| < \frac{|L|}{2} + |a_n|,$$

so $|a_n| > \frac{|L|}{2}$. Both quantities are positive, so we can take the reciprocal and get $\frac{1}{|a_n|} < \frac{2}{|L|}$.

Therefore, for a given ε, we have found N such that

$$\forall n > N, \ \left|\frac{1}{a_n} - \frac{1}{L}\right| = \left|\frac{L - a_n}{a_n L}\right| = \frac{|L - a_n|}{|a_n| \, |L|} = \frac{|a_n - L|}{|a_n| \, |L|} < \frac{\varepsilon |L|^2}{2} \cdot \frac{2}{|L|} \cdot \frac{1}{|L|} = \varepsilon,$$

so $\lim_{n \to \infty} \frac{1}{a_n} = \frac{1}{L}$. □

Corollary 4.3.17 (Quotient of Limits)
If $\lim_{n \to \infty} a_n = L$, $\lim_{n \to \infty} b_n = M$, and $M \neq 0$, then $\lim_{n \to \infty} \frac{a_n}{b_n} = \frac{L}{M}$.

Proof. The result follows by Theorem 4.3.15 and Theorem 4.3.16. □

A **corollary** is a result that is a quick consequence of a previously proven theorem. Here, we used the theorems of product and reciprocal of limits to immediately prove the quotient of limits.

Problem 4.3.18. If $\lim\limits_{n\to\infty} a_n = 0$, then $\lim\limits_{n\to\infty} \dfrac{1}{a_n}$ does not exist.

Proof. Assume for the sake of contradiction that $\lim\limits_{n\to\infty} \dfrac{1}{a_n} = L$. By Theorem 4.3.16, $\lim\limits_{n\to\infty} a_n = \dfrac{1}{L}$. We are given that this equals 0, so $\dfrac{1}{L} = 0 \implies 1 = 0$, which is clearly false. Thus, the limit does not exist. $\square$

Problem 4.3.19. Compute the following:

1. $\lim\limits_{n\to\infty} \dfrac{n}{n+1}$

2. $\lim\limits_{n\to\infty} 2 + \dfrac{3}{n} + \dfrac{5}{n^2} + 88^{-n} + \pi$

3. $\lim\limits_{n\to\infty} \dfrac{2n^2 + 3n + 4}{3n^2 + 5n - 2}$

Solution.

1. Divide the numerator and denominator by n. Then we have
$$\lim_{n\to\infty} \frac{1}{1 + \frac{1}{n}},$$
but notice that $\lim\limits_{n\to\infty} \dfrac{1}{n} = 0$, and 1 remains constant. Therefore, the limit is
$$\lim_{n\to\infty} \frac{1}{1 + \frac{1}{n}} = \lim_{n\to\infty} \frac{1}{1 + 0} = \boxed{1}.$$

2. Note that $\lim\limits_{n\to\infty} \dfrac{3}{n} = 0$, $\lim\limits_{n\to\infty} \dfrac{5}{n^2} = \lim\limits_{n\to\infty} 5 \cdot \dfrac{1}{n} \cdot \dfrac{1}{n} = 0$, and $\lim\limits_{n\to\infty} 88^{-n} = \lim\limits_{n\to\infty} \left(\dfrac{1}{88}\right)^n = 0$ by Theorem 4.3.14. We are left with $2 + 0 + 0 + 0 + \pi = \boxed{2 + \pi}$.

3. Divide the numerator and denominator by the highest degree of n, which in this case, is n^2. Then all the terms with a constant in the numerator and a power of n in the denominator tend to 0, and the limit becomes clear:
$$\lim_{n\to\infty} \frac{2n^2 + 3n + 4}{3n^2 + 5n - 2} = \lim_{n\to\infty} \frac{2 + \frac{3}{n} + \frac{4}{n^2}}{3 + \frac{5}{n} - \frac{2}{n^2}} = \boxed{\frac{2}{3}}.$$
$\square$

Problem 4.3.20. Compute the following:

1. $\lim\limits_{n\to\infty} \dfrac{2^n}{2^n + 3^n}$

2. $\lim\limits_{n\to\infty} \dfrac{3^n}{2^n + 3^n}$

3. $\lim\limits_{n\to\infty} \dfrac{5^n}{2^n + 3^n}$

Solution.

1. Divide the numerator and denominator by 3^n to get
$$\lim_{n\to\infty} \frac{\left(\frac{2}{3}\right)^n}{\left(\frac{2}{3}\right)^n + 1}.$$

By Theorem 4.3.14, $\lim\limits_{n\to\infty} \left(\dfrac{2}{3}\right)^n = 0$. By various properties of limits we had proven earlier,
$$\lim_{n\to\infty} \frac{\left(\frac{2}{3}\right)^n}{\left(\frac{2}{3}\right)^n + 1} = \frac{0}{0+1} = \boxed{0}.$$

2. Similarly, divide the numerator and denominator by 3^n to get
$$\lim_{n\to\infty} \frac{1}{\left(\frac{2}{3}\right)^n + 1}.$$

We know that $\lim\limits_{n\to\infty}\left(\dfrac{2}{3}\right)^n = 0$. Therefore,
$$\lim_{n\to\infty} \frac{1}{\left(\frac{2}{3}\right)^n + 1} = \lim_{n\to\infty} \frac{1}{0+1} = \boxed{1}.$$

3. We do the same thing to get $\lim\limits_{n\to\infty} \dfrac{\left(\frac{5}{3}\right)^n}{\left(\frac{2}{3}\right)^n + 1}$. By properties of limits, we have
$$\lim_{n\to\infty} \frac{\left(\frac{5}{3}\right)^n}{\left(\frac{2}{3}\right)^n + 1} = \frac{\lim\limits_{n\to\infty}\left(\frac{5}{3}\right)^n}{1+0} = \lim_{n\to\infty}\left(\frac{5}{3}\right)^n.$$

Note that $\left(\dfrac{5}{3}\right)^n = \left(1 + \dfrac{2}{3}\right)^n \geq 1 + \dfrac{2n}{3}$ by Bernoulli's Inequality. Since $1 + \dfrac{2n}{3}$ will go to infinity as n goes to infinity, so will $\left(\dfrac{5}{3}\right)^n$, therefore $\lim\limits_{n\to\infty}\left(\dfrac{5}{3}\right)^n = \boxed{\infty}$. □

4.4 Summation and Product Notation

Moving aside from sequences, series, and limits, another section will be dedicated to summation and product notation, which is useful shorthand to represent long sums and products in compact form.

Definition 4.4.1. Let $m, n \in \mathbb{Z}$, $m \leq n$. Then,

$$\sum_{i=m}^{n} a_i = a_m + a_{m+1} + \ldots + a_n,$$

where i is referred to as the *dummy variable*. This is read as "the **summation** from $i = m$ to n of a_i."

Here are some examples:

- $\sum_{r=3}^{7} r^2 = 9 + 16 + 25 + 36 + 49 = \boxed{135}$.

- $\sum_{k=-1}^{3} k^3 = -1 + 0 + 1 + 8 + 27 = \boxed{35}$.

- $\sum_{k=79}^{100} 7 = 22 \cdot 7 = \boxed{154}$.

- $\sum_{j=2}^{5} j = 2 + 3 + 4 + 5 = \boxed{14}$.

Theorem 4.4.2

We can add summations together and pull out constant factors.

1. $\sum_{k=m}^{n} a_k + \sum_{k=m}^{n} b_k = \sum_{k=m}^{n} (a_k + b_k)$

2. $c \sum_{k=m}^{n} a_k = \sum_{k=m}^{n} c a_k$

Proof. By using the definition, the proofs of these involve simple algebra:

1. Using the associative property yields:

$$\sum_{k=m}^{n} a_k + \sum_{k=m}^{n} b_k = (a_m + a_{m+1} + a_{m+2} + \ldots + a_n) + (b_m + b_{m+1} + b_{m+2} + \ldots + b_n)$$

$$= ((a_m + b_m) + (a_{m+1} + b_{m+1}) + (a_{m+2} + b_{m+2}) + \ldots + (a_n + b_n))$$

$$= \sum_{k=m}^{n} (a_k + b_k).$$

2. Likewise, we use the distributive property.

$$c \sum_{k=m}^{n} a_k = c(a_m + a_{m+1} + a_{m+2} + \ldots + a_n)$$

$$= ca_m + ca_{m+1} + ca_{m+2} + \ldots + ca_n$$
$$= \sum_{k=m}^{n} ca_k.$$

□

Problem 4.4.3. Write in summation form the general formulas for the sums of an arithmetic series and a geometric series.

Solution. For an arithmetic series, we have
$$\sum_{k=1}^{n} (a + (k-1)d) = na + \frac{n(n-1)}{2}d.$$

For a geometric series, we have
$$\sum_{k=1}^{n} ar^{k-1} = a \cdot \frac{1-r^n}{1-r}, \text{ provided } r \neq 1.$$

□

Problem 4.4.4. Write the following as a summation:
$$\frac{2}{3} + \frac{3}{4} + \frac{4}{5} + \frac{5}{6} + \ldots + \frac{79}{80}.$$

Solution. The denominator is simply the numerator plus 1, so this sum can be expressed as
$$\sum_{k=2}^{79} \frac{k}{k+1}.$$

Note that if we changed the starting value of the dummy variable, we can still 'shift over' the ending value and the expression itself to represent the same sum. For instance, if we had $k = 41$, we could express the same sum above as
$$\sum_{k=41}^{118} \frac{k-39}{k-38}.$$

□

Problem 4.4.5. Given the following formulas:
$$\sum_{k=1}^{n} k = \frac{n(n+1)}{2},$$
$$\sum_{k=1}^{n} 1 = n,$$
$$\sum_{k=1}^{n} k^2 = \frac{n(n+1)(2n+1)}{6}.$$

Find the sum:
$$\sum_{k=1}^{10} (2k^2 + 3k + 1).$$

Solution. We will eventually get around to proving the given formulas.

We can split the sum, by Theorem 4.4.2, and compute each separately:

$$\sum_{k=1}^{10}(2k^2 + 3k + 1) = 2\sum_{k=1}^{10}k^2 + 3\sum_{k=1}^{10}k + \sum_{k=1}^{10}1$$
$$= 2 \cdot \frac{10 \cdot 11 \cdot 21}{6} + 3 \cdot \frac{10 \cdot 11}{2} + 10 = \boxed{945}.$$

Problem 4.4.6. Compute $\sum_{i=1}^{4}\left(\sum_{j=1}^{3}i+j\right)$.

Solution. We evaluate the inner summation first, then the outer summation.

$$\sum_{i=1}^{4}\left(\sum_{j=1}^{3}i+j\right) = \sum_{j=1}^{3}1+j + \sum_{j=1}^{3}2+j + \sum_{j=1}^{3}3+j + \sum_{j=1}^{3}4+j$$
$$= (2+3+4) + (3+4+5) + (4+5+6) + (5+6+7)$$
$$= 9 + 12 + 15 + 18$$
$$= \boxed{54}.$$

Problem 4.4.7. Find another way to express $\sum_{k=400}^{1000}k^2$.

Solution. The complication is that our dummy variable k starts at 400. We can make $k = 1$ and either subtract what we don't want from the entire sum, or as shown before, 'shift' the ending value and the sequence formula as well:

$$\sum_{k=1}^{1000}k^2 - \sum_{k=1}^{399}k^2$$

$$\sum_{k=1}^{601}(k+399)^2$$

Try listing out the first few terms of each to convince yourself that all three ways represent the same sum.

Problem 4.4.8. Compute $\sum_{k=10}^{20}k^2$ in two ways by:

a) Subtracting two sums.

b) Reindexing the summation starting from 1 and breaking the sum into parts.

Solution.

a) The sum of $10^2 + 11^2 + \ldots + 20^2$ is the same as subtracting the sum $1^2 + 2^2 + \ldots + 9^2$ from the total sum $1^2 + 2^2 + \ldots + 20^2$, making this more manageable with the formulas we already know:

$$\sum_{k=10}^{20} k^2 = \sum_{k=1}^{20} k^2 - \sum_{k=1}^{9} k^2 = \frac{20 \cdot 21 \cdot 41}{6} - \frac{9 \cdot 10 \cdot 19}{6} = 2870 - 285 = \boxed{2585}.$$

b) Note that we can reindex the sum as:

$$\sum_{k=10}^{20} k^2 = \sum_{k=1}^{11} (k+9)^2 = \sum_{k=1}^{11} k^2 + 18k + 81$$

We can split $\sum_{k=1}^{11} k^2 + 18k + 81$ into a sum of partial sums, which we are able to compute individually using our formulas:

$$\sum_{k=1}^{11} k^2 + 18k + 81 = \sum_{k=1}^{11} k^2 + 18 \sum_{k=1}^{11} k + \sum_{k=1}^{11} 81$$
$$= \frac{11 \cdot 12 \cdot 23}{6} + 18 \left(\frac{11 \cdot 12}{2} \right) + 11(81)$$
$$= 506 + 1188 + 891 = \boxed{2585}. \qquad \square$$

You may recall from earlier that I represented an infinite geometric series by

$$a + ar + ar^2 + \ldots$$

Using this newly introduced summation notation, we can represent this same infinite sum as

$$\sum_{k=1}^{\infty} ar^k,$$

and when $|r| < 1$, we can state the general formula as

$$\sum_{k=1}^{\infty} ar^k = \frac{a}{1-r}.$$

Lastly, keep in mind that we can turn an infinite summation into a finite summation, with the limit attached in front of it, as such:

$$\sum_{k=1}^{\infty} a_k = \lim_{n \to \infty} \sum_{k=1}^{n} a_k.$$

In addition to summation, we also have a way to write the product of terms in shorthand form.

Definition 4.4.9 (Product Notation). Let $m, n \in \mathbb{Z}$, $m \leq n$. Then,

$$\prod_{k=m}^{n} a_k = a_m \cdot a_{m+1} \cdot a_{m+2} \cdots a_n,$$

and product notation is analogous to summation notation.

Here are some examples:

1. $\prod_{k=1}^{n} k = \boxed{n!}$.

2. $\prod_{k=1}^{n} r = \boxed{r^n}$.

3. $\prod_{k=2}^{79} \frac{k}{k+1} = \frac{2}{3} \cdot \frac{3}{4} \cdot \frac{4}{5} \cdots \frac{79}{80} = \frac{2}{80} = \boxed{\frac{1}{40}}$. This occurrence, when nearly all terms ultimately cancel each other out, is called *telescoping*.

4. $\sum_{k=40}^{80} \log k = \log \left(\prod_{k=40}^{80} k \right)$, if you recall that $\log(ab) = \log a + \log b$.

> **Theorem 4.4.10**
>
> Likewise, we can multiply two products together, and the power of the product is equal to the product of the powers.
>
> 1. $\prod_{k=m}^{n} a_k \prod_{k=m}^{n} b_k = \prod_{k=m}^{n} a_k b_k$.
>
> 2. $\left(\prod_{k=m}^{n} a_k \right)^r = \prod_{k=m}^{n} (a_k)^r$.

Exercise 4.4.11. Prove Theorem 4.4.10 (it should be relatively straightforward).

Chapter 5

Mathematical Induction

This chapter is dedicated to an essential technique of proof for certain claims, particularly when the claim should be true for all positive integers (and variants). Then, we will transition to a brief discussion in combinatorics about the "choose" function, and we show how induction can be used to prove some theorems (in particular, the Binomial Theorem) in this area.

5.1 Standard Applications

Recall the following valid argument form, which underlies the principle of mathematical induction.

$$P(1)$$
$$\forall n \in \mathbb{Z}^+, \ P(n) \to P(n+1)$$
$$\therefore \forall n \in \mathbb{Z}^+, \ P(n).$$

We have already demonstrated that this argument is true at the end of Chapter 1. If we show that $P(1)$ is true and the implication is true, then we get $P(2)$, $P(3)$, $P(4)$, etc. for the rest of the positive integers.

Suppose you have a statement you are trying to prove for all positive integers n. Here are the steps you should take in a proof by induction:

1. Prove the statement for $n = 1$. This is called the **base case**.

2. Assume that the statement is true for $n = k$. This is called the **inductive hypothesis**.

3. Prove that if the inductive hypothesis is true, then the statement is also true for $n = k+1$. This is the **inductive step**.

This kind of proof may seem mechanic, but this established, reliable structure is what makes induction proofs relatively straightforward.

> **Example 5.1.1**
> Prove $\sum_{k=1}^{n} k = \dfrac{n(n+1)}{2}$.

Proof. For clarity, let $P(n)$ denote the assertion that $\sum_{k=1}^{n} k = \frac{n(n+1)}{2}$.

<u>Base Case</u>: $P(1) : \sum_{k=1}^{1} k = \frac{1(1+1)}{2} = 1$.

We have $1 = 1$, which is clearly true.

<u>Inductive Step</u>: Suppose $P(n) : \sum_{k=1}^{n} k = \frac{n(n+1)}{2}$, i.e. $1 + 2 + 3 + \ldots + n = \frac{n(n+1)}{2}$, is true.

We want to prove that $P(n+1) : 1 + 2 + 3 + \ldots + n + (n+1) = \frac{(n+1)(n+2)}{2}$ is true.

We have

$$1 + 2 + 3 + \ldots + n + (n+1) = \frac{n(n+1)}{2} + (n+1)$$
$$= (n+1)\left(\frac{n}{2} + 1\right)$$
$$= (n+1)\left(\frac{n+2}{2}\right)$$
$$= \frac{(n+1)(n+2)}{2}.$$

Therefore our inductive step holds and we are done. $\square$

Problem 5.1.2. Prove $\sum_{k=1}^{n} k^2 = \frac{n(n+1)(2n+1)}{6}$.

Proof. Let $P(n) : \sum_{k=1}^{n} k^2 = \frac{n(n+1)(2n+1)}{6}$.

<u>Base Case</u>: $P(1) : \sum_{k=1}^{1} k^2 = \frac{1 \cdot 2 \cdot 3}{6} = 1$.

We have $1^2 = 1$, so we're done.

<u>Inductive Step</u>: Suppose $P(n) : \sum_{k=1}^{n} k^2 = \frac{n(n+1)(2n+1)}{6}$ is true.

We want to prove that $P(n+1) : 1^2 + 2^2 + 3^2 + \ldots + n^2 + (n+1)^2 = \frac{(n+1)(n+2)(2n+3)}{6}$.

We have

$$1^2 + 2^2 + 3^2 + \ldots + n^2 + (n+1)^2 = \frac{n(n+1)(2n+1)}{6} + (n+1)^2$$
$$= (n+1)\left(\frac{n(2n+1)}{6} + (n+1)\right)$$
$$= (n+1)\left(\frac{2n^2+n}{6} + \frac{6n+6}{6}\right)$$
$$= (n+1)\left(\frac{2n^2+7n+6}{6}\right)$$

$$= (n+1)\left(\frac{(2n+3)(n+2)}{6}\right)$$
$$= \frac{(n+1)(n+2)(2n+3)}{6}.$$

Our inductive step holds, so we are done. □

Problem 5.1.3.

1. Prove $\sum_{i=1}^{n} i^3 = \frac{n^2(n+1)^2}{4}$ by induction.

2. Then compute $\sum_{i=1}^{10} 2i^3 - 3i^2 + 5i - 7$.

Proof. For the induction proof, let $P(n) : \sum_{i=1}^{n} i^3 = \frac{n^2(n+1)^2}{4}$.

<u>Base Case</u>: $P(1) : \sum_{i=1}^{1} i^3 = \frac{1^2(1+1)^2}{4} = \frac{4}{4} = 1$.

We have $1^3 = 1$, which is clearly true.

<u>Inductive Step</u>: Suppose $P(n) : \sum_{i=1}^{n} i^3 = \frac{n^2(n+1)^2}{4}$.

We must prove that $P(n+1) : 1^3 + 2^3 + 3^3 + \ldots + n^3 + (n+1)^3 = \frac{(n+1)^2(n+2)^2}{4}$.

Then, note that

$$1^3 + 2^3 + 3^3 + \ldots + n^3 + (n+1)^3 = \frac{n^2(n+1)^2}{4} + (n+1)^3$$
$$= (n+1)^2 \left(\frac{n^2}{4} + (n+1)\right)$$
$$= (n+1)^2 \left(\frac{n^2}{4} + \frac{4n+4}{4}\right)$$
$$= (n+1)^2 \left(\frac{n^2 + 4n + 4}{4}\right)$$
$$= (n+1)^2 \left(\frac{(n+2)^2}{4}\right)$$
$$= \frac{(n+1)^2(n+2)^2}{4},$$

which completes the proof.

For part 2, simply split up the sum as follows:

$$\sum_{i=1}^{10} 2i^3 - 3i^2 + 5i - 7 = 2\sum_{i=1}^{10} i^3 - 3\sum_{i=1}^{10} i^2 + 5\sum_{i=1}^{10} i - \sum_{i=1}^{10} 7$$

$$= 2 \cdot \frac{10^2 \cdot 11^2}{4} - 3 \cdot \frac{10 \cdot 11 \cdot 21}{6} + 5 \cdot \frac{10 \cdot 11}{2} - 70$$
$$= 6050 - 1155 + 275 - 70$$
$$= \boxed{5100}. \qquad \square$$

Problem 5.1.4. Let $a_n = \sum_{i=1}^{n} \frac{1}{i(i+1)}$.

1. Compute $a_1, a_2, a_3, a_4,$ and a_5.

2. Hypothesize a formula for a_n.

3. Prove that formula using induction.

4. What is $\sum_{i=1}^{\infty} \frac{1}{i(i+1)}$?

Solution.

1. This is just direct computation of the summation.

$$a_1 = \frac{1}{2}$$
$$a_2 = \frac{1}{2} + \frac{1}{6} = \frac{2}{3}$$
$$a_3 = \frac{1}{2} + \frac{1}{6} + \frac{1}{12} = \frac{3}{4}$$
$$a_4 = \frac{1}{2} + \frac{1}{6} + \frac{1}{12} + \frac{1}{20} = \frac{4}{5}$$
$$a_5 = \frac{1}{2} + \frac{1}{6} + \frac{1}{12} + \frac{1}{20} + \frac{1}{30} = \frac{5}{6}$$

2. Noticing that the denominator is always one more than the numerator, we can hypothesize that the formula is $a_n = \frac{n}{n+1}$.

3. We proceed to prove $\sum_{i=1}^{n} \frac{1}{i(i+1)} = \frac{n}{n+1}$ by induction.

   Let $P(n) : \sum_{i=1}^{n} \frac{1}{i(i+1)} = \frac{n}{n+1}$.

   <u>Base Case:</u> $P(1) : \sum_{i=1}^{1} \frac{1}{i(i+1)} = \frac{1}{2}$.

   We also have that $\frac{n}{n+1} = \frac{1}{1+1} = \frac{1}{2}$, so the base case is true.

   <u>Inductive Step:</u> Suppose that $P(n) : \sum_{i=1}^{n} \frac{1}{i(i+1)} = \frac{n}{n+1}$.

   We wish to prove that $P(n+1) : \sum_{i=1}^{n+1} \frac{1}{i(i+1)} = \frac{n+1}{n+2}$, i.e.

$$\frac{1}{1(1+1)} + \frac{1}{2(2+1)} + \ldots + \frac{1}{n(n+1)} + \frac{1}{(n+1)(n+2)} = \frac{n+1}{n+2}.$$

Note that

$$\frac{1}{1(1+1)} + \frac{1}{2(2+1)} + \ldots + \frac{1}{n(n+1)} + \frac{1}{(n+1)(n+2)} = \frac{n}{n+1} + \frac{1}{(n+1)(n+2)}$$
$$= \frac{n(n+2)+1}{(n+1)(n+2)}$$
$$= \frac{n^2+2n+1}{(n+1)(n+2)}$$
$$= \frac{(n+1)^2}{(n+1)(n+2)}$$
$$= \frac{n+1}{n+2}.$$

This holds the inductive step, and we're done.

4. Recall that we can rewrite an infinite summation as the limit of a finite summation:

$$\sum_{i=1}^{\infty} \frac{1}{i(i+1)} = \lim_{n \to \infty} \sum_{i=1}^{n} \frac{1}{i(i+1)} = \lim_{n \to \infty} \frac{n}{n+1}.$$

Divide the numerator and denominator by n:

$$\lim_{n \to \infty} \frac{n}{n+1} = \lim_{n \to \infty} \frac{1}{1+\frac{1}{n}}.$$

Then $\frac{1}{n}$ tends to 0 as n gets arbitrarily large, so we are left with $\frac{1}{1+0} = 1$. Therefore $\sum_{i=1}^{\infty} \frac{1}{i(i+1)} = \boxed{1}$. □

Problem 5.1.5. Let $f(n) = \prod_{k=1}^{n} \left(1 - \frac{1}{k+1}\right)$.

i) Compute $f(n)$ for $n = 1, 2, 3, 4, 5$.

ii) Hypothesize a formula.

iii) Prove your formula by induction.

iv) Compute $\prod_{k=1}^{\infty} \left(1 - \frac{1}{k+1}\right)$.

Solution.

i) This time, we have a product instead of a summation to evaluate.

$$f(1) = \left(1 - \frac{1}{2}\right) = \boxed{\frac{1}{2}}$$

$$f(2) = \left(1 - \frac{1}{2}\right)\left(1 - \frac{1}{3}\right) = \frac{1}{2} \cdot \frac{2}{3} = \boxed{\frac{1}{3}}$$

$$f(3) = \left(1 - \frac{1}{2}\right)\left(1 - \frac{1}{3}\right)\left(1 - \frac{1}{4}\right) = \frac{1}{2} \cdot \frac{2}{3} \cdot \frac{3}{4} = \boxed{\frac{1}{4}}$$

$$f(4) = \left(1 - \frac{1}{2}\right)\left(1 - \frac{1}{3}\right)\left(1 - \frac{1}{4}\right)\left(1 - \frac{1}{5}\right) = \frac{1}{2} \cdot \frac{2}{3} \cdot \frac{3}{4} \cdot \frac{4}{5} = \boxed{\frac{1}{5}}$$

$$f(5) = \left(1 - \frac{1}{2}\right)\left(1 - \frac{1}{3}\right)\left(1 - \frac{1}{4}\right)\left(1 - \frac{1}{5}\right)\left(1 - \frac{1}{6}\right) = \frac{1}{2} \cdot \frac{2}{3} \cdot \frac{3}{4} \cdot \frac{4}{5} \cdot \frac{5}{6} = \boxed{\frac{1}{6}}$$

ii) The pattern of the first five terms suggests that the formula is $f(n) = \boxed{\dfrac{1}{n+1}}$.

iii) The statement we must prove is: $\prod_{k=1}^{n}\left(1 - \dfrac{1}{k+1}\right) = \dfrac{1}{n+1}$.

Let $P(n) : \prod_{k=1}^{n}\left(1 - \dfrac{1}{k+1}\right) = \dfrac{1}{n+1}$.

<u>Base Case</u>: $P(1) : \prod_{k=1}^{1}\left(1 - \dfrac{1}{k+1}\right) = 1 - \dfrac{1}{2} = \dfrac{1}{2}$

But $\dfrac{1}{n+1}$ where $n = 1$ is $\dfrac{1}{2}$, so the base case is true.

<u>Inductive Step</u>: Assume $P(n) : \prod_{k=1}^{n}\left(1 - \dfrac{1}{k+1}\right) = \dfrac{1}{n+1}$.

We want to prove: $P(n+1) : \prod_{k=1}^{n+1}\left(1 - \dfrac{1}{k+1}\right) = \dfrac{1}{n+2}$.

We have

$$\left(1 - \frac{1}{2}\right)\left(1 - \frac{1}{3}\right)\left(1 - \frac{1}{4}\right) \cdots \left(1 - \frac{1}{n+1}\right)\left(1 - \frac{1}{n+2}\right) = \left(\frac{1}{n+1}\right)\left(1 - \frac{1}{n+2}\right)$$

$$= \left(\frac{1}{n+1}\right)\left(\frac{n+1}{n+2}\right)$$

$$= \frac{1}{n+2}.$$

So the statement for $P(n+1)$ is true, which concludes the proof by induction.

iv) Like before, we can rewrite an infinite product as the limit of a finite product, and evaluate as such:

$$\prod_{k=1}^{\infty}\left(1 - \frac{1}{k+1}\right) = \lim_{n \to \infty} \prod_{k=1}^{n}\left(1 - \frac{1}{k+1}\right) = \lim_{n \to \infty} \frac{1}{n+1} = \boxed{0}. \qquad \square$$

However, proofs by induction are not limited to summations. For the next few problems, we establish a few facts about divisibility first.

Lemma 5.1.6 (Divisibility Lemmas)
Recall that $a \mid b$ means "a divides b," or "a is a factor of b." Then,

1. $a \mid b \wedge b \mid c \longrightarrow a \mid c$
2. $a \mid b \wedge a \mid c \longrightarrow a \mid (b+c)$
3. $a \mid b \wedge a \mid c \longrightarrow a \mid (b-c)$
4. $a \mid b \longrightarrow a \mid (bc)$

Problem 5.1.7. Using induction, prove $\forall n \in \mathbb{Z}^+$, $7 \mid (8^n - 1)$.

Proof. Let $P(n) : 7 \mid (8^n - 1)$.

Base Case: $P(1) : 7 \mid (8^1 - 1)$ i.e. $7 \mid 7$, which is true.

Inductive Step: We assume $P(n) : 7 \mid (8^n - 1)$. We wish to prove $P(n+1) : 7 \mid (8^{n+1} - 1)$.

Note that $8^{n+1} = 8^n \cdot 8$. To prove $P(n+1)$, note that $7 \mid (8^n - 1) \longrightarrow 7 \mid (8 \cdot (8^n - 1))$, i.e. $7 \mid (8^{n+1} - 8)$. As $7 \mid 7$, we have $7 \mid ((8^{n+1} - 8) + 7)$ i.e. $7 \mid (8^{n+1} - 1)$, and we're done. □

Problem 5.1.8. Prove $\forall n \in \mathbb{Z}^+$, $5 \mid (8^n - 3^n)$.

Proof. $\forall n \in \mathbb{Z}^+$, let $P(n) : 5 \mid (8^n - 3^n)$.

Base Case: $P(1) : 5 \mid (8^1 - 3^1) \longrightarrow 5 \mid (8-3)$ i.e. $5 \mid 5$, which is true.

Inductive Step: Suppose $P(n) : 5 \mid (8^n - 3^n)$.

We wish to prove $P(n+1) : 5 \mid (8^{n+1} - 3^{n+1})$.

Note that $5 \mid (8^n - 3^n) \to 5 \mid (8 \cdot (8^n - 3^n))$, i.e. $5 \mid (8^{n+1} - 8 \cdot 3^n)$.

Using the fact that $3^{n+1} = 3 \cdot 3^n$ and $5 \mid (5 \cdot 3^n)$, we have

$$5 \mid (5 \cdot 3^n) \wedge 5 \mid (8^{n+1} - 8 \cdot 3^n) \longrightarrow 5 \mid ((8^{n+1} - 8 \cdot 3^n) + (5 \cdot 3^n))$$
$$\text{i.e. } 5 \mid (8^{n+1} - 3 \cdot 3^n)$$
$$\text{i.e. } 5 \mid (8^{n+1} - 3^{n+1}).$$

We have reached the conclusion that $P(n+1) : 5 \mid (8^{n+1} - 3^{n+1})$ is true, so our proof is complete. □

Problem 5.1.9. Prove for all positive odd integers n, $11 \mid (8^n + 3^n)$.

Proof. There is something different about this problem - we must prove it for all positive odd integers n. In this case, it suffices to prove $P(1)$ and then $P(n) \to P(n+2)$.

Let $P(n) : 11 \mid (8^n + 3^n)$.

Base Case: $P(1) : 11 \mid (8^1 + 3^1) \to 11 \mid 11$, which is true.

Inductive Step: Suppose that $P(n) : 11 \mid (8^n + 3^n)$ is true.

Then we must prove $P(n+2) : 11 \mid (8^{n+2} + 3^{n+2})$.

First note that $11 \mid (8^n + 3^n) \to 11 \mid (8^2(8^n + 3^n))$ i.e. $11 \mid (8^{n+2} + 64 \cdot 3^n)$.

However, notice that $64 = 55 + 9$, then we have
$$11 \mid (8^{n+2} + 64 \cdot 3^n) \longrightarrow 11 \mid (8^{n+2} + (55 + 9) \cdot 3^n)$$
$$\text{i.e. } 11 \mid (8^{n+2} + 55 \cdot 3^n + 9 \cdot 3^n).$$

As $11 \mid 55$, it must also be true that $11 \mid (55 \cdot 3^n)$, therefore
$$11 \mid (55 \cdot 3^n) \wedge 11 \mid (8^{n+2} + 55 \cdot 3^n + 9 \cdot 3^n) \to 11 \mid ((8^{n+2} + 55 \cdot 3^n + 9 \cdot 3^n) - 55 \cdot 3^n)$$
$$\text{i.e. } 11 \mid (8^{n+2} + 9 \cdot 3^n)$$
$$\text{i.e. } 11 \mid (8^{n+2} + 3^{n+2}),$$

and our proof by induction is complete. $\square$

Problem 5.1.10. Prove that for all n which are positive odd multiples of 3, $91 \mid (3^n + 4^n)$.

Proof. Let $P(n) : 91 \mid (3^n + 4^n)$.

<u>Base Case</u>: Since we are talking about positive odd multiples of 3, our base case is $n = 3$. We have $P(3) : 91 \mid (3^3 + 4^3)$, or $91 \mid 91$, which is true.

<u>Inductive Step</u>: For a given positive odd multiple of 3, say n, we must increment it by 6 to get to the next positive odd multiple of 3. Thus, we want to demonstrate $P(n) \longrightarrow P(n+6)$.

Suppose $P(n) : 91 \mid (3^n + 4^n)$. We must prove that $P(n+6) : 91 \mid (3^{n+6} + 4^{n+6})$.

First, we can show that $91 \mid (3^n + 4^n) \longrightarrow 91 \mid (4^6(3^n + 4^n))$ i.e. $91 \mid (4^6 \cdot 3^n + 4^{n+6})$.

Note that $4^6 - 3^6 = 4096 - 729 = 3367 = (4^3 + 3^3)(4^3 - 3^3) = 91 \cdot 37$.

Therefore, $91 \mid 3367$ or $91 \mid (4^6 - 3^6)$ i.e. $91 \mid (4^6 \cdot 3^n - 3^6 \cdot 3^n)$. Then we have
$$91 \mid (4^6 \cdot 3^n - 3^6 \cdot 3^n) \wedge 91 \mid (4^6 \cdot 3^n + 4^{n+6}) \longrightarrow 91 \mid (4^6 \cdot 3^n - (4^6 \cdot 3^n - 3^6 \cdot 3^n) + 4^{n+6})$$
$$\text{i.e. } 91 \mid (3^6 \cdot 3^n + 4^{n+6})$$
$$\text{i.e. } 91 \mid (3^{n+6} + 4^{n+6}).$$

The statement $P(n+6) : 91 \mid (3^{n+6} + 4^{n+6})$ is true, and therefore our inductive step holds, and the proof is done. $\square$

Problem 5.1.11. Prove $\forall n \in \mathbb{Z}^+, 3 \mid (n^3 - n)$.

Proof. Let $P(n) : 3 \mid (n^3 - n)$.

<u>Base Case</u>: $P(1) : 3 \mid (1 - 1)$ i.e. $3 \mid 0$, which is true.

<u>Inductive Step</u>: Suppose $P(n) : 3 \mid (n^3 - n)$. We must prove $P(n+1) : 3 \mid ((n+1)^3 - (n+1))$.

We know that $3 \mid (3 \cdot (n^2 + n))$ i.e. $3 \mid (3n^2 + 3n)$. Therefore,
$$3 \mid (3n^2 + 3n) \wedge 3 \mid (n^3 - n) \longrightarrow 3 \mid (n^3 - n + 3n^2 + 3n)$$
$$\text{i.e. } 3 \mid (n^3 + 3n^2 + 3n - n)$$
$$\text{i.e. } 3 \mid (n^3 + 3n^2 + 3n + 1 - n - 1)$$
$$\text{i.e. } 3 \mid ((n+1)^3 - (n+1)).$$

We have proven $P(n+1)$, which completes the inductive step, so we are done. $\square$

Problem 5.1.12. Prove $\sum_{i=1}^{n} \frac{1}{i^2} \leq 2 - \frac{1}{n}$ $\forall n \in \mathbb{Z}^+$ (and by implication $\sum_{i=1}^{n} \frac{1}{i^2} < 2$).

Proof. Let $P(n) : \sum_{i=1}^{n} \frac{1}{i^2} \leq 2 - \frac{1}{n}$.

<u>Base Case</u>: $P(1) : \sum_{i=1}^{1} \frac{1}{i^2} = 1 \leq 2 - \frac{1}{1^2}$.

We have $1 \leq 1$, which is true.

<u>Inductive Step</u>: Assume $P(n) : \sum_{i=1}^{n} \frac{1}{i^2} \leq 2 - \frac{1}{n}$.

We wish to prove that $P(n+1) : \sum_{i=1}^{n+1} \frac{1}{i^2} \leq 2 - \frac{1}{n+1}$.

In other words, given $\frac{1}{1^2} + \frac{1}{2^2} + \frac{1}{3^2} + \ldots + \frac{1}{n^2} \leq 2 - \frac{1}{n}$, we should prove that $\frac{1}{1^2} + \frac{1}{2^2} + \frac{1}{3^2} + \ldots + \frac{1}{n^2} + \frac{1}{(n+1)^2} \leq 2 - \frac{1}{n+1}$. As a first step, we can manipulate what our assumption into something similar to our goal, as follows:

$$\frac{1}{1^2} + \frac{1}{2^2} + \frac{1}{3^2} + \ldots + \frac{1}{n^2} \leq 2 - \frac{1}{n} \qquad \text{(by inductive hypothesis)}$$

$$\frac{1}{1^2} + \frac{1}{2^2} + \frac{1}{3^2} + \ldots + \frac{1}{n^2} + \frac{1}{(n+1)^2} \leq 2 - \frac{1}{n} + \frac{1}{(n+1)^2}$$

How would we use this inequality to get a result like $\frac{1}{1^2} + \frac{1}{2^2} + \frac{1}{3^2} + \ldots + \frac{1}{n^2} + \frac{1}{(n+1)^2} \leq 2 - \frac{1}{n+1}$? Try to find a relation between $2 - \frac{1}{n} + \frac{1}{(n+1)^2}$ and $2 - \frac{1}{n+1}$ that would quickly enable us to finish the proof.

In fact, we want the inequality $2 - \frac{1}{n} + \frac{1}{(n+1)^2} \leq 2 - \frac{1}{n+1}$ to be true.

Why? If the above is true, then $\frac{1}{1^2} + \frac{1}{2^2} + \frac{1}{3^2} + \ldots + \frac{1}{n^2} + \frac{1}{(n+1)^2} \leq 2 - \frac{1}{n} + \frac{1}{(n+1)^2} \leq 2 - \frac{1}{n+1} \implies \frac{1}{1^2} + \frac{1}{2^2} + \frac{1}{3^2} + \ldots + \frac{1}{n^2} + \frac{1}{(n+1)^2} \leq 2 - \frac{1}{n+1}$, allowing us to quickly finish the proof.

Indeed, this is true, and the proof is as follows:

As n is positive, $n^2 + 2n + 1 \geq n^2 + 2n$. Then, we have

$$(n+1)^2 \geq n(n+2)$$

$$1 \geq \frac{n(n+2)}{(n+1)^2}$$

$$\frac{1}{n} \geq \frac{n+2}{(n+1)^2}$$

$$\frac{1}{n} \geq \frac{(n+1)+1}{(n+1)^2}$$

$$\frac{1}{n} \geq \frac{n+1}{(n+1)^2} + \frac{1}{(n+1)^2}$$

$$\frac{1}{n} \geq \frac{1}{n+1} + \frac{1}{(n+1)^2}$$

$$\frac{1}{n} - \frac{1}{(n+1)^2} \geq \frac{1}{n+1}$$

$$-\frac{1}{n} + \frac{1}{(n+1)^2} \leq -\frac{1}{n+1}$$

$$\therefore 2 - \frac{1}{n} + \frac{1}{(n+1)^2} \leq 2 - \frac{1}{n+1}$$

Since $2 - \frac{1}{n} + \frac{1}{(n+1)^2} \leq 2 - \frac{1}{n+1}$, we have therefore proven that $\frac{1}{1^2} + \frac{1}{2^2} + \frac{1}{3^2} + \ldots + \frac{1}{n^2} + \frac{1}{(n+1)^2} \leq 2 - \frac{1}{n+1}$. Our inductive step holds true, and so our proof is complete. $\square$

Problem 5.1.13. Prove $\sum_{k=1}^{n} \frac{1}{\sqrt{k}} < 2\sqrt{n}, \forall n \in \mathbb{Z}^+$.

Proof. Let $P(n) : \sum_{k=1}^{n} \frac{1}{\sqrt{k}} < 2\sqrt{n}$.

<u>Base Case</u>: $P(1) : \sum_{k=1}^{1} \frac{1}{\sqrt{k}} = 1$.

Then 1 is less than $2\sqrt{1} = 2$, so the base case is true.

<u>Inductive Step</u>: Suppose $P(n) : \sum_{k=1}^{n} \frac{1}{\sqrt{k}} < 2\sqrt{n}$ is true.

We want to prove: $P(n+1) : \sum_{k=1}^{n+1} \frac{1}{\sqrt{k}} < 2\sqrt{n+1}$.

By assumption we have

$$\frac{1}{\sqrt{1}} + \frac{1}{\sqrt{2}} + \frac{1}{\sqrt{3}} + \ldots + \frac{1}{\sqrt{n}} < 2\sqrt{n}.$$

Add $\frac{1}{\sqrt{n+1}}$ to both sides. Then,

$$\frac{1}{\sqrt{1}} + \frac{1}{\sqrt{2}} + \frac{1}{\sqrt{3}} + \ldots + \frac{1}{\sqrt{n}} + \frac{1}{\sqrt{n+1}} < 2\sqrt{n} + \frac{1}{\sqrt{n+1}}.$$

We need $2\sqrt{n} + \frac{1}{\sqrt{n+1}} < 2\sqrt{n+1}$ to be true in order to complete the proof. Below, we will prove this fact.

Note that $n \in \mathbb{Z}^+$. Then,

$$\left(\sqrt{n} - \sqrt{n+1}\right)^2 > 0$$

$$n - 2\sqrt{n(n+1)} + n + 1 > 0$$
$$2\sqrt{n(n+1)} < 2n + 1$$
$$2\sqrt{n(n+1)} + 1 < 2n + 2$$
$$2\sqrt{n(n+1)} + 1 < 2(n+1)$$
$$2\sqrt{n}\sqrt{n+1}\left(\frac{1}{\sqrt{n+1}}\right) + 1\left(\frac{1}{\sqrt{n+1}}\right) < 2(n+1)\left(\frac{1}{\sqrt{n+1}}\right)$$
$$2\sqrt{n} + \frac{1}{\sqrt{n+1}} < 2(n+1)\left(\frac{\sqrt{n+1}}{n+1}\right)$$
$$\therefore 2\sqrt{n} + \frac{1}{\sqrt{n+1}} < 2\sqrt{n+1}.$$

Thus,
$$\frac{1}{\sqrt{1}} + \frac{1}{\sqrt{2}} + \frac{1}{\sqrt{3}} + \ldots + \frac{1}{\sqrt{n}} + \frac{1}{\sqrt{n+1}} < 2\sqrt{n} + \frac{1}{\sqrt{n+1}} < 2\sqrt{n+1},$$
or
$$\frac{1}{\sqrt{1}} + \frac{1}{\sqrt{2}} + \frac{1}{\sqrt{3}} + \ldots + \frac{1}{\sqrt{n}} + \frac{1}{\sqrt{n+1}} < 2\sqrt{n+1},$$
which concludes the inductive step, so our proof by induction is complete. $\square$

Here is an arrangement of various results that are provable using induction.

Exercise 5.1.14. Prove $\forall n \in \mathbb{Z}^+$, $7 \mid (13^n - 6^n)$.

Exercise 5.1.15. Prove $\forall n \in \mathbb{Z}^+$, $4 \mid (5^n - 1)$.

Exercise 5.1.16. Prove $\forall n \in \mathbb{Z}^+$, $3 \mid (n^3 + 2n)$.

Exercise 5.1.17. Prove for all positive odd integers n, $3 \mid (2^n + 1)$.

Exercise 5.1.18. Prove $\forall n \in \mathbb{Z}^+$, $\sum_{k=0}^{n} 2^k = 2^{n+1} - 1$.

Exercise 5.1.19. Prove $\forall n \geq 0$, $7 \mid (5^{2n+1} + 2^{2n+1})$.

Exercise 5.1.20. Prove for all positive odd integers n, $8 \mid (n^2 - 1)$.

Exercise 5.1.21. Prove for all positive odd integers n, $16 \mid (n^4 - 1)$.

Exercise 5.1.22. Prove $\forall n \in \mathbb{Z}^+$, $6 \mid (17n^3 + 103n)$.

Exercise 5.1.23. Prove $\forall n \in \mathbb{Z}^+$, $\sum_{k=1}^{n} (2k-1)^2 = \frac{4n^3 - n}{3}$.

Exercise 5.1.24. Prove $\forall n \in \mathbb{Z}^+$, $\sum_{k=1}^{n} \frac{1}{(2k-1)(2k+1)} = \frac{n}{2n+1}$.

Exercise 5.1.25. Prove $\forall n \in \mathbb{Z}^+$, $5 \mid (6^n + 4)$.

Exercise 5.1.26. Prove $\forall n \in \mathbb{Z}^+$, $8 \mid (9^n - 1)$.

Exercise 5.1.27. Prove $\forall n \in \mathbb{Z}^+$, $3 \mid (5^n - 2^n)$.

Exercise 5.1.28. Prove Lemma 4.3.13. That is, given $\forall n \in \mathbb{N}_0$, $h \geq -1$, prove that $(1+h)^n \geq 1+hn$.

Exercise 5.1.29. Prove that if n is an integer greater than 3, then $n! > 2^n$.

Exercise 5.1.30. Prove $\forall n \in \mathbb{Z}^+$, $\displaystyle\prod_{k=1}^{n}\left(\frac{2k-1}{2k}\right) \leq \frac{1}{\sqrt{3n+1}}$.

Induction is not necessarily limited to simply one inductive step. Consider the following argument form:

$$\forall n \in \mathbb{Z}^+ \ P(n) \longrightarrow P(2n)$$
$$\forall n \in \mathbb{Z}^+ \ P(n) \longrightarrow P(n-1)$$
$$P(2)$$
$$\therefore \forall n \in \mathbb{Z}^+ \ P(n)$$

Given $P(2)$, we know that $P(4)$ must be true. If $P(4)$ is true, then $P(3)$ is true.

Given $P(4)$, we know that $P(8)$ must be true. If $P(8)$ is true, then $P(7)$, $P(6)$, and $P(5)$ are true.

Given $P(8)$, we know that $P(16)$ must be true. If $P(16)$, then $P(15)$, ... all the way down to $P(9)$ are true.

In other words, we can use $P(n) \longrightarrow P(2n)$ to increase our scope while $P(n) \longrightarrow P(n-1)$ will take care of all the statements in the gap between $P(n)$ and $P(2n)$.

Thus, it follows that this argument form, called **Cauchy Induction**, is indeed valid. This form will aid us in proving the following major result:

Theorem 5.1.31 (AM-GM Inequality)

The Arithmetic Mean-Geometric Mean Inequality states that $\forall n \in \mathbb{Z}^+$ and $a_1, a_2, a_3, \ldots, a_n > 0$,

$$\frac{a_1 + a_2 + a_3 + \ldots + a_n}{n} \geq \sqrt[n]{a_1 a_2 a_3 \cdots a_n},$$

where the left hand side is the arithmetic mean and the right hand side is the geometric mean.

Proof. Let $P(n) : \frac{a_1+a_2+a_3+\ldots+a_n}{n} \geq \sqrt[n]{a_1 a_2 a_3 \cdots a_n}$.

<u>Base Case</u>: We want to prove that $P(2) : \dfrac{a_1 + a_2}{2} \geq \sqrt{a_1 a_2}$.

First, as the square of any number is nonnegative, we know that $(a_1 - a_2)^2 \geq 0$. Then,

$$a_1^2 - 2a_1 a_2 + a_2^2 \geq 0$$
$$a_1^2 + 2a_1 a_2 + a_2^2 \geq 4a_1 a_2$$
$$(a_1 + a_2)^2 \geq 4a_1 a_2.$$

As both sides are positive, we can take the square root to get $a_1 + a_2 \geq 2\sqrt{a_1 a_2}$, and this rearranges to the desired inequality, proving our base case.

<u>Inductive Step</u>: Assume $P(n): \dfrac{a_1 + a_2 + a_3 + \ldots + a_n}{n} \geq \sqrt[n]{a_1 a_2 a_3 \cdots a_n}$ is true.

First, we will prove $P(n) \to P(2n)$.

Consider the positive terms $\dfrac{a_1 + a_2 + a_3 + \ldots + a_n}{n}$ and $\dfrac{b_1 + b_2 + b_3 + \ldots + b_n}{n}$. Then as the base case suggests, we have

$$\frac{\frac{a_1+a_2+a_3+\ldots+a_n}{n} + \frac{b_1+b_2+b_3+\ldots+b_n}{n}}{2} \geq \sqrt{\frac{a_1+a_2+a_3+\ldots+a_n}{n} \cdot \frac{b_1+b_2+b_3+\ldots+b_n}{n}},$$

which simplifies to

$$\frac{a_1+a_2+\ldots+a_n+b_1+b_2+\ldots+b_n}{2n} \geq \sqrt{\frac{a_1+a_2+\ldots+a_n}{n} \cdot \frac{b_1+b_2+\ldots+b_n}{n}}.$$

By assumption of $P(n)$, we know that $\dfrac{a_1+a_2+a_3+\ldots+a_n}{n} \geq \sqrt[n]{a_1 a_2 a_3 \cdots a_n}$, and similarly, $\dfrac{b_1+b_2+b_3+\ldots+b_n}{n} \geq \sqrt[n]{b_1 b_2 b_3 \cdots b_n}$.

As all terms are positive, we can multiply the inequalities together to get

$$\frac{a_1+a_2+a_3+\ldots+a_n}{n} \cdot \frac{b_1+b_2+b_3+\ldots+b_n}{n} \geq \sqrt[n]{a_1 a_2 a_3 \cdots a_n} \cdot \sqrt[n]{b_1 b_2 b_3 \cdots b_n}.$$

Take the square root of both sides to get

$$\sqrt{\frac{a_1+a_2+a_3+\ldots+a_n}{n} \cdot \frac{b_1+b_2+b_3+\ldots+b_n}{n}} \geq \sqrt{\sqrt[n]{a_1 a_2 a_3 \cdots a_n} \cdot \sqrt[n]{b_1 b_2 b_3 \cdots b_n}}.$$

Thus, we have

$$\begin{aligned}\frac{a_1+a_2+\ldots+a_n+b_1+b_2+\ldots+b_n}{2n} &\geq \sqrt{\frac{a_1+a_2+\ldots+a_n}{n} \cdot \frac{b_1+b_2+\ldots+b_n}{n}} \\ &\geq \sqrt{\sqrt[n]{a_1 a_2 a_3 \cdots a_n} \cdot \sqrt[n]{b_1 b_2 b_3 \cdots b_n}} \\ &\geq \sqrt{\sqrt[n]{a_1 a_2 a_3 \cdots a_n b_1 b_2 b_3 \cdots b_n}} \\ &\geq \sqrt[2n]{a_1 a_2 a_3 \cdots a_n b_1 b_2 b_3 \cdots b_n}.\end{aligned}$$

We have now established that

$$P(2n): \frac{a_1+a_2+a_3+\ldots+a_n+b_1+b_2+b_3+\ldots+b_n}{2n} \geq \sqrt[2n]{a_1 a_2 a_3 \cdots a_n b_1 b_2 b_3 \cdots b_n},$$

so we conclude the proof of our first inductive step.

Next, we need to demonstrate that $P(n) \to P(n-1)$.

Consider the terms $a_1, a_2, a_3, \ldots, a_{n-1}$, and $\dfrac{a_1 + a_2 + \ldots + a_{n-1}}{n-1}$, where the last term is the arithmetic mean of the previous terms. By assumption of $P(n)$, we have

$$\frac{a_1 + a_2 + a_3 + \ldots + a_{n-1} + \frac{a_1+a_2+\ldots+a_{n-1}}{n-1}}{n} \geq \sqrt[n]{a_1 a_2 a_3 \cdots a_{n-1} \cdot \left(\frac{a_1 + a_2 + \ldots + a_{n-1}}{n-1}\right)}.$$

Let $S = a_1 + a_2 + \ldots + a_{n-1}$. Then we rewrite the above as

$$\frac{S + \frac{S}{n-1}}{n} \geq \sqrt[n]{a_1 a_2 a_3 \cdots a_{n-1} \cdot \left(\frac{S}{n-1}\right)}.$$

We can simplify this expression further:

$$\frac{S + \frac{S}{n-1}}{n} \geq \sqrt[n]{a_1 a_2 a_3 \cdots a_{n-1} \cdot \left(\frac{S}{n-1}\right)}$$

$$\frac{S}{n-1} \geq \sqrt[n]{a_1 a_2 a_3 \cdots a_{n-1} \cdot \left(\frac{S}{n-1}\right)}$$

$$\frac{\frac{S}{n-1}}{\left(\frac{S}{n-1}\right)^{\frac{1}{n}}} \geq (a_1 a_2 \cdots a_{n-1})^{\frac{1}{n}}$$

$$\left(\frac{S}{n-1}\right)^{\frac{n-1}{n}} \geq (a_1 a_2 \cdots a_{n-1})^{\frac{1}{n}}.$$

Take both sides to the $\dfrac{n}{n-1}$ power.

$$\left(\left(\frac{S}{n-1}\right)^{\frac{n-1}{n}}\right)^{\frac{n}{n-1}} \geq \left((a_1 a_2 \cdots a_{n-1})^{\frac{1}{n}}\right)^{\frac{n}{n-1}}$$

$$\frac{S}{n-1} \geq (a_1 a_2 \cdots a_{n-1})^{\frac{1}{n-1}}$$

$$\frac{S}{n-1} \geq \sqrt[n-1]{a_1 a_2 \cdots a_{n-1}}$$

$$\therefore \frac{a_1 + a_2 + \ldots + a_{n-1}}{n-1} \geq \sqrt[n-1]{a_1 a_2 \cdots a_{n-1}}.$$

We obtain the result $\dfrac{a_1 + a_2 + \ldots + a_{n-1}}{n-1} \geq \sqrt[n-1]{a_1 a_2 \cdots a_{n-1}}$, proving that $P(n-1)$ is true.

It has been proven that $P(n) \longrightarrow P(2n)$, and $P(n) \longrightarrow P(n-1)$. The base case, $P(2)$, was already proven. Thus, by Cauchy Induction, $P(n)$ for all $n \in \mathbb{Z}^+$, and we may conclude the proof. $\square$

5.2 The Binomial Theorem

Relevant to our discussion of mathematical induction, we take a brief look into combinatorics, a branch of mathematics that deals with counting objects in an efficient manner.

Definition 5.2.1. Let $n, k \in \mathbb{Z}$ such that $n \geq k \geq 0$. Then,

$$\binom{n}{k} = \frac{n!}{k!(n-k)!} \quad \text{where } 0! = 1,$$

and this is pronounced "n choose k."

For example, if you had a bag of n balls, there would be $\binom{n}{k}$ ways to choose k out of n balls from the bag.

Problem 5.2.2. How many different 3-member committees can be formed from a group of 15 people?

Solution. Out of the total 15 people, we want to select 3 of them. Then the total number of ways is $\binom{15}{3} = \frac{15!}{3!12!} = \frac{15 \cdot 14 \cdot 13}{3 \cdot 2} = \boxed{455}$. □

Theorem 5.2.3 (Pascal's Identity)

$$\binom{n}{k} + \binom{n}{k+1} = \binom{n+1}{k+1}$$

Proof. We can go for an algebra-based approach:

$$\frac{n!}{k!(n-k)!} + \frac{n!}{(k+1)!(n-k-1)!} = \frac{n!(k+1)}{k!(k+1)(n-k)!} + \frac{n!(n-k)}{(k+1)!(n-k-1)!(n-k)}$$

$$= \frac{n!(k+1)}{(k+1)!(n-k)!} + \frac{n!(n-k)}{(k+1)!(n-k)!}$$

$$= \frac{n!(k+1+n-k)}{(k+1)!(n-k)!}$$

$$= \frac{n!(n+1)}{(k+1)!(n-k)!}$$

$$= \frac{(n+1)!}{(k+1)!((n+1)-(k+1))!}$$

$$= \binom{n+1}{k+1}.$$

□

Alternative Proof. In fact, we can also prove this identity using a combinatorial argument.

Consider a group of $n+1$ people and we want to choose $k+1$ of them to form a committee. Now focus on a particular person - call that person A.

We can either include or not include person A in the committee. If we do choose to include person A, then there are $\binom{n}{k}$ ways to choose k remaining people for the committee out of the n remaining people, since person A took one spot on the committee.

If we choose to exclude person A, then we still have to select $k+1$ people out of the remaining n people, and the number of ways to do this is $\binom{n}{k+1}$.

As person A is definitely either in or not in the committee, there are no other possibilities. We also know that these possibilities do not overlap, i.e. they are mutually exclusive. Then, we can establish that adding $\binom{n}{k}$ and $\binom{n}{k+1}$ will give us the total number of ways to select a committee of $k+1$ people from $n+1$ people in total. Thus,
$$\binom{n}{k} + \binom{n}{k+1} = \binom{n+1}{k+1}.$$
□

Problem 5.2.4. Prove that $\binom{n}{k} \in \mathbb{Z}$, where $0 \le k \le n$ and $n, k \in \mathbb{Z}$.

Proof. At first, it seems unclear how to prove this by induction, because we have two variables n and k to deal with. One approach may use *double induction*, where we let $P(n,k) : \binom{n}{k} \in \mathbb{Z}$ and then prove $P(n,k) \to P(n+1,k)$ and $P(n,k) \to P(n, k+1)$.

However, this seems tedious, and in fact there is a more elegant solution. Let $Q(n) : \binom{n}{k} \in \mathbb{Z}$ for $k = 0, 1, 2, \ldots, n$. Then we only have to worry about n as the variable in question. By letting $Q(n)$ refer to a collection of statements, as such:
$$Q(n) \equiv P(n, 0) \wedge P(n, 1) \wedge \ldots \wedge P(n, n),$$
if we are able to prove that $Q(n)\ \forall n$ is true, then $P(n, k)\ \forall n,\ k \le n$ will be true. This will finish the proof cleanly.

Now, we proceed by induction on n of $Q(n)$.

<u>Base Case</u>: $Q(1) : \binom{1}{0} = \frac{1!}{0!1!} = 1$, and $\binom{1}{1} = \frac{1!}{1!0!} = 1$, which are integers, so the base case is done.

<u>Inductive Step</u>: Suppose $Q(n) : \binom{n}{k} \in \mathbb{Z}$ for $k = 0, 1, 2, \ldots, n$ is true.

We want to prove $Q(n+1) : \binom{n+1}{k} \in \mathbb{Z}$ for $k = 0, 1, 2, \ldots, n+1$.

Writing out the terms for $\binom{n+1}{k}$, $k = 0, 1, 2, \ldots, n, n+1$, we have:
$$\binom{n+1}{0}, \binom{n+1}{1}, \binom{n+1}{2}, \ldots, \binom{n+1}{n}, \binom{n+1}{n+1}.$$

By Theorem 5.2.3, each of these can be expressed as the sum of two terms from $\binom{n}{k}$, $k = 0, 1, 2, \ldots, n$, as follows:
$$\binom{n+1}{0}, \binom{n}{0} + \binom{n}{1}, \binom{n}{1} + \binom{n}{2}, \ldots, \binom{n}{n-1} + \binom{n}{n}, \binom{n+1}{n+1}.$$

Note that $\binom{n+1}{0} = \binom{n+1}{n+1} = 1$, and obviously are integers. From assumption of $Q(n)$, we have thereby assumed that each of $\binom{n}{0}, \binom{n}{1}, \binom{n}{2}, \ldots, \binom{n}{n}$ are integers. Then any sum of some terms from these is also an integer. Therefore, each term from $\binom{n+1}{k}$, $k = 0, 1, 2, \ldots, n, n+1$ (except $\binom{n+1}{0}$ and $\binom{n+1}{n+1}$, which are integers anyway) can be expressed as the sum of two integers, and must necessarily be an integer. $\square$

Problem 5.2.5. Prove that $\forall n \in \mathbb{Z}^+$, $n!$ divides the product of n consecutive integers.

Proof. Consider $\binom{n}{k}$, where $k \leq n$. Then,

$$\binom{n}{k} = \frac{n!}{(n-k)!k!}$$
$$= \frac{n(n-1)(n-2)\cdots(n-k+1)(n-k)(n-k-1)\cdots 3 \cdot 2 \cdot 1}{(n-k)(n-k-1)(n-k-2)\cdots 3 \cdot 2 \cdot 1 \cdot k!}$$
$$= \frac{n(n-1)(n-2)\cdots(n-k+1)}{k!}.$$

There are k consecutive terms in the numerator, and this is divided by $k!$ in the denominator. However, by Problem 5.2.4, this quotient is an integer, thus $k!$ divides the k consecutive terms in the numerator, so we are done. $\square$

Now, we finally move on to the main theorem that is provable by induction.

Theorem 5.2.6 (The Binomial Theorem)
Let $n \in \mathbb{Z}^+$. Then,
$$(x+y)^n = \sum_{k=0}^{n} \binom{n}{k} x^{n-k} y^k.$$

Proof. We proceed by induction on n.

<u>Base Case</u>: Consider $n = 1$. We have

$$\sum_{k=0}^{1} \binom{1}{k} x^{1-k} y^k = \binom{1}{0} x^1 y^0 + \binom{1}{1} x^0 y^1$$
$$= x^1 + y^1$$
$$= x + y.$$

Clearly $(x+y)^1 = x+y$, so therefore $(x+y)^1 = \sum_{k=0}^{1} \binom{1}{k} x^{1-k} y^k$, and the base case is true.

<u>Inductive Step</u>: Assume $(x+y)^n = \sum_{k=0}^{n} \binom{n}{k} x^{n-k} y^k$ is true.

We want to prove: $(x+y)^{n+1} = \sum_{k=0}^{n+1} \binom{n+1}{k} x^{n+1-k} y^k$.

We use Theorem 5.2.3 to proceed with the inductive step.

$$(x+y)^{n+1} = (x+y) \sum_{k=0}^{n} \binom{n}{k} x^{n-k} y^k$$

$$= x \sum_{k=0}^{n} \binom{n}{k} x^{n-k} y^k + y \sum_{k=0}^{n} \binom{n}{k} x^{n-k} y^k$$

$$= \sum_{k=0}^{n} \binom{n}{k} x^{n+1-k} y^k + \sum_{k=0}^{n} \binom{n}{k} x^{n-k} y^{k+1}$$

$$= \left[\binom{n}{0} x^{n+1} + \binom{n}{1} x^n y + \binom{n}{2} x^{n-1} y^2 + \binom{n}{3} x^{n-2} y^3 + \ldots + \binom{n}{n} xy^n \right]$$

$$+ \left[\binom{n}{0} x^n y + \binom{n}{1} x^{n-1} y^2 + \binom{n}{2} x^{n-2} y^3 + \ldots + \binom{n}{n} y^{n+1} \right]$$

$$= \binom{n}{0} x^{n+1} + \left[\binom{n}{1} x^n y + \binom{n}{0} x^n y \right] + \left[\binom{n}{2} x^{n-1} y^2 + \binom{n}{1} x^{n-1} y^2 \right]$$

$$+ \left[\binom{n}{3} x^{n-2} y^3 + \binom{n}{2} x^{n-2} y^3 \right] + \ldots + \left[\binom{n}{n} x^1 y^n + \binom{n}{n-1} x^1 y^n \right] + \binom{n}{n} y^{n+1}$$

$$= \binom{n}{0} x^{n+1} + \left[\binom{n}{1} + \binom{n}{0} \right] x^n y + \left[\binom{n}{2} + \binom{n}{1} \right] x^{n-1} y^2$$

$$+ \left[\binom{n}{3} + \binom{n}{2} \right] x^{n-2} y^3 + \ldots + \left[\binom{n}{n} + \binom{n}{n-1} \right] x^1 y^n + \binom{n}{n} y^{n+1}$$

$$= \binom{n}{0} x^{n+1} + \binom{n+1}{1} x^n y + \binom{n+1}{2} x^{n-1} y^2 + \ldots + \binom{n+1}{n} xy^n + \binom{n}{n} y^{n+1}.$$

Note that $\binom{n}{0} = \binom{n+1}{0} = \binom{n}{n} = 1 = \binom{n+1}{n+1} = 1$. Then,

$$(x+y)^{n+1} = \binom{n+1}{0} x^{n+1} + \binom{n+1}{1} x^n y + \binom{n+1}{2} x^{n-1} y^2 + \ldots + \binom{n+1}{n} xy^n + \binom{n+1}{n+1} y^{n+1}$$

$$= \sum_{k=0}^{n+1} \binom{n+1}{k} x^{n+1-k} y^k,$$

which concludes our inductive step. $\square$

Problem 5.2.7. Expand the following:

1. $(x+y)^4$
2. $(2x+3y)^3$

Solution. This problem is an exercise in directly applying the Binomial Theorem.

$$(x+y)^4 = \binom{4}{0} x^4 y^0 + \binom{4}{1} x^{4-1} y^1 + \binom{4}{2} x^{4-2} y^2 + \binom{4}{1} x^{4-3} y^3 + \binom{4}{0} x^{4-4} y^4$$

$$= \boxed{x^4 + 4x^3y + 6x^2y^2 + 4xy^3 + y^4}.$$

$$(2x+3y)^3 = \binom{3}{0}(2x)^3(3y)^0 + \binom{3}{1}(2x)^2(3y)^1 + \binom{3}{2}(2x)^1(3y)^2 + \binom{3}{3}(2x)^0(3y)^3$$
$$= (2x)^3 + 3(2x)^2(3y) + 3(2x)(3y)^2 + (3y)^3$$
$$= \boxed{8x^3 + 36x^2y + 54xy^2 + 27y^3}.$$

□

Problem 5.2.8. When expanded, what is the constant term of $\left(5x^3 - \dfrac{7}{x^2}\right)^{150}$?

Solution. According to the binomial theorem, a single term for an arbitrary k is

$$\binom{150}{k}(5x^3)^{150-k}\left(-\frac{7}{x^2}\right)^k.$$

We must solve for the value of k which cancels the $(5x^3)^{150-k}$ term with the $\left(-\dfrac{7}{x^2}\right)^k$ term, as the latter has a power of x in the denominator which will cancel with the power of the first x, guaranteeing the existence of a constant term.

Ignoring coefficients, the power of the first x is $3(150-k)$ and the power of the second x, which is in the denominator, is $-2k$.

Therefore, the overall power of x will be the sum of these two powers. Since we are searching for the constant term, we want this overall power to be 0. Therefore, we solve the equation $3(150-k) - 2k = 0$, which gives $k = 90$.

Substituting this back into the general form given earlier, our constant term is

$$\binom{150}{90}(5x^3)^{60}\left(-\frac{7}{x^2}\right)^{90} = \boxed{\binom{150}{90}5^{60}7^{90}}.$$

□

Problem 5.2.9. When expanded, what is the full term of the form $kx^{1776}y^r$ in $(4x - 5y)^{2017}$?

Solution. The Binomial Theorem states that a general term in a binomial expansion to the n power is of the form

$$\binom{n}{k}x^{n-k}y^k.$$

Clearly $n = 2017$ and $n - k = 1776$, so $k = 241$. Therefore the term we have to find is

$$\binom{2017}{241}(4x)^{1776}(-5y)^{241},$$

which simplifies to

$$\boxed{-\binom{2017}{241}\left(4^{1776}\right)\left(5^{241}\right)x^{1776}y^{241}}.$$

□

Problem 5.2.10. Find and prove a formula for:

a) $\sum_{k=0}^{n} \binom{n}{k}$

b) $\sum_{k=0}^{n} (-1)^k \binom{n}{k}$

c) $\sum_{k=0}^{n} \binom{2n}{2k}$

Proof. We consider special cases of the Binomial Theorem.

a) Consider the quantity $(1+1)^n$.
$$(1+1)^n = \sum_{k=0}^{n} \binom{n}{k} 1^{n-k} 1^k.$$

But also note that $(1+1)^n = 2^n$, therefore, $\sum_{k=0}^{n} \binom{n}{k} = \boxed{2^n}$.

b) Similarly, consider $(1+-1)^n$.
$$(1+-1)^n = \sum_{k=0}^{n} \binom{n}{k} 1^{n-k} (-1)^k$$
$$= \sum_{k=0}^{n} \binom{n}{k} (-1)^k.$$

We have $(1+-1)^n = 0^n = 0$, therefore, $\sum_{k=0}^{n} (-1)^k \binom{n}{k} = \boxed{0}$.

c) Based on the two previous examples, we know that $\sum_{k=0}^{2n} \binom{2n}{k} = 2^{2n}$ and $\sum_{k=0}^{2n} (-1)^k \binom{2n}{k} = 0$. We can split these sums based on their parity (even or odd).

For $\sum_{k=0}^{2n} \binom{2n}{k}$, if k is even, then $k = 2i$ for some integer i, so the sum of all the even terms is $\binom{2n}{0} + \binom{2n}{2} + \binom{2n}{4} + \ldots + \binom{2n}{2n}$, or $\sum_{i=0}^{n} \binom{2n}{2i}$. If k is odd, then $k = 2i+1$, so the sum of all the odd terms is $\binom{2n}{1} + \binom{2n}{3} + \binom{2n}{5} + \ldots + \binom{2n}{2n-1}$ or $\sum_{i=0}^{n-1} \binom{2n}{2i+1}$. Since k can only be even or odd,

$$\sum_{k=0}^{2n} \binom{2n}{k} = \sum_{i=0}^{n} \binom{2n}{2i} + \sum_{i=0}^{n-1} \binom{2n}{2i+1} = 2^{2n}.$$

It is nearly the same thing for $\sum_{k=0}^{2n}(-1)^k\binom{2n}{k}$, except that when k is odd, $(-1)^k = -1$, so we have

$$\sum_{k=0}^{2n}(-1)^k\binom{2n}{k} = \sum_{i=0}^{n}\binom{2n}{2i} + \sum_{i=0}^{n-1}-\binom{2n}{2i+1} = 0.$$

Adding these two together, we get

$$\sum_{k=0}^{2n}\binom{2n}{k} + \sum_{k=0}^{2n}(-1)^k\binom{2n}{k} = \sum_{i=0}^{n}\binom{2n}{2i} + \sum_{i=0}^{n-1}\binom{2n}{2i+1} + \sum_{i=0}^{n}\binom{2n}{2i} + \sum_{i=0}^{n-1}-\binom{2n}{2i+1}$$

$$= \sum_{i=0}^{n}\binom{2n}{2i} + \sum_{i=0}^{n-1}\binom{2n}{2i+1} + \sum_{i=0}^{n}\binom{2n}{2i} + -1\cdot\sum_{i=0}^{n-1}\binom{2n}{2i+1}$$

$$= \sum_{i=0}^{n}\binom{2n}{2i} + \sum_{i=0}^{n}\binom{2n}{2i}$$

$$= 2\sum_{i=0}^{n}\binom{2n}{2i}$$

$$2^{2n} + 0 = 2\sum_{i=0}^{n}\binom{2n}{2i}$$

$$\therefore \sum_{i=0}^{n}\binom{2n}{2i} = \boxed{2^{2n-1}}.$$ □

Problem 5.2.11. What is wrong with the following proof?

Claim: All horses are the same color.

We proceed with proof by induction: Let $P(n)$: Any set of n horses is the same color.

Base Case: $P(1)$: Any set of 1 horse is the same color.

This is obviously true, as each horse has its own color.

Inductive Step: Assume $P(n)$: any set of n horses is the same color.

Consider a set of n horses and let x refer to one of the horses in that set, and let H refer to the rest of the horses.

Consider another set of n horses consisting of H horses plus another horse (distinct from x) that we shall call y.

Because x is in a set with H, horse x and the horses H have the same color. Because y is also in a set with H, horse y and the horses H have the same color. Therefore, $x, y,$ and H have the same color.

Therefore, we can construct a set of $n + 1$ horses containing $x, y,$ and H. The inductive step holds, so all horses are the same color.

Solution. This proof by induction makes a critical logical error in that $P(1) \to P(2)$ is false. If we have a set of 1 horse, then there is no H ("rest of the horses") from which we could compare the colors of x and y. To 'fix' this, if you're thinking about starting the induction with $P(2) \to P(3)$, remember that $P(2)$ itself is false because one can choose two differently colored horses for a set of 2 horses. Overall, if the base case cannot imply the next statement, then the inductive form of reasoning cannot be applied, so this argument is invalid. □

Chapter 6

Basic Trigonometry

The reader is expected to have some experience with basic right triangle trigonometry, but a brief review of it is given first, for the convenience of the reader and for the sake of completeness. A basic understanding of simple concepts in geometry is expected. Then, we will delve into how the trigonometric functions are intertwined with the unit circle, and investigate its consequences in great depth.

6.1 Review

First, we review the 6 trigonometric functions.

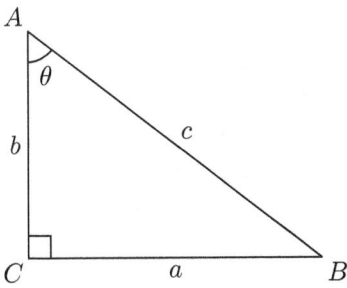

Consider $\triangle ABC$ where $\angle ACB$ is a right angle and let $\angle CAB = \theta$. Then, we may define our 6 trigonometric functions given this angle, as follows:

$$\sin \theta = \frac{a}{c} \qquad \csc \theta = \frac{c}{a}$$

$$\cos \theta = \frac{b}{c} \qquad \sec \theta = \frac{c}{b}$$

$$\tan \theta = \frac{a}{b} \qquad \cot \theta = \frac{b}{a}$$

To remember these, one can use the famous acronym **SOH CAH TOA**:

1. **S**ine-**O**pposite-**H**ypotenuse: $\sin\theta$ refers to the ratio $\frac{\text{opposite}}{\text{hypotenuse}}$, where the sides in discussion are in relation to θ. In this diagram, a would be the opposite side to θ and c would be the hypotenuse, so $\sin\theta = \frac{a}{c}$.

2. **C**osine-**A**djacent-**H**ypotenuse: $\cos\theta$ refers to the ratio $\frac{\text{adjacent}}{\text{hypotenuse}}$, where the sides in discussion are in relation to θ. In this diagram, b would be the adjacent side to θ and c is still the hypotenuse, so $\cos\theta = \frac{b}{c}$.

3. **T**angent-**O**pposite-**A**djacent: $\tan\theta$ refers to the ratio $\frac{\text{opposite}}{\text{adjacent}}$, where the sides in discussion are in relation to θ. In this diagram, as previously mentioned, a is the opposite, and b is the adjacent, so $\tan\theta = \frac{a}{b}$.

In addition, recall the following definitions (and vice-versa):

$$\sin\theta = \frac{1}{\csc\theta}$$
$$\cos\theta = \frac{1}{\sec\theta}$$
$$\tan\theta = \frac{1}{\cot\theta}$$

Noting that cosecant, secant, and cotangent are the reciprocals of sine, cosine, and tangent respectively, their definitions become obvious:

$$\csc\theta = \frac{1}{\frac{\text{opposite}}{\text{hypotenuse}}} = \frac{\text{hypotenuse}}{\text{opposite}} \text{ or } \frac{c}{a}$$
$$\sec\theta = \frac{1}{\frac{\text{adjacent}}{\text{hypotenuse}}} = \frac{\text{hypotenuse}}{\text{adjacent}} \text{ or } \frac{c}{b}$$
$$\cot\theta = \frac{1}{\frac{\text{opposite}}{\text{adjacent}}} = \frac{\text{adjacent}}{\text{opposite}} \text{ or } \frac{b}{a}$$

By using the helpful acronym **SOH CAH TOA** and remembering the reciprocal relationships between each pair, we can intuitively derive the corresponding ratios for all of the functions.

Now, there are special angles associated with these trigonometric functions that you should memorize.

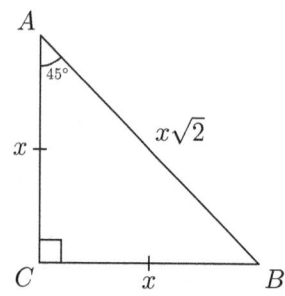

Consider an isosceles right triangle ABC with right angle C, and let the common length of the legs be x. Then, we can derive the well-known side length proportions of this particular triangle using the Pythagorean Theorem, as follows:

$$AB^2 = AC^2 + BC^2$$
$$AB^2 = x^2 + x^2$$
$$AB^2 = 2x^2$$
$$\therefore AB = x\sqrt{2}.$$

We know that $\angle A = 45°$, so we can find out the trigonometric ratios of the angle $45°$ using the proportions of the sides we have just proven. Note that the x terms cancel out in the numerator and denominator.

$\sin 45° = \frac{\sqrt{2}}{2}$	$\csc 45° = \sqrt{2}$
$\cos 45° = \frac{\sqrt{2}}{2}$	$\sec 45° = \sqrt{2}$
$\tan 45° = 1$	$\cot 45° = 1$

Here is the other special triangle:

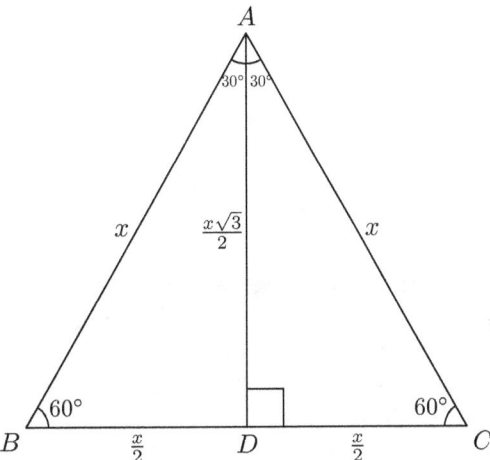

Consider an equilateral triangle ABC with common side length x. Drop the altitude from A to BC, and let the foot be D. Note that AD is also the median, as $AB = AC$. Furthermore, it is not hard to see that AD is the angle bisector of $\angle BAC$. Therefore, D is the midpoint of BC, so $BD = CD = \frac{x}{2}$. We also have that $\angle BAD = \angle CAD = 30°$. We can then compute AD by using the Pythagorean theorem on either $\triangle ABD$ or $\triangle ACD$.

$$AD^2 + \left(\frac{x}{2}\right)^2 = x^2$$
$$AD^2 = x^2 - \frac{x^2}{4}$$
$$\therefore AD = \frac{x\sqrt{3}}{2}.$$

The resulting proportions of the sides of the smaller triangle inside the larger equilateral triangle yield the 30-60-90 triangle:

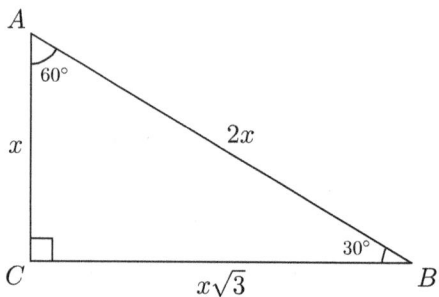

We can now derive the trigonometric values for angles 60° and 30° respectively:

$\sin 60° = \frac{\sqrt{3}}{2}$	$\csc 60° = \frac{2\sqrt{3}}{3}$
$\cos 60° = \frac{1}{2}$	$\sec 60° = 2$
$\tan 60° = \sqrt{3}$	$\cot 60° = \frac{\sqrt{3}}{3}$

$\sin 30° = \frac{1}{2}$	$\csc 30° = 2$
$\cos 30° = \frac{\sqrt{3}}{2}$	$\sec 30° = \frac{2\sqrt{3}}{3}$
$\tan 30° = \frac{\sqrt{3}}{3}$	$\cot 30° = \sqrt{3}$

Lastly, we have the notion of radians vs. degrees, two ways of measuring angles. We define 2π **radians** to be equivalent to 360°, or in simpler terms, π radians = 180°.

Exercise 6.1.1. Convert 0°, 30°, 45°, 60°, and 90° to radians. You should be familiar with all of the radian equivalents for these special angles.

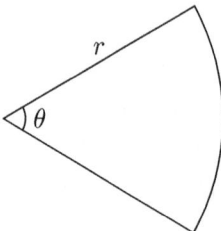

Sector of a circle with radius r and subtended angle θ

We can derive the formulae for the arc length and area of this sector of a circle for radians and degrees:

	Degrees	Radians
Arc length	$\dfrac{\pi r \theta}{180°}$	$r\theta$
Area	$\pi r^2 \cdot \dfrac{\theta}{360°}$	$\dfrac{r^2 \theta}{2}$

Why should we use radians over degrees? As a start, the formulae in terms of radians is clearly more aesthetically pleasing. However, it is not until we begin the topic of calculus that we realize the true benefits of using radians.

In this chapter, if the symbol ° is specified, then the angle is in degrees. Otherwise, it is in radians.

6.2 The Unit Circle

Now, we tie this idea of right triangle trigonometry to the unit circle. Consider the diagram below:

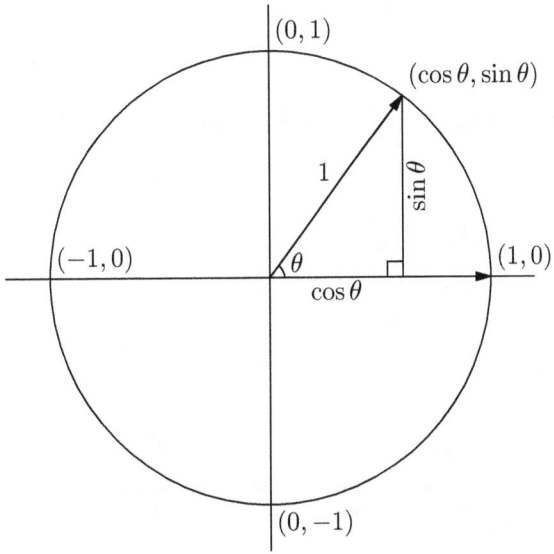

Draw a ray from the origin to some point on the graph of $x^2 + y^2 = 1$, i.e. the unit circle. For clarity I will illustrate such a ray in the first quadrant. If we drop a perpendicular from the point to the x-axis, we actually form a right triangle, with the hypotenuse being the ray, which must be length 1 since it is a radius of the circle.

Let θ be the angle between the hypotenuse and the x-axis. We start at $\theta = 0°$, which is the point $(1, 0)$, and move counter-clockwise (in order of the four quadrants).

Definition 6.2.1. An **angle** will represent the rotation of a ray through the origin of the unit circle.

Definition 6.2.2. Two angles will be called **coterminal** if they end up at the same position on the unit circle. In other words, angle x and angle y are coterminal $\longleftrightarrow 360° \mid (x - y)$, in terms of degrees.

The **terminal side** is the hypotenuse of the triangle, which is 1.

This means that rotating the ray by a full circle, or 360°, will not change the point (x, y) on the circle. Thus, $\sin(120°) = \sin(480°) = \sin(840°) = \ldots$, so the trigonometric functions are periodic. We will revisit this property later.

Since the hypotenuse is 1, the side adjacent to θ would be $\cos\theta$, the side opposite to θ would be $\sin\theta$, and the slope of the hypotenuse would be $\tan\theta$, using the mnemonic 'SOH CAH TOA.'

Definition 6.2.3. For any angle θ, let the terminal side of θ hit the unit circle at (x, y). Then we define

$$x = \cos\theta,$$
$$y = \sin\theta.$$

Keep in mind that the domains of cosine and sine are necessarily all real numbers.

Definition 6.2.4. Although we have already stated these in the last section, I will emphasize that the following remain the same under the context of the unit circle.

$$\csc\theta = \frac{1}{\sin\theta} \quad \sec\theta = \frac{1}{\cos\theta}$$

$$\tan\theta = \frac{\sin\theta}{\cos\theta} \quad \cot\theta = \frac{\cos\theta}{\sin\theta}$$

Definition 6.2.5. Quadrantal angles are angles that terminate on the x or y axis. For example, we call the angles $90°, 180°, 270°, 360°, 450°, 540°, \ldots$ quadrantal, as each of them lie on one of the four points $(1, 0)$, $(0, 1)$, $(-1, 0)$, or $(0, -1)$.

First, we can take advantage of the reflective/rotational symmetry that the circle offers in order to develop our first few trigonometric identities.

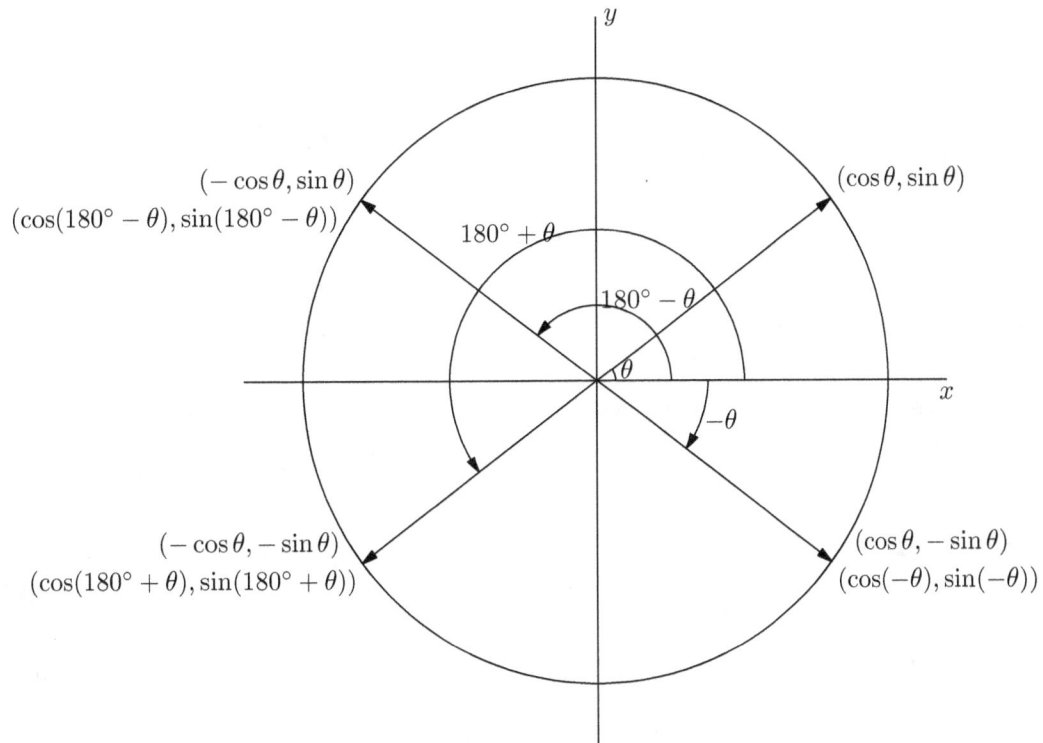

Reflections of the ray from $(0,0)$ to $(\cos\theta, \sin\theta)$ to the four quadrants

Recall the following facts: If a point (x, y) in the first quadrant is reflected across ...

1. ...the *y-axis*, then the new point is $(-x, y)$.

2. ...the *origin*, then the new point is $(-x, -y)$.

3. ...the *x-axis*, then the new point is $(x, -y)$.

Applying these facts to the point $(\cos\theta, \sin\theta)$, as shown in the diagram, we can express the three other points in two ways each: the first way considering the reflection applied to the original, and the second way considering the angle of the new point.

For the point in quadrant 2, notice how we have reflected $(\cos\theta, \sin\theta)$ across the *y-axis*, so this new point can be represented as $(-\cos\theta, \sin\theta)$. However, this point is also the result of rotating a ray $180° - \theta$ in the counterclockwise direction, so the point can also be expressed as $(\cos(180° - \theta), \sin(180° - \theta))$. As these two coordinates refer to the same point, we have the following identities:

$$\cos(180° - \theta) = -\cos\theta$$
$$\sin(180° - \theta) = \sin\theta$$

Similarly, the point in the third quadrant can be represented as either $(-\cos\theta, -\sin\theta)$ or $(\cos(180° + \theta), \sin(180° + \theta))$. As a result, we can derive similar identities:

$$\cos(180° + \theta) = -\cos\theta$$

$$\sin(180° + \theta) = -\sin\theta$$

Lastly, the point in the fourth quadrant is either $(\cos\theta, -\sin\theta)$ or $(\cos(-\theta), \sin(-\theta))$. So we have the following identities:

$$\cos(-\theta) = \cos\theta$$
$$\sin(-\theta) = -\sin\theta$$

Thus, we put together our first set of trigonometric identities:

$\cos(180° - \theta) = -\cos\theta$	$\cos(180° + \theta) = -\cos\theta$	$\cos(-\theta) = \cos\theta$
$\sin(180° - \theta) = \sin\theta$	$\sin(180° + \theta) = -\sin\theta$	$\sin(-\theta) = -\sin\theta$

As you solve more problems, you will get used to these identities. However, if you imagine reflecting and rotating angles on the unit circle, then it won't be hard to rederive these relationships again if you forget.

It is important that you remember that $\cos\theta$ is an even function, while $\sin\theta$ is an odd function.

Definition 6.2.6. The **reference angle** for a non-quadrantal angle θ is the measure of the acute angle that the terminal side makes with the x-axis.

Remember that the actual angle and the reference angle *are not the same*. Consider the diagram below:

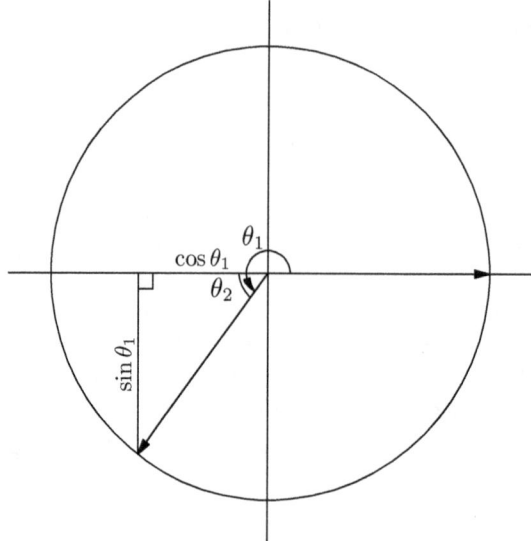

In this example, $\pi \leq \theta_1 \leq \dfrac{3\pi}{2}$ would be the overall angle that we base cosine and sine on, while $0 \leq \theta_2 < \dfrac{\pi}{2}$ would be the reference angle.

Problem 6.2.7. Find the reference angles for the following (which are in radians):

a) $\dfrac{7\pi}{11}$

b) $\dfrac{19\pi}{5}$

c) 8

Solution. Make sure you keep in mind the main quadrantal angles in radians: $0, \dfrac{\pi}{2}, \pi, \dfrac{3\pi}{2}, 2\pi$, and further multiples of $\dfrac{\pi}{2}$. Multiples of π lie on the x-axis, so pay attention to those when looking for the reference angle. Also remember to reduce a given radian measure larger than 2π by subtracting the appropriate multiple of 2π. To visualize the angle, try drawing it on the unit circle and then the appropriate right triangle for it.

a) $\dfrac{7\pi}{11}$ is between $\dfrac{\pi}{2}$ and π, so the reference angle is $\pi - \dfrac{7\pi}{11} = \boxed{\dfrac{4\pi}{11}}$.

b) $\dfrac{19\pi}{5}$ is larger than 2π, so subtract 2π to get $\dfrac{9\pi}{5}$, which is coterminal to $\dfrac{19\pi}{5}$. Then, notice that $\dfrac{9\pi}{5}$ is between $\dfrac{3\pi}{2}$ and 2π, so the reference angle is $2\pi - \dfrac{9\pi}{5} = \boxed{\dfrac{\pi}{5}}$.

c) In this case, we should figure out estimated values for π and $\dfrac{\pi}{2}$, which are 3.14 and 1.57 respectively. 8 is larger than 2π, so subtract ≈ 6.28 to get 1.72, which is between 1.57 and 3.14, or $\dfrac{\pi}{2}$ and π. So the reference angle is $\pi - (8 - 2\pi) = \boxed{3\pi - 8}$. Note that we are merely using these estimates for π and its fractions so we can determine which quadrant the angle 8 (in radians) is located in. □

From our definitions, the following are true:

1. If two angles are coterminal, then they have the same trigonometric values.

2. If two angles have the same reference angle, then they have the same trigonometric functions up to the sign. For example, $\sin(111°) = \pm \sin(69°)$.

Take a moment to convince yourself why these are true, especially the second result.

Now, we derive another important trigonometric identity by another kind of reflection.

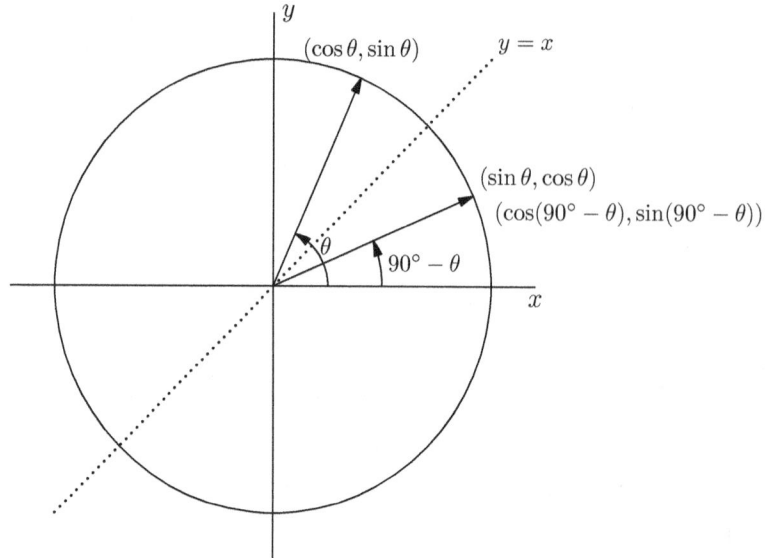

Reflecting the point $(\cos\theta, \sin\theta)$ over the line $y = x$

Similar to the reflections across the *x-axis*, *y-axis*, and origin, we can also reflect a point $(\cos\theta, \sin\theta)$ across the line $y = x$, yielding the point $(\sin\theta, \cos\theta)$. Reflections also maintain angles, so we can express the reflected point as $(\cos(90° - \theta), \sin(90° - \theta))$. These two coordinates refer to the same point, so we have now derived the following identities:

$$\sin(90° - \theta) = \cos\theta$$
$$\cos(90° - \theta) = \sin\theta$$

Taking the reciprocal of these equations, we get

$$\csc(90° - \theta) = \sec\theta$$
$$\sec(90° - \theta) = \csc\theta$$

Furthermore, note that $\tan(90° - \theta) = \dfrac{\sin(90° - \theta)}{\cos(90° - \theta)} = \dfrac{\cos\theta}{\sin\theta} = \cot\theta$, and vice-versa.

Therefore, we can conclude that if f is a trigonometric function, then

$$f(\theta) = \underbrace{cof}_{\text{cofunction of } f}(90° - \theta),$$

where the cofunction pairs are sine and cosine, secant and cosecant, and tangent and cotangent. Their relationships express the notion of the **cofunction identities**.

Definition 6.2.8. A function is **periodic** if $\exists p > 0$ s.t. $f(x + p) = f(x)\ \forall x$. If p is the smallest positive number satisfying this, then p is called the **period**.

Problem 6.2.9. What is the period of sine and cosine? What about tangent?

Solution. As previously stated regarding coterminal angles, rotating a ray by a full circle, which is 360°, will not change the point that the ray is pointing to. Thus, $\sin\theta = \sin(\theta + 360°)$ and $\cos\theta = \cos(\theta + 360°)$. It can then be confirmed that 360° is the period.

However, for tangent, notice that the slope of the ray from the origin is the same when it is reflected across the origin. In other words, the tangent is the same when 180° is added to the current angle. The period of tangent is thus 180°.

We can also demonstrate this using some identities. Note that

$$\tan(\theta + 180°) = \frac{\sin(\theta + 180°)}{\cos(\theta + 180°)} = \frac{-\sin\theta}{-\cos\theta} = \tan\theta. \qquad \square$$

Problem 6.2.10. Find all six trig values for each angle:

a) 150°

b) 225°

c) 300°

Then find the sum of all eighteen values.

Solution.

a) $\sin 150° = \dfrac{1}{2}$

$\cos 150° = -\dfrac{\sqrt{3}}{2}$

$\tan 150° = -\dfrac{\sqrt{3}}{3}$

$\csc 150° = 2$

$\sec 150° = -\dfrac{2\sqrt{3}}{3}$

$\cot 150° = -\sqrt{3}$

b) $\sin 225° = -\dfrac{\sqrt{2}}{2}$

$\cos 225° = -\dfrac{\sqrt{2}}{2}$

$\tan 225° = 1$

$\csc 225° = -\sqrt{2}$

$\sec 225° = -\sqrt{2}$

$\cot 225° = 1$

c) $\sin 300° = -\dfrac{\sqrt{3}}{2}$

$\cos 300° = \dfrac{1}{2}$

$\tan 300° = -\sqrt{3}$

$\csc 300° = -\dfrac{2\sqrt{3}}{3}$

$\sec 300° = 2$

$\cot 300° = -\dfrac{\sqrt{3}}{3}$

The sums in part a, b, and c respectively are $\dfrac{5}{2} - \dfrac{5\sqrt{3}}{2}$, $2 - 3\sqrt{2}$, and $\dfrac{5}{2} - \dfrac{5\sqrt{3}}{2}$, so the total sum would be $\boxed{7 - 5\sqrt{3} - 3\sqrt{2}}$. The important idea to consider is that we should take advantage of the identities to simplify the problem and reduce the workload. Note that the sum for 150° and 300° were the same, and this is because

$$\begin{aligned} f(150°) &= cof(90° - 150°) \\ &= cof(-60°) \\ &= cof(-60° + 360°) \\ &= cof(300°), \end{aligned}$$

according to our cofunction identities. Therefore, the six trig values for 150° will be the same for 300°, but for cofunctions of each other. We could have sped up the process of computing the sum by finding the sum of either 150° or 300° and multiplying by two, then adding the sum for 225°. $\square$

Problem 6.2.11. Write the following in terms of a trig function of an angle between 0° and 45°:

1. $\sin(73°)$

2. $\tan(109°)$

3. $\sec(2017°)$

4. $\cos\left(\dfrac{11\pi}{7}\right)$

Solution. Apply the identities we have covered so far:

1.
$$\sin(73°) = \cos(90° - 73°)$$
$$= \boxed{\cos(17°)}.$$

2.
$$\tan(109°) = \cot(90° - 109°)$$
$$= \cot(-19°)$$
$$= \boxed{-\cot(19°)}.$$

3.
$$\sec(2017°) = \sec(217°)$$
$$= \sec(217° - 360°)$$
$$= \sec(-143°)$$
$$= \sec(143°)$$
$$= \boxed{-\sec(37°)}.$$

4.
$$\cos\left(\frac{11\pi}{7}\right) = -\cos\left(\pi - \frac{11\pi}{7}\right)$$
$$= -\cos\left(-\frac{4\pi}{7}\right)$$
$$= -\cos\left(\frac{4\pi}{7}\right)$$
$$= -\sin\left(\frac{\pi}{2} - \frac{4\pi}{7}\right)$$
$$= -\sin\left(-\frac{\pi}{14}\right)$$
$$= \boxed{\sin\left(\frac{\pi}{14}\right)}. \qquad \square$$

Problem 6.2.12. Write the following in terms of a trig function of an angle between 0° and 45°:

1. $\sin(177°)$

2. $\cos(111°)$

3. $\tan(620°)$

Solution.

1.
$$\sin(177°) = \sin(180° - 177°)$$
$$= \boxed{\sin(3°)}.$$

2.
$$\cos(111°) = -\cos(180° - 111°)$$
$$= -\cos(69°)$$
$$= -\sin(90° - 69°)$$
$$= \boxed{-\sin(21°)}.$$

3.
$$\tan(620°) = \tan(620° - 360°)$$
$$= \tan(260°)$$
$$= \frac{\sin(260°)}{\cos(260°)}$$
$$= \frac{\sin(180° + 80°)}{\cos(180° + 80°)}$$
$$= \frac{-\sin(80°)}{-\cos(80°)}$$
$$= \frac{\cos(90° - 80°)}{\sin(90° - 80°)}$$
$$= \boxed{\cot(10°)}. \qquad \square$$

Now consider the right triangle of the unit circle once again. The legs of the triangle are $\cos\theta$ and $\sin\theta$, and the hypotenuse is 1. Then, by the Pythagorean Theorem, we have

$$\sin^2\theta + \cos^2\theta = 1.$$

Furthermore, if we divide both sides by $\sin^2\theta$, we get

$$\cot^2\theta + 1 = \csc^2\theta,$$

and if we chose to divide both sides by $\cos^2\theta$ instead, we get

$$1 + \tan^2\theta = \sec^2\theta.$$

These three equations are known as the **Pythagorean Identities**.

Problem 6.2.13. Find the rest of the trigonometric values for $\sin\theta = \frac{4}{5}$.

Solution. First, it is obvious that $\boxed{\csc\theta = \frac{5}{4}}$, as it is the reciprocal of $\sin\theta$.

Furthermore, we use the identity $\cos^2\theta + \sin^2\theta = 1$ to have $\cos^2\theta + \left(\frac{4}{5}\right)^2 = 1 \longrightarrow \boxed{\cos\theta = \pm\frac{3}{5}}$.

Since secant is the reciprocal of cosine, we have $\boxed{\sec\theta = \pm\frac{5}{3}}$. Lastly, $\tan\theta = \frac{\sin\theta}{\cos\theta}$, so $\boxed{\tan\theta = \pm\frac{4}{3}}$.

Then $\boxed{\cot\theta = \pm\frac{3}{4}}$.

Keep in mind that if the quadrant of this angle is not specified, then some trig values can either be positive or negative, so make sure you consider the sign as well. $\square$

For the following problems, we will use *I*, *II*, *III*, and *IV* to refer to the four quadrants.

Problem 6.2.14. Find the remaining trigonometric values when $\csc\theta = -\dfrac{20}{17}$, and $\theta \in \text{III}$.

Solution. We can instantly see that $\boxed{\sin\theta = -\dfrac{17}{20}}$. Furthermore, we can use the identity $\csc^2\theta = 1+\cot^2\theta$. We get $\dfrac{400}{289} = 1+\cot^2\theta$, or $\cot\theta = \pm\dfrac{\sqrt{111}}{17}$. However, as θ is in quadrant III, tangent must be positive, so cotangent is also positive. Therefore, $\boxed{\cot\theta = \dfrac{\sqrt{111}}{17}}$. This implies $\boxed{\tan\theta = \dfrac{17}{\sqrt{111}}}$.

We also use the Pythagorean identity $\cos^2\theta + \sin^2\theta = 1$. This yields $\dfrac{289}{400} + \cos^2\theta = 1$, or $\boxed{\cos\theta = -\dfrac{\sqrt{111}}{20}}$, as cosine is negative in the third quadrant. Since secant is the reciprocal of cosine, we have $\boxed{\sec\theta = -\dfrac{20}{\sqrt{111}}}$. $\square$

While we have been simply applying identities in order to find the rest of the values, choosing the sign can be a hassle. We could opt for the alternative method of *reference triangles* for a cleaner and more straightforward solution.

For example, consider $\sin\theta = \dfrac{4}{5}$ where $\theta \in I$. We can construct a reference triangle in the first quadrant, as such:

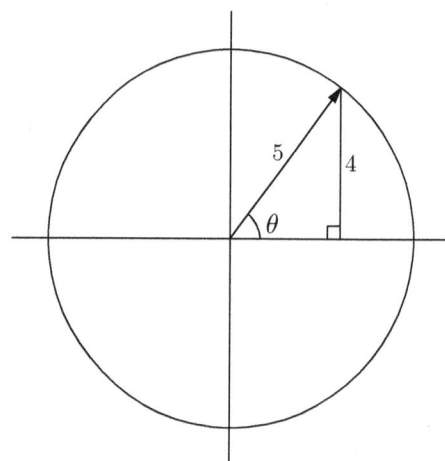

We fill in the triangle with the given information. For simplicity, we let the opposite side be 4 and the hypotenuse be 5. We could then use the Pythagorean Theorem to get the remaining leg of the right triangle.

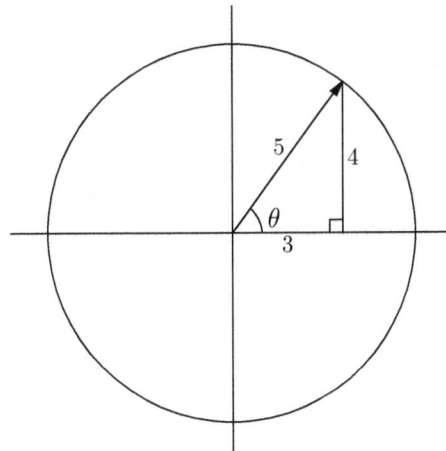

Now, we can read our information from the resulting reference triangle to derive the rest of the trigonometric values. From the triangle above, we have

$$\csc\theta = \frac{5}{4},$$
$$\cos\theta = \frac{3}{5},$$
$$\sec\theta = \frac{5}{3},$$
$$\tan\theta = \frac{4}{3},$$
$$\cot\theta = \frac{3}{4}.$$

It is much easier to read the information off a visual cue like a triangle, and this method is less error-prone than applying identities and worrying over which sign to choose.

The true strength of reference triangles is shown for examples in other quadrants.

Consider $\sin\theta = \frac{4}{5}$, but this time $\theta \in II$. Then our reference triangle would look different:

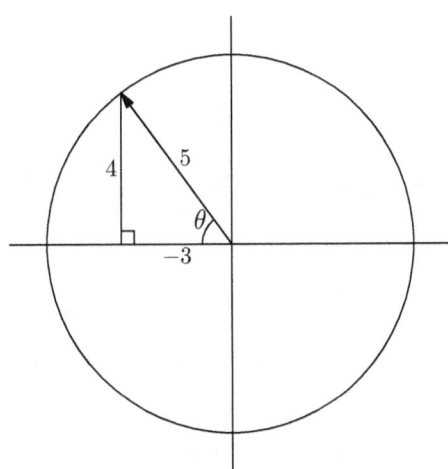

As $\theta \in II$, it should be true that $90° < \theta < 180°$. However, in the context of a reference triangle, we let θ in discussion be the *reference angle* of the triangle, so our calculations proceed smoothly.

As the triangle is to the left of the y-axis, the horizontal leg must be negative. Hence, we let it be -3 instead of 3 after we apply Pythagorean's Theorem to the given sides 4 and 5.

By drawing a diagram which clearly represents which parts are positive and negative, it is easily to identify the rest of the trigonometric values. For this example, the rest would be:

$$\csc \theta = \frac{5}{4},$$
$$\cos \theta = -\frac{3}{5},$$
$$\sec \theta = -\frac{5}{3},$$
$$\tan \theta = -\frac{4}{3},$$
$$\cot \theta = -\frac{3}{4}.$$

Exercise 6.2.15. Find the rest of the trigonometric values for $\cos \theta = \frac{4}{5}$, $\theta \in IV$.

Exercise 6.2.16. Find the rest of the trigonometric values for $\tan \theta = \frac{12}{5}$, $\theta \in III$.

Exercise 6.2.17. Find the rest of the trigonometric values for $\tan \theta = -\frac{7}{11}$, $\theta \in II$.

Exercise 6.2.18. Find the rest of the trigonometric values for $\tan \theta = -\frac{1}{2}$, $\theta \in II$.

Problem 6.2.19. Simplify $(4 \sin \theta - 7 \cos \theta)^2 + (7 \sin \theta + 4 \cos \theta)^2$.

Solution. Expand and simplify:

$$(4 \sin \theta - 7 \cos \theta)^2 + (7 \sin \theta + 4 \cos \theta)^2$$
$$= 16 \sin^2 \theta - 56 \sin \theta \cos \theta + 49 \cos^2 \theta + 49 \sin^2 \theta + 56 \sin \theta \cos \theta + 16 \cos^2 \theta$$
$$= 65 \sin^2 \theta + 65 \cos^2 \theta$$
$$= 65(\sin^2 \theta + \cos^2 \theta)$$
$$= \boxed{65}.$$
□

Exercise 6.2.20. Simplify $(2 \sin \theta - 3 \cos \theta)^2 + (3 \sin \theta + 2 \cos \theta)^2$.

Problem 6.2.21. If $\sin \theta + \cos \theta = \frac{1}{3}$, find all possible values of $\cos \theta$.

Solution. If $\sin \theta + \cos \theta = \frac{1}{3}$, then $(\sin \theta + \cos \theta)^2 = \frac{1}{9}$. We expand and simplify this to get

$$\sin^2 \theta + 2 \sin \theta \cos \theta + \cos^2 \theta = \frac{1}{9}$$

$$2\sin\theta\cos\theta = -\frac{8}{9}$$
$$\sin\theta\cos\theta = -\frac{4}{9}.$$

Furthermore, from the original equation, we have $\sin\theta = \frac{1}{3} - \cos\theta$. We substitute this into the equation above to get $\cos\theta\left(\frac{1}{3} - \cos\theta\right) = -\frac{4}{9}$. This expands to

$$\frac{1}{3}\cos\theta - \cos^2\theta + \frac{4}{9} = 0.$$

For legibility, let $x = \cos\theta$. Then we want to solve the quadratic $\frac{1}{3}x - x^2 + \frac{4}{9} = 0$. Multiply by -9 to get $9x^2 - 3x - 4 = 0$, and by the quadratic formula, we get

$$x = \cos\theta = \boxed{\frac{1 \pm \sqrt{17}}{6}}.$$

□

Problem 6.2.22. Find all values of $\sin x$ when $\sin x + \cos x = \frac{1}{2}$.

Solution. Square both sides of $\sin x + \cos x = \frac{1}{2}$ to get:

$$\sin^2 x + \cos^2 x + 2\sin x\cos x = \frac{1}{4}$$
$$1 + 2\sin x\cos x = \frac{1}{4}$$
$$\sin x\cos x = -\frac{3}{8}.$$

From the original equation, we know that $\cos x = \frac{1}{2} - \sin x$. Then we have:

$$\sin x\left(\frac{1}{2} - \sin x\right) = -\frac{3}{8}.$$

Let $y = \sin x$. Then we solve for the quadratic $\frac{1}{2}y - y^2 = -\frac{3}{8}$, or $8y^2 - 4y - 3 = 0$. By the quadratic formula, we have $y = \sin x = \boxed{\frac{1 \pm \sqrt{7}}{4}}$.

□

Problem 6.2.23. Prove the following identities:

1. $\sec x - \cos x = \sin x \tan x$
2. $\frac{\sin x}{1 + \cos x} = \csc x - \cot x$

Proof.

1. We can simply combine fractions and use the Pythagorean Identity:

$$\sec x - \cos x = \frac{1}{\cos x} - \cos x$$
$$= \frac{1 - \cos^2 x}{\cos x}$$
$$= \frac{\sin^2 x}{\cos x}$$
$$= \sin x \tan x.$$

2. The denominator $1 + \cos x$ motivates us to multiply the top and bottom by $1 - \cos x$, so we can apply the Pythagorean Identity:

$$\frac{\sin x}{1 + \cos x} = \frac{\sin x}{1 + \cos x} \cdot \frac{1 - \cos x}{1 - \cos x}$$
$$= \frac{\sin x (1 - \cos x)}{1 - \cos^2 x}$$
$$= \frac{\sin x (1 - \cos x)}{\sin^2 x}$$
$$= \frac{1 - \cos x}{\sin x}$$
$$= \frac{1}{\sin x} - \frac{\cos x}{\sin x}$$
$$= \csc x - \cot x. \qquad \square$$

Problem 6.2.24. $\tan x + \cot x$ equals the product of two trigonometric functions, both in terms of x. What is this product?

Solution. Simply rewrite the given expression in terms of sine and cosine, then apply appropriate identities:

$$\tan x + \cot x = \frac{\sin x}{\cos x} + \frac{\cos x}{\sin x}$$
$$= \frac{\sin^2 x + \cos^2 x}{\cos x \sin x}$$
$$= \frac{1}{\cos x \sin x}$$
$$= \boxed{\csc x \sec x}. \qquad \square$$

Lastly, there is one more identity to discover, based on previous identities that we have already found.

We have $\cos \theta = \sin(90° - \theta)$. If we substitute $\theta \to -\theta$, we get $\cos(-\theta) = \sin(90° + \theta)$. But notice that $\cos(-\theta) = \cos \theta$, therefore

$$\cos \theta = \sin(\theta + 90°).$$

This identity will play a significant role for the next section.

6.3 Graphing

First observe the behavior of $y = \sin x$ as x goes from $0°$ to $90°$. When we go counter-clockwise on the unit circle from $(1,0)$, the y-coordinate, which is $\sin x$, is increasing from 0 to 1. This can be illustrated by the approximations,

$$\sin 0° = 0,$$
$$\sin 30° = \frac{1}{2} = 0.5,$$
$$\sin 45° = \frac{\sqrt{2}}{2} \approx 0.7,$$
$$\sin 60° = \frac{\sqrt{3}}{2} \approx 0.9,$$
$$\sin 90° = 1.$$

Then, when x goes from $90°$ to $180°$, $\sin x$ goes from 1 back to 0. In fact,

$$\sin 120° = \frac{\sqrt{3}}{2} \approx 0.9,$$
$$\sin 135° = \frac{\sqrt{2}}{2} = 0.7,$$
$$\sin 150° = \frac{1}{2} \approx 0.5,$$
$$\sin 180° = 0.$$

These are symmetric with the previous values. Notice that the identity $\sin(180° - \theta) = \sin \theta$ confirms this.

Thus, as x goes from $0°$ to $180°$, $\sin x$ rises from 0 to 1, then back to 0. This can be graphed as:

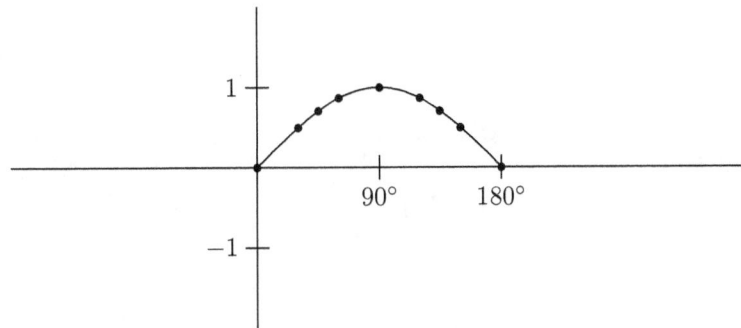

What happens when x goes from $180°$ to $360°$? By the identity $\sin(180° + \theta) = -\sin \theta$, the graph of $\sin x$ from $180°$ to $360°$ is basically the reflection of the graph from $0°$ to $180°$ over the x-axis, as such:

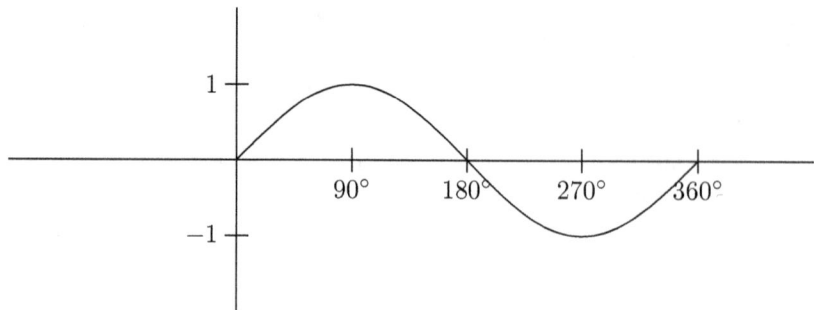

Now remember that the period of sine is 2π, or $360°$. Thus, the entire graph of $\sin x$ repeats indefinitely (oscillating between 0 and 1) in both directions:

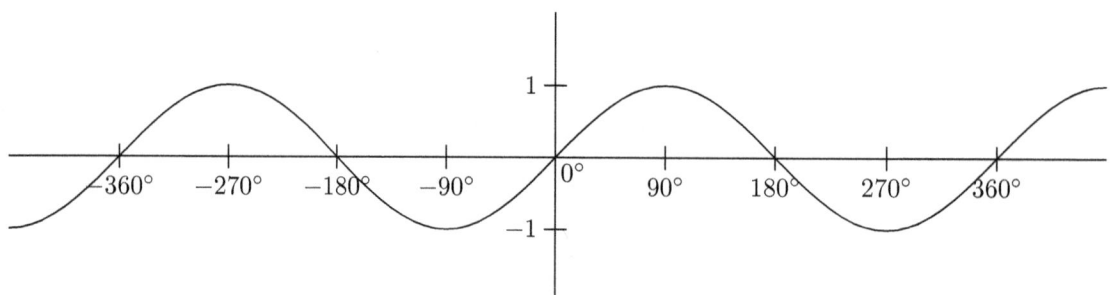

The graph of $\sin x$

Now, recall the identity $\cos\theta = \sin(\theta + 90°)$. This indicates that the graph of $\cos x$ is just the graph of $\sin\theta$ shifted $90°$ to the *left*! Thus, the entire graph of $\cos x$ would be:

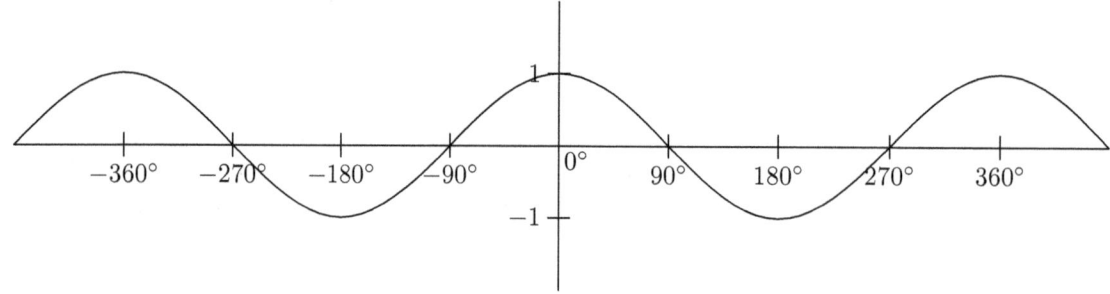

The graph of $\cos x$

We usually express these graphs in radians, as such:

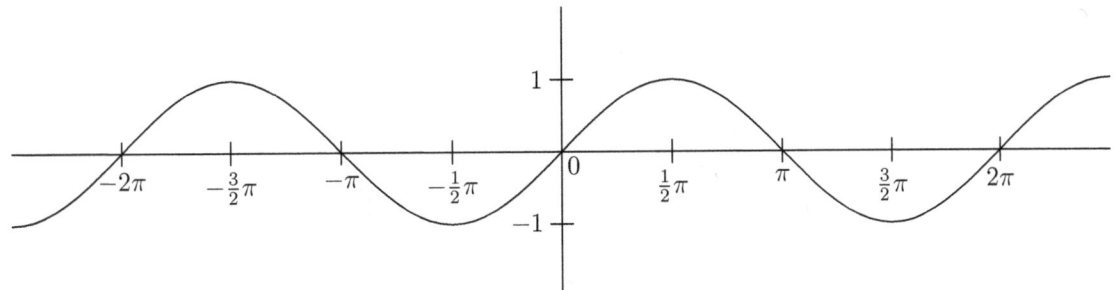

The graph of $\sin x$ in radians

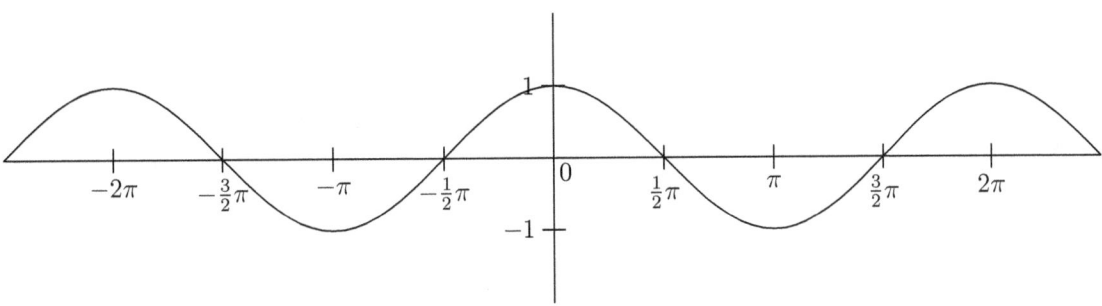

The graph of $\cos x$ in radians

Notice how the graph of $\sin x$ is consistent with the earlier discovery that $\sin x$ is an odd function, meaning that it is symmetric around the origin. Likewise, notice how the graph of $\cos x$ is symmetric across the y-axis, since $\cos x$ is an odd function.

As both functions continue oscillating between -1 and 1 in both directions forever, we can conclude the following:

	Domain	Range
$\sin x$	$\mathbb{R}$	$[-1, 1]$
$\cos x$	$\mathbb{R}$	$[-1, 1]$

To graph $\csc x$ and $\sec x$, we should use the fact that they are reciprocals of $\sin x$ and $\cos x$ respectively.

Let's look at $\csc x$ first. As $\sin x$ goes from 1 to an arbitrarily small positive number close to 0, notice that $\csc x = \dfrac{1}{\sin x}$ goes from 1 to some arbitrarily large number. In other words, as $\sin x$ goes from 1 to 0, $\csc x$ goes from 1 to ∞.

Similarly, as $\sin x$ goes from 0 to 1, $\csc x$ goes from ∞ to 1. Keeping this behavior in mind, here is the graph $\csc x$ along with $\sin x$ for one part:

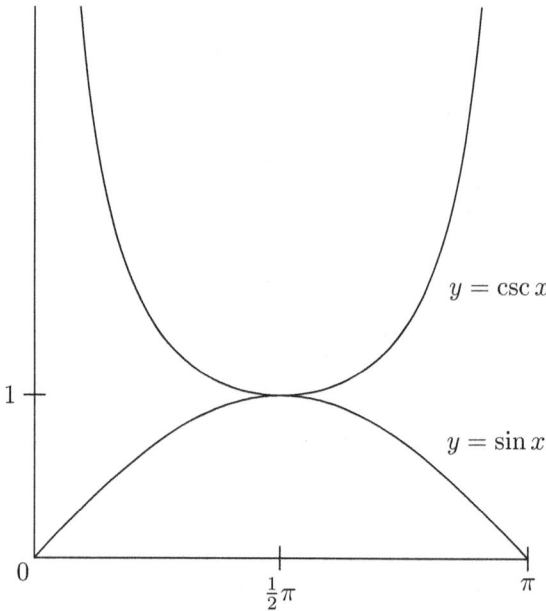

Make sure you understand how $\sin x$ and $\csc x$ are related to each other with respect to their graphs. Thus, our whole graph of $\csc x$ over many periods looks like this (the vertical asymptotes are represented by dashed lines):

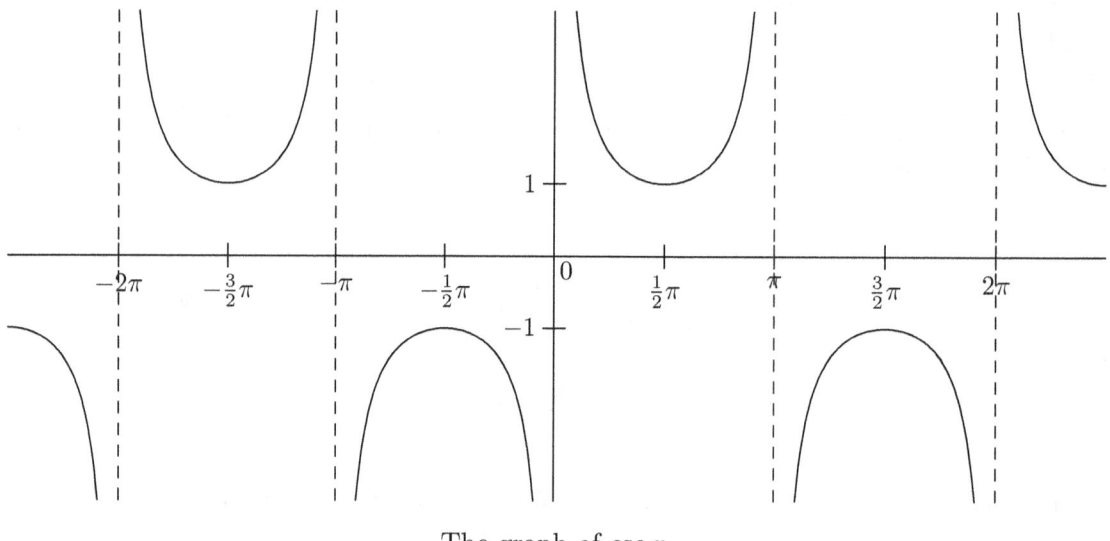

The graph of $\csc x$

Sketch $\sin x$ over this graph to reinforce your understanding of their relations.

Likewise, $\sec x$ has an analogous relationship to $\cos x$, as such:

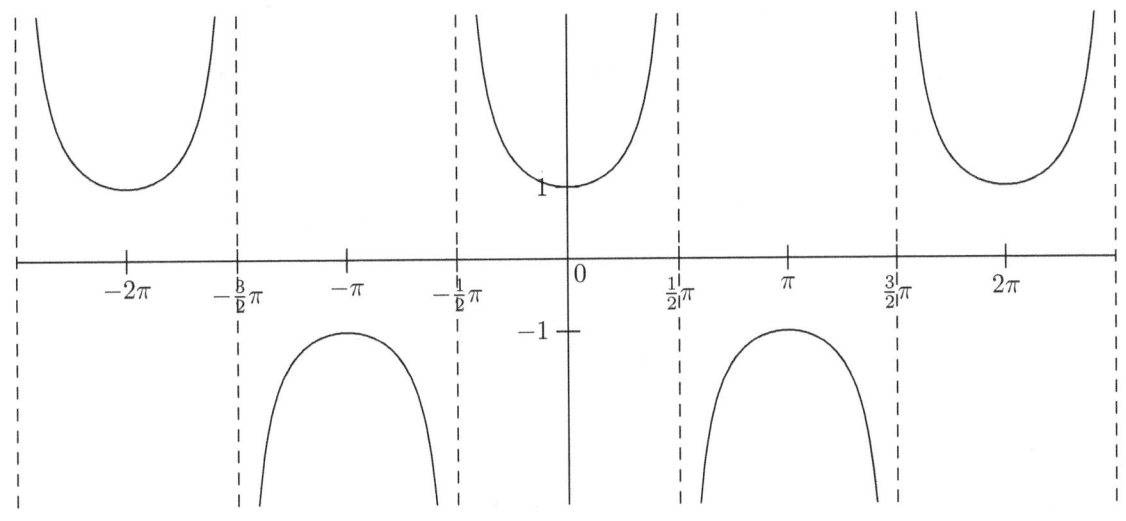

The graph of sec x

Here, we also used dashed lines to denote the vertical asymptotes of sec x.

Again, sketch cos x over the graph of sec x as an exercise.

Now, as long as you remember the graphs of sin x and cos x, you should be able to easily graph csc x and sec x as well.

Notice that csc x has vertical asymptotes at $x = -2\pi$, $x = -\pi$, $x = 0$, $x = \pi$, $x = 2\pi$, etc. At those values of x, csc x is not defined. In other words, the domain of csc x is the real numbers excluding any multiple of π. This can be expressed as $\mathbb{R} - \{\pi k \mid k \in \mathbb{Z}\}$.

What about the range of csc x? Notice that csc x never becomes any number between -1 and 1 exclusive. Thus, its range can be expressed as $(-\infty, -1] \cup [1, +\infty)$.

Similarly, sec x has vertical asymptotes at $x = -\frac{3}{2}\pi$, $x = -\frac{1}{2}\pi$, $x = \frac{1}{2}\pi$, $x = \frac{3}{2}\pi$, etc. Thus the domain of sec x is $\mathbb{R} - \left\{\pi k + \frac{\pi}{2} \mid k \in \mathbb{Z}\right\}$. Since sec x is merely csc x with a horizontal shift, their ranges are the same.

	Domain	Range
csc x	$\mathbb{R} - \{\pi k \mid k \in \mathbb{Z}\}$	$(-\infty, -1] \cup [1, +\infty)$
sec x	$\mathbb{R} - \left\{\pi k + \frac{\pi}{2} \mid k \in \mathbb{Z}\right\}$	$(-\infty, -1] \cup [1, +\infty)$

For the graph of tan x, let's consider the function's behavior as x goes from 0 inclusive to $\frac{\pi}{2}$ exclusive.

Since $\tan x = \frac{\sin x}{\cos x}$, notice that sin x is going from 0 to 1 while cos x is going from 1 to 0. Thus, tan x is increasing without bound, i.e. it is going to ∞ as x goes to $\frac{\pi}{2}$.

We can think about this in another way: $\tan x$ is the slope of the hypotenuse of the triangle in the unit circle, so as the angle approaches $\frac{\pi}{2}$, the hypotenuse gets steeper (until it becomes vertical at $x = \frac{\pi}{2}$). This indicates that the slope, which is $\tan x$, is tremendously increasing.

Then, let's graph $\tan x$ over $\left[0, \frac{\pi}{2}\right)$. We plug in some common values:

$$\tan 0 = 0,$$
$$\tan \frac{\pi}{6} = \frac{\sqrt{3}}{3} \approx 0.6,$$
$$\tan \frac{\pi}{4} = 1,$$
$$\tan \frac{\pi}{3} = \sqrt{3} \approx 1.7.$$

Then we consider the fact that $\tan x$ goes to ∞ as x approaches $\frac{1}{2}\pi$ from the left.

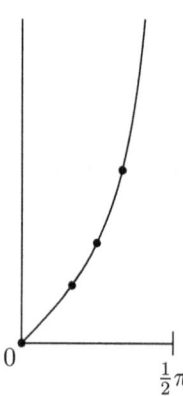

How would we sketch the rest of the graph? We can take advantage of a few identities.

Recall that $\tan x = \tan(x + \pi)$. Thus, the graph above will repeat for $x = \frac{1}{2}\pi$ to $\frac{3}{2}\pi$, etc.

Furthermore, note that

$$\tan(-x) = \frac{\sin(-x)}{\cos(-x)} = \frac{-\sin x}{\cos x} = -\tan x,$$

so $\tan x$ is an odd function, indicating that it is symmetric around the origin.

Using these two pieces of information, we can sketch the rest of the graph (the dashed lines are vertical asymptotes):

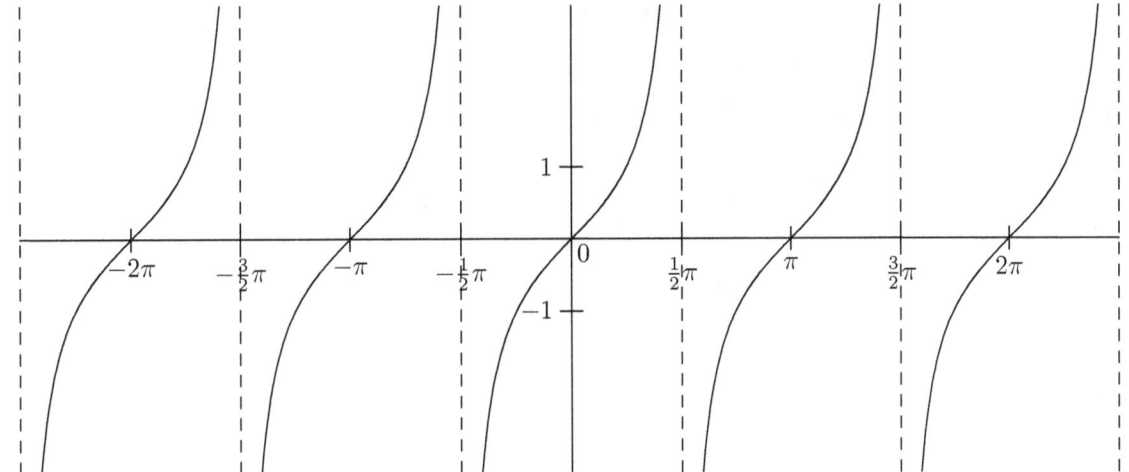

The graph of $\tan x$

What about $\cot x$? It turns out that it is relatively simple to sketch $\cot x$ once you know how to sketch $\tan x$.

Recall the cofunction identity $\tan\left(\frac{\pi}{2} - x\right) = \cot x$ (since $90° = \frac{\pi}{2}$). Replacing x with $-x$ gives us $\tan\left(\frac{\pi}{2} + x\right) = \cot(-x)$. But note that $\cot(-x) = \dfrac{\cos(-x)}{\sin(-x)} = \dfrac{\cos x}{-\sin x} = -\cot x$, so we have

$$\cot x = -\tan\left(\frac{\pi}{2} + x\right).$$

This indicates that the graph of $\cot x$ is the result of shifting the graph of $\tan x$ to the left by $\dfrac{\pi}{2}$, then flipping it over the x-axis. Thus, we end up with:

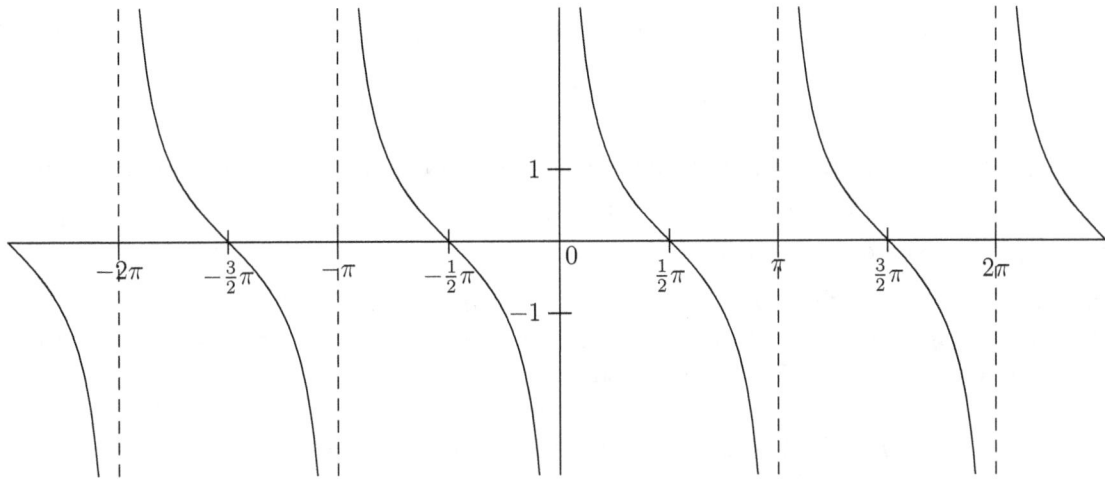

The graph of $\cot x$

Notice that $\tan x$ has the same vertical asymptotes as $\sec x$, so the domain of $\tan x$ is also $\mathbb{R} - \left\{\pi k + \dfrac{\pi}{2} \mid k \in \mathbb{Z}\right\}$. However, if we look at the graph of $\tan x$, we can see that $\tan x$ can be any real number. Thus, the range of $\tan x$ is $\mathbb{R}$.

Likewise, cot x has the same vertical asymptotes as csc x, so the domain of cot x is $\mathbb{R} - \{\pi k \mid k \in \mathbb{Z}\}$. For the same reason as tan x, the range of cot x is also $\mathbb{R}$.

Thus, we have the following results:

	Domain	Range
tan x	$\mathbb{R} - \left\{\pi k + \dfrac{\pi}{2} \mid k \in \mathbb{Z}\right\}$	$\mathbb{R}$
cot x	$\mathbb{R} - \{\pi k \mid k \in \mathbb{Z}\}$	$\mathbb{R}$

I will summarize all the discoveries made about the domain and range of every trigonometric function below:

	Domain	Range
$\sin \theta$	$\mathbb{R}$	$[-1, 1]$
$\cos \theta$	$\mathbb{R}$	$[-1, 1]$
$\tan \theta$	$\mathbb{R} - \left\{\pi k + \dfrac{\pi}{2} \mid k \in \mathbb{Z}\right\}$	$\mathbb{R}$
$\cot \theta$	$\mathbb{R} - \{\pi k \mid k \in \mathbb{Z}\}$	$\mathbb{R}$
$\sec \theta$	$\mathbb{R} - \left\{\pi k + \dfrac{\pi}{2} \mid k \in \mathbb{Z}\right\}$	$(-\infty, -1] \cup [1, +\infty)$
$\csc \theta$	$\mathbb{R} - \{\pi k \mid k \in \mathbb{Z}\}$	$(-\infty, -1] \cup [1, +\infty)$

It will not always be the case that you will be tasked with sketching a simple graph of $\sin x$. You may be asked to graph more complicated trigonometric functions. Consider the general equation of sine,

$$y = A\sin(Bx + C) + D.$$

Note that all equations defined in this form will have a "wave"-like form, which we call **sinusoidal**.

The following will still apply for an equation like $y = A\cos(Bx + C) + D$, since sine and cosine are merely phase shifts of each other.

Assume that $B > 0$ (whenever B is negative, we can always use the fact that sine is an odd function and manipulate the equation into the given form above). With respect to these variables, we define the following properties of the equation:

- The **midline** is $y = D$. It is the horizontal, center line on which the sinusoidal wave oscillates above and below. Here is an example:

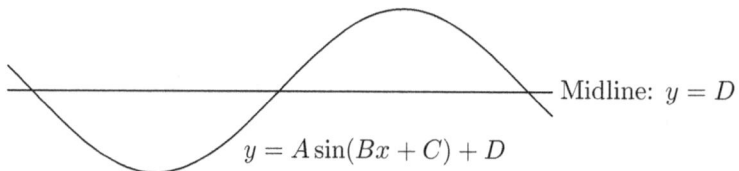

- The **amplitude** is $|A|$. This represents the vertical distance from the midline to either the highest or the lowest point on the graph.

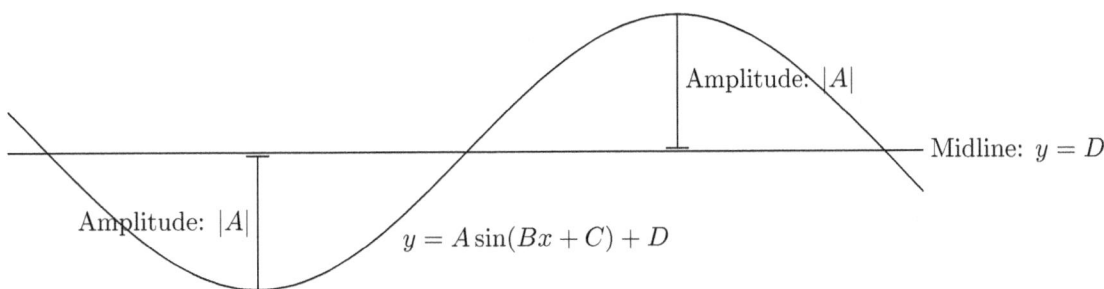

- The **frequency** is B. This denotes the number of **cycles** completed in an interval of 2π or $360°$. One cycle is the part of the graph that serves as a repeated pattern, since all trigonometric functions are periodic. Here is an example of one cycle:

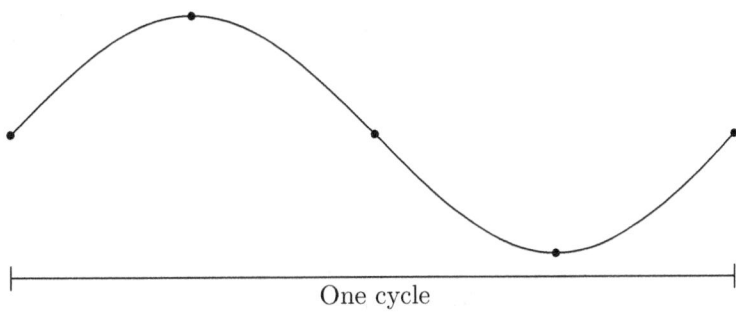

For $y = \sin x$, one cycle happens every 2π, so the frequency of $\sin x$ is 1.

- The **period** is $\dfrac{2\pi}{B}$. This is simply the horizontal length of one cycle. This is consistent with the definition of frequency: we divide the interval 2π by the number of cycles completed in that interval, which is B, to get the length of each cycle.

- The **phase shift** is $-\dfrac{C}{B}$. This can be derived from the observation that $y = A\sin(Bx + C) + D \implies y = A\sin\left(B\left(x + \dfrac{C}{B}\right)\right) + D$. This represents how far the original sine function (if you are given $y = A\sin(Bx + C) + D$) or cosine function (if you are given $y = A\cos(Bx + C) + D$) has been shifted right, if the phase shift is positive, or left, if the phase shift is negative.

- The **minimum** is $D - |A|$, while the **maximum** is $D + |A|$. This follows from our understanding of the midline and amplitude:

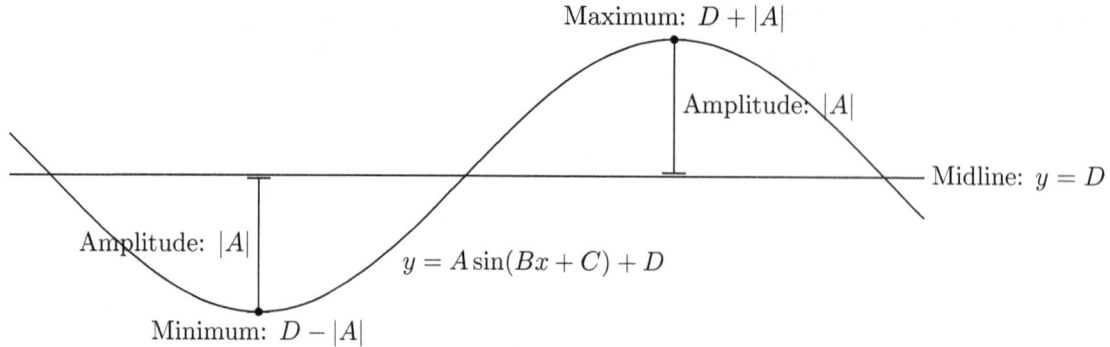

Since graphs of trigonometric functions can go on forever, we will establish some criteria for a 'sufficiently' drawn graph (in the context of this book; this is NOT official or conventional). When a problem asks for a sketch of some variant of $\sin x$, then draw a curve of this form:

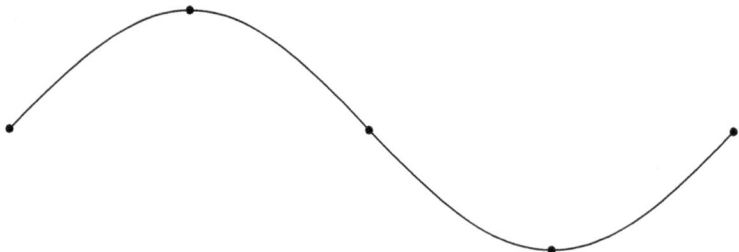

Then, label the coordinates of the five dotted points on that one period.

We will denote this portion of the graph as the **first period**. The first of the five points will always have its x-coordinate equal to the phase shift (remember this, it is a useful tip!).

For some variant of $-\sin x$, the first period would be:

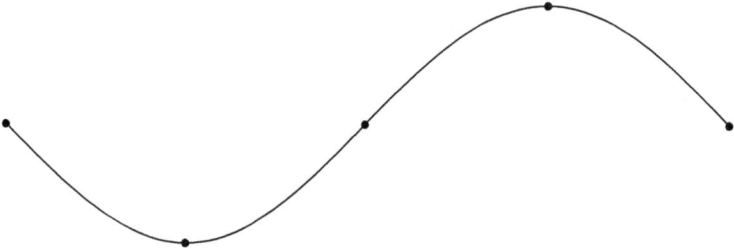

For some variant of $\cos x$, the first period would be:

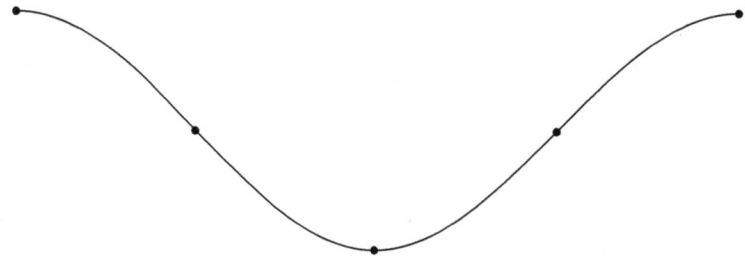

For some variant of $-\cos x$, the first period would be:

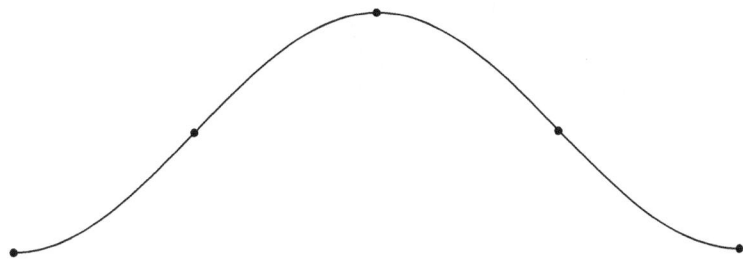

Example 6.3.1
Sketch $y = 2\sin(3x + 15) - 117$.

Solution. For simplicity, we will use degrees.

First, notice that the phase shift is $-\dfrac{15}{3} = -5$, so the x-coordinate of the first point is $-5°$. Since we are sketching a variant of $\sin x$, the first point lies on the midline, which is $y = -117$, so the coordinates of the first point is $(-5°, -117)$.

The period is $\dfrac{360°}{3} = 120°$, so the last point will have an x-coordinate of $-5° + 120° = 115°$.

Notice that the five special points are equally spaced away with respect to their x-coordinates. Then, we can deduce that each point is horizontally a quarter of a full period away from its adjacent points.

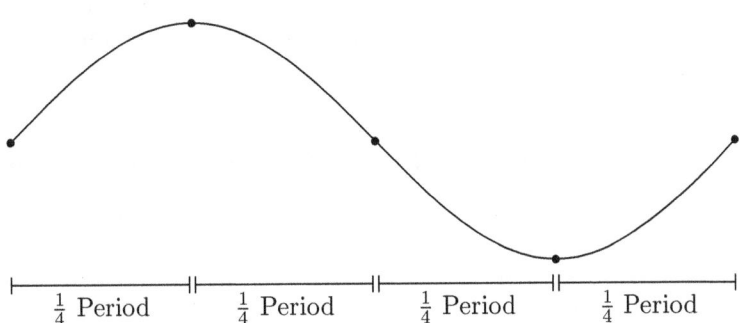

Since the period is $120°$, each point will horizontally be $30°$ away from its adjacent points.

Thus, the second point will have an x-coordinate of $-5° + 30° = 25°$, the third point will have an x-coordinate of $25° + 30° = 55°$, and the fourth point will have an x-coordinate of $55° + 30° = 85°$. We can also confirm that the x-coordinate of the last point is indeed $115°$ by adding $30°$ to $85°$.

Now, we just have to find the y-coordinates. Here, we observe that the minimum is $-117 - |2| = -119$ and the maximum is $-117 + |2| = -115$. Then, we can assign y-coordinates to the points according to which are maximums, minimums, or lie on the midline. Thus, our first period sketch is:

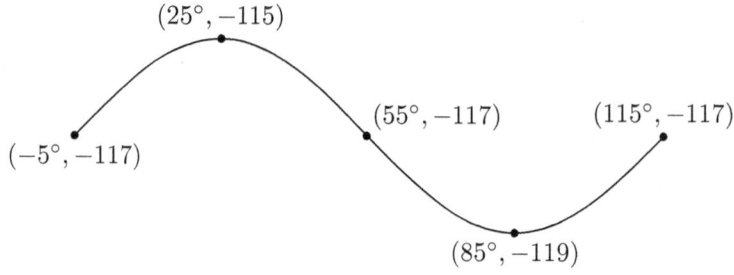

Exercise 6.3.2. Sketch $y = 2 - 3\cos\left(5x + \dfrac{\pi}{3}\right)$.

Example 6.3.3

Consider a portion of a sinusoidal function:

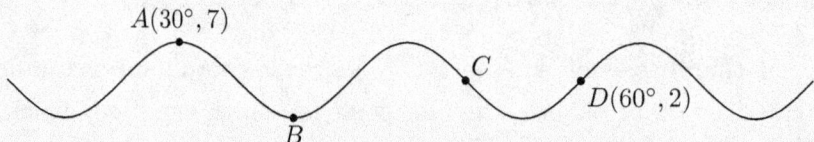

Given that points C and D lie on the midline, find the coordinates of B and C. Then, find four equations for the graph with the plane shift at A, B, C, and D.

Solution. Recall that a period can be broken up into four 'quarters.' While we are not directly dealing with a single cycle this time, notice that there are seven 'quarter' pieces between points A and D. Since the x-coordinate of points A and D are respectively 30° and 60°, each 'quarter' piece will be $\dfrac{60° - 30°}{7} = \dfrac{30°}{7}$ long.

Since point B is two 'quarter' pieces away from point A, its x-coordinate will be $30° + 2 \cdot \dfrac{30°}{7} = \dfrac{270°}{7}$. Likewise, point C is 5 'quarter' pieces away from point A, its x-coordinate will then be $30° + 5 \cdot \dfrac{30°}{7} = \dfrac{360°}{7}$.

Now, we just have to find the y-coordinates. Notice that point C also lies on the midline, so its y-coordinate will be the same as point D, which is 2.

Since B lies on a minimum of the wave, its y-coordinate will be the midline minus the amplitude. The amplitude is also the distance from the midline to the maximum, and since point A lies on a maximum of 7, the amplitude must be $7 - 2 = 5$. Thus, the minimum is $2 - 5 = -3$, so the y-coordinate of point B must be -3.

Thus, point B has coordinates $\boxed{\left(\dfrac{270°}{7}, -3\right)}$ and point C has coordinates $\boxed{\left(\dfrac{360°}{7}, 2\right)}$.

To find an equation for this graph, we need the following information:

- We have already found the amplitude to be 5.

- The period is four 'quarters,' which is $4 \cdot \frac{30°}{7} = \frac{120°}{7}$.

- Since the period is $\frac{120°}{7} = \frac{360°}{21}$, the frequency must be 21.

- The midline is $y = 2$.

All we need now is the phase shift. We look back to the four different shapes of 'first periods' for $\sin x$, $-\sin x$, $\cos x$, and $-\cos x$ to determine which function should be used for which point.

1. If the phase shift is at point A, then the function must be some variant of $\cos x$. The phase shift itself must be 30° (it is positive because we are shifting cosine to the right). Putting together all the information, we have the equation,

$$y = 5\cos(21(x - 30°)) + 2 \implies \boxed{y = 5\cos(21x - 630°) + 2}.$$

2. Likewise, the phase shift at point B must be $\frac{270°}{7}$. The function that should be used is some variant of $-\cos x$. Thus, our equation is

$$y = -5\cos\left(21\left(x - \frac{270°}{7}\right)\right) + 2 \implies \boxed{y = -5\cos(21x - 810°) + 2}.$$

3. The phase shift at point C must be $\frac{360°}{7}$. Our function at this point must be some variant of $-\sin x$, so the equation is

$$y = -5\sin\left(21\left(x - \frac{360°}{7}\right)\right) + 2 \implies \boxed{y = -5\sin(21x - 1080°) + 2}.$$

4. The phase shift at point D is $\frac{360°}{7}$. The function must be some variant of $\sin x$, so the equation is

$$y = 5\sin(21(x - 60°)) + 2 \implies \boxed{y = 5\sin(21x - 1260°) + 2}. \qquad \square$$

6.4 Inverse Trigonometric Functions

Clearly, the graphs of these trigonometric functions fail the *horizontal line test*: if any horizontal line intersects the function at more than one point, then an inverse function does not exist.

Then how could there possibly be inverse trigonometric functions? It turns out that the only reason for the failure of the horizontal line test is that the graph of the function repeats itself periodically.

However, there is no need to consider all the repeated periods. We just need to look at one period of the graph in order to define an appropriate inverse function.

Consider the graph of $\sin x$ on the interval $\left[-\frac{\pi}{2}, \frac{\pi}{2}\right]$.

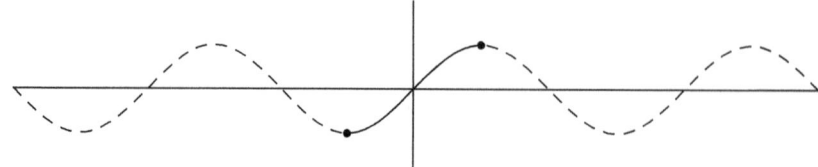

If we just consider this single portion of the graph, we can see that we have covered all possible points of $\sin x$ between -1 and 1. In other words, every distinct value of x is mapped to its corresponding, distinct value of $\sin x$. This is the condition needed for the existence of an inverse function.

By limiting the graph to this interval, the horizontal line test is satisfied, i.e. there exists an inverse for this function.

So, if we limit the domain of $\sin x$ to $\left[-\frac{\pi}{2}, \frac{\pi}{2}\right]$, then there exists an inverse function. We could have chosen $\left[\frac{\pi}{2}, \frac{3\pi}{2}\right]$ or $\left[-\frac{3\pi}{2}, -\frac{\pi}{2}\right]$, but it is most convenient to select the interval centered at the origin.

We will call this inverse function $\sin^{-1} x$. It can also be called $\arcsin x$. It is universally agreed that to define $\sin^{-1} x$, we will restrict the domain of $\sin x$ to $\left[-\frac{\pi}{2}, \frac{\pi}{2}\right]$.

Then, the domain of $\sin^{-1} x$ is simply the range of $\sin x$, which remains to be $[-1, 1]$, and the range of $\sin^{-1} x$ is the newly restricted domain of $\sin x$, which is $\left[-\frac{\pi}{2}, \frac{\pi}{2}\right]$.

We can easily graph $\sin^{-1} x$ by reflecting the limited graph of $\sin x$ over the line $y = x$.

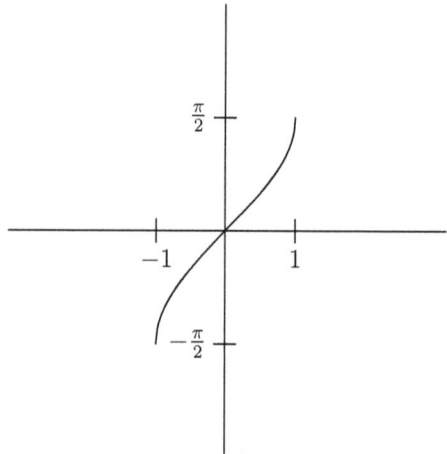

Now, let's consider $\cos x$. Like before, we want to restrict the domain so we can define $\cos^{-1} x$.

This time, if we try to limit the domain to $\left[-\frac{\pi}{2}, \frac{\pi}{2}\right]$, we run into couple of problems. First, that portion of the graph still fails the horizontal line test! Second, we would completely leave out the negative values of $\cos x$. Remember, it is our goal to include every possible value of $\cos x$ between -1 and 1 without repeated values.

However, if we limit the domain of $\cos x$ to $[0, \pi]$, then the resulting portion of the graph accomplishes what we wanted: it passes the horizontal line test, and it covers all possible values of $\cos x$ between -1 and 1.

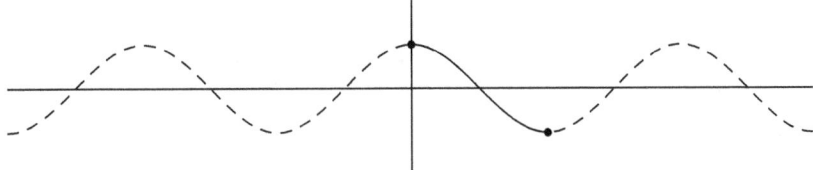

Thus, we define $\cos^{-1} x$ (or $\arccos x$, if you prefer) to be the inverse of $\cos x$, when the domain of $\cos x$ is restricted to $[0, \pi]$.

Of course, this interval is chosen for convenience - we could've chosen $[-\pi, 0]$, but the negative bounds may complicate matters in the future. It is nice to stick with a positive interval starting at 0. As with $\sin x$, it is generally agreed that the domain of $\cos x$ should be limited to $[0, \pi]$ in order to define $\cos^{-1} x$.

Therefore, if the domain of $\cos x$ was limited to $[0, \pi]$, then the range of $\cos^{-1} x$ should be $[0, \pi]$. As the range of $\cos x$ is still $[-1, 1]$, the domain of $\cos^{-1} x$ is $[-1, 1]$.

Again, we graph $\cos^{-1} x$ by reflecting through the line $y = x$.

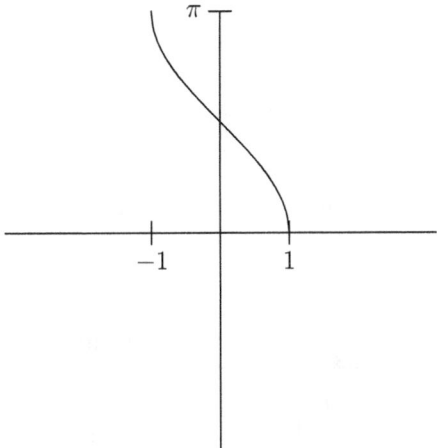

Lastly, let's move on to $\tan x$. We still have the same problem as before, but now you should be able to tell what slight modification is necessary.

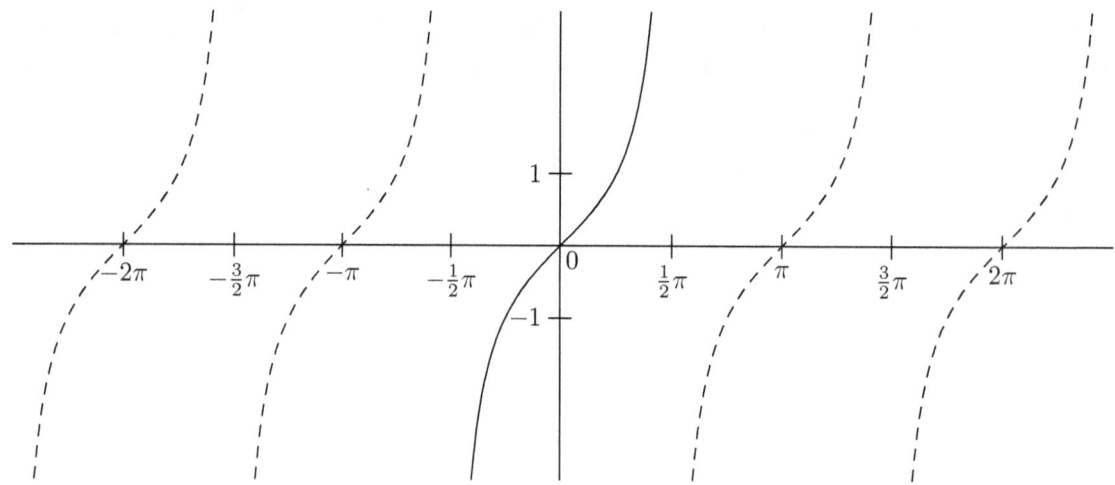

We should limit the domain to $\left(-\frac{\pi}{2}, \frac{\pi}{2}\right)$. It is unnecessary to include more than one period of tangent, since this selected portion already covers all values of $\tan x$.

Then, since the range of $\tan x$ is $\mathbb{R}$, the domain of $\tan^{-1} x$ is $\mathbb{R}$. Likewise, the restricted domain of $\tan x$ is $\left(-\frac{\pi}{2}, \frac{\pi}{2}\right)$, so the range of $\tan^{-1} x$ is $\left(-\frac{\pi}{2}, \frac{\pi}{2}\right)$.

By reflecting by the line $y = x$, we can graph $\tan^{-1} x$. The dashed lines represent the horizontal asymptotes of $\tan^{-1} x$.

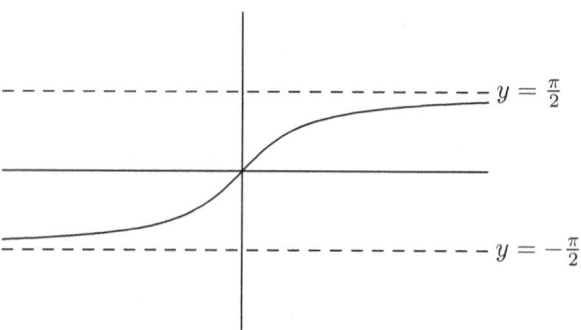

To recap what we have done so far, here are the domains and ranges of the three trigonometric inverse functions.

	Domain	Range
$\sin^{-1} x$	$[-1, 1]$	$\left[-\frac{\pi}{2}, \frac{\pi}{2}\right]$
$\cos^{-1} x$	$[-1, 1]$	$[0, \pi]$
$\tan^{-1} x$	$\mathbb{R}$	$\left(-\frac{\pi}{2}, \frac{\pi}{2}\right)$

You should grow accustomed to some common values for these functions.

x	$\sin^{-1} x$	$\cos^{-1} x$
1	$\dfrac{\pi}{2}$	0
$\dfrac{\sqrt{3}}{2}$	$\dfrac{\pi}{3}$	$\dfrac{\pi}{6}$
$\dfrac{\sqrt{2}}{2}$	$\dfrac{\pi}{4}$	$\dfrac{\pi}{4}$
$\dfrac{1}{2}$	$\dfrac{\pi}{6}$	$\dfrac{\pi}{3}$
0	0	$\dfrac{\pi}{2}$
$-\dfrac{1}{2}$	$-\dfrac{\pi}{6}$	$\dfrac{2\pi}{3}$
$-\dfrac{\sqrt{2}}{2}$	$-\dfrac{\pi}{4}$	$\dfrac{3\pi}{4}$
$-\dfrac{\sqrt{3}}{2}$	$-\dfrac{\pi}{3}$	$\dfrac{5\pi}{6}$
-1	$-\dfrac{\pi}{2}$	π

x	$\tan^{-1} x$
$\sqrt{3}$	$\dfrac{\pi}{3}$
1	$\dfrac{\pi}{4}$
$\dfrac{1}{\sqrt{3}}$	$\dfrac{\pi}{6}$
0	0
$-\dfrac{1}{\sqrt{3}}$	$-\dfrac{\pi}{6}$
-1	$-\dfrac{\pi}{4}$
$-\sqrt{3}$	$-\dfrac{\pi}{3}$

Take a moment to confirm that these values of x give the correct values of $\sin^{-1} x$, $\cos^{-1} x$, and $\tan^{-1} x$.

Problem 6.4.1. Find the values of the following:

1. $\sin^{-1}\left(\sin \dfrac{\pi}{7}\right)$

2. $\cos^{-1}\left(\cos \dfrac{\pi}{7}\right)$

3. $\tan^{-1}\left(\tan \dfrac{\pi}{7}\right)$

4. $\sin^{-1}\left(\sin 2\pi\right)$

5. $\sin^{-1}\left(\sin 3\right)$

Solution. Understand that the basic definition of an inverse implies $f^{-1}(f(x)) = x$. But be careful of the domains and ranges of the inverse trig functions!

1. $\sin^{-1}\left(\sin \dfrac{\pi}{7}\right) = \boxed{\dfrac{\pi}{7}}$.

2. $\cos^{-1}\left(\cos \dfrac{\pi}{7}\right) = \boxed{\dfrac{\pi}{7}}$.

3. $\tan^{-1}\left(\tan \dfrac{\pi}{7}\right) = \boxed{\dfrac{\pi}{7}}$.

4. The answer is not 2π, because the range of inverse sine is $\left[-\frac{\pi}{2}, \frac{\pi}{2}\right]$. So we must find a $\theta \in \left[-\frac{\pi}{2}, \frac{\pi}{2}\right]$ such that $\sin \theta = \sin(2\pi)$, which is $\theta = 0$. Therefore, $\sin^{-1}(\sin 2\pi) = \sin^{-1}(\sin 0) = \boxed{0}$.

5. Similarly, 3 would not be the correct answer. But note that $\sin 3 = \sin(\pi - 3)$, by the identity $\sin(180 - \theta) = \sin \theta$. Since $\pi - 3 \in \left[-\frac{\pi}{2}, \frac{\pi}{2}\right]$, $\sin^{-1}(\sin 3) = \sin^{-1}(\sin(\pi - 3)) = \boxed{\pi - 3}$. □

Example 6.4.2

Find the values of the following:

1. $\sin^{-1}\left(\cos\left(\frac{\pi}{7}\right)\right)$

2. $\sin^{-1}\left(\cos\left(-\frac{\pi}{7}\right)\right)$

3. $\sin\left(\cos^{-1}\left(\frac{\pi}{7}\right)\right)$

4. Find a general form for $\sin(\cos^{-1} x)$.

5. $\sin\left(\cos^{-1}\left(\frac{\pi}{2}\right)\right)$

6. $\sec(\tan^{-1}(2017))$

Solution.

1. Use the cofunction identities to make the problem more manageable:

$$\sin^{-1}\left(\cos\left(\frac{\pi}{7}\right)\right) = \sin^{-1}\left(\sin\left(\frac{\pi}{2} - \frac{\pi}{7}\right)\right)$$
$$= \sin^{-1}\left(\sin\left(\frac{5\pi}{14}\right)\right)$$
$$= \boxed{\frac{5\pi}{14}}.$$

2. Note that $\cos(-\theta) = \cos \theta$. Thus, $\sin^{-1}\left(\cos\left(-\frac{\pi}{7}\right)\right) = \sin^{-1}\left(\cos\left(\frac{\pi}{7}\right)\right) = \boxed{\frac{5\pi}{14}}$, based on the previous problem.

3. We introduce another technique that is commonly applied to this type of problem. Let $\theta = \cos^{-1}\left(\frac{\pi}{7}\right)$. This means that $\cos \theta = \frac{\pi}{7}$. We must find $\sin \theta$, and now the problem becomes familiar:

$$\sin^2 \theta + \cos^2 \theta = 1$$
$$\sin^2 \theta = 1 - \frac{\pi^2}{49}$$

$$\sin\theta = \pm\frac{\sqrt{49-\pi^2}}{7}.$$

Which sign do we choose? Now, we have to consider the domain and range of $\cos^{-1} x$. Since the range is $[0, \pi]$, we must have $\theta \in [0, \pi]$. Then, in that interval, $\sin\theta$ is always positive. Therefore, we choose the positive square root to get $\boxed{\dfrac{\sqrt{49-\pi^2}}{7}}$.

4. First, note that
$$\sin^2\theta + \cos^2\theta = 1$$
$$\sin^2\theta = 1 - \cos^2\theta$$
$$\sin\theta = \pm\sqrt{1-\cos^2\theta}.$$

Then, let $\theta = \cos^{-1} x$. So, we have
$$\sin(\cos^{-1}(x)) = \pm\sqrt{1 - \cos^2(\cos^{-1}(x))},$$
$$= \pm\sqrt{1-x^2}.$$

However, $\cos^{-1}(x)$ has range $[0, \pi]$, and sin is always positive in this interval, so we choose the positive square root: $\sin(\cos^{-1}(x)) = \boxed{\sqrt{1-x^2}}$.

5. The domain of $\cos^{-1}(x)$ is $[-1, 1]$, but we are given $x = \dfrac{\pi}{2}$, which is greater than 1. Therefore, there is $\boxed{\text{no solution}}$.

6. Using the identity $\tan^2\theta + 1 = \sec^2\theta$ and letting $\theta = \tan^{-1}(2017)$ or $\tan\theta = 2017$, we get $\sec\theta = \pm\sqrt{2017^2 + 1}$. Note that $\theta \in \left(-\dfrac{\pi}{2}, \dfrac{\pi}{2}\right)$, so $\sec\theta$, being the reciprocal of $\cos\theta$, must be positive, so we choose the positive square root: $\boxed{\sqrt{2017^2+1}}$. $\square$

Exercise 6.4.3. Compute and simplify $\sin\left(\cos^{-1}\left(-\dfrac{3}{5}\right) + \sin^{-1}\left(-\dfrac{4}{5}\right)\right)$.

Exercise 6.4.4. Compute and simplify $\sin\left(\sin^{-1}\left(\dfrac{5}{13}\right) + \cos^{-1}\left(-\dfrac{5}{13}\right)\right)$.

Problem 6.4.5. Prove that $\sin^{-1} x + \cos^{-1} x = \dfrac{\pi}{2}$.

Proof. Let $\sin^{-1} x = \theta$, or $\sin\theta = x$. By the cofunction identities, $\sin\theta = \cos\left(\dfrac{\pi}{2} - \theta\right) = x$, so $\cos^{-1} x = \dfrac{\pi}{2} - \theta$, or $\cos^{-1} x = \dfrac{\pi}{2} - \sin^{-1} x$. This rearranges to $\sin^{-1} x + \cos^{-1} x = \dfrac{\pi}{2}$, and we're done. $\square$

Problem 6.4.6. Find the following values:

1. $\sin\left(\cos^{-1}\left(-\dfrac{1}{3}\right)\right)$

2. $\csc(\tan^{-1}(-2))$

3. $\sec(\sin^{-1} x)$

Solution. It is essential that you understand the domains and ranges of the inverse functions so that you are able to choose the proper sign.

1. Let $\theta = \cos^{-1}\left(-\frac{1}{3}\right)$. Then $\cos\theta = -\frac{1}{3}$. Because the range of $\cos^{-1}$ is $[0, \pi]$, and sin is always nonnegative in that interval, $\sin\theta$ must be nonnegative. Using the identity $\sin^2\theta + \cos^2\theta = 1$, we get that $\sin\theta = \pm\frac{2\sqrt{2}}{3}$, so choose the positive square root: $\sin\theta = \boxed{\frac{2\sqrt{2}}{3}}$.

2. This is a challenging problem.

    First, let $\theta = \tan^{-1}(-2)$. Then $\tan\theta = -2$. Using the identity $\tan^2\theta + 1 = \sec^2\theta$, we get that $\sec\theta = \pm\sqrt{5}$. We know that $\tan\theta < 0$, so therefore $\theta \in \left(-\frac{\pi}{2}, 0\right)$. $\cos\theta$ must be positive in that interval, so $\sec\theta$ is also positive. Thus, $\sec\theta = \sqrt{5}$, and $\cos\theta = \frac{1}{\sqrt{5}}$. Using the identity $\sin^2\theta + \cos^2\theta = 1$, we get $\sin\theta = \pm\frac{2}{\sqrt{5}}$, but since $\theta \in \left(-\frac{\pi}{2}, 0\right)$, $\sin\theta < 0$, so we choose $\sin\theta = -\frac{2}{\sqrt{5}}$. Therefore, $\csc\theta = \boxed{-\frac{\sqrt{5}}{2}}$.

3. Note that $\sec(\sin^{-1} x) = \dfrac{1}{\cos(\sin^{-1} x)}$. Let $\theta = \sin^{-1} x$, so $\sin\theta = x$. The range of inverse sine implies that $\theta \in \left[-\frac{\pi}{2}, \frac{\pi}{2}\right]$, and therefore $\cos\theta$ is always positive in that interval. Using the identity $\sin^2\theta + \cos^2\theta = 1$, $\cos\theta = \sqrt{1-x^2}$ (we choose the positive square root). Thus, $\sec(\sin^{-1} x) = \boxed{\dfrac{1}{\sqrt{1-x^2}}}$. □

6.5 More Trigonometric Identities

So far, we have only discovered identities that dealt with 90° or 180°. What if we wanted to find an expression for $\sin(\theta + 30°)$? If we know $\sin\theta$ and $\sin 30°$, it seems reasonable that we should also get $\sin(\theta + 30°)$.

To develop our first set of new, useful identities, we first consider the following two triangles which lie on the unit circle:

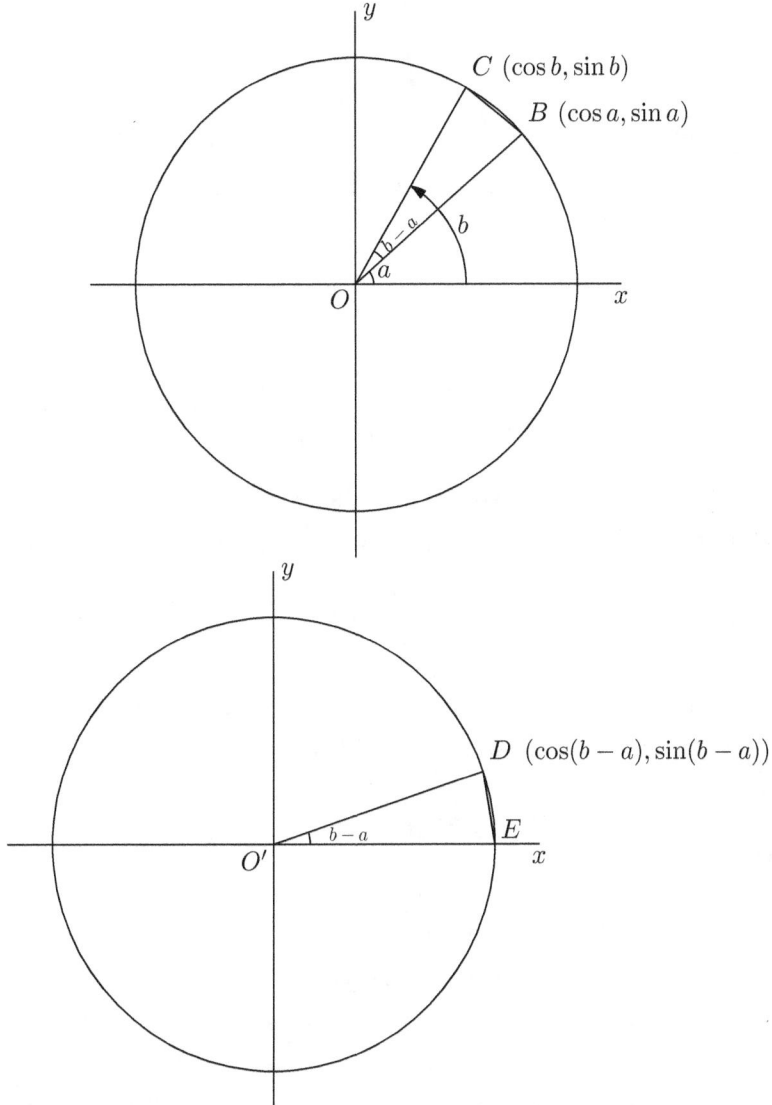

Notice that $\overline{OC} \cong \overline{O'D}$ and $\overline{OB} \cong \overline{O'E}$, as they are radii of the unit circle. We have also constructed the triangles to have same angle $m\angle COB = m\angle DO'E = b - a$. Therefore, by SAS, $\triangle OBC \cong \triangle O'ED$. Then, $\overline{BC} \cong \overline{ED}$, implying that $m\overline{BC} = m\overline{ED}$.

These are equal, so now we have basic algebraic manipulation:

$$\sqrt{(\cos b - \cos a)^2 + (\sin b - \sin a)^2} = \sqrt{(\cos(b-a) - 1)^2 + \sin^2(b-a)}$$
$$(\cos b - \cos a)^2 + (\sin b - \sin a)^2 = (\cos(b-a) - 1)^2 + \sin^2(b-a).$$

Expanding gives

$$\cos^2 b - 2\cos b \cos a + \cos^2 a + \sin^2 b - 2\sin b \sin a + \sin^2 a$$
$$= \cos^2(b-a) - 2\cos(b-a) + 1 + \sin^2(b-a).$$

This reduces to
$$2 - 2(\cos b \cos a + \sin b \sin a) = 2 - 2\cos(b - a).$$

From here, we finally get our first new identity:
$$\cos(b - a) = \cos b \cos a + \sin b \sin a.$$

Now, observe that $\cos(b + a) = \cos(b - (-a))$. Then,
$$\cos(b + a) = \cos(b - (-a))$$
$$\cos(b + a) = \cos b \cos(-a) + \sin b \sin(-a)$$
$$\cos(b + a) = \cos b \cos a - \sin b \sin a,$$

using the identities $\cos(-a) = \cos a$ and $\sin(-a) = -\sin a$.

To find the formula for $\sin(b + a)$, apply the cofunction identity $\sin(b + a) = \cos(90° - (b + a))$.

$$\sin(b + a) = \cos(90° - (b + a))$$
$$\sin(b + a) = \cos((90° - b) - a))$$
$$\sin(b + a) = \cos(90° - b) \cos a + \sin(90° - b) \sin a$$
$$\sin(b + a) = \sin b \cos a + \cos b \sin a.$$

The angle difference for sine is similar to that of cosine: use the facts that $\sin(-\theta) = -\sin \theta$ and $\cos(-\theta) = \cos \theta$. We have,

$$\sin(b - a) = \sin(b + (-a))$$
$$\sin(b - a) = \sin b \cos(-a) + \cos b \sin(-a)$$
$$\sin(b - a) = \sin b \cos a - \cos b \sin a.$$

The four identities we have just discovered are known as the **sum and difference identities**:

$$\sin(x \pm y) = \sin x \cos y \pm \cos x \sin y$$
$$\cos(x \pm y) = \cos x \cos y \mp \sin x \sin y$$

Here are some exercises that require the use of these formulas.

Problem 6.5.1. Compute the following values:

1. $\cos(15°)$

2. $\sin(195°)$

3. $\cos\left(\cos^{-1}\dfrac{3}{5} + \cos^{-1}\dfrac{5}{13}\right)$

Solution.

1. $\cos(15°) = \cos(45° - 30°)$
$$= \cos 45° \cos 30° + \sin 45° \sin 30°$$
$$= \frac{\sqrt{2}}{2} \cdot \frac{\sqrt{3}}{2} + \frac{\sqrt{2}}{2} \cdot \frac{1}{2}$$
$$= \frac{\sqrt{2}}{2} \left(\frac{\sqrt{3}+1}{2} \right)$$
$$= \boxed{\frac{\sqrt{6}+\sqrt{2}}{4}}.$$

2. $\sin(195°) = \sin(150° + 45°)$
$$= \sin 150° \cos 45° + \cos 150° \sin 45°$$
$$= \frac{\sqrt{2}}{2} \left(\frac{1}{2} - \frac{\sqrt{3}}{2} \right)$$
$$= \frac{\sqrt{2}}{2} \left(\frac{1-\sqrt{3}}{2} \right)$$
$$= \boxed{\frac{\sqrt{2}-\sqrt{6}}{4}}.$$

3. $\cos\left(\cos^{-1}\frac{3}{5} + \cos^{-1}\frac{5}{13}\right) = \cos\left(\cos^{-1}\frac{3}{5}\right)\cos\left(\cos^{-1}\frac{5}{13}\right) - \sin\left(\cos^{-1}\frac{3}{5}\right)\sin\left(\cos^{-1}\frac{5}{13}\right)$
$$= \frac{3}{5} \cdot \frac{5}{13} - \frac{4}{5} \cdot \frac{12}{13}$$
$$= \boxed{-\frac{33}{65}}.$$

$\square$

Using these identities, we can also find the sum and difference formulas for tangent:
$$\tan(x \pm y) = \frac{\sin(x \pm y)}{\cos(x \pm y)}$$
$$= \frac{\sin x \cos y \pm \cos x \cos y}{\cos x \cos y \mp \sin x \sin y}.$$

Divide the numerator and denominator by $\cos x \cos y$ to get the desired relation:
$$\tan(x \pm y) = \frac{\tan x \pm \tan y}{1 \mp \tan x \tan y}.$$

Problem 6.5.2. Compute the following values:

1. $\tan(15°)$

2. $\tan^{-1}\frac{1}{2} + \tan^{-1}\frac{1}{3}$

Solution.

1. $\tan(15°) = \tan(45° - 30°)$
$$= \frac{\tan 45° - \tan 30°}{1 + \tan 45° \tan 30°}$$
$$= \frac{1 - \frac{1}{\sqrt{3}}}{1 + \frac{1}{\sqrt{3}}}$$
$$= \boxed{2 - \sqrt{3}}.$$

2. The addition of these inverse tan values suggest that we should take the tangent of this sum and analyze its result. Note that

$$\tan\left(\tan^{-1}\frac{1}{2} + \tan^{-1}\frac{1}{3}\right) = \frac{\tan\left(\tan^{-1}\frac{1}{2}\right) + \tan\left(\tan^{-1}\frac{1}{3}\right)}{1 - \tan\left(\tan^{-1}\frac{1}{2}\right)\tan\left(\tan^{-1}\frac{1}{3}\right)}$$
$$= \frac{\frac{1}{2} + \frac{1}{3}}{1 - \frac{1}{6}}$$
$$= 1.$$

If the slope (which is the tangent) is less than 1, then the angle must be less than $\frac{\pi}{4}$. Thus, $\tan^{-1}\frac{1}{2} < \frac{\pi}{4}$ and $\tan^{-1}\frac{1}{3} < \frac{\pi}{4}$, so $\tan^{-1}\frac{1}{2} + \tan^{-1}\frac{1}{3} < \frac{\pi}{2}$.

Combining this with the result that $\tan\left(\tan^{-1}\frac{1}{2} + \tan^{-1}\frac{1}{3}\right) = 1$, we see that the only value possible for $\tan^{-1}\frac{1}{2} + \tan^{-1}\frac{1}{3}$ is $\boxed{\frac{\pi}{4}}$. □

Using the sum and difference formulas, we can derive formulas for $\sin 2x$, $\cos 2x$, and $\tan 2x$ in terms of $\sin x$, $\cos x$, and $\tan x$.

Observe that $2x = x + x$. Then,

$$\sin(2x) = \sin(x + x)$$
$$= \sin x \cos x + \cos x \sin x$$
$$= \boxed{2 \sin x \cos x}.$$
$$\cos(2x) = \cos(x + x)$$
$$= \cos x \cos x - \sin x \sin x$$
$$= \boxed{\cos^2 x - \sin^2 x}.$$

The result for $\cos(2x)$ reminds us of the Pythagorean Identity $\sin^2 x + \cos^2 x = 1$. In fact, this equation can be rewritten in two ways: $\sin^2 x = 1 - \cos^2 x$, and $\cos^2 x = 1 - \sin^2 x$. We then substitute these two relations into the result $\cos^2 x - \sin^2 x$ to derive two new double angle identities for cosine:

$$\cos(2x) = \boxed{\cos^2 x - \sin^2 x}$$
$$= \cos^2 x - (1 - \cos^2 x) = \boxed{2\cos^2 x - 1},$$
$$= (1 - \sin^2 x) - \sin^2 x = \boxed{1 - 2\sin^2 x}.$$

Deriving the double angle identity for tangent is straightforward:

$$\tan(2x) = \tan(x+x)$$
$$= \frac{\tan x + \tan x}{1 - \tan x \tan x}$$
$$= \boxed{\frac{2\tan x}{1 - \tan^2 x}}.$$

Thus, our **double angle** identities for sine, cosine, and tangent are:

$$\sin 2x = 2\sin x \cos x$$
$$\cos 2x = \cos^2 x - \sin^2 x$$
$$= 2\cos^2 x - 1$$
$$= 1 - 2\sin^2 x$$
$$\tan 2x = \frac{2\tan x}{1 - \tan^2 x}$$

Problem 6.5.3. Answer the following:

1. If $\cos x = \frac{1}{3}$, what is $\cos 2x$?

2. If $\sin x = \frac{3}{5}$, what is $\sin 2x$?

3. If $\tan x = \frac{1}{3}$, what is $\tan 2x$?

4. Compute the value $\tan\left(2\tan^{-1}\frac{1}{2}\right)$.

5. Compute $\cos(2\tan^{-1} 5)$.

Solution.

1. Directly apply the double angle formula for cosine: $\cos 2x = 2\cos^2 x - 1 = 2\left(\frac{1}{3}\right)^2 - 1 = \boxed{-\frac{7}{9}}$.

2. Since $\sin 2x = 2\sin x \cos x$, we also have to find the value of $\cos x$. Using the Pythagorean Identity $\sin^2 x + \cos^2 x = 1$, we see that $\cos x = \pm\frac{4}{5}$. We must be careful as there are two possible values for $\sin 2x$ when we consider the sign of $\cos x$:

- If $\cos x > 0$, then $\sin 2x = 2 \cdot \dfrac{3}{5} \cdot \dfrac{4}{5} = \boxed{\dfrac{24}{25}}$.

- If $\cos x < 0$, then $\sin 2x = 2 \cdot \dfrac{3}{5} \cdot -\dfrac{4}{5} = \boxed{-\dfrac{24}{25}}$.

3. Again, we can directly apply the half angle formula for tangent: $\tan 2x = \dfrac{2 \cdot \frac{1}{3}}{1 - \left(\frac{1}{3}\right)^2} = \boxed{\dfrac{3}{4}}$.

4. We treat $\tan^{-1} \dfrac{1}{2}$ as the angle we are doubling. Applying the half angle formula in this fashion, we have

$$\tan\left(2 \tan^{-1} \dfrac{1}{2}\right) = \dfrac{2 \tan\left(\tan^{-1} \dfrac{1}{2}\right)}{1 - \tan^2\left(\tan^{-1} \dfrac{1}{2}\right)}$$

$$= \dfrac{2 \cdot \dfrac{1}{2}}{1 - \left(\dfrac{1}{2}\right)^2}$$

$$= \boxed{\dfrac{4}{3}}.$$

5. By the double angle identity for cosine, $\cos(2\tan^{-1} 5) = 2\cos^2\left(\tan^{-1} 5\right) - 1$. Now we must compute the value $\cos(\tan^{-1} 5)$ to find the answer.

   Let $\theta = \tan^{-1} 5$, implying $\tan \theta = 5$. Using the identity $\tan^2 \theta + 1 = \sec^2 \theta$, we get $\sec \theta = \pm\sqrt{26}$. However, as θ is equal to an inverse tangent function, the range of inverse tangent implies that $\theta \in \left(-\dfrac{\pi}{2}, \dfrac{\pi}{2}\right)$. In this interval, $\cos \theta$, and therefore, $\sec \theta$, are always positive, so $\sec \theta = \sqrt{26}$ and $\cos \theta = \dfrac{1}{\sqrt{26}}$.

   Therefore, $\cos(2\tan^{-1} 5) = 2\cos^2\left(\tan^{-1} 5\right) - 1 = 2\left(\dfrac{1}{\sqrt{26}}\right)^2 - 1 = \dfrac{1}{13} - 1 = \boxed{-\dfrac{12}{13}}$. □

If we can double an angle, we can also halve an angle. This will lead us to our next set of identities.

First, we can express $\sin \theta$ in terms of $\cos 2\theta$:

$$\cos 2\theta = 1 - 2\sin^2 \theta$$

$$\sin \theta = \pm\sqrt{\dfrac{1 - \cos 2\theta}{2}}.$$

Then, we can substitute $\theta \to \dfrac{\theta}{2}$ to get

$$\sin \dfrac{\theta}{2} = \pm\sqrt{\dfrac{1 - \cos \theta}{2}}.$$

Likewise, for cosine:

$$\cos 2\theta = 2\cos^2\theta - 1$$

$$\cos\theta = \pm\sqrt{\frac{1+\cos 2\theta}{2}}$$

$$\cos\frac{\theta}{2} = \pm\sqrt{\frac{1+\cos\theta}{2}}.$$

There are two half angle identities for tangent, derived in different ways:

$$\tan\frac{\theta}{2} = \frac{\sin\frac{\theta}{2}}{\cos\frac{\theta}{2}}$$

$$= \frac{\sin\frac{\theta}{2}}{\cos\frac{\theta}{2}} \cdot \frac{2\cos\frac{\theta}{2}}{2\cos\frac{\theta}{2}}$$

$$= \frac{2\sin\frac{\theta}{2}\cos\frac{\theta}{2}}{2\cos^2\frac{\theta}{2}}$$

$$= \boxed{\frac{\sin\theta}{1+\cos\theta}}.$$

$$\tan\frac{\theta}{2} = \frac{\sin\frac{\theta}{2}}{\cos\frac{\theta}{2}}$$

$$= \frac{\sin\frac{\theta}{2}}{\cos\frac{\theta}{2}} \cdot \frac{2\sin\frac{\theta}{2}}{2\sin\frac{\theta}{2}}$$

$$= \frac{2\sin^2\frac{\theta}{2}}{2\sin\frac{\theta}{2}\cos\frac{\theta}{2}}$$

$$= \boxed{\frac{1-\cos\theta}{\sin\theta}}.$$

Thus, the **half angle** identities for sine, cosine, and tangent are:

$$\sin\frac{\theta}{2} = \pm\sqrt{\frac{1-\cos\theta}{2}}$$

$$\cos\frac{\theta}{2} = \pm\sqrt{\frac{1+\cos\theta}{2}}$$

$$\tan\frac{\theta}{2} = \frac{\sin\theta}{1+\cos\theta}$$

$$= \frac{1-\cos\theta}{\sin\theta}$$

Problem 6.5.4. Answer the following:

1. If $\cos\theta = \frac{1}{5}$ and $\theta \in I$, what is $\cos\frac{\theta}{2}$?

2. Compute and simplify $\tan \dfrac{\pi}{8}$.

Solution.

1. The half angle formula for cosine gives us $\cos \dfrac{\theta}{2} = \pm\sqrt{\dfrac{1+\frac{1}{5}}{2}} = \boxed{\pm\sqrt{\dfrac{3}{5}}}$. Be careful, $\cos \dfrac{\pi}{2}$ may not always be positive! Note that $\theta \in I$ implies that $0° + 360k° < \theta < 90° + 360k°$, which could suggest $360° < \theta < 450°$, leading to $180° < \dfrac{\theta}{2} < 225°$, and $\cos \dfrac{\theta}{2}$ is negative in this interval. Therefore $\cos \dfrac{\theta}{2}$ can either be positive or negative, even though θ is in quadrant I.

2. We simply use the half angle formula for tangent: $\tan \dfrac{\pi}{8} = \dfrac{\sin \frac{\pi}{4}}{1 + \cos \frac{\pi}{4}} = \dfrac{\frac{\sqrt{2}}{2}}{\frac{2+\sqrt{2}}{2}} = \dfrac{\sqrt{2}}{2+\sqrt{2}} = \boxed{\sqrt{2} - 1}$. □

Exercise 6.5.5. Compute $\tan 67.5°$ and simplify your answer.

Problem 6.5.6. Compute $\tan\left(\dfrac{1}{2}\tan^{-1}(2)\right)$.

Solution. If we let $\theta = \tan^{-1}(2)$, then we have to compute $\tan \dfrac{\theta}{2}$. By our half angle identity, we have

$$\tan \dfrac{\theta}{2} = \dfrac{\sin \theta}{1 + \cos \theta}.$$

Now we have to find $\sin \theta$ and $\cos \theta$. Note that $\theta = \tan^{-1}(2) \implies \tan \theta = 2$. Now we have a simple reference triangle problem.

Note that $\tan^2 \theta + 1 = \sec^2 \theta$, so $\sec^2 \theta = 2^2 + 1 = 5 \implies \sec \theta = \pm\sqrt{5}$.

Recall that the range of $\tan^{-1}$ is $\left(-\dfrac{\pi}{2}, \dfrac{\pi}{2}\right)$. Since $\theta = \tan^{-1}(2)$ and 2 is a positive slope, we must conclude that θ is in the first quadrant, i.e. $\theta \in \left(0, \dfrac{\pi}{2}\right)$. Then $\cos \theta$ and $\sec \theta$ must be positive on that interval. Thus, we choose $\sec \theta = \sqrt{5}$, and thus $\cos \theta = \dfrac{1}{\sqrt{5}}$. Likewise, $\sin \theta$ will also be positive on this interval, so $\sin \theta = \sqrt{1 - \left(\dfrac{1}{\sqrt{5}}\right)^2} = \dfrac{2}{\sqrt{5}}$.

Finally, we can plug in to get

$$\tan \dfrac{\theta}{2} = \dfrac{\frac{2}{\sqrt{5}}}{1 + \frac{1}{\sqrt{5}}} = \boxed{\dfrac{\sqrt{5}-1}{2}}.$$ □

In addition to the double angle identities, we also have the **triple angle identities**:

$$\sin 3\theta = -4\sin^3 \theta + 3\sin \theta$$

$$\cos 3\theta = 4\cos^3\theta - 3\cos\theta$$
$$\tan 3\theta = \frac{3\tan\theta - \tan^3\theta}{1 - 3\tan^2\theta}$$

Problem 6.5.7. Prove the triple angle identities.

Proof. Using the fact that $3\theta = 2\theta + \theta$, we can use the sum formulas for sine and cosine, then repeatedly apply double angle identities and Pythagorean identities $\sin^2\theta = 1 - \cos^2\theta$ and $\cos^2\theta = 1 - \sin^2\theta$ to finish the proof.

$$\begin{aligned}
\sin 3\theta &= \sin(2\theta + \theta) \\
&= \sin 2\theta \cos\theta + \cos 2\theta \sin\theta \\
&= (2\sin\theta\cos\theta)\cos\theta + (1 - 2\sin^2\theta)\sin\theta \\
&= 2\sin\theta\cos^2\theta + \sin\theta - 2\sin^3\theta \\
&= 2\sin\theta(1 - \sin^2\theta) + \sin\theta - 2\sin^3\theta \\
&= 2\sin\theta - 2\sin^3\theta + \sin\theta - 2\sin^3\theta \\
&= -4\sin^3\theta + 3\sin\theta. \\
\cos 3\theta &= \cos(2\theta + \theta) \\
&= \cos 2\theta \cos\theta - \sin 2\theta \sin\theta \\
&= (2\cos^2\theta - 1)\cos\theta - (2\sin^2\theta \cos\theta) \\
&= 2\cos^3\theta - \cos\theta - (1 - \cos^2\theta)(2\cos\theta) \\
&= 2\cos^3\theta - \cos\theta - 2\cos\theta + 2\cos^3\theta \\
&= 4\cos^3\theta - 3\cos\theta. \\
\tan 3\theta &= \tan(2\theta + \theta) \\
&= \frac{\tan 2\theta + \tan\theta}{1 - \tan 2\theta \tan\theta} \\
&= \frac{\frac{2\tan\theta}{1 - \tan^2\theta} + \tan\theta}{1 - \frac{2\tan\theta}{1 - \tan^2\theta} \cdot \tan\theta} \\
&= \frac{\frac{2\tan\theta + \tan\theta(1 - \tan^2\theta)}{1 - \tan^2\theta}}{\frac{1 - 3\tan^2\theta}{1 - \tan^2\theta}} \\
&= \frac{2\tan\theta + \tan\theta - \tan^3\theta}{1 - 3\tan^2\theta} \\
&= \frac{3\tan\theta - \tan^3\theta}{1 - 3\tan^2\theta}. \qquad \square
\end{aligned}$$

Now, here are some review problems that will require the use of the identities discovered in this section.

Problem 6.5.8. If $\sin\theta + \cos\theta = \dfrac{1}{2}$, what's $\sin 2\theta$?

Solution. If we square both sides of the equation $\sin\theta + \cos\theta = \dfrac{1}{2}$, we get

$$\sin^2\theta + 2\sin\theta\cos\theta + \cos^2\theta = \dfrac{1}{4}.$$

Note that $\sin^2\theta + \cos^2\theta = 1$ and $\sin 2\theta = 2\sin\theta\cos\theta$. Therefore, $\sin 2\theta = \boxed{-\dfrac{3}{4}}$. □

Problem 6.5.9. Simplify $\cos^4 T - \sin^4 T$ as much as possible.

Solution. We have that $\cos^4 T - \sin^4 T = (\cos^2 T + \sin^2 T)(\cos^2 T - \sin^2 T)$. However, $\cos^2 T + \sin^2 T = 1$, and $\cos^2 T - \sin^2 T = \cos 2T$, thus $\cos^4 T - \sin^4 T = \boxed{\cos 2T}$. □

Problem 6.5.10. Prove $\cot\dfrac{\theta}{2} = \csc\theta + \cot\theta$.

Proof. Recall that $\tan\dfrac{\theta}{2} = \dfrac{\sin\theta}{1+\cos\theta}$. Then, $\cot\dfrac{\theta}{2} = \dfrac{1}{\tan\frac{\theta}{2}} = \dfrac{1+\cos\theta}{\sin\theta} = \dfrac{1}{\sin\theta} + \dfrac{\cos\theta}{\sin\theta} = \csc\theta + \cot\theta$, as desired. □

Problem 6.5.11. Derive a formula for $\cot(\alpha+\beta)$ in terms of $\cot\alpha$ and $\cot\beta$.

Solution. We can use the tangent sum identity:

$$\begin{aligned}
\cot(\alpha+\beta) &= \dfrac{1}{\tan(\alpha+\beta)} \\
&= \dfrac{1-\tan\alpha\tan\beta}{\tan\alpha+\tan\beta} \\
&= \dfrac{1 - \dfrac{1}{\cot\alpha\cot\beta}}{\dfrac{1}{\cot\alpha} + \dfrac{1}{\cot\beta}} \\
&= \dfrac{\dfrac{\cot\alpha\cot\beta - 1}{\cot\alpha\cot\beta}}{\dfrac{\cot\alpha+\cot\beta}{\cot\alpha\cot\beta}} \\
&= \boxed{\dfrac{\cot\alpha\cot\beta - 1}{\cot\alpha + \cot\beta}}.
\end{aligned}$$

□

Problem 6.5.12. If $\tan\theta = 2$, find all possible values of $\tan\dfrac{\theta}{2}$.

Solution. As $\tan\theta$ is positive, θ is in either quadrant I or III.

If $\theta \in I$, then $\sin\theta = \dfrac{2}{\sqrt{5}}$ and $\cos\theta = \dfrac{1}{\sqrt{5}}$, so $\tan\dfrac{\theta}{2} = \dfrac{\frac{2}{\sqrt{5}}}{1+\frac{1}{\sqrt{5}}} = \dfrac{2}{\sqrt{5}+1} = \boxed{\dfrac{\sqrt{5}-1}{2}}$.

If $\theta \in III$, then $\sin\theta = -\dfrac{2}{\sqrt{5}}$ and $\cos\theta = -\dfrac{1}{\sqrt{5}}$, so $\tan\dfrac{\theta}{2} = \dfrac{-\frac{2}{\sqrt{5}}}{1-\frac{1}{\sqrt{5}}} = -\dfrac{2}{\sqrt{5}-1} = \boxed{\dfrac{-\sqrt{5}-1}{2}}$.

□

Problem 6.5.13. If $\sin\theta = \dfrac{3}{5}$, what is $\sin 3\theta$?

Solution. The triple angle identity for sine is $\sin 3\theta = -4\sin^3\theta + 3\sin\theta$. Therefore, when $\sin\theta = \dfrac{3}{5}$, $\sin 3\theta = -4\left(\dfrac{3}{5}\right)^3 + 3\cdot\dfrac{3}{5} = \boxed{\dfrac{117}{125}}$. $\square$

Problem 6.5.14. Prove $\cos 20° \cos 40° \cos 80° = \dfrac{1}{8}$.

Proof. Using $\sin(180° - \theta) = \sin\theta$ and the double angle identity for sine, notice that

$$\cos 20° \cos 40° \cos 80° \sin 20° = \dfrac{1}{2} \sin 40° \cos 40° \cos 80°$$
$$= \dfrac{1}{4} \sin 80° \cos 80°$$
$$= \dfrac{1}{8} \sin 160°$$
$$= \dfrac{1}{8} \sin 20°.$$

Since $\cos 20° \cos 40° \cos 80° \sin 20° = \dfrac{1}{8}\sin 20°$, $\cos 20° \cos 40° \cos 80° = \dfrac{1}{8}$, so we're done. $\square$

Problem 6.5.15. Prove $\cos 36° \cos 72° = \dfrac{1}{4}$. Then, use this result to find the value of $\cos 36°$.

Solution. Similar to the previous problem,

$$\cos 36° \cos 72° \sin 36° = \dfrac{1}{2} \sin 72° \cos 72°$$
$$= \dfrac{1}{4} \sin 144°$$
$$= \dfrac{1}{4} \sin 36°,$$

implying $\cos 36° \cos 72° = \dfrac{1}{4}$.

To find $\cos 36°$, rewrite $\cos 36° \cos 72° = \dfrac{1}{4}$ in terms of $\cos 36°$ only. To do this, notice that 72 is $2 \cdot 36$, so we can use the double angle formula to get: $\cos 72° = 2\cos^2 36° - 1$, so we have:

$$\cos 36°(2\cos^2 36° - 1) = \dfrac{1}{4}$$

Letting $\cos 36° = x$ for convenience, the above equation leaves us with the polynomial $8x^3 - 4x - 1 = 0$. This factors into $2\left(x + \dfrac{1}{2}\right)(4x^2 - 2x - 1) = 0$, and since $\cos 36°$ clearly does not equal $-\dfrac{1}{2}$, we must find the roots of $4x^2 - 2x - 1$. Using the quadratic formula, we get $x = \dfrac{1 \pm \sqrt{5}}{4}$. Since $\cos 36° > 0$, we choose the positive value, i.e. $\cos 36° = \boxed{\dfrac{1 + \sqrt{5}}{4}}$. $\square$

Problem 6.5.16. Prove $-\sqrt{2} \leq \sin\theta + \cos\theta \leq \sqrt{2}\ \forall \theta$.

Proof. Given the range of sine, we have that $\sin 2\theta \leq 1$, which implies $\sin 2\theta + 1 \leq 2$. However, note that $\sin 2\theta + 1 = \sin 2\theta + \sin^2\theta + \cos^2\theta = 2\sin\theta\cos\theta + \sin^2\theta + \cos^2\theta = (\sin\theta + \cos\theta)^2$. Therefore, we have $(\sin\theta + \cos\theta)^2 \leq 2$, which means that $-\sqrt{2} \leq \sin\theta + \cos\theta \leq \sqrt{2}$, and we are done. □

Problem 6.5.17. What's the domain and range of $\cos^{-1}\left(\cos^{-1} x\right)$?

Solution. For $\cos^{-1}(\cos^{-1} x)$ to be defined, the domain of the outer $\cos^{-1}$ must be $[-1, 1]$. Note that the range of the inner $\cos^{-1} x$ is $[0, \pi]$; this does not fit inside the domain of the outer $\cos^{-1}$, so we must restrict the range of the inner $\cos^{-1} x$ to $[0, 1]$.

If the range of $\cos^{-1} x$ is $[0, 1]$, then $0 \leq \cos^{-1} x \leq 1$. Taking the cosine of this inequality yields $1 \geq x \geq \cos 1$. We flip the inequality signs because $\cos 1$ is clearly less than 1.

Therefore the domain of $\cos^{-1}(\cos^{-1} x)$ is $\boxed{[\cos 1, 1]}$.

Because the range of $\cos^{-1} x$ is $[0, 1]$, the range of $\cos^{-1}(\cos^1 x)$ would be $[\cos^{-1} 1, \cos^{-1} 0]$ (because $\cos^1 1 < \cos^{-1} 0$), or $\boxed{\left[0, \dfrac{\pi}{2}\right]}$. □

Problem 6.5.18. Prove $\tan \dfrac{\theta}{2} + \cot \dfrac{\theta}{2} = 2\csc\theta$.

Proof.
$$\tan \frac{\theta}{2} + \cot \frac{\theta}{2} = \frac{\sin\theta}{1 + \cos\theta} + \frac{1 + \cos\theta}{\sin\theta}$$
$$= \frac{\sin^2\theta + 1 + 2\cos\theta + \cos^2\theta}{(1 + \cos\theta)(\sin\theta)}$$
$$= \frac{2 + 2\cos\theta}{(1 + \cos\theta)(\sin\theta)}$$
$$= \frac{2(1 + 1\cos\theta)}{(1 + \cos\theta)(\sin\theta)}$$
$$= \frac{2}{\sin\theta}$$
$$= 2\csc\theta.$$
□

Problem 6.5.19. Find all θ in radians such that $\sin\theta = \dfrac{1}{2}$.

Solution. It may be tempting to immediately declare $\theta = \dfrac{\pi}{6}$ as the solution. However, recall that all trigonometric functions are periodic, and thus there are an infinite number of solutions. Since sine has a period of 2π (and thus the value does not change when adding or subtracting multiples of 2π), we see that $\theta = \dfrac{\pi}{6} + 2\pi k\ \forall k \in \mathbb{Z}$.

However, we are not finished. Note that $\sin\theta = \sin(\pi - \theta)$. Therefore, $\theta = \dfrac{5\pi}{6}$ is also a valid solution. We cannot forget that sine is periodic, so θ can actually be $\dfrac{5\pi}{6} + 2\pi k\ \forall k \in \mathbb{Z}$.

Combining these, we see that all solutions can be represented as:

$$\theta = \boxed{\frac{\pi}{6} + 2\pi k, \ \frac{5\pi}{6} + 2\pi k \ \forall k \in \mathbb{Z}}.$$

It may be hard to see that $\theta = \frac{5\pi}{6}$ is also a solution. A helpful tip is to visualize the unit circle on the coordinate plane, then plot the line $y = \frac{1}{2}$ and notice that it intersects the circle at two places, namely $\left(\cos\frac{\pi}{6}, \sin\frac{\pi}{6}\right)$ and $\left(\cos\frac{5\pi}{6}, \sin\frac{5\pi}{6}\right)$. We can then proceed from here. □

Problem 6.5.20. Find all $0° \leq x < 360°$ in degrees such that $\cos x = \frac{1}{3}$. A calculator may be used.

Solution. First, we calculate $x = \cos^{-1}\left(\frac{1}{3}\right) \approx 70.5°$. Then, observe that $\cos(360° - \theta) = \cos\theta$, so we also have $x = 360° - 70.5° = 289.5°$. All together, our solutions are $\boxed{70.5°, \ 289.5°}$.

Like the previous problem, notice that the line $x = \frac{1}{3}$ intersects the unit circle at two places (the first and fourth quadrants), so there must be two values of $x \in [0°, 360°)$. □

Problem 6.5.21. Find all $0 \leq x < 2\pi$ in radians such that $\sin 2x = \sin x$.

Solution. First, we can use the double angle identity to get $2\sin x \cos x = \sin x$. You may be tempted to divide both sides by $\sin x$, but this ignores the possibility that $\sin x = 0$. It is better to rearrange the equation to $2\sin x \cos x - \sin x = 0$, from we factor out $\sin x$ to get $\sin x(2\cos x - 1) = 0$. Now, we can notice that either $\sin x = 0$ or $\cos x = \frac{1}{2}$. We can then get our solutions $x = \boxed{0, \frac{\pi}{3}, \pi, \frac{5\pi}{3}}$. □

Problem 6.5.22. Find all $0° \leq \theta < 360°$ in degrees such that $\cos 3\theta = -\frac{1}{2}$.

Solution. If $0° \leq \theta < 360°$, then $0° \leq 3\theta < 1080°$. Therefore, solving for all solutions of 3θ in that range for the equation $\cos 3\theta = -\frac{1}{2}$, we have $3\theta = 120°, 240°, 480°, 600°, 840°, 960°$ (these are obtained by determining the principal values $120°$ and $240°$, then adding multiples of $360°$ to each). Dividing by 3, we have: $\theta = \boxed{40°, 80°, 160°, 200°, 280°, 320°}$. □

Problem 6.5.23. Find all $0° \leq x < 360°$ such that $\sin(2x + 44°) = \frac{1}{2}$.

Solution. Let $y = 2x + 44$.

If $0° \leq x < 360°$, then $44° \leq y < 764°$.

If we only consider $0 \leq y < 360°$, then we can get the solutions $\sin y = \frac{1}{2}$ as $y = 30°, 150°$. To get all possible solutions $44° \leq y < 764°$, we can simply add multiples of $360°$ to $30°$ and $150°$ respectively.

We end up with $y = 150°, 390°, 510°, 750°$ as our solutions when we take into account the given restrictions.

Then, we replace y with $2x + 44$ and solve for x, resulting in $x = \boxed{53°, 173°, 233°, 353°}$. □

Problem 6.5.24. Find all $0° \leq x < 360°$ in degrees such that $\cos 2x = \cos x$.

Solution. By the double angle identity for cosine, we have $2\cos^2 x - 1 = \cos x$, which rearranges to $2\cos^2 x - \cos x - 1 = 0$. We can factor this as $(2\cos x + 1)(\cos x - 1) = 0$, from we get $\cos x = \dfrac{1}{2}$ and 1 as roots. Within the interval $0° \leq x < 360°$, we have the solutions $x = \boxed{0°, 120°, 240°}$. □

Exercise 6.5.25. Find all $0 \leq \theta < 2\pi$ such that $\cos 3\theta = \cos \theta$.

Problem 6.5.26. Classify all cases in which a, b, c and $\cos a, \cos b, \cos c$ are both arithmetic sequences.

Solution. Let $a = b - d_1$, $c = b + d_1$, and $\cos a = \cos b - d_2$, $\cos c = \cos b + d_2$. Then we have the relations:

$$\cos(b - d_1) = \cos b - d_2,$$
$$\cos(b + d_1) = \cos b + d_2.$$

Adding these, we eventually get $2\cos b \cos d_1 = 2\cos b$, or $2\cos b(\cos d_1 - 1) = 0$. This implies $\cos d_1 = 1$ or $\cos b = 0$. For the former, we get that $\boxed{d_1 = 360k° \; \forall k \in \mathbb{Z}}$ (d_1 is the common difference between a, b, c) and for the latter, $\boxed{b = 90° + 180k° \; \forall k \in \mathbb{Z}}$. □

Problem 6.5.27. If $\sin x + \cos x = \dfrac{1}{2}$ and $\dfrac{\pi}{2} < x < \pi$, what is $\tan x$?

Solution. First, note that

$$(\sin x + \cos x)^2 = \sin^2 x + 2\sin x \cos x + \cos^2 x = 1 + \sin 2x = \left(\dfrac{1}{2}\right)^2,$$

from which we get $\sin 2x = -\dfrac{3}{4}$.

If we know $\sin x + \cos x$, it may be helpful to also find out $\sin x - \cos x$. Observe that

$$(\sin x - \cos x)^2 = \sin^2 x - 2\sin x \cos x + \cos^2 x = 1 - \sin 2x = \dfrac{7}{4}.$$

Thus, we can take the square root of both sides of $\sin x - \cos x = \pm\dfrac{\sqrt{7}}{2}$. Now, we use the fact that $\dfrac{\pi}{2} < x < \pi$. On this interval, $\sin x > \cos x$ (this can be seen from looking at the unit circle or comparing graphs of sine and cosine). Thus, since $\sin x - \cos x > 0$, we choose the positive sign: $\sin x - \cos x = \dfrac{\sqrt{7}}{2}$.

Now we have the equations $\sin x + \cos x = \dfrac{1}{2}$ and $\sin x - \cos x = \dfrac{\sqrt{7}}{2}$. If we add them together, we get $2\sin x = \dfrac{1+\sqrt{7}}{2}$. If we subtract either equation from the other, we get $2\cos x = \dfrac{1-\sqrt{7}}{2}$.

Finally, we can compute

$$\tan x = \frac{2\sin x}{2\cos x} = \frac{1+\sqrt{7}}{1-\sqrt{7}} = \frac{(1+\sqrt{7})^2}{-6} = \frac{8+2\sqrt{7}}{-6} = \boxed{-\frac{4+\sqrt{7}}{3}}.$$ □

6.6   Areas, Law of Sines, Law of Cosines

Theorem 6.6.1
The area of a triangle $\triangle ABC$ with side a opposite angle A, side b opposite angle B, and side c opposite angle C is $\dfrac{1}{2}ab\sin C$.

Proof. We consider several cases: an acute triangle, a right triangle, an obtuse triangle in which angle C is obtuse, and an obtuse triangle in which angle C is acute.

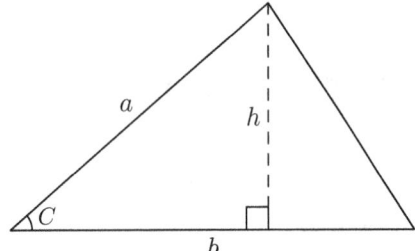

The area of this acute triangle above is $\dfrac{1}{2}bh$, where h is the altitude dropped to the base. Using our knowledge of right triangle trig, it is clear that $\sin C = \dfrac{h}{a}$, which rearranges to $h = a\sin C$. Therefore, substituting h in the original area formula, the area is $\dfrac{1}{2}ab\sin C$.

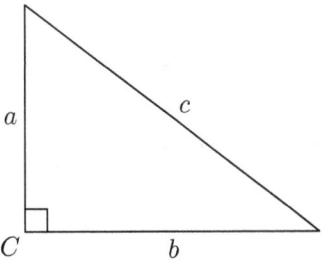

Similarly, the area of this right triangle is $\dfrac{1}{2}ab$. Note that $\sin 90° = 1$, so $\sin C = 1$. Therefore, the area is $\dfrac{1}{2}ab = \dfrac{1}{2}ab\sin C$.

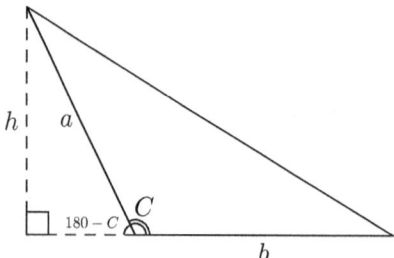

The area of this obtuse triangle with obtuse angle C is $\frac{1}{2}bh$, when altitude h is dropped to the same level as base b. Note that $h = a\sin(180° - C) = a(\sin 180° \cos C - \sin C \cos 180°) = a(0 - \sin C \cdot -1) = a\sin C$, leading to the desired formula $\frac{1}{2}ab\sin C$.

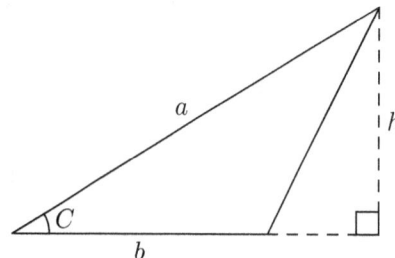

Lastly, we consider the case of an obtuse triangle with acute angle C, with an area of $\frac{1}{2}bh$. Note that $\sin C = \frac{h}{a} \implies h = a\sin C$, so the area can also be expressed by $\frac{1}{2}ab\sin C$, as desired. □

We will henceforth use the notation $[ABC]$ to denote the area of $\triangle ABC$.

> **Theorem 6.6.2 (Law of Sines)**
>
> The **law of sines** states that for any given triangle $\triangle ABC$ and appropriate side lengths a, b, c, the following relationships hold:
> $$\frac{\sin A}{a} = \frac{\sin B}{b} = \frac{\sin C}{c}$$

Proof. Recall that $[ABC] = \frac{1}{2}ab\sin C$. It is evident that $[ABC] = \frac{1}{2}bc\sin A$ and $[ABC] = \frac{1}{2}ac\sin B$. Therefore, we have
$$\frac{1}{2}ab\sin C = \frac{1}{2}bc\sin A = \frac{1}{2}ac\sin B.$$
Dividing everything by $\frac{1}{2}abc$ yields
$$\frac{\sin C}{c} = \frac{\sin A}{a} = \frac{\sin B}{b},$$
as desired. □

Theorem 6.6.3 (Law of Cosines)

The **law of cosines** states that for any given triangle $\triangle ABC$ with side lengths a, b, c, the following equation is true:
$$c^2 = a^2 + b^2 - 2ab\cos C.$$

Proof. Similar as before, we consider various cases depending on the triangle.

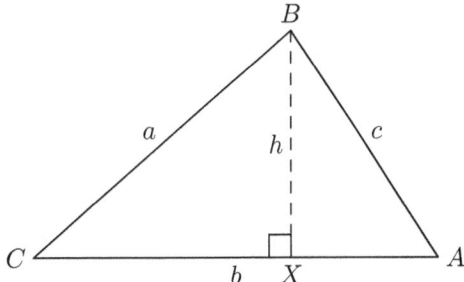

Consider acute $\triangle ABC$. We have $\sin C = \dfrac{h}{a}$, so $h = a \sin C$. We also have $\cos C = \dfrac{CX}{a}$, so $CX = a \cos C$. Therefore, $AX = AC - CX = b - a \cos C$. Then, apply the Pythagorean Theorem to $\triangle ABX$ to get $c^2 = h^2 + AX^2$. Substituting $h = a \sin C$ and $AX = b - a \cos C$, we have

$$\begin{aligned} c^2 &= a^2 \sin^2 C + (b - a\cos C)^2 \\ &= a^2 \sin^2 C + b^2 - 2ab \cos C + a^2 \cos^2 C \\ &= a^2 \left(\sin^2 C + \cos^2 C\right) + b^2 - 2ab \cos C \\ &= a^2 + b^2 - 2ab \cos C. \end{aligned}$$

Secondly, for the case of a right triangle $\triangle ABC$ with right angle at C, it suffices to show that $\cos C = \cos 90° = 0$, combined with the already given relationship $c^2 = a^2 + b^2$ by the Pythagorean Theorem. $c^2 = a^2 + b^2 \implies c^2 = a^2 + b^2 + 0 \implies c^2 = a^2 + b^2 - 2ab \cos C$, so the right triangle case is done.

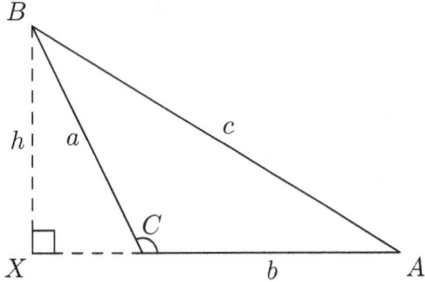

Consider an obtuse triangle $\triangle ABC$ where $\angle C$ is obtuse. Drop the altitude from B to X such that it forms a perpendicular with line AC. Notice that $\angle BCX = 180° - \angle BCA = 180° - \angle C$. Furthermore, as $\cos \angle BCX = \dfrac{CX}{a}$, $CX = a \cos \angle BCX = a \cos(180° - C) = -a \cos C$. Similarly, $h = a \sin \angle BCX = a \sin(180° - C) = a \sin C$.

Applying Pythagorean Theorem on $\triangle BXA$, we know that $c^2 = h^2 + AX^2$. It has already been shown that $h = a\sin C$ and $CX = -a\cos C$. Note that $AX = b + CX$, so $AX = b - a\cos C$. Substitute in the necessary values to get our desired result:

$$c^2 = (a\sin C)^2 + (b - a\cos C)^2$$
$$= a^2\sin^2 C + b^2 - 2ab\cos C + a^2\cos^2 C$$
$$= a^2\left(\sin^2 C + \cos^2 C\right) + b^2 - 2ab\cos C$$
$$= a^2 + b^2 - 2ab\cos C.$$

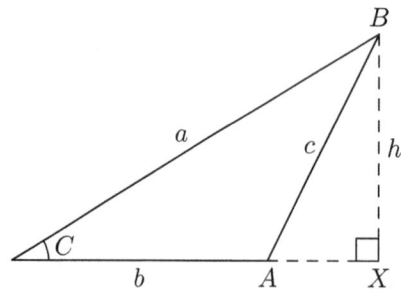

Lastly, consider an obtuse triangle $\triangle ABC$ where $\angle C$ is acute, and dropped altitude h to line AC. First, given right triangle $\triangle CBX$ yields $\sin C = \dfrac{h}{a} \implies h = a\sin C$. Furthermore, $\cos C = \dfrac{b + AX}{a} \implies AX = a\cos C - b$.

Apply Pythagorean Theorem on $\triangle ABX$ to get $c^2 = AX^2 + h^2$. However, we know what AX and h are, so we substitute in their respective values:

$$c^2 = (a\cos C - b)^2 + a^2\sin^2 C$$
$$= a^2\cos^2 C - 2ab\cos C + b^2 + a^2\sin^2 C$$
$$= a^2 + b^2 - 2ab\cos C.$$

We have covered all possible cases and have shown that the Law of Cosines works on any given triangle. $\square$

Recall the several triangle congruence laws:

1. SAS: Side-Angle-Side

2. SSS: Side-Side-Side

3. ASA: Angle-Side-Angle

4. AAS: Angle-Angle-Side

We also have HL (Hypotenuse-Leg), a special case of the SSS congruence law, but for right triangles (as the third side is predetermined by Pythagorean Theorem).

These congruence laws suggest that when we are given 3 particular pieces of the triangle, we are able to 'solve' the rest of the triangle (determining all remaining side lengths and angles). Here are some examples:

ASA and AAS:

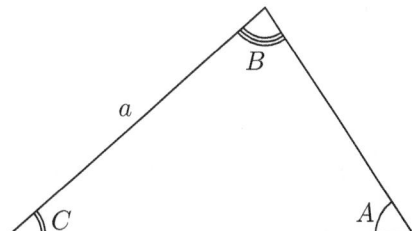

When given 2 angles and a side length included between them, we can use the Law of Sines to find the rest of the information. We actually have four pieces of information (that we need in order to solve the proportions) because we can always find the third angle using the fact that there are always 180° degrees in a triangle. This is why ASA and AAS are essentially the same.

$$\frac{\boxed{\sin A}}{\boxed{a}} = \frac{\boxed{\sin B}}{b} = \frac{\boxed{\sin C}}{c}$$

Thus, we can compute side lengths b and c (which are not known to us immediately) using Law of Sines.

SSS and SAS:

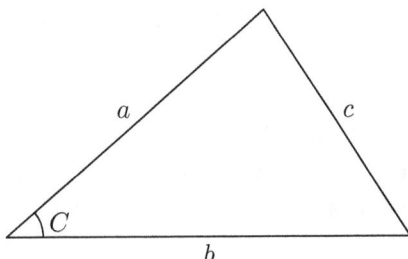

When given two side lengths and an angle included between them (SAS), we can use the Law of Cosines to solve for the third side. Then once the third side is known, we can use the Law of Sines to find the rest of the angles:

$$\frac{\boxed{\sin A}}{\boxed{a}} = \frac{\sin B}{\boxed{b}} = \frac{\sin C}{\boxed{c}}$$

We can then solve for $\sin A$ and $\sin B$, then take the inverse sine of those, to get our angles A and B.

If we are given three side lengths but no angle measurements (SSS), we can find the measurement of one of the angles using the Law of Cosines ($c^2 = a^2 + b^2 - 2ab\cos C$) and solving for $\cos C$. Then, like before, we can use Law of Sines to find the rest of the angles.

For the following problems, a calculator is required.

Problem 6.6.4. Solve for the rest of the side lengths and angles for the following triangles. Round angles in degrees to the nearest tenth and side lengths to the nearest hundredth.

1. $\triangle ABC$ with $m\angle A = 73°$, $m\angle B = 42°$, and $b = 7$
2. $\triangle ABC$ with $m\angle C = 12°$, $b = 7$, and $a = 11$

Solution.

1. As all angles in a triangle add up to 180°, we can easily get that $m\angle C = \boxed{65°}$. Then using the Law of Sines,
$$\frac{\sin 73°}{a} = \frac{\sin 42°}{7} = \frac{\sin 65°}{c}$$
we can calculate the rest of the side lengths:
$$a = \frac{7 \sin 73°}{\sin 42°} \approx \boxed{10.00}$$
$$b = \frac{7 \sin 65°}{\sin 42°} \approx \boxed{9.48}$$

2. Using the Law of Cosines, we get that $c \approx \boxed{4.40}$. By the Law of Sines, we have
$$\frac{\sin 12°}{c} = \frac{\sin A}{11} = \frac{\sin B}{7}.$$

Here is a caveat: we must use the exact answer to c (that is still stored in the calculator; not the approximate 4.40) to find the *smaller* of the two remaining angles. Why?

As inverse sine only returns values in the interval $[-90°, 90°]$, we could incorrectly label an obtuse angle acute. Therefore, we should choose the smaller angle of the two because we know for sure that a triangle cannot have two angles both greater than 90°. After calculating the smaller angle, we can then calculate the larger angle of the two by using the fact that all angles add up to 180°.

As $\angle B$ is the smaller of the two, we calculate $m\angle B = \sin^{-1}\left(\frac{7 \sin 12°}{c}\right) \approx \boxed{19.3°}$. Then $m\angle A = 180° - 12° - 19.3° = \boxed{148.7°}$. □

Problem 6.6.5. Find all triangles with sides in arithmetic progression that have an angle of 60°.

Solution. If the triangle has an angle of 60°, then either the triangle is equiangular (and thus equilateral) or for the other two angles, one is greater than 60° and one is less than 60°. Since this angle of 60° is the average of the three angles in this kind of triangle, it must be between the 'smallest' and 'largest' side lengths (as the problem states that the sides are in arithmetic progression). Therefore, if we let the side lengths be $x - d, x$, and $x + d$ with a common difference of d, then this angle of 60° is between $x - d$ and $x + d$ and is opposite the side x. We then apply Law of Cosines:
$$x^2 = (x-d)^2 + (x+d)^2 - 2(x-d)(x+d)\cos 60°$$
$$= 2x^2 + 2d^2 - (x^2 - d^2)$$

$$= x^2 + 3d^2$$
$$\therefore d = 0.$$

Therefore, the only kind of triangle that has sides in arithmetic progression and contains an angle of 60° is an equilateral triangle. □

Why isn't SSA considered a valid triangle congruence law? In fact, when given two sides and an angle *not* included between them, there can be multiple scenarios. Henceforth, for $\triangle ABC$, we will denote sides $a = \overline{BC}$, $b = \overline{AC}$, and $c = \overline{AB}$. Consider this diagram:

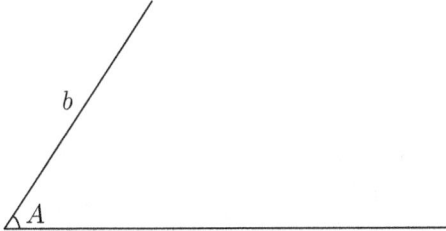

The line that forms an angle A with side length b will contain side c, depending on the side length a. The following cases will demonstrate the various situations which can occur depending on the length of a.

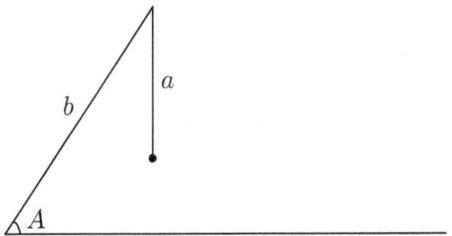

Case 1: $a < b \sin A$ **Possible Triangles:** 0

If we choose a side length a that is smaller than $b \sin A$ (which is the length of the perpendicular dropped from angle C to the long line), then we will not be able to create any triangle. One can visualize this by constructing a circle of radius a around point C, and realize that this circle will never intersect with the long line.

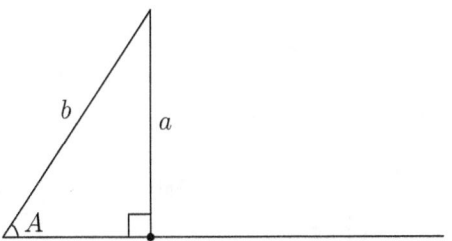

Case 2: $a = b \sin A$ **Possible Triangles:** 1

If we let a be that perpendicular, notice that we can construct exactly one triangle, which is the right triangle with altitude a. Note that the shortest distance from a point to a line is the perpendicular dropped from the point to the line.

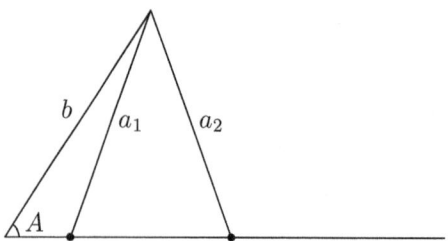

Case 3: $b > a > b \sin A$ **Possible Triangles: 2**

If we have a side length a be between the length of the altitude $b \sin A$ and the side length b, then there are actually two possible triangles. As mentioned in case 1, it is easier to visualize this and understand the reasoning by constructing a circle of radius a and seeing that it intersects the long line at two points.

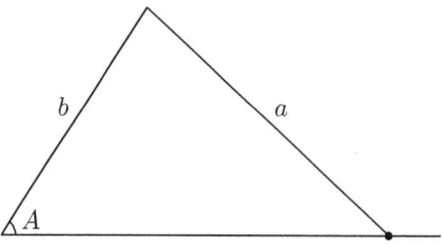

Case 4: $a \geq b$ **Possible Triangles: 1**

If we make side length a longer than side length b, then we can only make 1 triangle where side length a is 'pushed outward' and cannot be 'pushed inward' like what happened in Case 3.

Problem 6.6.6. Consider a triangle $\triangle ABC$ where $A = 30°$ and $b = 10$. How many possible triangles are there for $a = 4, 5, 8,$ and 12 respectively?

Solution. Note that $\sin A = \dfrac{1}{2}$. If we solve the proportion (from Law of Sines) $\dfrac{\sin B}{10} = \dfrac{\frac{1}{2}}{a}$ for $\sin B$, we get $\sin B = \dfrac{5}{a}$.

1. $a = 4$: We end up with $\sin B = \dfrac{5}{4} > 1$, which is clearly impossible as the range of sine is $[-1, 1]$. Therefore, there is no solution.

2. $a = 5$: We have $\sin B = \dfrac{5}{5} = 1$, so $B = 90°$ is the only option. This corresponds to a right triangle with hypotenuse 10 and angle 30°.

3. $a = 8$: We have $\sin B = \dfrac{5}{8}$. Taking the inverse sine of this, we get $B \approx 38.7°$. Using the identity $\sin(180 - \theta) = \sin \theta$, we see that angle B could also be $141.3°$. If angle B was $141.3°$,

such a triangle would be possible because $m\angle A + m\angle B = 30° + 141.3° < 180°$. Therefore, there are two possible triangles here.

4. $a = 12$: This yields $\sin B = \dfrac{5}{12}$. Taking inverse sine and applying the identity $\sin(180 - \theta) = \sin\theta$, we get $B \approx 24.6°, 155.4°$. However, if $m\angle B = 155.4°$, then such a triangle would be impossible, because $m\angle A + m\angle B = 30° + 155.4° > 180°$. Therefore, $B \approx 155.4°$ is not valid, so there is only one possible triangle at $B \approx 24.6°$. □

Problem 6.6.7. Solve the following SSA scenario for $\triangle ABC$: $A = 38°$, $a = 4$, $b = 9$.

Solution. By the Law of Sines, we have
$$\frac{\sin 38°}{4} = \frac{\sin B}{9},$$
yielding $\sin B = \dfrac{9}{4}\sin 38° \approx 1.39$. However, this is impossible, as $1.39 \notin [-1, 1]$, which is the range of sine. Therefore, there exists $\boxed{\text{no triangle}}$. □

Exercise 6.6.8. Solve the following triangle: $a = 5$, $b = 6$, and $A = 50°$.

Problem 6.6.9. Find the angles of a triangle with side lengths $12, 13$, and 14.

Solution. Given $\triangle ABC$, we let $c = 12, b = 13, a = 14$. By the Law of Cosines, we get
$$14^2 = 12^2 + 13^2 - 2 \cdot 12 \cdot 13 \cdot \cos A,$$
which yields $\cos A = \dfrac{14^2 - (12^2 + 13^2)}{-2 \cdot 12 \cdot 13} = \dfrac{3}{8}$. Using the Pythagorean identity $\sin^2 A + \cos^2 A = 1$, we get $\sin A = \dfrac{\sqrt{55}}{8}$. Taking inverse sine of this, we get $A \approx \boxed{68.0°}$. Now that we know the value of $\sin A$, we can use the Law of Sines:
$$\frac{\sin A}{14} = \frac{\sin B}{13} = \frac{\sin C}{12}.$$

Solve for $\sin B$ and $\sin C$, then take inverse sine, as necessary:
$$\frac{\frac{\sqrt{55}}{8}}{14} = \frac{\sin B}{13} \implies B \approx \boxed{59.4°}.$$
$$\frac{\frac{\sqrt{55}}{8}}{14} = \frac{\sin C}{12} \implies C \approx \boxed{52.6°}.$$
□

Exercise 6.6.10. Compute the largest angle in a triangle with side lengths $13, 15$, and 17.

Chapter 7

Advanced Trigonometry

This is simply a continuation of the previous chapter; however, this chapter will focus on the other ways of representing the coordinate plane, introducing more advanced concepts. The following material will require secure understanding and foundation of the trigonometry covered earlier.

7.1 Polar Coordinates

In the Cartesian plane, we represent points by (x, y) according to an xy coordinate grid. Polar coordinates are another way of representing these points.

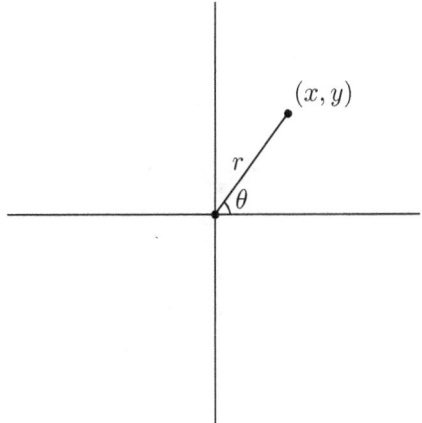

Definition 7.1.1. We denote a point $(r; \theta)$ as a **polar coordinate**, where r is the length of the ray from the origin and θ is the angle which represents the rotation of the ray through the origin of the unit circle, analogous to the definitions of the unit circle stated earlier.

On the Cartesian plane, the unit circle contains all points of the form $(\cos \theta, \sin \theta)$. This can be generalized to circles for any radius k: $(k \cos \theta, k \sin \theta)$. Therefore, we have that $(r \cos \theta, r \sin \theta)$ in Cartesian coordinates is $(r; \theta)$ in polar coordinates, or in other words: $(x, y) \longleftrightarrow (r \cos \theta, r \sin \theta) \longleftrightarrow (r; \theta)$, implying:

$$x = r \cos \theta,$$

$$y = r\sin\theta.$$

This suggests that $\frac{y}{x} = \tan\theta$. Furthermore, note that $x^2 + y^2 = r^2\cos^2\theta + r^2\sin^2\theta = r^2(\sin^2\theta + \cos^2\theta) = r^2$. To simplify our work for converting between polar and Cartesian coordinates, we could establish $r \geq 0$ and $0 \leq \theta \leq 2\pi$ as stipulations, in which case, $r = \sqrt{x^2 + y^2}$ and $\theta = \tan^{-1}\left(\frac{y}{x}\right)$, adding or subtracting multiples of π as necessary (because inverse tan can return negative values, and it depends on which quadrant the point lies).

Problem 7.1.2. Plot the following points and convert them into Cartesian coordinates.

1. $A\left(3; \frac{\pi}{2}\right)$
2. $B\left(2; \frac{5\pi}{6}\right)$
3. $C\left(4; -\frac{\pi}{3}\right)$
4. $D\left(0; 10^{10}\pi + 2\right)$
5. $E(-1; \pi)$

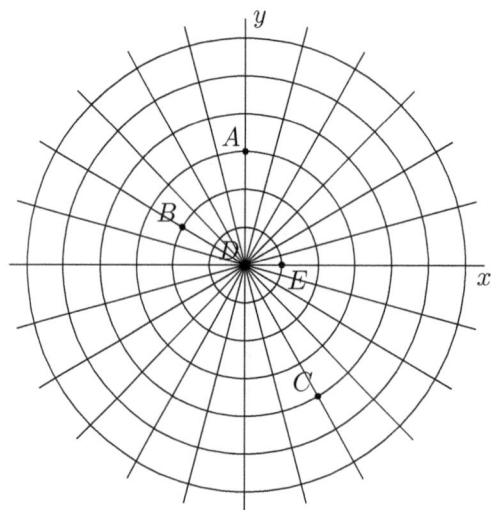

Solution. For point A, we plot the point that is 3 away from the origin and $\frac{\pi}{2}$ radians from the starting line, which is the x-axis. To convert this into a point in the form (x, y), recall that $x = r\cos\theta$ and $y = r\sin\theta$, so $x = 3\cos\frac{\pi}{2} = 0$ and $y = 3\sin\frac{\pi}{2} = 3$, so the Cartesian coordinate would be $\boxed{(0,3)}$.

Similarly, for point B, note that $\left(2; \frac{5\pi}{6}\right) \longleftrightarrow \left(2\cos\frac{5\pi}{6}, 2\sin\frac{5\pi}{6}\right)$. We compute $\cos\frac{5\pi}{6} = -\frac{\sqrt{3}}{2}$ and $\sin\frac{5\pi}{6} = \frac{1}{2}$. Thus, $B = \boxed{(-\sqrt{3}, 1)}$.

Likewise, Point $C = \left(4; -\frac{\pi}{3}\right) = \left(4\cos\left(-\frac{\pi}{3}\right), 4\sin\left(-\frac{\pi}{3}\right)\right)$. We have $\cos\left(-\frac{\pi}{3}\right) = \frac{1}{2}$ and $\sin\left(-\frac{\pi}{3}\right) = -\frac{\sqrt{3}}{2}$, so $C = \boxed{(2, -2\sqrt{3})}$.

For point D, note that $r = 0$. In this case, D clearly has to be the origin, $\boxed{(0,0)}$, regardless of the angle given.

We are given a negative radius for point E. By intuition we can see that a point with $-r$ reflects the original point with r over the origin. Thus, $(-1; \pi)$ is the same point as $(1; 0)$, or $\boxed{(1,0)}$ in Cartesian coordinates. □

Problem 7.1.3. Convert these Cartesian coordinates into polar coordinates, with the stipulations $r \geq 0$ and $0 \leq \theta \leq 2\pi$.

1. $(7, -7)$

2. $(-4, 3)$

Solution. For $(7, -7)$, we use the relation $r = \sqrt{x^2 + y^2}$ to get $r = 7\sqrt{2}$. Then, $\theta = \tan^{-1}\left(\frac{7}{-7}\right) = \tan^{-1}(-1) = -\frac{\pi}{4}$. However, the point lies in quadrant IV, so $\frac{3\pi}{2} < \theta < 2\pi$. Therefore, we add 2π to get $\theta = \frac{7\pi}{4}$. Then the polar coordinate is $\boxed{\left(7\sqrt{2}; \frac{7\pi}{4}\right)}$.

Similarly, for point $(-4, 3)$, we get $r = 5$ and $\theta = \tan^{-1}\left(-\frac{3}{4}\right)$. However, $\tan^{-1}\left(-\frac{3}{4}\right)$ is clearly negative, so add π to get $\theta = \pi + \tan^{-1}\left(-\frac{3}{4}\right)$. Therefore the polar coordinate is $\boxed{\left(5; \pi + \tan^{-1}\left(-\frac{3}{4}\right)\right)}$. □

Now that we have dealt with plotting polar coordinates, it is time to graph *polar functions*.

First, we address some obvious special cases:

- An equation of the form $r = k$ for some $k \in \mathbb{R}$ is simply a circle centered at the origin with radius k.

- An equation of the form $\theta = \alpha$ where α is in radians or degrees is a ray from the origin rotated by the angle θ around the origin.

For the remainder of the section, we will discuss the general $r = f(\theta)$ form for some function f regarding θ.

Consider the graph of $r = 2\sin\theta$. Using the approximations $\sqrt{2} \approx 1.4$ and $\sqrt{3} \approx 1.7$, we can determine some points to plot:

θ	r
0°	0
30°	1
45°	≈ 1.4
60°	≈ 1.7
90°	2
120°	≈ 1.7
135°	≈ 1.4
150°	1
180°	0

θ	r
210°	−1
225°	≈ −1.4
240°	≈ −1.7
270°	−2
300°	≈ −1.7
315°	≈ −1.4
330°	−1
360°	0

We can then develop a basic sketch on the polar coordinate plane.

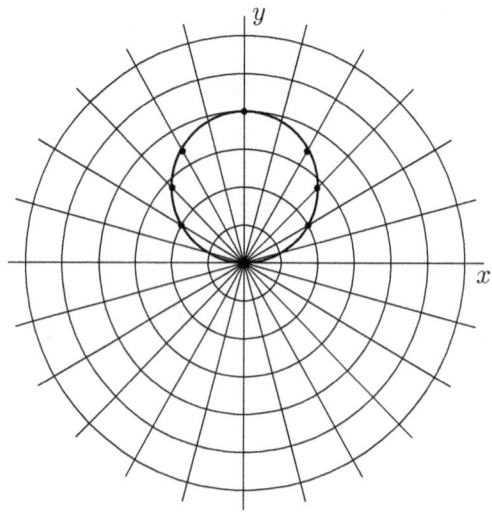

Scale: 0.5

Note that the negative values on the right table result in the same points in the left table (recall the identity $\sin(180° + \theta) = -\sin\theta$). After we plot these points and sketch the graph, notice that it resembles a circle! We can then prove that this equation's graph is a circle, by converting the polar equation into a regular Cartesian equation:

$$r = 2\sin\theta$$
$$r^2 = 2r\sin\theta$$
$$x^2 + y^2 = 2r\sin\theta$$
$$x^2 + y^2 = 2y$$
$$x^2 + y^2 - 2y = 0$$

$$x^2 + y^2 - 2y + 1 = 1$$
$$x^2 + (y-1)^2 = 1.$$

Thus, the graph is actually a circle of radius 1 centered at $(0, 1)$.

Consider the graph of $r = 1 + \cos\theta$. Using the approximations $\dfrac{\sqrt{3}}{2} \approx 0.9$ and $\dfrac{\sqrt{2}}{2} \approx 0.7$:

θ	r
$0°$	2
$30°$	≈ 1.9
$45°$	≈ 1.7
$60°$	1.5
$90°$	1
$120°$	0.5
$135°$	≈ 0.3
$150°$	≈ 0.1
$180°$	0

θ	r
$210°$	≈ 0.1
$225°$	≈ 0.3
$240°$	0.5
$270°$	1
$300°$	1.5
$315°$	≈ 1.7
$330°$	≈ 1.9
$360°$	2

Then, we sketch:

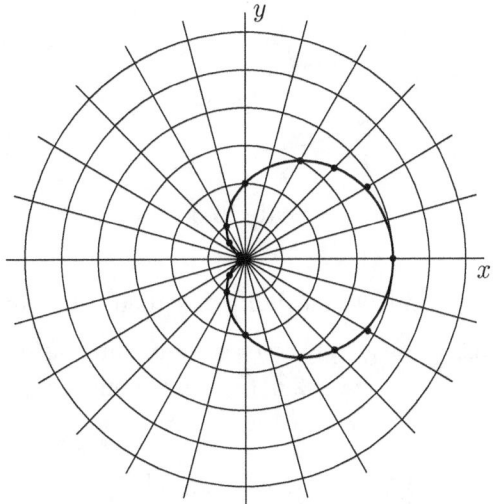

Scale: 0.5

This 'heart-shaped' graph is called a **cardioid**.

Now let's graph $r = \dfrac{1}{2} + \cos\theta$.

θ	r
0°	1.5
30°	≈ 1.4
45°	≈ 1.2
60°	1
90°	0.5
120°	0
135°	≈ −0.2
150°	≈ −0.4
180°	−0.5

θ	r
210°	≈ −0.4
225°	≈ −0.2
240°	0
270°	0.5
300°	1
315°	≈ 1.2
330°	≈ 1.4
360°	1.5

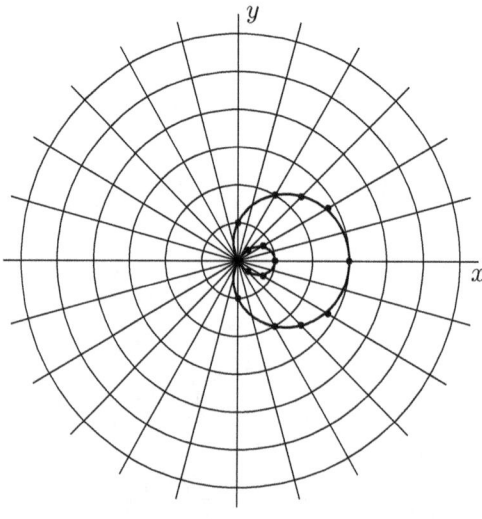

Scale: 0.5

The shape of this graph (a generalized cardioid) is called a **limaçon**.

There is a faster way to sketch these graphs; we analyze r increasing or decreasing as we increment θ. For instance, consider the graph of $r = \sin 2\theta$. For some common values of θ, look at the behavior of r:

0°	45°	90°	135°	180°	225°	270°	315°	360°
0	1	0	−1	0	1	0	−1	0

The value of r is increasing from 0 to 1 as θ goes from 0° to 45°, then r decreases from 1 back to 0 as θ goes from 45° to 90°. This forms the quadrant I 'petal' of the graph, with a 'peak' at point $(1; 45°)$.

We then see that r goes negative (from 0 to -1) when θ goes from 90° to 135°, and r goes back to 0 as θ approaches 180°. As r is negative in this part, the petal which would have been in quadrant II has been reflected across the origin, resulting in a petal that is in quadrant IV, with a peak at $(-1; 135°)$.

We continue with the rest of the values of r, leaving us with four petals.

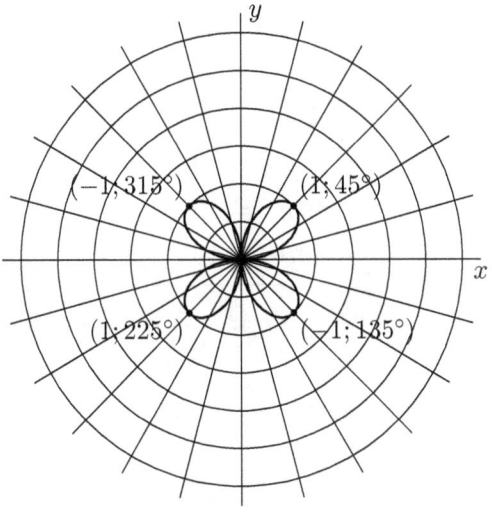

Scale: 0.5

Exercise 7.1.4. Sketch the following polar functions:

1. $r = \sin 3\theta$
2. $r = \theta$
3. $r = \dfrac{1}{\theta}$
4. $r = 2 + \cos 2\theta$
5. $r = 2 + \cos 3\theta$

Problem 7.1.5. Sketch $r = \sec \theta$.

Solution. Rearranging $r = \dfrac{1}{\cos \theta}$, we get $r \cos \theta = 1$. But $x = r \cos \theta$, so our graph is simply a line, $x = 1$. □

Problem 7.1.6. Let a, b not be simultaneously 0. What do all graphs of the form $r = a \sin \theta + b \cos \theta$ have in common?

Solution. Multiply both sides of the equation by r to get: $r^2 = a \cdot r \sin \theta + b \cdot r \cos \theta$. Substitute in the definitions $x^2 + y^2 = r^2$, $x = r \cos \theta$, and $y = r \sin \theta$, so we have: $x^2 + y^2 = ay + bx$. Rearranging this and completing the square yields:

$$\left(x - \frac{b}{2}\right)^2 + \left(y - \frac{a}{2}\right)^2 = \frac{a^2 + b^2}{4},$$

which is an equation for a circle, centered at $\left(\dfrac{b}{2}, \dfrac{a}{2}\right)$ with radius $\dfrac{\sqrt{a^2+b^2}}{2}$. Therefore, all polar graphs of the form $r = a\sin\theta + b\cos\theta$ are circles which vary depending on the values of a and b. Furthermore, note that all these circles *go through the origin*. □

Exercise 7.1.7. Convert $r = 2\sin\theta - 4\cos\theta$ into Cartesian form, and describe fully the graph.

Problem 7.1.8. Convert $x + y = 10$ into a polar equation $r = f(\theta)$ if possible.

Solution. Simply use the definitions $x = r\cos\theta$ and $y = r\sin\theta$:

$$x + y = 10$$
$$r\cos\theta + r\sin\theta = 10$$
$$r(\cos\theta + \sin\theta) = 10$$
$$\boxed{r = \dfrac{10}{\cos\theta + \sin\theta}}.$$

□

Problem 7.1.9. Given the graph of $r = f(\theta)$, describe the transformation that results in

a) $r = f(-\theta)$.

b) $r = k \cdot f(\theta)$, $k \in \mathbb{R}$.

c) $r = f(\theta + \alpha)$, $\alpha \in \mathbb{R}$.

Solution.

a) Recall that a ray on the unit circle with an angle $-\theta$ is rotated by θ clockwise from the initial starting place (which is the *x-axis*) rather than counter-clockwise. Therefore, the graph of $r = f(-\theta)$ is a reflection of $r = f(\theta)$ over the x-axis.

b) We have a little casework:

- If $k > 0$, then we simply scale the graph of $r = f(\theta)$ by a factor of k from the origin.
- If $k = 0$, then the graph becomes $r = 0$, which is simply the origin, $(0,0)$.
- If $k < 0$, then we first reflect the graph on the origin, *then* we scale the graph by a factor of $|k|$ from the origin.

c) The graph $r = f(\theta + \alpha)$ is a rotation of $r = f(\theta)$ by an angle of $|\alpha|$, clockwise when α is positive and counter-clockwise when α is negative. This is analogous to left and right shifts for normal graphs $y = f(x)$, $y = f(x + k)$ $k \in \mathbb{R}$ on the Cartesian plane. □

Problem 7.1.10. If f is odd, what can you say about the graph of $r = f(\theta)$? What about if f is even?

Solution. Suppose we have a point $P = (r; \theta)$. We know that if f is odd, then $r = f(\theta) = -f(-\theta)$, or $-r = f(-\theta)$. This implies that $(-r; -\theta)$ lies on the graph as well. However, the point $(-r; -\theta)$ is actually the reflection of point P across the y-axis.

To see why this is the case, note that $(-r; \theta)$ is a reflection of P across the origin, and $(-r; -\theta)$ is the reflection of $(-r; \theta)$ across the x-axis. These two transformations ultimately result in a reflection across the y-axis.

If f is even, then $f(\theta) = f(-\theta)$. It has been established that $f(-\theta)$ is a reflection of $f(\theta)$ over the x-axis. But if $f(-\theta)$ and $f(\theta)$ are the same graph, then we can say that a graph with even function f is symmetric over the x-axis. □

Problem 7.1.11. Convert the following polar equations into Cartesian equations:

1. $r = \cos \theta$

2. $r = 1 + \cos \theta$

Solution.

1. Multiply both sides by r, perform the necessary substitutions, then complete the square:

$$r = \cos \theta$$
$$r^2 = r \cos \theta$$
$$x^2 + y^2 = x$$
$$x^2 - x + y^2 = 0$$
$$x^2 - x + \frac{1}{4} + y^2 = \frac{1}{4}$$
$$\boxed{\left(x - \frac{1}{2}\right)^2 + y^2 = \frac{1}{4}}.$$

2. Similar steps, however the resulting equation is more complicated:

$$r = 1 + \cos \theta$$
$$r^2 = r + r \cos \theta$$
$$x^2 + y^2 = r + x$$
$$r = x^2 + y^2 - x$$
$$r^2 = (x^2 + y^2 - x)^2$$
$$\boxed{x^2 + y^2 = (x^2 + y^2 - x)^2}.$$

□

Problem 7.1.12. Convert $x^2 - y^2 = 1$ into a polar equation.

Solution. Use the relations $x = r \cos \theta$ and $y = r \sin \theta$:

$$x^2 - y^2 = 1$$
$$r^2 \cos^2 \theta - r^2 \sin^2 \theta = 1$$
$$r^2(\cos^2 \theta - \sin^2 \theta) = 1$$
$$r^2(\cos 2\theta) = 1$$

$$r^2 = \sec 2\theta$$
$$\boxed{r = \sqrt{\sec 2\theta}}.$$

Note that we do not put "$\pm$" before $\sqrt{\sec 2\theta}$ because there's no difference whether r is negative or not (all points $(r; \theta)$ can be represented as $(-r; \theta + \pi)$). □

7.2 Parametric Equations

This section will introduce another way we can represent Cartesian points and graphs, by the use of a third variable. Previous experience with conic sections is required.

Definition 7.2.1. Given some rectangular equation using variables x and y, we can relate x and y to each other by expressing each in terms of a third variable t, the **parameter**. Given some arbitrary functions f and g, we have the parametric equations:

$$x = f(t)$$
$$y = g(t)$$

The **parametric curve** is the collection of all points $(f(t), g(t))$ as t runs through some domain.

I present a well-known example: the unit circle. It can be represented by the parametric equations $x = \cos\theta$, $y = \sin\theta$. In this case, θ would be the parameter.

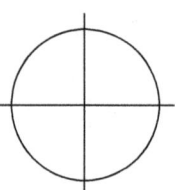

- Let $x = \cos\theta$, $y = \sin\theta$ and suppose $0 \le \theta \le 2\pi$.

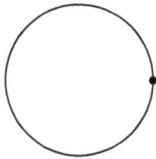

The parametric curve would start at the point $(1, 0)$ (the dot), go counter-clockwise in a circular motion, and finish back at $(1, 0)$.

- $-\pi \le \theta \le \pi$

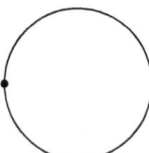

The curve starts at $(-1, 0)$, go counter-clockwise in a circular motion and finish at $(-1, 0)$.

- $0 \leq \theta \leq 4\pi$

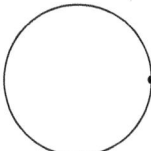

The course of motion is similar to the first one ($0 \leq \theta \leq 2\pi$) except that after the curve starts at $(1,0)$, it goes around the same circle twice counter-clockwise and finishes at $(1,0)$.

- $\dfrac{\pi}{4} \leq \theta \leq \dfrac{\pi}{3}$

The result would be an arc of angle $\dfrac{\pi}{12}$ drawn clockwise, as θ increases from $\dfrac{\pi}{4}$ to $\dfrac{\pi}{3}$. For clarity, the rest of the unit circle is shown through a dashed curve.

Consider the parametric equations $x = \cos 2\theta$, $y = \sin 2\theta$.

a) If there was no restriction on θ, then we would have the normal *unit circle*, because $x^2 + y^2 = 1$, based on the Pythagorean Identity.

b) If we suppose that $0 \leq \theta \leq 2\pi$, then we would end up with a graph that starts at $(1,0)$, goes counter-clockwise around the unit circle twice and finishes at $(1,0)$. Then how is it any different than the parametric curve $x = \cos \theta$, $y = \sin \theta$, $0 \leq \theta \leq 4\pi$?

The curve for $x = \cos 2\theta$, $y = \sin 2\theta$ is drawn *twice as fast*. For clarification, notice that when $\theta = 2\pi$, the graph for $x = \cos 2\theta$, $y = \sin 2\theta$ is already complete (circle drawn over twice), but for $x = \cos \theta$, $y = \sin \theta$, the circle has only been drawn once, with the 'second circle' remaining.

If we had parametric equations $x = \cos(-\theta)$, $y = \sin(-\theta)$, and restrictions $0 \leq \theta \leq 2\pi$, the parametric curve would be the unit circle but drawn clockwise (going backwards), as opposed to earlier examples.

Now, what if we defined $x = \sin \theta$, $y = \cos \theta$ with $0 \leq \theta \leq 2\pi$? In fact, the graph would look the same (but 'drawn' differently).

The graph would be a circle starting from $(0,1)$, going clockwise around the unit circle and ending up back at $(0,1)$.

This can also result from reflecting the graph determined by $x = \cos\theta$, $y = \sin\theta$ over the line $y = x$, since we have switched the parametric functions assigned to x and y respectively.

Problem 7.2.2. Find the Cartesian equation represented by the parametric equations $x = 1 + \cos\theta$, $y = 2 + \sin\theta$, with $0 \leq \theta \leq 2\pi$.

Solution. We use the Pythagorean identity $\sin^2\theta + \cos^2\theta = 1$. Note that $\cos\theta = x - 1$ and $\sin\theta = y - 2$. Substituting these into the identity, we therefore have $\boxed{(x-1)^2 + (y-2)^2 = 1}$, a circle of radius 1 centered at $(1, 2)$. $\square$

Problem 7.2.3. Find the Cartesian equation represented by the parametric equations $x = 88\cos\theta$, $y = 88\sin\theta$ with $0 \leq \theta \leq 2\pi$, with $0 \leq \theta \leq 2\pi$.

Solution. Similarly, note that $\cos\theta = \dfrac{x}{88}$ and $\sin\theta = \dfrac{y}{88}$, yielding the equation $\left(\dfrac{x^2}{88^2}\right) + \left(\dfrac{y^2}{88^2}\right) = 1$, or $\boxed{x^2 + y^2 = 7744}$, a circle centered at the origin with radius 88. $\square$

Problem 7.2.4. Find the Cartesian equation represented by the parametric equations $x = 88\cos\theta$, $y = 89\sin\theta$, with $0 \leq \theta \leq 2\pi$.

Solution. We once again use our Pythagorean identity $\sin^2\theta + \cos^2\theta = 1$. Note that $x^2 = 88^2 \cdot \cos^2\theta \implies \cos^2\theta = \dfrac{x^2}{88^2}$ and $y^2 = 89^2 \cdot \sin^2\theta \implies \sin^2\theta = \dfrac{y^2}{89^2}$, yielding the equation $\boxed{\dfrac{x^2}{88^2} + \dfrac{y^2}{89^2} = 1}$, which is an ellipse. $\square$

Problem 7.2.5. Represent the ellipse with equation $\dfrac{(x+2)^2}{25} + \dfrac{(y-3)^2}{16} = 1$ with parametric equations.

Solution. Given the reasoning presented in the solution of the previous problem, we can work backwards. Using the identity $\sin^2\theta + \cos^2\theta = 1$, we have the relations $\dfrac{(x+2)^2}{25} = \cos^2\theta$ and $\dfrac{(y-3)^2}{16} = \sin^2\theta$, and solve to get the parametric equations $\boxed{x = 5\cos\theta - 2}$ and $\boxed{y = 4\sin\theta + 3}$. $\square$

Problem 7.2.6. Find parametric equations for the graph $x^2 - y^2 = 9$.

Solution. The form of the given equation is similar to another Pythagorean identity: $\sec^2\theta = 1 + \tan^2\theta$. Since we can rearrange the equation to $\dfrac{x^2}{3^2} - \dfrac{y^2}{3^2} = 1$, we then solve for the parametric equations $\boxed{x = 3\sec\theta}$ and $\boxed{y = 3\tan\theta}$. $\square$

Problem 7.2.7. Graph the parametric curve $x = \cos t$, $y = \cos 2t$.

Solution. Using the double-angle formulas, we have that $y = 2\cos^2 t - 1$, or $y = 2x^2 - 1$. At first glance the graph may seem like a normal parabola. However, we must consider the ranges of x and y: as x is equal to the cosine function of parameter t, x necessarily has a range of $[-1, 1]$, so we must limit the graph to x-values from -1 to 1 only.

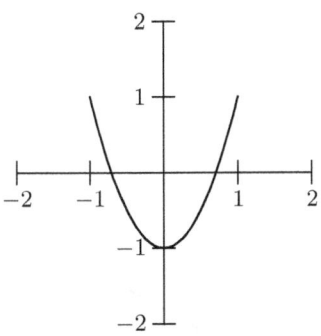

$\square$

Problem 7.2.8. Find the Cartesian equation for parametric equations $x = \sin t$, $y = \sin 2t$.

Solution. The double-angle formula for sine states that $\sin 2x = 2 \sin x \cos x$. Combining this with the fact that $\cos x = \pm\sqrt{1 - \sin^2 x}$, we have the equation $y = \pm 2x\sqrt{1 - x^2}$. To get rid of the plus-minus sign, we square both sides to get: $\boxed{y^2 = 4x^2(1 - x^2)}$. $\square$

Problem 7.2.9. Sketch the parametric curve for equations $x = t^2 - t$, $y = t^2 + t$.

Solution. There is no clear relationship between x and y, so first set up a table and calculate various x and y values:

t	x	y
-3	12	6
-2	6	2
-1	2	0
$-\dfrac{1}{2}$	$\dfrac{3}{4}$	$-\dfrac{1}{4}$
0	0	0
$\dfrac{1}{2}$	$-\dfrac{1}{4}$	$\dfrac{3}{4}$
1	0	2
2	2	6
-3	6	12

Then, we can produce a basic sketch:

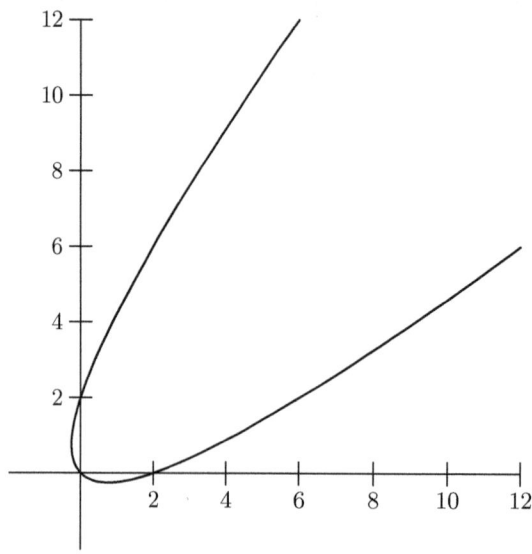

The graph looks like a rotated parabola. We can investigate this by finding the Cartesian equation for this parametric curve. Given the parametric equations,

$$x = t^2 - t,$$
$$y = t^2 + t,$$

we can add these to get $t^2 = \dfrac{x+y}{2}$, and subtract these to get $t = \dfrac{y-x}{2}$. Therefore, we have:

$$\left(\dfrac{y-x}{2}\right)^2 = \dfrac{x+y}{2}$$
$$\dfrac{y^2 - 2xy + x^2}{4} = \dfrac{x+y}{2}$$
$$4x + 4y = 2(y^2 - 2xy + x^2)$$
$$4x + 4y = 2y^2 - 4xy + 2x^2,$$

so we end up with the equation

$$2x^2 - 4xy + 2y^2 - 4x - 4y = 0.$$

We are left with an equation for a conic section. The conic discriminant is $(-4)^2 - 4(2)(2) = 0$, so we can confirm that it represents an oblique parabola.

Don't worry if you don't know about the conic discriminant, as it will be covered in depth in a later chapter (Theorem 7.3.34). □

Suppose that in the following diagram,

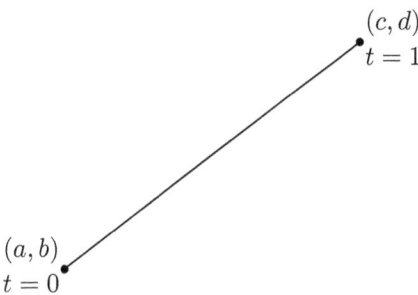

we must find a set of parametric equations for x and y such that the parametric curve is this line segment starting from point (a,b) at $t=0$ and ending at point (c,d) with $t=1$ (i.e. $0 \leq t \leq 1$).

To start, we drop altitudes and form right triangles:

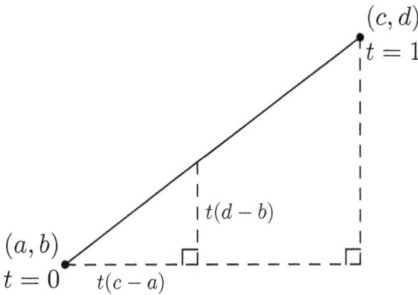

Note that since t goes from 0 to 1 and the graph in discussion is linear, t is the ratio of the line segment that has been drawn starting from point (a,b). Therefore, the distance covered on the x-axis would be t multiplied by the width difference $c - a$, and the distance covered on the y-axis would be t multiplied by the height difference $d - b$.

Recall that we are starting from point (a,b), so the x-coordinate would be $t(c-a)$ *added to* a and the y-coordinate would be $t(d-b)$ *added to* b. Therefore, we have the parametric equations:

$$x = f(t) = a + t(c - a),$$
$$y = g(t) = b + t(d - b).$$

Problem 7.2.10. Find parametric equations for the line segment connecting $(1,0)$ and $(7,-5)$ where

1. $(1,0)$ is the starting point.

2. $(7,-5)$ is the starting point.

Solution.

1. Using the relationship proven in the previous example, we have the equations $x = 1 + t(7-1)$ and $y = 0 + t(-5 - 0)$, or:

$$x = 1 + 6t,$$
$$y = -5t,$$

for $0 \leq t \leq 1$.

2. Similarly, the parametric equations would be:

$$x = 7 - 6t,$$
$$y = -5 + 5t,$$

for $0 \leq t \leq 1$. □

Problem 7.2.11. Sketch the following graphs:

1. $x = e^t$, $y = e^{-t}$

2. $x = 2^t$, $y = 4^t$

3. $x = \sin t$, $y = \sin t$

Solution.

1. At first, one might conclude that the graph is simply the hyperbola $y = \dfrac{1}{x}$. However, remember that $x, y > 0$, as a positive number raised to an exponent is always greater than zero. Therefore, we only draw the graph for positive x and y values, as such:

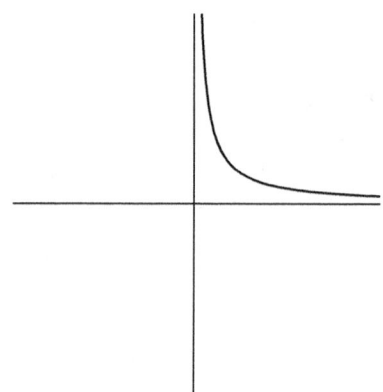

2. It is clear that $y = x^2$. However, keep in mind that $x, y > 0$ (because a positive number raised to any exponent is always positive). Therefore we only draw the right side of the parabola:

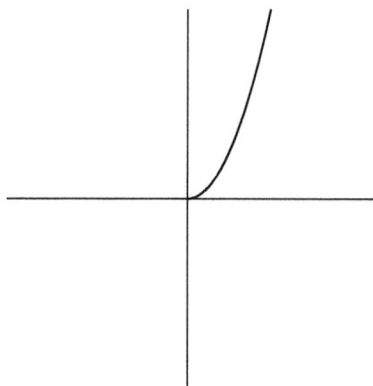

3. The line is obviously $y = x$, but remember that the range of sine is $[-1, 1]$, therefore we limit x, y to the interval $[-1, 1]$. Thus we are left with a line segment:

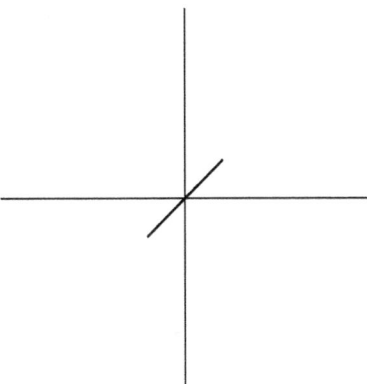

$\square$

Exercise 7.2.12. Graph the parametric curve for equations $x = \sqrt{t+1}$, $y = \sqrt{t-1}$.

Problem 7.2.13. Find a parametric expression for the graph $2(x-1)^2 + 3(y+2)^2 = 11$.

Solution. We strive to turn this equation into a standard equation for a conic section. Therefore, divide both sides of the equation by 11 to make the RHS equal to 1, then express the LHS as the sum of fractions where only the terms $(x-1)^2$ and $(y+2)^2$ are the numerators, as such:

$$2(x-1)^2 + 3(y+2)^2 = 11$$
$$\frac{2(x-1)^2}{11} + \frac{3(y+2)^2}{11} = 1$$
$$\frac{(x-1)^2}{\frac{11}{2}} + \frac{(y+2)^2}{\frac{11}{3}} = 1$$

This is an ellipse! Just like examples shown earlier in the section, the parametric equations for x and y rely on the identity $\sin^2 \theta + \cos^2 \theta = 1$:

$$x = \sqrt{\frac{11}{2}} \cos \theta + 1,$$
$$y = \sqrt{\frac{11}{3}} \sin \theta - 2.$$

$\square$

Problem 7.2.14. Sketch the parametric graph $x = 2 = 4\cos\theta$, $y = -1 + 3\sin\theta$.

We conclude this section with one famous example:

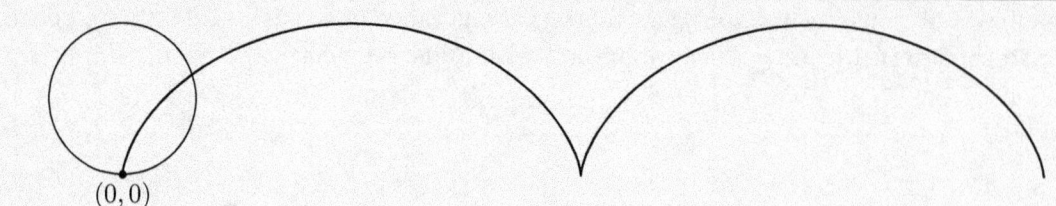

Example 7.2.15 (The Cycloid)

Consider a circle of radius 1, centered at $(0, 1)$, rolling across a line. Let us trace the path of a certain point (in this case, let it be initially $(0, 0)$) of the circle, as the circle rolls. What are the parametric equations to describe this path?

Solution. First, let's consider a circle of radius r, centered at $(0, 0)$, to simplify the problem. Given an angle of θ (in radians) from the point $(0, -r)$ to the point A, what would be the coordinates of A?

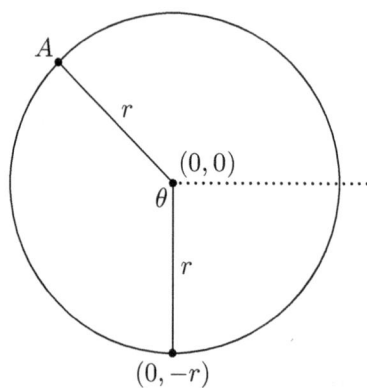

Well, remember that the functions $\sin x$ and $\cos x$ start from the 'east pole' (denoted by the dotted line in the diagram) and go counter-clockwise. Therefore, the point $(0, -r)$ would be $\left(r\cos\left(-\frac{\pi}{2}\right), r\sin\left(-\frac{\pi}{2}\right)\right)$ (it is $-\frac{\pi}{2}$ instead of $\frac{\pi}{2}$ because we went clockwise).

Point A is simply rotating the point $(0, -r)$ further θ degrees clockwise, so we subtract θ to get $A = \left(r\cos\left(-\frac{\pi}{2} - \theta\right), r\sin\left(-\frac{\pi}{2} - \theta\right)\right)$.

However, note that

$$\cos\left(-\frac{\pi}{2} - \theta\right) = \cos\left(\frac{\pi}{2} + \theta\right) = \cos\frac{\pi}{2}\cos\theta - \sin\frac{\pi}{2}\sin\theta = -\sin\theta,$$

and

$$\sin\left(-\frac{\pi}{2} - \theta\right) = -\sin\left(\frac{\pi}{2} + \theta\right) = -\left(\sin\frac{\pi}{2}\cos\theta + \cos\frac{\pi}{2}\sin\theta\right) = -\cos\theta,$$

therefore $A = (-r\sin\theta, -r\cos\theta)$.

To get the graph that we want, we must translate this circle upwards by r. Therefore, we add r to the y-coordinate of all points on the circle.

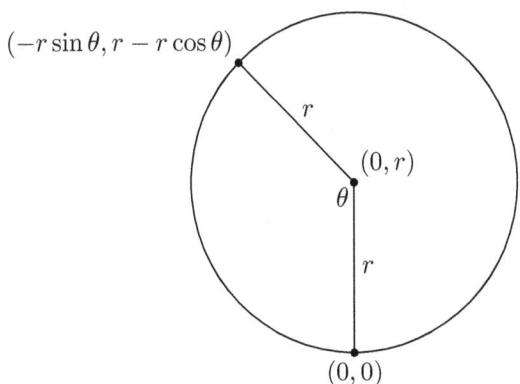

This results in the point $(-r\sin\theta, r - r\cos\theta)$ to describe the point on a circle with angle θ. However, we're not done yet. We have yet to factor in the circle moving sideways, on the x-axis.

If a circle 'rolls' on its surface by an angle θ, we are really just translating the circle horizontally by the length of the arc that the angle θ subtends. For example, in this diagram, the length of the arc between the point $(0,0)$ and $(-r\sin\theta, r - r\cos\theta)$ is the horizontal distance that the initial point $(0,0)$ will cover when that point becomes $(-r\sin\theta, r - r\cos\theta)$ as a result of the circle rolling.

We can compute this length as $\dfrac{\theta}{2\pi} \cdot 2\pi r = r\theta$. We add this to the x-coordinate of $(-r\sin\theta, r - r\cos\theta)$ to get the point $(r\theta - r\sin\theta, r - r\cos\theta)$, which is the correct representation of the point on the rolling circle. Therefore, our parametric equations would be:

$$x = r(\theta - \sin\theta),$$
$$y = r(1 - \cos\theta).$$
$\square$

7.3 Complex Numbers

This section assumes some prior experience of complex numbers.

7.3.1 Review

We define $i = \sqrt{-1}$. A **complex number** can be expressed as $z = a + bi$, where a is the **real part** and b is the **imaginary part**. All real numbers are complex numbers, with their imaginary part equal to 0.

If $i = \sqrt{-1}$, then $i^2 = -1$, $i^3 = -i$, and $i^4 = 1$. When multiplying complex numbers together, make sure you get used to various powers of i.

Problem 7.3.1. Compute $\dfrac{2+3i}{4+5i}$ and $(2+3i)^3$.

Solution. For the first one, multiply the numerator and denominator by the conjugate of the denominator:

$$\frac{2+3i}{4+5i} \cdot \frac{4-5i}{4-5i} = \boxed{\frac{23+2i}{41}}.$$

For the second one, use the Binomial Theorem to expand and simplify:

$$(2+3i)^3 = 2^3 + 3 \cdot 2^2 \cdot 3i + 3 \cdot 2 \cdot (3i)^2 + (3i)^3$$
$$= 8 + 36i - 54 - 27i$$
$$= \boxed{-46 + 9i}.$$

□

Given a complex number $z = a + bi$, define the **conjugate** of z as $\bar{z} = a - bi$.

Problem 7.3.2. Given $w, z \in \mathbb{C}$, prove:

a) $\overline{w + z} = \bar{w} + \bar{z}$.

b) $\overline{wz} = \bar{w} \cdot \bar{z}$.

c) $\dfrac{1}{\bar{z}} = \overline{\left(\dfrac{1}{z}\right)}$.

Proof.

a) Let $w = a + bi$ and $z = c + di$. Then $\overline{w + z} = \overline{(a+c) + (b+d)i} = (a+c) - (b+d)i$, and $\bar{w} + \bar{z} = \overline{a+bi} + \overline{c+di} = a - bi + c - di = (a+c) - (b+d)i$, therefore $\overline{w+z} = \bar{w} + \bar{z}$.

b) Similarly, let $w = a + bi$ and $z = c + di$. Expand both $\overline{wz}$ and $\bar{w} \cdot \bar{z}$ using the definitions of w and z and simplify, separating the real and imaginary parts.

$$\bar{w} \cdot \bar{z} = \overline{a+bi} \cdot \overline{c+di}$$
$$= (a - bi)(c - di)$$
$$= ac - adi - bci - bd$$
$$= ac - bd - adi - bci$$
$$= (ac - bd) - (ad + bc)i.$$

$$\overline{wz} = \overline{(a+bi)(c+di)}$$
$$= \overline{ac + adi + bci - bd}$$
$$= \overline{ac - bd + adi + bci}$$
$$= \overline{(ac - bd) + (ad + bc)i}$$
$$= (ac - bd) - (ad + bc)i.$$

We can compare the two and conclude that they are equal.

c) This time, let $z = a + bi$, and the structure of this proof is similar to the previous two:

$$\overline{\left(\frac{1}{z}\right)} = \overline{\left(\frac{1}{a+bi}\right)}$$
$$= \overline{\left(\frac{1}{a+bi}\right) \cdot \left(\frac{a-bi}{a-bi}\right)}$$

$$= \overline{\left(\frac{a-bi}{a^2+b^2}\right)}$$
$$= \overline{\left(\frac{a}{a^2+b^2} - \frac{b}{a^2+b^2}i\right)}$$
$$= \frac{a}{a^2+b^2} + \frac{b}{a^2+b^2}i$$

$$\frac{1}{\overline{z}} = \frac{1}{\overline{a+bi}}$$
$$= \frac{1}{a-bi}$$
$$= \frac{1}{a-bi} \cdot \frac{a+bi}{a+bi}$$
$$= \frac{a+bi}{a^2+b^2}$$
$$= \frac{a}{a^2+b^2} + \frac{b}{a^2+b^2}i$$

We find that they are equal, so we are done. □

Problem 7.3.3. Prove that if $P(x)$ is a polynomial with real coefficients and z is a root of $P(x)$, then $\overline{z}$ is also a root of $P(x)$.

Proof. Let $P(x) = \sum_{k=0}^{n} a_k x^k$ where $a_k \in \mathbb{R}$. Let $0 = P(z) = \sum_{k=0}^{n} a_k z^k$. Then,

$$\overline{0} = \overline{P(z)} = \overline{\sum_{k=0}^{n} a_k z^k} = \sum_{k=0}^{n} \overline{a_k} \overline{(z^k)}.$$

It is evident that $\overline{(z^k)} = (\overline{z})^k$. It is also true that the conjugate of any real number is itself, since $a + 0i = a - 0i$. Using those facts, we can conclude that $\overline{0} = \sum_{k=0}^{n} a_k (\overline{z})^k = P(\overline{z})$, i.e. $P(\overline{z}) = 0$. Thus, $\overline{z}$ is a root of $P(x)$. □

Problem 7.3.4. Define $|a+bi| = \sqrt{a^2+b^2}$. $\forall w, z \in \mathbb{C}$, prove:

a) $|wz| = |w||z|$.

b) $|w+z| \leq |w| + |z|$.

Proof.

a) First, $|w||z| = |a+bi||c+di| = \sqrt{a^2+b^2} \cdot \sqrt{c^2+d^2} = \sqrt{a^2c^2 + a^2d^2 + b^2c^2 + b^2d^2}$.
Then,
$$|wz| = |(a+bi)(c+di)|$$

$$= |ac - bd + (ad + bc)i|$$
$$= \sqrt{(ac-bd)^2 + (ad+bc)^2}$$
$$= \sqrt{a^2c^2 + a^2d^2 + b^2c^2 + b^2d^2},$$

so they are equal.

b) First, note that $(|w+z|)^2 = (a+c)^2 + (b+d)^2 = a^2 + b^2 + c^2 + d^2 + 2ac + 2bd$.
Also, $(|w|+|z|)^2 = |w|^2 + |z|^2 + 2|w||z| = a^2 + b^2 + c^2 + d^2 + 2\sqrt{(a^2+b^2)(c^2+d^2)}$.

Using terms ad and bc, we can apply the AM-GM inequality to get $\dfrac{ad+bc}{2} \geq \sqrt{abcd}$, which rearranges to $a^2d^2 + b^2c^2 \geq 2abcd$.

Therefore, by adding $a^2c^2 + b^2d^2$ to both sides of that result, we have $a^2c^2 + a^2d^2 + b^2c^2 + b^2d^2 \geq a^2c^2 + 2abcd + b^2d^2$, which factors into $(a^2+b^2)(c^2+d^2) \geq (ac+bd)^2$ i.e. $\sqrt{(a^2+b^2)(c^2+d^2)} \geq ac+bd$.

Now, we can apply that result on the expanded forms of $|w+z|$ and $|w|+|z|$ stated in the beginning of the proof; it is now clear that $a^2 + b^2 + c^2 + d^2 + 2\sqrt{(a^2+b^2)(c^2+d^2)} \geq a^2 + b^2 + c^2 + d^2 + 2ac + 2bd$, and so $(|w|+|z|)^2 \geq (|z+w|)^2$. Since magnitude is always nonnegative, we take square root of both sides to get the intended result $|w+z| \leq |w|+|z|$. $\square$

7.3.2 The Complex Plane

Now, we introduce a new coordinate system using complex numbers.

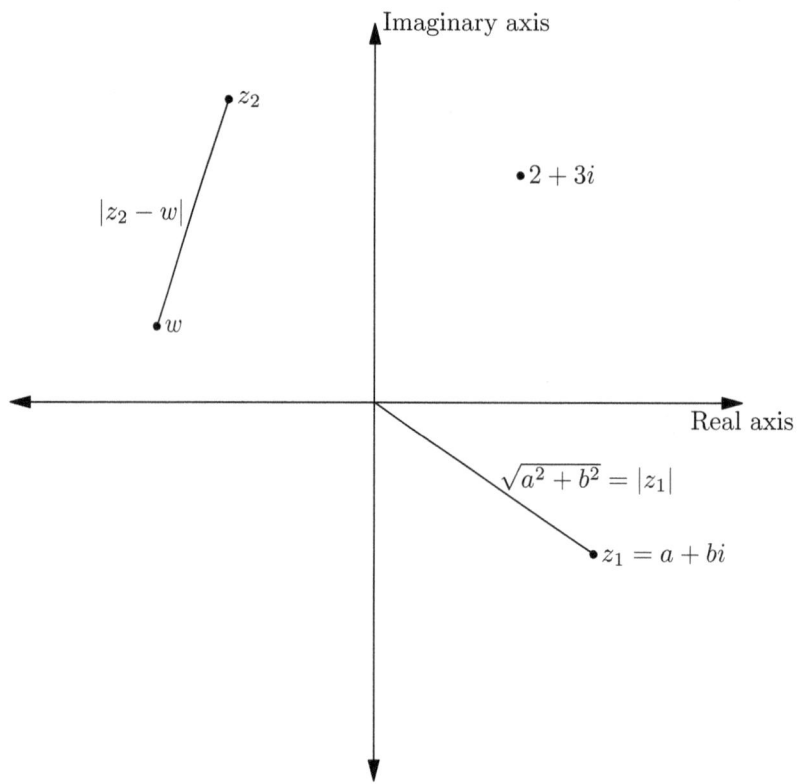

We have the Cartesian point (a, b) correspond to the point $a + bi$ on the **complex plane**, where the x-axis is the real part and the y-axis is the imaginary part of the complex number.

For instance, the point $(2, 3)$ on the Cartesian plane would be represented as $2 + 3i$ on the complex plane. Here are a couple of observations: We have the Cartesian point (a, b) correspond to the point $a + bi$ on the complex plane, where the x-axis is the real part and the y-axis is the imaginary part of the complex number. For instance, the point $(2, 3)$ on the Cartesian plane would be represented as $2 + 3i$ on the complex plane. Here are a couple of observations:

a) Given a point $z_1 \in \mathbb{C}$, $|z_1|$ is the distance from the origin to z_1. This is obvious as $|z_1| = \sqrt{a^2 + b^2} = \sqrt{(a-0)^2 + (b-0)^2}$ which is simply the Cartesian distance formula with points (a, b) and $(0, 0)$ plugged in.

b) Given two points z_2 and w, the distance between them is $|z_2 - w|$. For a brief proof, let $z_2 = a + bi$ (which denotes (a, b)) and $w = c + di$ (which denotes (c, d)). The Cartesian distance formula gives $\sqrt{(a-c)^2 + (b-d)^2}$, which is equivalent to $|(a-c) + (b-d)i|$, or $|z_2 - w|$.

Problem 7.3.5. Describe the graphs of the following equations in the complex plane:

1. $z = \bar{z}$

2. $|z - 1| = |z|$

3. $|z - 2| + |z + 3i| = 10$

4. $|z - 2| = 2|z|$

Solution.

a) If we let $z = a + bi$, then we have the equation $a + bi = a - bi$, and we solve to get $b = 0$, implying that z must be real. Therefore the graph would simply be the real axis.

b) Like before, let $z = a + bi$. We algebraically simplify the equation:

$$|a + bi - 1| = |a + bi|$$
$$\sqrt{(a-1)^2 + b^2} = \sqrt{a^2 + b^2}$$
$$(a-1)^2 = a^2$$
$$a^2 - 2a + 1 = a^2$$
$$2a = 1$$
$$a = \frac{1}{2}$$

Therefore the graph is a line of z such that the real part of z is $\frac{1}{2}$.

c) Recall the definition of an ellipse, which is the set of points such that the sum of the distances from any point to the two certain points (foci) is constant. In this equation, we are given that the sum of the distance from z to 2 and the distance from z to $3i$ is always 10. Therefore this graph is an ellipse with foci at 2 and $-3i$.

d) Let $z = a + bi$. We simplify this equation algebraically:

$$|a + bi - 2| = 2|a + bi|$$
$$\sqrt{(a-2)^2 + b^2} = 2\sqrt{a^2 + b^2}$$
$$(a-2)^2 + b^2 = 4a^2 + 4b^2$$
$$a^2 - 4a + 4 + b^2 = 4a^2 + 4b^2$$
$$3a^2 + 4a + 3b^2 = 4$$
$$3\left(a^2 + \frac{4}{3}a\right) + 3b^2 = 4$$
$$3\left(a^2 + \frac{4}{3}a + \frac{4}{9}\right) + 3b^2 = 4 + \frac{4}{3}$$
$$3\left(a + \frac{2}{3}\right)^2 + 3b^2 = \frac{16}{3}$$
$$\left(a + \frac{2}{3}\right)^2 + b^2 = \frac{16}{9}$$

Therefore the graph is a circle centered at $\left(-\frac{2}{3}, 0\right)$ with radius $\frac{4}{3}$. □

Recall the relationship between the Cartesian plane and the polar plane: $(a, b) \iff (r; \theta)$. We had defined $a = r \cos \theta$ and $b = r \sin \theta$. We can now establish a relationship between the polar plane and the complex plane:

$$a + bi = r \cos \theta + i \cdot r \sin \theta$$
$$= r(\cos \theta + i \sin \theta)$$
$$= r \operatorname{cis} \theta.$$

We denote the **polar form** of the complex number $a + bi$ as $r \operatorname{cis} \theta$, where r is the **magnitude** and θ is the **argument**. If z is the complex number, then we can denote $\theta = \operatorname{Arg} z$. For notation purposes, $\operatorname{cis} \theta$ is the abbreviation for $\cos \theta + i \sin \theta$.

We now have four ways to represent a point in two-dimensional space:

$$a + bi \longleftrightarrow (a, b) \longleftrightarrow (r; \theta) \longleftrightarrow r \operatorname{cis} \theta.$$

It turns out that $|\operatorname{cis} \theta| = |\cos \theta + i \sin \theta| = \sqrt{\cos^2 \theta + \sin^2 \theta} = 1$, so $|r \operatorname{cis} \theta| = |r||\operatorname{cis} \theta| = |r|$. Thus,

$$a + bi = r \operatorname{cis} \theta \longrightarrow |a + bi| = |r \operatorname{cis} \theta|$$
$$\longrightarrow |a + bi| = |r|$$
$$\longrightarrow |r| = \sqrt{a^2 + b^2}.$$

This concept of the 'magnitude' of a number is consistent throughout various representations.

Problem 7.3.6. Convert the following complex numbers from polar form to standard form $(a+bi)$:

a) $6\operatorname{cis}\left(\dfrac{\pi}{6}\right)$

b) $8\operatorname{cis}(-\pi)$

c) $4\operatorname{cis}\left(\dfrac{3\pi}{4}\right)$

Solution.

a)
$$6\operatorname{cis}\left(\frac{\pi}{6}\right) = 6\left(\cos\frac{\pi}{6} + i\sin\frac{\pi}{6}\right)$$
$$= 6\left(\frac{\sqrt{3}}{2} + \frac{1}{2}i\right)$$
$$= \boxed{3\sqrt{3} + 3i}.$$

b)
$$8\operatorname{cis}(-\pi) = 8(\cos(-\pi) + i\sin(-\pi))$$
$$= 8(-1 + i \cdot 0)$$
$$= \boxed{-8}.$$

c)
$$4\operatorname{cis}\left(\frac{3\pi}{4}\right) = 4\left(\cos\frac{3\pi}{4} + i\sin\frac{3\pi}{4}\right)$$
$$= 4\left(-\frac{\sqrt{2}}{2} + \frac{\sqrt{2}}{2}i\right)$$
$$= \boxed{-2\sqrt{2} + 2\sqrt{2}i}.$$
□

Problem 7.3.7. Convert $18 - 18\sqrt{3}i$ to polar form.

Solution.
$$18 - 18\sqrt{3}i = 36\left(\frac{1}{2} - \frac{\sqrt{3}}{2}i\right)$$
$$= 36\left(\cos\left(\frac{5\pi}{3}\right) - i\sin\left(\frac{5\pi}{3}\right)\right)$$
$$= \boxed{36\operatorname{cis}\left(\frac{5\pi}{3}\right)}.$$
□

Problem 7.3.8. Convert $3 + 4i$ to polar form.

Solution. Note that $3 + 4i$ is in the first quadrant, so $\tan^{-1}\dfrac{4}{3}$ gives the correct angle. The magnitude is $\sqrt{3^2 + 4^2} = 5$, therefore $3 + 4i$ in polar form is $\boxed{5\operatorname{cis}\left(\tan^{-1}\dfrac{4}{3}\right)}$. □

Lemma 7.3.9

Given two complex numbers $r_1 \operatorname{cis} \theta_1$ and $r_2 \operatorname{cis} \theta_2$,
$$(r_1 \operatorname{cis} \theta_1)(r_2 \operatorname{cis} \theta_2) = r_1 r_2 \operatorname{cis}(\theta_1 + \theta_2).$$

Proof. Expand and simplify using the trigonometric angle addition formulas.
$$\begin{aligned}
(\operatorname{cis} \alpha)(\operatorname{cis} \beta) &= (\cos \alpha + i \sin \alpha)(\cos \beta + i \sin \beta) \\
&= \cos \alpha \cos \beta + i \cos \alpha \sin \beta + i \cos \beta \sin \alpha - \sin \alpha \sin \beta \\
&= \cos(\alpha + \beta) + i \sin(\alpha + \beta) \\
&= \operatorname{cis}(\alpha + \beta).
\end{aligned}$$

Therefore, the statement $(r_1 \operatorname{cis} \theta_1)(r_2 \operatorname{cis} \theta_2) = r_1 r_2 \operatorname{cis}(\theta_1 + \theta_2)$ follows. □

Problem 7.3.10. Compute $(3\sqrt{3} + 3i)(18 - 18\sqrt{3}i)$ using Lemma 7.3.9, then compute it directly to confirm that it works.

Solution. First, we use Lemma 7.3.9:
$$\begin{aligned}
(3\sqrt{3} + 3i)(18 - 18\sqrt{3}i) &= 6 \operatorname{cis} \frac{\pi}{6} \cdot 36 \operatorname{cis} \frac{5\pi}{3} \\
&= 6 \cdot 36 \cdot \operatorname{cis}\left(\frac{\pi}{6} + \frac{5\pi}{3}\right) \\
&= 216 \operatorname{cis} \frac{11\pi}{6} \\
&= 216 \left(\cos \frac{11\pi}{6} + i \sin \frac{11\pi}{6}\right) \\
&= 216 \left(\frac{\sqrt{3}}{2} - \frac{1}{2}i\right) \\
&= \boxed{108\sqrt{3} - 108i}.
\end{aligned}$$

Then, we confirm by directly expanding the product:
$$\begin{aligned}
(3\sqrt{3} + 3i)(18 - 18\sqrt{3}i) &= 54\sqrt{3} - 162i + 54i + 54\sqrt{3} \\
&= \boxed{108\sqrt{3} - 108i}.
\end{aligned}$$
□

Lemma 7.3.11

$\operatorname{cis}(-\theta) = (\operatorname{cis} \theta)^{-1}$.

Proof. By Lemma 7.3.9, we have $\operatorname{cis}(-\theta) \operatorname{cis} \theta = \operatorname{cis}(-\theta + \theta) = \operatorname{cis} 0$, which is equal to 1. Since $\operatorname{cis}(-\theta) \operatorname{cis} \theta = 1$, $\operatorname{cis}(-\theta) = \dfrac{1}{\operatorname{cis} \theta} = (\operatorname{cis} \theta)^{-1}$. □

Problem 7.3.12. Compute $(\operatorname{cis}\theta)^2$ and $(\operatorname{cis}\theta)^3$.

Solution.
$$(\operatorname{cis}\theta)^2 = \operatorname{cis}\theta \operatorname{cis}\theta = \operatorname{cis}(\theta+\theta) = \operatorname{cis}2\theta$$
$$(\operatorname{cis}\theta)^2 = (\operatorname{cis}\theta)^2 \operatorname{cis}\theta = \operatorname{cis}2\theta + \operatorname{cis}\theta = \operatorname{cis}(2\theta+\theta) = \operatorname{cis}3\theta$$

The pattern suggests that $(\operatorname{cis}\theta)^n$ and $\operatorname{cis} n\theta$ are equal, which will be proven in the following theorem. $\square$

Theorem 7.3.13 (De Moivre's Theorem)
Let $n \in \mathbb{Z}^+$. Then, $(\operatorname{cis}\theta)^n = \operatorname{cis}(n\theta)$.

Proof. We proceed by induction. Let $P(n): (\operatorname{cis}\theta)^n = \operatorname{cis} n\theta$.

<u>Base Case</u>: $P(1): (\operatorname{cis}\theta)^1 = \operatorname{cis}\theta = \operatorname{cis}(\theta \cdot 1)$ so the base case is true.

<u>Inductive Step</u>: Assume $P(n): (\operatorname{cis}\theta)^n = \operatorname{cis} n\theta$ is true.

We want to prove $P(n+1): (\operatorname{cis}\theta)^{n+1} = \operatorname{cis}((n+1)\theta)$. By Lemma 7.3.9, we have

$$\begin{aligned}(\operatorname{cis}\theta)^{n+1} &= (\operatorname{cis}\theta)^n(\operatorname{cis}\theta) \\ &= (\operatorname{cis} n\theta)(\operatorname{cis}\theta) \\ &= \operatorname{cis}(n\theta + \theta) \\ &= \operatorname{cis}((n+1)\theta),\end{aligned}$$

which concludes the inductive step. $\square$

Corollary 7.3.14
$\forall n \in \mathbb{Z}, (\operatorname{cis}\theta)^n = \operatorname{cis} n\theta$.

Proof. We have already proven the case when $n > 0$, shown in the proof of Theorem 7.3.13.

If $n = 0$, then $(\operatorname{cis}\theta)^0 = 1$, and $\operatorname{cis}(0 \cdot \theta) = \operatorname{cis} 0 = 1$, so they are equal.

If $n < 0$, then $n + |n| = 0$. Then,

$$\begin{aligned}(\operatorname{cis}\theta)^n(\operatorname{cis}\theta)^{|n|} &= (\operatorname{cis}\theta)^{n+|n|} \\ &= (\operatorname{cis}\theta)^0 \\ &= 1.\end{aligned}$$

Therefore, we finish the proof for case $n < 0$ by using Lemma 7.3.9, Lemma 7.3.11, Theorem 7.3.13, and the fact that $-|n| = n$:

$$(\operatorname{cis}\theta)^n(\operatorname{cis}\theta)^{|n|} = 1$$
$$(\operatorname{cis}\theta)^n = \frac{1}{(\operatorname{cis}\theta)^{|n|}}$$

$$= \left(\left(\operatorname{cis}\theta\right)^{|n|}\right)^{-1}$$
$$= (\operatorname{cis}(|n|\theta))^{-1}$$
$$= \operatorname{cis}(-|n|\theta)$$
$$= \operatorname{cis} n\theta. \qquad \square$$

Problem 7.3.15. Compute $(\sqrt{3}+i)^{10}$.

Solution. First, we convert the complex number to cis form.

$$\sqrt{3}+i = 2\left(\frac{\sqrt{3}}{2}+\frac{1}{2}i\right)$$
$$= 2\left(\cos\frac{\pi}{6}+i\sin\frac{\pi}{6}\right)$$
$$= 2\operatorname{cis}\frac{\pi}{6}.$$

Therefore, by De Moivre's Theorem,

$$\left(2\operatorname{cis}\frac{\pi}{6}\right)^{10} = 2^{10}\cdot\left(\operatorname{cis}\frac{\pi}{6}\right)^{10}$$
$$= 1024\cdot\operatorname{cis}\frac{5\pi}{3}$$
$$= 1024\left(\cos\frac{5\pi}{3}+i\sin\frac{5\pi}{3}\right)$$
$$= 1024\left(\frac{1}{2}-\frac{\sqrt{3}}{2}i\right)$$
$$= \boxed{512-512\sqrt{3}i}. \qquad \square$$

Problem 7.3.16. Compute $(\sqrt{3}-i)^{11}$.

Solution.
$$(\sqrt{3}-i)^{11} = \left(2\left(\frac{\sqrt{3}}{2}-\frac{1}{2}i\right)\right)^{11}$$
$$= \left(2\operatorname{cis}\left(-\frac{\pi}{6}\right)\right)^{11}$$
$$= 2^{11}\operatorname{cis}\left(-\frac{11\pi}{6}\right)$$
$$= 2^{11}\operatorname{cis}\left(\frac{\pi}{6}\right)$$
$$= 2048\left(\frac{\sqrt{3}}{2}+\frac{1}{2}i\right)$$
$$= \boxed{1024\sqrt{3}+1024i}. \qquad \square$$

Problem 7.3.17. Now, $\operatorname{cis} 3\theta = (\operatorname{cis}\theta)^3$. By expanding $(\cos\theta+i\sin\theta)^3$ using the Binomial Theorem, derive formulas for $\cos 3\theta$ and $\sin 3\theta$ entirely in terms of $\cos\theta$ and $\sin\theta$ respectively.

Solution. By the Binomial Theorem,
$$(\cos\theta + i\sin\theta)^3 = \cos^3\theta + 3\cos^2\theta \cdot i\sin\theta - 3\cos\theta\sin^2\theta - i\sin^3\theta.$$

By De Moivre's Theorem, we have
$$\cos^3\theta + 3\cos^2\theta \cdot i\sin\theta - 3\cos\theta\sin^2\theta - i\sin^3\theta = \cos 3\theta + i\sin 3\theta.$$

We equate the real and imaginary parts, then simplify to get the triple angle formulas:
$$\begin{aligned}\cos 3\theta &= \cos^3\theta - 3\cos\theta\sin^2\theta \\ &= \cos^3\theta - 3\cos\theta(1 - \cos^2\theta) \\ &= \cos^3\theta - 3\cos\theta + 3\cos^3\theta \\ \cos 3\theta &= 4\cos^3\theta - 3\cos\theta.\end{aligned}$$

$$\begin{aligned}i\sin 3\theta &= 3\cos^2\theta \cdot i\sin\theta - i\sin^3\theta \\ &= i\left(3\cos^2\theta\sin\theta - \sin^3\theta\right) \\ &= i\left(3(1 - \sin^2\theta)\sin\theta - \sin^3\theta\right) \\ &= i\left(3\sin\theta - 3\sin^3\theta - \sin^3\theta\right) \\ \sin 3\theta &= -4\sin^3\theta + 3\sin\theta.\end{aligned}$$ □

Problem 7.3.18. By expanding $(\cos\theta + i\sin\theta)^5$ and rewriting, find polynomials in terms of $\cos\theta$, $\sin\theta$ respectively for $\cos 5\theta$, $\sin 5\theta$.

Solution. We expand $(\cos\theta + i\sin\theta)^5$ using the Binomial Theorem:
$$\cos^5\theta + 5\cos^4\theta \cdot i\sin\theta - 10\cos^3\theta\sin^2\theta - 10\cos^2\theta \cdot i\sin^3\theta + 5\cos\theta\sin^4\theta + i\sin^5\theta.$$

By De Moivre's Theorem, this equals $\cos 5\theta + i\sin 5\theta$.

Then, we equate real and imaginary parts:
$$\begin{aligned}\cos 5\theta &= \cos^5\theta - 10\cos^3\theta\sin^2\theta + 5\cos\theta\sin^4\theta \\ &= \cos^5\theta - 10\cos^3\theta(1 - \cos^2\theta) + 5\cos\theta(1 - \cos^2\theta)^2 \\ &= \cos^5\theta - 10\cos^3\theta + 10\cos^5\theta + 5\cos\theta(1 - 2\cos^2\theta + \cos^4\theta) \\ &= 11\cos^5\theta - 10\cos^3\theta + 5\cos\theta - 10\cos^3\theta + 5\cos^5\theta \\ &= 16\cos^5\theta - 20\cos^3\theta + 5\cos\theta.\end{aligned}$$

$$\begin{aligned}i\sin 5\theta &= 5\cos^4\theta \cdot i\sin\theta - 10\cos^2\theta \cdot i\sin^3\theta + i\sin^5\theta \\ \sin 5\theta &= 5\cos^4\theta\sin\theta - 10\cos^2\theta\sin^3\theta + \sin^5\theta \\ &= 5(1 - \sin^2\theta)^2\sin\theta - 10(1 - \sin^2\theta)\sin^3\theta + \sin^5\theta \\ &= 5(1 - 2\sin^2\theta + \sin^4\theta)\sin\theta - 10\sin^3\theta + 10\sin^5\theta + \sin^5\theta \\ &= 5\sin\theta - 10\sin^3\theta + 5\sin^5\theta - 10\sin^3\theta + 11\sin^5\theta \\ &= 16\sin^5\theta - 20\sin^3\theta + 5\sin\theta.\end{aligned}$$ □

> **Theorem 7.3.19**
>
> We have certain relationships between $\cos n\theta$, $\cos\theta$ and $\sin n\theta$, $\sin\theta$:
>
> a) $\cos n\theta$ can be written as a polynomial in $\cos\theta$ $\forall n \in \mathbb{Z}^+$.
>
> b) $\sin n\theta$ can be written as a polynomial in $\sin\theta$ $\forall$ odd $n \in \mathbb{Z}^+$.

Proof. Consider the binomial expansion of $(\cos\theta + i\sin\theta)^n$:

$$\cos^n\theta + \binom{n}{1}\cos^{n-1}\theta \cdot i\sin\theta - \binom{n}{2}\cos^{n-2}\theta \cdot \sin^2\theta - \binom{n}{3}\cos^{n-3}\theta \cdot i\sin^3\theta + \binom{n}{4}\cos^{n-4}\theta\sin^4\theta + \ldots$$

If we consider the real parts only, we have

$$\cos n\theta = \cos^n\theta - \binom{n}{2}\cos^{n-2}\theta\sin^2\theta + \binom{n}{4}\cos^{n-4}\theta\sin^4\theta + \ldots$$

Notice that all powers of $\sin\theta$ are even. We can use the identity $\sin^2\theta = 1 - \cos^2\theta$ to be able to express any $\sin^{2k}\theta$ as $(1-\cos^2\theta)^k$ $\forall k \in \mathbb{Z}^+$. Therefore, since all $\sin\theta$ raised to an even power can be expressed in terms of $\cos\theta$, we are left with $\cos n\theta$ being equal to a polynomial in terms of $\cos\theta$.

Likewise, consider the imaginary parts:

$$\sin(n\theta) = \binom{n}{1}\cos^{n-1}\theta\sin\theta - \binom{n}{3}\cos^{n-3}\theta\sin^3\theta + \binom{n}{5}\cos^{n-5}\theta\sin^5\theta - \ldots$$

When we consider all *odd* n in $\mathbb{Z}^+$, n minus some other odd number ($n - (2k+1)$ $\forall k \in \mathbb{Z}$) must be *even*. Note that the powers of $\cos\theta$ in this expression are all of that form, therefore all $\cos\theta$ are raised to an even power.

We can then apply the identity $\cos^2\theta = 1 - \sin^2\theta$ similar to the $\cos(n\theta)$ example above, to establish that all even powers of $\cos\theta$ can be expressed in terms of $\sin\theta$. We can then conclude that $\sin(n\theta)$ can be expressed as a polynomial in terms of $\sin\theta$ only, for all odd positive integers n. $\square$

Problem 7.3.20. Given the equation $(a+bi)^2 = i$, solve for all such possible complex numbers.

Solution. We are given
$$a^2 + 2abi - b^2 = i.$$

We equate the real and imaginary parts, resulting in the equations $a^2 - b^2 = 0$ and $ab = \dfrac{1}{2}$.

From the latter, we have $b = \dfrac{1}{2a}$, so we substitute this into the former equation, and simplify:

$a^2 - \left(\dfrac{1}{2a}\right)^2 = 0 \implies a^2 = \dfrac{1}{4a^2} \implies 4a^4 = 1$, solving for a we get $\pm\dfrac{\sqrt{2}}{2}$. Therefore we have two solutions:

- $a = \dfrac{\sqrt{2}}{2} \implies b = \dfrac{\sqrt{2}}{2} \implies \boxed{\dfrac{\sqrt{2}}{2} + \dfrac{\sqrt{2}}{2}i}$.

- $a = -\dfrac{\sqrt{2}}{2} \implies b = -\dfrac{\sqrt{2}}{2} \implies \boxed{-\dfrac{\sqrt{2}}{2} - \dfrac{\sqrt{2}}{2}i}$. □

Problem 7.3.21. Solve the equation $z^2 = i$ (given $z \in \mathbb{C}$) using the polar form of complex numbers.

Solution. First, note that $|i| = 1$ and $\operatorname{Arg} i = \dfrac{\pi}{2}$ (the complex number i on the complex plane is the same as point $(0, 1)$, or $\left(\cos \dfrac{\pi}{2}, \sin \dfrac{\pi}{2}\right)$ on the Cartesian plane). Therefore, $i = 1 \cdot \operatorname{cis} \dfrac{\pi}{2}$. We let $z = r \operatorname{cis} \theta$ for arbitrary r and θ, so we have the equation

$$(r \operatorname{cis} \theta)^2 = 1 \cdot \operatorname{cis} \dfrac{\pi}{2}.$$

Using De Moivre's Theorem, this results in $r^2 \operatorname{cis} 2\theta = 1 \cdot \operatorname{cis} \dfrac{\pi}{2}$. We assume r to be positive, so $r = 1$. We also have $\operatorname{cis} 2\theta = \operatorname{cis} \dfrac{\pi}{2}$. Because sine and cosine functions are periodic by a value of 2π, we conclude that $2\theta = \dfrac{\pi}{2} + 2\pi k \ \forall k \in \mathbb{Z}$, or $\theta = \dfrac{\pi}{4} + \pi k \ \forall k \in \mathbb{Z}$. Therefore, limiting θ to $[0, 2\pi)$ we have the solutions $\theta = \dfrac{\pi}{4}, \dfrac{5\pi}{4}$. Our final solutions are $z = \boxed{1 \cdot \operatorname{cis} \dfrac{\pi}{4}}, \boxed{1 \cdot \operatorname{cis} \dfrac{5\pi}{4}}$. □

Exercise 7.3.22. Confirm that the answers in Problem 7.3.20 and Problem 7.3.21 are equivalent.

Problem 7.3.23. Solve for $z \in \mathbb{C}$: $z^3 = 8$.

Solution. We can solve this in two ways, as follows:

1. *Algebra.* We rewrite the equation into a polynomial $z^3 - 8 = 0$, which can then be factored into $(z-2)(z^2 + 2z + 4) = 0$. Using the quadratic formula, we find that the roots are $z = \boxed{2}, \boxed{-1 + i\sqrt{3}}, \boxed{-1 - i\sqrt{3}}$.

2. *Using Polar Form.* We know that $8 = 8 \operatorname{cis} 0$, therefore if we let $z = r \operatorname{cis} \theta$, then we have the equation $(r \operatorname{cis} \theta)^3 = 8 \operatorname{cis} 0$, or $r^3 \operatorname{cis} 3\theta = 8 \operatorname{cis} 0$. This implies $r^3 = 8$ and $\operatorname{cis} 3\theta = \operatorname{cis} 0$, thus $r = 3$ and $3\theta = 0 + 2\pi k \ \forall k \in \mathbb{Z}$ (as cis has a period of 2π). Thus $\theta = \dfrac{2\pi}{3}k$ i.e. $\theta = 0, \dfrac{2\pi}{3}, \dfrac{4\pi}{3}$ when $\theta \in [0, 2\pi)$. Finally we bring all information together to state all solutions $z = \boxed{2 \operatorname{cis} 0}$, $\boxed{2 \operatorname{cis} \dfrac{2\pi}{3}}$, and $\boxed{2 \operatorname{cis} \dfrac{4\pi}{3}}$.

Check that both sets of answers are the same. □

Problem 7.3.24. Write down all solutions to $z^5 = -243$.

Solution. As usual, rewrite -243 as $243 \operatorname{cis} \pi$. Letting $z = r \operatorname{cis} \theta$, we get $(r \operatorname{cis} \theta)^5 = 243 \operatorname{cis} \pi$, or $r^5 \operatorname{cis} 5\theta = 243 \operatorname{cis} \pi$ using De Moivre's Theorem. We have $z = 3$ and $5\theta = \pi + 2\pi k$, or $\theta = \dfrac{\pi}{5} + \dfrac{2\pi}{5}k$, and when restricting θ to the interval $[0, 2\pi)$, we have the solutions $\theta = \dfrac{\pi}{5}, \dfrac{3\pi}{5}, \pi, \dfrac{7\pi}{5}$, and $\dfrac{9\pi}{5}$. Therefore all the solutions to z are $\boxed{3 \operatorname{cis} \dfrac{\pi}{5}}, \boxed{3 \operatorname{cis} \dfrac{3\pi}{5}}, \boxed{3 \operatorname{cis} \pi}, \boxed{3 \operatorname{cis} \dfrac{7\pi}{5}}$, and $\boxed{3 \operatorname{cis} \dfrac{9\pi}{5}}$. □

Problem 7.3.25. What are the five fifth roots of i? Then, find their sum and product.

Solution. Following the usual procedure: $z^5 = i \implies (r\operatorname{cis}\theta)^5 = 1 \cdot \operatorname{cis}\frac{\pi}{2} \implies r^5 \operatorname{cis} 5\theta = 1 \cdot \operatorname{cis}\frac{\pi}{2}$, yielding $r = 1$ and $\theta = \frac{\pi}{10} + \frac{2\pi}{5}k$, i.e. $\theta = \frac{\pi}{10}, \frac{\pi}{2}, \frac{9\pi}{10}, \frac{13\pi}{10}, \frac{17\pi}{10}$. Therefore the solutions to z are $\boxed{\operatorname{cis}\frac{\pi}{10}}, \boxed{\operatorname{cis}\frac{\pi}{2}}, \boxed{\operatorname{cis}\frac{9\pi}{10}}, \boxed{\operatorname{cis}\frac{13\pi}{10}}, \boxed{\operatorname{cis}\frac{17\pi}{10}}$.

To find their sum and product, we must recall that the fifth roots of i are essentially the roots of the equation $z^5 - i = 0$. This is a polynomial! Therefore we can apply Vieta's Formulas to determine that the sum is $\boxed{0}$ and the product is $\boxed{i}$. □

Problem 7.3.26. If the five fifth roots of i are $\omega_1, \omega_2, \omega_3, \omega_4$, and ω_5, what is $\prod_{k=1}^{5}(2 - \omega_k)$?

Solution. As previously stated, the polynomial that has these roots is $z^5 - i = 0$. Therefore

$$z^5 - i = (z - \omega_1)(z - \omega_2)(z - \omega_3)(z - \omega_4)(z - \omega_5) = \prod_{k=1}^{5}(z - \omega_k).$$

Thus our answer is simply plugging in $z = 2$, which gives us $\boxed{32 - i}$. □

Problem 7.3.27. Find all solutions to $z^5 = 16\sqrt{3} - 16i$.

Solution. As usual, we use De Moivre's Theorem and compare the magnitude and argument:

$$(r\operatorname{cis}\theta)^5 = 32\left(\frac{\sqrt{3}}{2} - \frac{1}{2}i\right)$$
$$r^5 \operatorname{cis} 5\theta = 32 \operatorname{cis}\left(-\frac{\pi}{6}\right)$$
$$r = 2,\ 5\theta = -\frac{\pi}{6} + 2\pi k$$
$$\theta = -\frac{\pi}{30} + \frac{2\pi}{5}k.$$

Therefore $z = \boxed{2\operatorname{cis}\frac{11\pi}{30}}, \boxed{2\operatorname{cis}\frac{23\pi}{30}}, \boxed{2\operatorname{cis}\frac{35\pi}{30}}, \boxed{2\operatorname{cis}\frac{47\pi}{30}}$, and $\boxed{2\operatorname{cis}\frac{59\pi}{30}}$. □

Exercise 7.3.28. Write in polar form all solutions to $z^5 = -1 + i$, $z \in \mathbb{C}$.

Exercise 7.3.29. Write the six solutions to $z^6 = -64i$ in polar form, then convert two of them to complex form.

7.3.3 Rotation

Expressing complex numbers in polar form allows us to easily rotate points. Consider the following diagram:

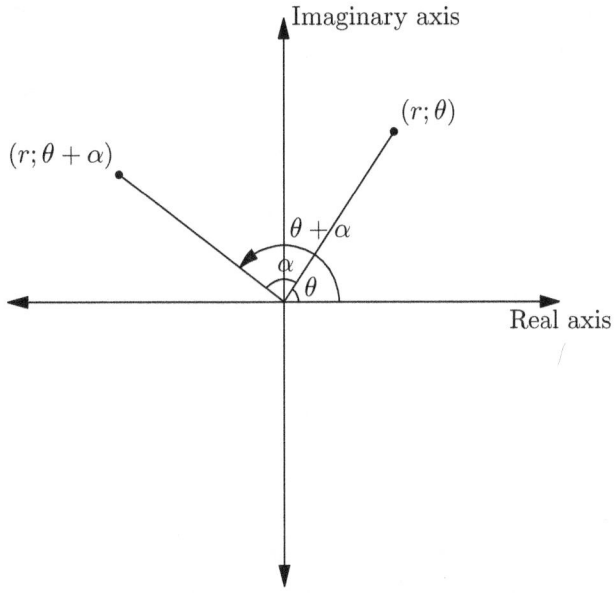

Recall that $r \operatorname{cis}(\theta + \alpha) = (r \operatorname{cis} \theta) \cdot \operatorname{cis} \alpha$. Thus, if we are given some complex number $z = a + bi = r \operatorname{cis} \theta$, we can easily rotate it around the origin counter-clockwise by an angle α by multiplying z by $\operatorname{cis} \alpha$.

Thus, the complex number that results from rotating $a + bi$ by an angle of α counterclockwise is:

$$(a + bi)(\cos \alpha + i \sin \alpha) = (a \cos \alpha - b \sin \alpha) + (a \sin \alpha + b \cos \alpha)i.$$

Then, if we convert this complex number back to coordinates, we conclude that the rotation of the point (a, b) by the angle α around the origin is

$$(a \cos \alpha - b \sin \alpha, a \sin \alpha + b \cos \alpha).$$

Problem 7.3.30. Rotate $(3, 4)$ around the origin by $60°$ counter-clockwise.

Solution. Simple application of the formula yields:

$$(3 \cos 60° - 4 \sin 60°, 3 \sin 60° + 4 \cos 60°) = \boxed{\left(\frac{3}{2} - 2\sqrt{3}, \frac{3\sqrt{3}}{2} + 2\right)}.$$ □

Problem 7.3.31. Rotate (x, y) $90°$ counter-clockwise.

Solution. Another straightforward application of the formula:

$$(x \cos 90° - y \sin 90°, x \sin 90° + y \cos 90°) = \boxed{(-y, x)}.$$ □

Problem 7.3.32. Rotate $(1, -4)$ around $(2, 3)$ counterclockwise by $60°$.

Solution. We must turn this problem into something we know how to do, which is rotating around the origin.

Observe how we can shift all points by -2 on the x-axis and -3 on the y-axis in order to have $(2, 3)$ 'become' the origin. Therefore this problem is equivalent to rotating $(1 - 2, -4 - 3) = (-1, -7)$ around the origin by $60°$ counter-clockwise, then shifting the point back 2 right and 3 up. Using the formula, we have

$$(-1 \cdot \cos 60° + 7 \sin 60°, -1 \cdot \sin 60° - 7 \cos 60°) = \left(\frac{7\sqrt{3} - 1}{2}, -\frac{7 + \sqrt{3}}{2}\right)$$

as the rotated point from $(-1, -7)$ around the origin. Now we can shift the point by adding 2 to the x-coordinate and 3 to the y-coordinate to get our answer:

$$\left(\frac{7\sqrt{3} - 1}{2} + 2, -\frac{7 + \sqrt{3}}{2} + 3\right) = \boxed{\left(\frac{7\sqrt{3} + 3}{2}, -\frac{1 + \sqrt{3}}{2}\right)}. \qquad \square$$

Now we shift our focus to conic sections. The method of rotating points that we have discovered earlier can be utilized in a certain fashion (also known as a *coordinate substitution*) to rotate general functions, particularly conics.

While functions from complex numbers to complex numbers are impossible to graph, functions of the form $f(z) = 0$ are possible. Graphs of $f(z) = 0$ correspond to graphs of $f(x, y) = 0$ in the Cartesian plane, so we will instead deal with those. Consider the following diagram.

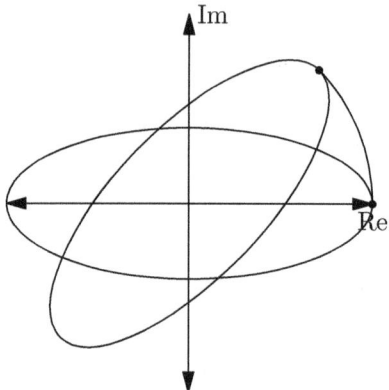

In this figure, let the original ellipse be horizontal along the x-axis. The ellipse is rotated some angle α counterclockwise. Note that if we rotate any point on the rotated ellipse clockwise by α, then we get a point on the original ellipse.

For example, the point on the rotated ellipse gives us the point on the original ellipse when rotated. Therefore, if the equation of the original ellipse is $f(x, y) = 0$, then the equation of the rotated ellipse should be $f(\text{the point } (x, y) \text{ rotated } \alpha \text{ clockwise}) = 0$. However, we now have a coordinate substitution that gives us the coordinates after rotation! Substituting in our formulas (and noting that rotating clockwise by α is the same as rotating counterclockwise by $-\alpha$), the equation for the rotated ellipse is

$$f(x\cos(-\alpha) - y\sin(-\alpha), x\sin(-\alpha) + y\cos(-\alpha)) = 0.$$

In general, we can conclude that given a function $f(x, y) = 0$, the new equation

$$f(x\cos(-\alpha) - y\sin(-\alpha), x\sin(-\alpha) + y\cos(-\alpha)) = 0$$

is a rotation of $f(x, y) = 0$ by an angle of α.

Problem 7.3.33. Rotate $y = 2x$ by $60°$ counter-clockwise.

Solution. For clarity, rearrange this to $y - 2x = 0$. We then use the stated formula and make appropriate substitutions to x and y:

$$(x\sin(-60°) + y\cos(-60°)) - 2(x\cos(-60°) - y\sin(-60°)) = 0.$$

This rearranges to $\left(-\dfrac{x\sqrt{3}}{2} + \dfrac{y}{2}\right) - 2\left(\dfrac{x}{2} + \dfrac{y\sqrt{3}}{2}\right) = 0$, or $\dfrac{y}{2} - y\sqrt{3} = x + \dfrac{x\sqrt{3}}{2}$. After much simplification, we end up with $\boxed{y = -\dfrac{8 + 5\sqrt{3}}{11}x}$. □

Theorem 7.3.34

Consider the general equation for a conic section:

$$Ax^2 + Bxy + Cy^2 + Dx + Ey + F = 0.$$

We call the value $B^2 - 4AC$ the **conic discriminant**. Assuming that the conic is not degenerate:

- If $B^2 - 4AC < 0$, then the conic is an ellipse.
- If $B^2 - 4AC = 0$, then the conic is a parabola.
- If $B^2 - 4AC > 0$, then the conic is a hyperbola.

Proof. We first attempt to get rid of the x and y terms of that general conic equation by translating it. Translations are characterized by the transformations $x \to x - r$ and $y \to y - s$. Substituting, we have this equation:

$$A(x-r)^2 + B(x-r)(y-s) + C(y-s)^2 + D(x-r) + E(y-s) + F = 0.$$

After expanding, the resulting coefficient of x is $D - 2Ar - Bs$ and the y coefficient is $E - 2Cs - Br$. In order for both of these to equal 0 (and therefore eliminate those terms), we have

$$D = 2Ar + Bs,$$

$$E = Br + 2Cs.$$

We then solve for r and s, which are the translations necessary to get rid of the x and y terms:

$$r = \frac{BE - 2CD}{B^2 - 4AC},$$
$$s = \frac{BD - 2AE}{B^2 - 4AC}.$$

Thus, if the quantity $B^2 - 4AC \neq 0$, then we can translate the conic such that there are no x nor y terms. Note also that the coefficients A, B, and C all stay the same under this transformation. We now split into two different cases: $4AC - B^2 = 0$ and $4AC - B^2 \neq 0$.

- Case 1: $B^2 - 4AC \neq 0$

  Assuming $B^2 - 4AC \neq 0$, then we have successfully eliminated the x and y terms, so we just want to deal with equations of the form $Ax^2 + Bxy + Cy^2 + F = 0$ (remember, the values A, B, C, and F all stayed the same under that transformation, so we can still use these variables for this new equation).

  We now try to rotate the conic by some angle θ to get rid of the xy term. As stated in Theorem 8, we can make the transformations $x \to x\cos\theta - y\sin\theta$ and $y \to x\sin\theta + y\cos\theta$. Making our substitutions, we have the equation

  $$A(x\cos\theta - y\sin\theta)^2 + B(x\cos\theta - y\sin\theta)(x\sin\theta + y\cos\theta) + C(x\sin\theta + y\cos\theta)^2 + F$$

  Expanding and rearranging according to our x^2, xy, and y^2 terms, we are left with:

  $$(A\cos^2\theta + B\sin\theta\cos\theta + C\sin^2\theta)x^2$$
  $$+ (B\cos 2\theta + (C - A)\sin 2\theta)xy$$
  $$+ (A\sin^2\theta - B\sin\theta\cos\theta + C\cos^2\theta)y^2 + K = 0$$

  Our original purpose was to eliminate the xy term, so we set the coefficient of the xy term equal to 0:

  $$B\cos 2\theta + (C - A)\sin 2\theta = 0.$$

  Rearranging, we have:

  $$B\cos 2\theta = (A - C)\sin 2\theta.$$

  If $A \neq C$, then we can conclude that

  $$\tan 2\theta = \frac{B}{A - C}.$$

  If $A = C$, then we have $\cos 2\theta = 0$, or $\theta = 45°$. Either way, we have found an expression for θ that can eliminate the xy term.

  After finally eliminating the xy term, we now have the new conic equation $\tilde{a}x^2 + \tilde{c}y^2 + F = 0$ (we cannot use the initial A, B, C variables again because the coefficients of x^2 and y^2 have changed due to the rotation by θ). Based on what we know about conic sections so far:

- If $\tilde{a}, \tilde{c}$ have the same sign, then the conic is an ellipse.
- If $\tilde{a}, \tilde{c}$ have opposite signs, then the conic is a hyperbola.

To figure out whether $\tilde{a}$ and $\tilde{c}$ have same signs or not, we multiply them together: if the product is negative, then they have different signs, and if the product is positive, then they have the same signs.

Recall from the expanded equation stated earlier that $\tilde{a} = A\cos^2\theta + B\sin\theta\cos\theta + C\sin^2\theta$ and $\tilde{c} = A\sin^2\theta - B\sin\theta\cos\theta + C\cos^2\theta$. We have to figure out the sign of this unwieldy product:

$$(A\cos^2\theta + B\sin\theta\cos\theta + C\sin^2\theta) \cdot (A\sin^2\theta - B\sin\theta\cos\theta + C\cos^2\theta).$$

Without loss of generality, we can double each of these expressions, because multiplying by 2 would not influence the sign of the product.

$$(A \cdot 2\cos^2\theta + B \cdot 2\sin\theta\cos\theta + C \cdot 2\sin^2\theta) \cdot (A \cdot 2\sin^2\theta - B \cdot 2\sin\theta\cos\theta + C \cdot 2\cos^2\theta).$$

As one may observe, doubling these expressions has enabled us to be able to conveniently apply our known trigonometric identities:

$$(A \cdot (\cos 2\theta + 1) + B\sin 2\theta + C \cdot (1 - \cos 2\theta)) \cdot (A \cdot (1 - \cos 2\theta) - B\sin 2\theta + C \cdot (1 + \cos 2\theta)).$$

Simplifying further, we have:

$$((A+C) + (A-C)\cos 2\theta + B\sin 2\theta) \cdot ((A+C) - (A-C)\cos 2\theta - B\sin 2\theta).$$

At this point, we cannot proceed without discussing the value of θ. As concluded earlier, we have either $\tan 2\theta = \dfrac{B}{A-C}$ or $\theta = 45°$. Consider both cases:

- Case 1.1: $\tan 2\theta = \dfrac{B}{A-C}$.

  We must find the expressions of $\sin 2\theta$ and $\cos 2\theta$ in terms of A, B, and C. We can accomplish this with the use of a reference triangle (constructed such that the tangent of an angle 2θ is equal to the ratio of the opposite side to the adjacent side), as shown:

  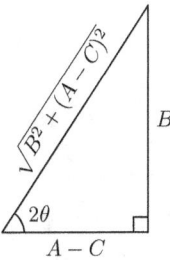

  We can then read our values:

  $$\sin 2\theta = \frac{B}{\sqrt{B^2 + (A-C)^2}},$$

$$\cos 2\theta = \frac{A-C}{\sqrt{B^2+(A-C)^2}}.$$

Looking back at our expression,

$$((A+C)+(A-C)\cos 2\theta + B\sin 2\theta) \cdot ((A+C)-(A-C)\cos 2\theta - B\sin 2\theta),$$

we substitute in $\sin 2\theta$ and $\cos 2\theta$ to get:

$$\left((A+C)+\sqrt{B^2+(A-C)^2}\right)\left((A+C)-\sqrt{B^2+(A-C)^2}\right).$$

This is simply a difference of squares, and we simplify to end up with:

$$(A+C)^2 - (B^2+(A-C))^2 = 4AC - B^2.$$

If $4AC - B^2$ is positive, then $\tilde{a}$ and $\tilde{c}$ have the same sign, therefore the conic is an ellipse. Note that $4AC - B^2 > 0 \implies B^2 - 4AC < 0$, and so we have proven the 'ellipse' of the theorem.

If $4AC - B^2$ is negative, then $\tilde{a}$ and $\tilde{c}$ have different signs, therefore the conic is a hyperbola. Note that $4AC - B^2 < 0 \implies B^2 - 4AC > 0$, and so we have proven the 'hyperbola' of the theorem.

– Case 1.2: $\theta = 45°$.

Our expression,

$$((A+C)+(A-C)\cos 2\theta + B\sin 2\theta) \cdot ((A+C)-(A-C)\cos 2\theta - B\sin 2\theta),$$

is simplified tremendously when $\theta = 45°$ is plugged in:

$$(A+B+C)(A-B+C).$$

However, recall that $\theta = 45°$ iff $A = C$. Therefore, the expression above is equal to $(2A+B)(2A-B) = 4A^2 - B^2 = 4AC - B^2$, and now we can make the same conclusion as Case 1.1.

- Case 2: $B^2 - 4AC = 0$

Let's go back to our original general equation of a conic section:

$$Ax^2 + Bxy + Cy^2 + Dx + Ey + F = 0.$$

Note that $Ax^2 + Bxy + Cy^2$ is a square if and only if $B^2 - 4AC = 0$. To see why this is true, recall the quadratic formula $\dfrac{-B \pm \sqrt{B^2 - 4AC}}{2A}$ (which is an expression for the roots of the quadratic). If $B^2 - 4AC = 0$, then the square root term is eliminated and there is no plus-minus case to consider, resulting in double roots (both roots are the same), so the expression is a square of another expression.

Thus, let $Ax^2 + Bxy + Cy^2 = (mx + ny)^2$ for arbitrary $m, n \in \mathbb{R}$. Substituting, we now have the equation

$$(mx+ny)^2 + Dx + Ey + F = 0.$$

We are trying to prove that $B^2 - 4AC = 0$ implies that the conic is a parabola. Therefore we seek to eliminate the y^2 term so we are left with an equation with only y, x^2, and x as variables. Like the first case, we perform the rotation $x \to x\cos\theta - y\sin\theta$ and $y \to x\sin\theta + y\cos\theta$ in hopes of getting rid of the y^2 term:

$$(m(x\cos\theta - y\sin\theta) + n(x\sin\theta + y\cos\theta))^2 + D(x\cos\theta - y\sin\theta) + E(x\sin\theta + y\cos\theta) + F = 0.$$

Rewrite this equation so that it is clear what the coefficients of x^2, y^2, x, and y are:

$$(x(m\cos\theta + n\sin\theta) + y(n\cos\theta - m\sin\theta))^2 + x(D\cos\theta + E\sin\theta) + y(E\cos\theta - D\sin\theta) + F = 0.$$

Now it is clear that the only source of the y^2 term is $n\cos\theta - m\sin\theta$ which is the coefficient of the y term inside the squared expression. Therefore we set $n\cos\theta - m\sin\theta = 0$, or $\tan\theta = \dfrac{n}{m}$.

Note that the equation now will resemble this:

$$(x \cdot (\text{some expression}))^2 + \widetilde{D}x + \widetilde{E}y + \widetilde{F} = 0,$$

for arbitrary coefficients $\widetilde{D}$, $\widetilde{E}$, and $\widetilde{F}$.

At last, we now have shown that we can rotate the conic by a chosen angle θ (such that $\tan\theta = \dfrac{n}{m}$), to end up with an equation that is a parabola. Therefore, $B^2 - 4AC = 0 \implies$ the conic is a parabola. $\square$

Exercise 7.3.35. Prove that the parametrically defined graph $x = t^2 + t$, $y = t^2 + 1$ is a parabola.

Chapter 8

Linear Algebra

In this chapter, we will touch upon the basics of linear algebra, particularly vectors and matrices. Then we discuss their applications in 2D and 3D geometry.

This chapter will only serve as a general introduction of linear algebra, so some proofs will be omitted as they would be beyond the scope of this book. More emphasis will be placed on showing how certain concepts are related to each other, as well as key observations to be made, rather than utmost mathematical rigor. For in-depth study of linear algebra, feel free to explore courses offered by universities or purchase books in Linear Algebra.

8.1 Vectors

Definition 8.1.1. A **vector** is characterized by its **magnitude** and **direction**.

The following would be some examples which constitute vectors:

- $\vec{v}$: 12 ft. east

- $\vec{w}$: 5 in. north

We represent the concept of vectors with arrows, however every vector is unique by its magnitude and direction. Although we can draw more than one arrow with the same length and direction, remember that they all denote the same vector. Some representations of vectors are illustrated below:

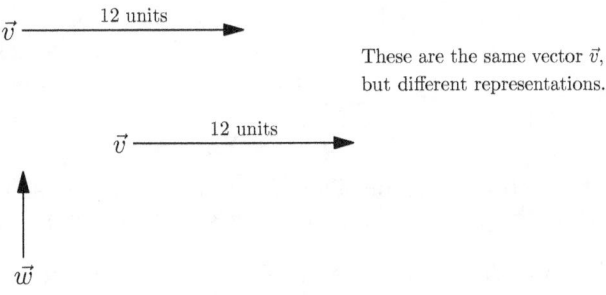

Furthermore, we define two important parts of the vector:

Now we consider the idea of adding two vectors together:

Definition 8.1.2 (Vector Addition). $\vec{v} + \vec{w}$ can be described as follows: Take a representation of $\vec{v}$. Create a representation of $\vec{w}$ by placing the tail of $\vec{w}$ at the tip of $\vec{v}$. We form a new vector by taking the tail of $\vec{v}$ to the tip of $\vec{w}$.

This is demonstrated in the following diagram:

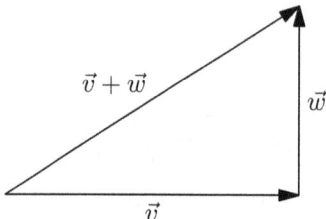

Example 8.1.3
Show that $\vec{v} + \vec{w}$ is unique.

Proof. Given the diagram below, we need to show that the lengths AC and $A'C'$ are equal (that $\vec{v} + \vec{w}$ has a concrete value no matter what representations of $\vec{v}$ and $\vec{w}$ are taken).

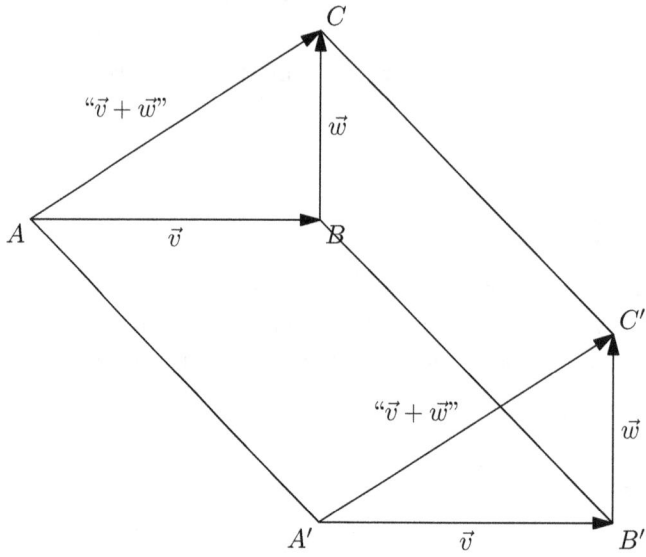

First, note that the both vectors $\vec{v}$ are parallel (i.e. pointing in the same direction) and equal in magnitude. So are the two $\vec{w}$ vectors. Therefore, $ABB'A$ and $BCC'B'$ are parallelograms.

This implies $AA' \cong BB'$ and $BB' \cong CC'$, and by the transitive property, $AA' \cong CC'$.

Furthermore, since $ABB'A$ and $BCC'B'$ are parallelograms, $AA' \parallel BB'$ and $BB' \parallel CC'$, therefore $AA' \parallel CC'$.

Since $AA' \cong CC'$ and $AA' \parallel CC'$, we can conclude that $ACC'A'$ is a parallelogram, therefore $AC = A'C' = \vec{v} + \vec{w}$, a well-defined value. $\square$

Problem 8.1.4. From this definition of vector addition, prove the following:

1. $\vec{v} + \vec{w} = \vec{w} + \vec{v}$

2. $\vec{u} + (\vec{v} + \vec{w}) = (\vec{u} + \vec{v}) + \vec{w}$

Proof.

1. Consider the following diagram:

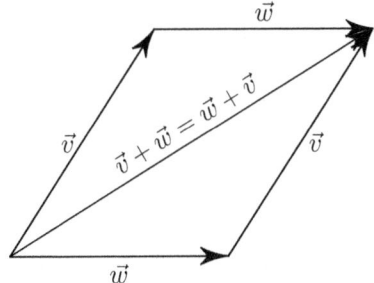

Simply use two different representations of vector $\vec{v}$ and two different representations of vector $\vec{w}$ such that the resulting vector $\vec{v} + \vec{w}$ is the same as $\vec{w} + \vec{v}$.

2. Consider the following diagram:

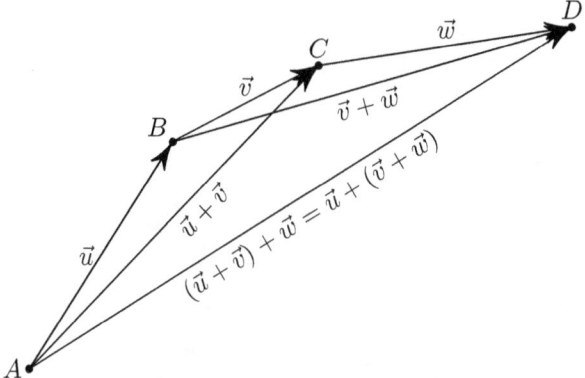

Let $\vec{u}$ be represented by $\overrightarrow{AB}$, $\vec{v}$ be represented by $\overrightarrow{BC}$, and $\vec{w}$ be represented by $\overrightarrow{CD}$. Therefore $\vec{u} + \vec{v}$ is represented by $\overrightarrow{AC}$, and we can conclude that $\overrightarrow{AD}$ represents $(\vec{u} + \vec{v}) + \vec{w}$, or $\overrightarrow{AC} + \overrightarrow{CD}$.

However, $\overrightarrow{AD}$ also represents $\vec{u} + (\vec{v} + \vec{w})$, or $\overrightarrow{AB} + \overrightarrow{BD}$. Since $\overrightarrow{AD}$ represents both $(\vec{u} + \vec{v}) + \vec{w}$ and $\vec{u} + (\vec{v} + \vec{w})$, we can conclude that these are the same vector. $\square$

Definition 8.1.5. Let a **scalar** be a real number. If $k \in \mathbb{R}^+$, we define $k\vec{v}$ to be the vector in the same direction as $\vec{v}$ but with k times the magnitude.

Exercise 8.1.6. From this definition of a scalar, two distributive properties follow:

1. $k(\vec{v} + \vec{w}) = k\vec{v} + k\vec{w}$

2. $(k + l)\vec{v} = k\vec{v} + l\vec{v}$

Prove these using similar triangles.

Definition 8.1.7. The **zero vector**, $\vec{0}$, is the vector of magnitude 0 in any direction.

Definition 8.1.8. $-\vec{v}$ is the vector which when added to $\vec{v}$, gives us $\vec{0}$ (i.e. $-\vec{v}$ is the same magnitude as $\vec{v}$, but in the opposite direction).

It follows that we have another associative property: $(kl)\vec{v} = k(l\vec{v})$ for $k, l \in \mathbb{R}$. Feel free to prove this on your own.

Problem 8.1.9. Prove $-1 \cdot \vec{v} = -\vec{v}$.

Proof. Using the distributive property, note that $-1 \cdot \vec{v} + 1 \cdot \vec{v} = (-1 + 1) \cdot \vec{v} = 0 \cdot \vec{v} = \vec{0}$. Therefore, $-1 \cdot v + \vec{v} = \vec{0}$, so by the previous definition, $-1 \cdot v = -\vec{v}$. □

Definition 8.1.10 (Vector Subtraction). Given $\vec{v}, \vec{w}$, we can define $\vec{v} - \vec{w}$ to be that vector, which when added to $\vec{w}$, gives us $\vec{v}$.

Here is a geometric interpretation:

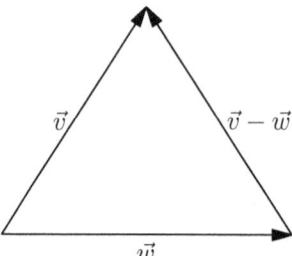

Furthermore, note that $-\vec{w}$ has the same magnitude as $\vec{w}$ but in the opposite direction, therefore we can have another representation:

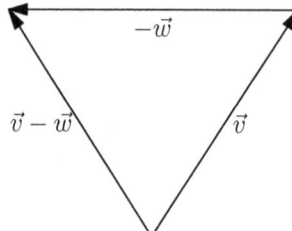

We can see that the vector $\vec{v} - \vec{w}$ is the same in both of these scenarios.

Definition 8.1.11. We now introduce new notation that is not universally standard, but we will be using this notation from now on:

In the two-dimensional plane, denote the vector $\langle a, b \rangle$ as the vector that represents the overall path taken when going a horizontally and b vertically from any starting point.

Here is a geometric example:

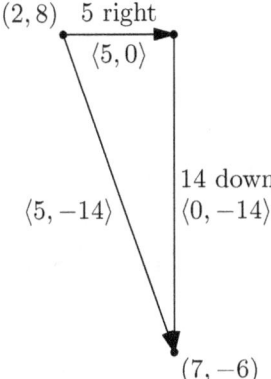

Given a vector $\langle a_1, a_2, \ldots, a_n \rangle$, we would call $a_1, a_2, \ldots, a_n$ the **components** of that vector.

Exercise 8.1.12. What would be the vector that connects the point (r, s) to the point (t, u)?

Definition 8.1.13. We define a set of special *unit* vectors:

- $\vec{i} = \langle 1, 0 \rangle$ in 2D and $\langle 1, 0, 0 \rangle$ in 3D.
- $\vec{j} = \langle 0, 1 \rangle$ in 2D and $\langle 0, 1, 0 \rangle$ in 3D.
- $\vec{k} = \langle 0, 0, 1 \rangle$ in 3D.

A vector of magnitude 1 is called a **unit vector**.

We can define more unit vectors for greater dimensions, and we will do so at a later part of this chapter.

Using these vectors, we can establish the relation

$$\langle a, b \rangle = a\vec{i} + b\vec{j},$$

allowing us to break down any vector in terms of the unit vectors. We will revisit this idea later in the chapter.

Definition 8.1.14. Let $\|\vec{v}\|$ denote the magnitude of $\vec{v}$.

For a two-dimensional vector $\langle a, b \rangle$, $\|\langle a, b \rangle\| = \sqrt{a^2 + b^2}$.

For a three-dimensional vector $\langle a, b, c \rangle$, $\|\langle a, b, c \rangle\| = \sqrt{a^2 + b^2 + c^2}$. The pattern follows for higher dimensions.

In accordance with this definition, $\|\vec{v}\| \geq 0$ with equality iff $\vec{v} = \vec{0}$.

Problem 8.1.15. Find $\|\langle 3, 4\rangle\|$, $\|\vec{i}\|$, and $\|\langle 1, 2, 3\rangle\|$.

Solution. The vector $\langle 3, 4\rangle$ means that we're going 3 up and 4 to the right, so we have $\|\langle 3, 4\rangle\| = \sqrt{3^2 + 4^2} = \sqrt{25} = \boxed{5}$. It is evident that $\|\vec{i}\| = \boxed{1}$, since we are only going 1 unit right. Lastly, $\|\langle 1, 2, 3\rangle\| = \sqrt{1^2 + 2^2 + 3^2} = \boxed{\sqrt{14}}$. □

The magnitude of a vector follows with a couple of properties:

1. $\|k\vec{v}\| = |k|\|\vec{v}\|$
2. $\|\vec{v} + \vec{w}\| \leq \|\vec{v}\| + \|\vec{w}\|$ with equality if and only if $\vec{v}, \vec{w}$ are in the same direction.

The first one is easily provable, while a proof for the second one is nearly identical to that of Problem 7.3.4.

Problem 8.1.16. Find vectors in the same direction as $\langle 2, 3\rangle$ of:

1. Magnitude 1.
2. Magnitude 7.

Solution.

1. We find that $\|\langle 2, 3\rangle\| = \sqrt{2^2 + 3^2} = \sqrt{13}$. Therefore we must scale our vector by a factor of $\dfrac{1}{\sqrt{13}}$ in order to scale its magnitude to 1. Therefore our new vector is $\dfrac{1}{\sqrt{13}} \langle 2, 3\rangle = \left\langle \dfrac{2}{\sqrt{13}}, \dfrac{3}{\sqrt{13}} \right\rangle$.

2. Similarly, since we have found our vector $\left\langle \dfrac{2}{\sqrt{13}}, \dfrac{3}{\sqrt{13}} \right\rangle$ of magnitude 1 in the same direction of the original vector, we can simply scale that vector by a factor of 7 to get: $\left\langle \dfrac{14}{\sqrt{13}}, \dfrac{21}{\sqrt{13}} \right\rangle$. □

Now, we introduce the concept of **angles** to vectors. Consider the following vectors:

The vectors $\vec{v}$, $\vec{w}$, and $\vec{v} - \vec{w}$ form a triangle. We can then apply the Law of Cosines to find out the value of angle θ between vectors $\vec{v}$ and $\vec{w}$:

$$\|\vec{v} - \vec{w}\|^2 = \|\vec{v}\|^2 + \|\vec{w}\|^2 - 2\|\vec{v}\|\|\vec{w}\|\cos\theta.$$

Solving for θ, this rearranges to

$$\cos\theta = \frac{\|\vec{v}\|^2 + \|\vec{w}\|^2 - \|\vec{v} - \vec{w}\|^2}{2\|\vec{v}\|\|\vec{w}\|}.$$

We arbitrarily let $\vec{v} = \langle a, b \rangle$ and $\vec{w} = \langle c, d \rangle$, which implies $\vec{v} - \vec{w} = \langle a - c, b - d \rangle$. Therefore, using the definition of magnitude, we make substitutions in the numerator (we will keep the denominator the same to keep our expression from becoming too messy):

$$\cos \theta = \frac{a^2 + b^2 + c^2 + d^2 - \left((a-c)^2 + (b-d)^2\right)}{2\|\vec{v}\|\|\vec{w}\|}$$

$$= \frac{2ac + 2bd}{2\|\vec{v}\|\|\vec{w}\|}$$

$$= \frac{ac + bd}{\|\vec{v}\|\|\vec{w}\|}.$$

Notice that $ac + bd$ is the result of taking the sum of the product of the first coordinates and the product of the second coordinates of $\vec{v}$ and $\vec{w}$. This quantity is extremely useful and significant in the use of vectors, and so we will define this unique operation:

Definition 8.1.17. Given vectors $\langle a_1, a_2, \ldots, a_n \rangle$ and $\langle b_1, b_2, \ldots, b_n \rangle$, the **dot product** is denoted as:

$$\langle a_1, a_2, \ldots, a_n \rangle \cdot \langle b_1, b_2, \ldots, b_n \rangle = \sum_{i=1}^{n} a_i b_i.$$

Then, we have the following properties:

1. $\forall a \in \mathbb{R}, \, a\vec{v} \cdot \vec{w} = a(\vec{v} \cdot \vec{w})$.

2. $\vec{u} \cdot (\vec{v} + \vec{w}) = \vec{u} \cdot \vec{v} + \vec{u} \cdot \vec{w}$.

   Proof. Let $\vec{u} = \langle a, b \rangle$, $\vec{v} = \langle c, d \rangle$, $\vec{w} = \langle e, f \rangle$. Then $\vec{u} \cdot (\vec{v} + \vec{w}) = \langle a, b \rangle \cdot (\langle c + e, d + f \rangle) = a(c + e) + b(d + f) = ac + ae + bd + bf$.
   Likewise, $\vec{u} \cdot \vec{v} + \vec{u} \cdot \vec{w} = \langle a, b \rangle \cdot \langle c, d \rangle + \langle a, b \rangle \cdot \langle e, f \rangle = ac + bd + ae + bf = ac + ae + bd + bf$, therefore $\vec{u} \cdot (\vec{v} + \vec{w}) = \vec{u} \cdot \vec{v} + \vec{u} \cdot \vec{w}$. □

3. $\vec{u} \cdot \vec{u} = \|\vec{u}\|^2$.

   Proof. When we let $\vec{u} = \langle a, b \rangle$, we end up with $\langle a, b \rangle \cdot \langle a, b \rangle = a \cdot a + b \cdot b = a^2 + b^2 = \|\vec{u}\|^2$. □

4. $(\vec{u} + \vec{v}) \cdot (\vec{u} - \vec{v}) = \|\vec{u}\|^2 - \|\vec{v}\|^2$.

   Proof. We use our previously declared definitions and make the proper substitutions.

   $$(\vec{u} + \vec{v})(\vec{u} - \vec{v}) = (\vec{u} + \vec{v}) \cdot \vec{u} + (\vec{u} + \vec{v}) \cdot (-\vec{v})$$
   $$= \vec{u} \cdot \vec{u} + \vec{u} \cdot \vec{v} + (\vec{u} + \vec{v}) \cdot (-1 \cdot \vec{v})$$
   $$= \|\vec{u}\|^2 + \vec{u} \cdot \vec{v} + (-1(\vec{u} + \vec{v})) \cdot \vec{v}$$
   $$= \|\vec{u}\|^2 + \vec{u} \cdot \vec{v} + (-\vec{u} - \vec{v}) \cdot \vec{v}$$
   $$= \|\vec{u}\|^2 + \vec{u} \cdot \vec{v} - \vec{u} \cdot \vec{v} - \vec{v} \cdot \vec{v}$$
   $$= \|\vec{u}\|^2 - \|\vec{v}\|^2.$$
   □

Now that we have defined the dot product, we can rewrite $\cos \theta$ with a simpler, cleaner expression.

Theorem 8.1.18

Given two vectors $\vec{v}$ and $\vec{w}$ and the angle θ between their representations such that they share the same tail, we have the following relationship:

$$\cos\theta = \frac{\vec{v}\cdot\vec{w}}{\|\vec{v}\|\|\vec{w}\|}.$$

This formula extends to higher dimensions.

Problem 8.1.19. What is the angle between $\langle 1,2\rangle$ and $\langle 2,1\rangle$?

Solution. The dot product $\langle 1,2\rangle\cdot\langle 2,1\rangle = 1\cdot 2+2\cdot 1 = 4$, $\|\langle 1,2\rangle\| = \sqrt{5}$, and $\|\langle 2,1\rangle\| = \sqrt{5}$, therefore $\cos\theta = \dfrac{4}{\sqrt{5}\cdot\sqrt{5}} = \dfrac{4}{5}$, and thus $\theta = \boxed{\cos^{-1}\left(\dfrac{4}{5}\right)}$ since $\langle 1,2\rangle$ and $\langle 2,1\rangle$ have representations in the first quadrant in the Cartesian plane when their tails are placed at the origin. $\square$

Problem 8.1.20. Find the angle between $\langle 1,2,3\rangle$ and $\langle 3,4,5\rangle$.

Solution. We have

$$\cos\theta = \frac{\langle 1,2,3\rangle\cdot\langle 3,4,5\rangle}{\|\langle 1,2,3\rangle\|\|\langle 3,4,5\rangle\|} = \frac{1\cdot 3+2\cdot 4+3\cdot 5}{\sqrt{1^2+2^2+3^2}\cdot\sqrt{3^2+4^2+5^2}} = \frac{13}{5\sqrt{7}}.$$

Therefore $\theta = \boxed{\cos^{-1}\left(\dfrac{13}{5\sqrt{7}}\right)}$. $\square$

Problem 8.1.21. Find all values of m for which the angle between vectors $\langle 1,1\rangle$ and $\langle 1,m\rangle$ is $60°$.

Solution. We have

$$\cos 60° = \frac{1+m}{\sqrt{2}\cdot\sqrt{1+m^2}}.$$

Since $\cos 60° = \dfrac{1}{2}$, we end up with $\sqrt{2+2m^2} = 2+2m$. After squaring both sides and simplifying, the equation reduces to $m^2+4m+1 = 0$. The quadratic formula yields $m = -2\pm\sqrt{3}$.

However, since $\cos 60° = \dfrac{1}{2} > 0$, we cannot have $\dfrac{1+m}{\sqrt{2}\cdot\sqrt{1+m^2}}$ be negative. When we plug in $m = -2-\sqrt{3}$, we end up with a negative value. Therefore $-2-\sqrt{3}$ cannot be a solution of m.

Then, $m = \boxed{-2+\sqrt{3}}$ yields a positive value and thus it is the only value of m which satisfies the conditions. $\square$

Definition 8.1.22. $\vec{v}$ and $\vec{w}$ are **orthogonal** if any representation of $\vec{v}$ is perpendicular to any representation of $\vec{w}$.

> **Theorem 8.1.23**
> $\vec{v}$ and $\vec{w}$ are orthogonal if and only if $\vec{v} \cdot \vec{w} = 0$.

Proof. If any representation of $\vec{v}$ is perpendicular to any representation of $\vec{w}$, then we can take a representation of $\vec{v}$ and align it with the representation of $\vec{w}$ such that they share the same tail. Then, the angle between those representations would be 90°. Therefore, we have $\cos 90° = \dfrac{\vec{v} \cdot \vec{w}}{\|\vec{v}\|\|\vec{w}\|}$, or $\vec{v} \cdot \vec{w} = 0$, so that concludes the first part.

If $\vec{v} \cdot \vec{w} = 0$, then $\cos \theta = 0$ such that θ is the angle between the representation of $\vec{v}$ and representation of $\vec{w}$ such that they share the same tail. The only angle θ that is less than or equal to 180° which satisfies $\cos \theta = 0$ would be $\theta = 90°$, therefore the representations of $\vec{v}$ and $\vec{w}$ would be perpendicular, and we're done. □

Problem 8.1.24. Prove that for any $k, l > 0$, the angle between $\vec{v}$ and $\vec{w}$ is the same as the angle between $k\vec{v}$ and $l\vec{w}$.

Proof. Let the angle between the representation of $\vec{v}$ and representation of $\vec{w}$ be θ_1, and likewise θ_2 for $k\vec{v}$ and $l\vec{w}$. Then,
$$\cos \theta_1 = \frac{\vec{v} \cdot \vec{w}}{\|\vec{v}\|\|\vec{w}\|}.$$

We now show that $\cos \theta_2 = \cos \theta_1$ assuming that $k, l > 0$ and using the various properties of magnitude and dot product that we have previously established:
$$\cos \theta_2 = \frac{k\vec{v} \cdot l\vec{w}}{\|k\vec{v}\|\|l\vec{w}\|} = \frac{kl(\vec{v} \cdot \vec{w})}{|k|\|\vec{v}\||l|\|\vec{w}\|} = \frac{kl(\vec{v} \cdot \vec{w})}{k\|\vec{v}\| \cdot l\|\vec{w}\|} = \frac{\vec{v} \cdot \vec{w}}{\|\vec{v}\|\|\vec{w}\|} = \cos \theta_1.$$

Therefore we can conclude that $\theta_1 = \theta_2$. □

Consider the following diagram:

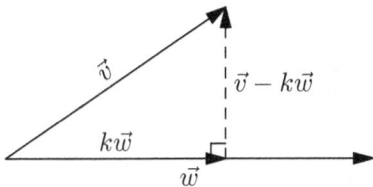

For some scalar k, we define the vector $k\vec{w}$ as the **projection** of $\vec{v}$ onto $\vec{w}$, where the vector that goes from the tip of $k\vec{w}$ to the tip of $\vec{v}$ is orthogonal to $\vec{w}$. By Theorem 8.1.23, we have
$$(\vec{v} - k\vec{w}) \cdot \vec{w} = 0,$$
allowing us to find an expression for k.

This rearranges to $\vec{v} \cdot \vec{w} = k(\vec{w} \cdot \vec{w})$, and we have previously discovered that $\vec{w} \cdot \vec{w} = \|\vec{w}\|^2$, therefore we end up with
$$k = \frac{\vec{v} \cdot \vec{w}}{\|\vec{w}\|^2}.$$

These results lead to the development of our next definition:

Definition 8.1.25. The **vector projection** of $\vec{v}$ onto $\vec{w}$ is defined as

$$\operatorname{proj}_{\vec{w}}(\vec{v}) = \frac{\vec{v} \cdot \vec{w}}{\|\vec{w}\|^2} \cdot \vec{w}.$$

This formula also works for vectors in higher dimensions.

Problem 8.1.26. Find $\operatorname{proj}_{\langle 1,2 \rangle}(\langle 3,4 \rangle)$, $\operatorname{proj}_{\langle 3,4 \rangle}(\langle 1,2 \rangle)$, and $\operatorname{proj}_{\vec{i}-\vec{j}+\vec{k}}\left(\vec{i}+\vec{j}+\vec{k}\right)$.

Solution. First, $\|\langle 1,2 \rangle\|^2 = 1^2 + 2^2 = 5$, and $\langle 1,2 \rangle \cdot \langle 3,4 \rangle = 1 \cdot 3 + 2 \cdot 4 = 11$, therefore

$$\operatorname{proj}_{\langle 1,2 \rangle}(\langle 3,4 \rangle) = \frac{11}{5} \cdot \langle 1,2 \rangle = \boxed{\left\langle \frac{11}{5}, \frac{22}{5} \right\rangle}.$$

Likewise, $\|\langle 3,4 \rangle\|^2 = 3^2 + 4^2 = 25$, therefore

$$\operatorname{proj}_{\langle 3,4 \rangle}(\langle 1,2 \rangle) = \frac{11}{25} \cdot \langle 3,4 \rangle = \boxed{\left\langle \frac{33}{25}, \frac{44}{25} \right\rangle}.$$

Lastly, note that $\vec{i} - \vec{j} + \vec{k} = \langle 1, -1, 1 \rangle$ and $\vec{i} + \vec{j} + \vec{k} = \langle 1, 1, 1 \rangle$. Therefore $\|\langle 1, -1, 1 \rangle\|^2 = 1^2 + (-1)^2 + 1^2 = 3$ and $\langle 1, -1, 1 \rangle \cdot \langle 1, 1, 1 \rangle = 1 - 1 + 1 = 1$, so we substitute in the appropriate values:

$$\operatorname{proj}_{\vec{i}-\vec{j}+\vec{k}}\left(\vec{i}+\vec{j}+\vec{k}\right) = \frac{1}{3}\langle 1, -1, 1 \rangle = \boxed{\left\langle \frac{1}{3}, -\frac{1}{3}, \frac{1}{3} \right\rangle} = \boxed{\frac{1}{3}\vec{i} - \frac{1}{3}\vec{j} + \frac{1}{3}\vec{k}}. \qquad \square$$

Problem 8.1.27. Find $\operatorname{proj}_{\langle 1,2,3 \rangle}(\langle 3,4,5 \rangle)$.

Solution. We have

$$\operatorname{proj}_{\langle 1,2,3 \rangle}(\langle 3,4,5 \rangle) = \frac{3 \cdot 1 + 4 \cdot 2 + 5 \cdot 3}{1^2 + 2^2 + 3^2}\langle 1,2,3 \rangle = \frac{13}{7}\langle 1,2,3 \rangle = \boxed{\left\langle \frac{13}{7}, \frac{26}{7}, \frac{39}{7} \right\rangle}. \qquad \square$$

8.2 Linear Transformations and Matrices

In this section, we will give vectors useful meaning by discussing how vectors of one set can be *transformed* into vectors of another set. The discussion of linear transformations will enable us to relate vectors to matrices, and to understand the purpose of matrices.

Definition 8.2.1. Let $\mathbb{R}^n$ denote the set of all *n-dimensional* vectors with components in $\mathbb{R}$.

A **linear transformation** from $\mathbb{R}^n$ to $\mathbb{R}^m$ is a map $L: \mathbb{R}^n \mapsto \mathbb{R}^m$ such that:

1. $\forall \vec{v}, \vec{w} \in \mathbb{R}^n, L(\vec{v} + \vec{w}) = L(\vec{v}) + L(\vec{w})$.

2. $\forall \vec{v} \in \mathbb{R}^n$ and $k \in \mathbb{R}, L(k\vec{v}) = kL(\vec{v})$.

The notation $L: \mathbb{R}^n \mapsto \mathbb{R}^m$ describes L as the name of the map, $\mathbb{R}^n$ as the domain, and $\mathbb{R}^m$ as the codomain. Values in the domain $\mathbb{R}^n$ are mapped, or associated, to values in the codomain $\mathbb{R}^m$.

Note that the codomain is the set consisting of all possible values that can come out of the function mapping, while the range is the actual set of all values that do come out of the mapping. Therefore we can say that the range is a subset of the codomain.

As an example, what would $L\left(\vec{0}\right)$ be? Clearly, $L\left(\vec{0}\right) = \vec{0}$, however the zero vector that is inputted into the linear transformation is different than the zero vector that is outputted. In other words, $\vec{0}$ given to L is in $\mathbb{R}^n$ while the $\vec{0}$ as the result is in $\mathbb{R}^m$.

Problem 8.2.2. We define the following transformation:

$$L: \mathbb{R}^2 \mapsto \mathbb{R}^1$$

$$L\left(\langle a, b \rangle\right) = a.$$

Is this a linear transformation?

Solution. Recalling back to the definition, we must show that the transformation satisfies two properties:

1. $\forall \vec{v}, \vec{w} \in \mathbb{R}^2, L(\vec{v} + \vec{w}) = L(\vec{v}) + L(\vec{w})$.

2. $\forall \vec{v} \in \mathbb{R}^2$ and $k \in \mathbb{R}, L(k\vec{v}) = kL(\vec{v})$.

Let $\vec{v} = \langle a, b \rangle$ and $\vec{w} = \langle c, d \rangle$. First, note that $L(\langle a, b \rangle) + L(\langle c, d \rangle) = a + c = L(\langle a+c, b+d \rangle)$, therefore $L(\langle a+c, b+d \rangle) = L(\langle a, b \rangle) + L(\langle c, d \rangle)$, and we have showed that the transformation satisfies the first property.

Then, note that $L(k \langle a, b \rangle) = L(\langle ka, kb \rangle) = ka = kL(\langle a, b \rangle)$, therefore $L(k \langle a, b \rangle) = kL(\langle a, b \rangle)$, and our second property is satisfied, therefore the transformation is linear. $\square$

Problem 8.2.3. Determine whether the following transformation is linear or not.

$$L: \mathbb{R}^2 \mapsto \mathbb{R}^2,$$

$$L(\langle a, b \rangle) = \langle 2a - 3b, 3b + 79a \rangle.$$

Solution. First, note that

$$\begin{aligned} L(\langle a, b \rangle) + L(\langle c, d \rangle) &= \langle 2a - 3b, 3b + 79a \rangle + \langle 2c - 3d, 3d + 79c \rangle \\ &= \langle 2a + 2c - 3b - 3d, 3b + 3d + 79a + 79c \rangle \\ &= \langle 2(a+c) - 3(b+d), 3(b+d) + 79(a+c) \rangle \\ &= L(\langle a+c, b+d \rangle) \\ &= L(\langle a, b \rangle + \langle c, d \rangle), \end{aligned}$$

which satisfies the first property of a linear transformation. Likewise, we show that the transformation holds for the second one as well:

$$kL(\langle a, b \rangle) = k \langle 2a - 3b, 3b + 79a \rangle$$

$$= \langle k(2a - 3b), k(3b + 79a) \rangle$$
$$= \langle 2(ka) - 3(kb), 3(kb) + 79(ka) \rangle$$
$$= L(\langle ka, kb \rangle)$$
$$= L(k \langle a, b \rangle).$$
$\square$

Problem 8.2.4. Is this a linear transformation?
$$\text{proj}_{\vec{w}} : \mathbb{R}^n \mapsto \mathbb{R}^m.$$

Solution. We essentially treat the vector projection function as a mapping from any vector of the n-dimension to an m-dimensional vector.

$$\text{proj}_{\vec{w}}(\vec{v_1} + \vec{v_2}) = \frac{(\vec{v_1} + \vec{v_2}) \cdot \vec{w}}{\|\vec{w}\|^2} \vec{w}$$
$$= \frac{\vec{v_1} \cdot \vec{w} + \vec{v_2} \cdot \vec{w}}{\|\vec{w}\|^2} \vec{w}$$
$$= \frac{\vec{v_1} \cdot \vec{w}}{\|\vec{w}\|^2} \vec{w} + \frac{\vec{v_2} \cdot \vec{w}}{\|\vec{w}\|^2} \vec{w}$$
$$= \text{proj}_{\vec{w}}(\vec{v_1}) + \text{proj}_{\vec{w}}(\vec{v_2}).$$
$$\text{proj}_{\vec{w}}(k\vec{v}) = \frac{k\vec{v} \cdot \vec{w}}{\|\vec{w}\|^2} \vec{w}$$
$$= k \left(\frac{\vec{v} \cdot \vec{w}}{\|\vec{w}\|^2} \vec{w} \right)$$
$$= k \, \text{proj}_{\vec{w}}(\vec{v}).$$

As it satisfies the two properties, the vector projection is a linear transformation. $\square$

Exercise 8.2.5. Given $L : \mathbb{R}^2 \mapsto \mathbb{R}^2$, $L(\langle a, b \rangle) = \langle x^2, y^2 \rangle$, is it a linear transformation?

Recall that we defined the special unit vectors $\vec{i}, \vec{j}$, and $\vec{k}$ of magnitude 1, and that we can express a two-dimensional vector $\langle a, b \rangle$ as $a\vec{i} + b\vec{j}$.

Since we are dealing with an arbitrary number of dimensions, we reestablish these definitions with a more generalized outlook:

Definition 8.2.6. If $\vec{v_1}, \vec{v_2}, \ldots, \vec{v_n}$ are vectors, a **linear combination** is any vector of the form $a_1 \vec{v_1} + a_2 \vec{v_2} + \ldots + a_n \vec{v_n}$ for $a_1, a_2, \ldots, a_n \in \mathbb{R}$.

Definition 8.2.7. The **standard basis** of $\mathbb{R}^n$ will be denoted as:

$$\vec{i_1} = \langle 1, 0, 0, \ldots, 0 \rangle,$$
$$\vec{i_2} = \langle 0, 1, 0, \ldots, 0 \rangle,$$
$$\vdots$$
$$\vec{i_n} = \langle 0, 0, 0, \ldots, 1 \rangle.$$

Using these two definitions, we can write any vector $\langle a_1, a_2, a_3, \ldots, a_n \rangle$ as a linear combination of the standard basis vectors:

$$\langle a_1, a_2, a_3, \ldots, a_n \rangle = \langle a_1, 0, 0, \ldots, 0 \rangle + \langle 0, a_2, 0, \ldots, 0 \rangle + \langle 0, 0, a_3, \ldots, 0 \rangle + \ldots + \langle 0, 0, 0, \ldots, a_n \rangle.$$

We factor out scalars from each vector to get

$$a_1 \langle 1, 0, 0, \ldots, 0 \rangle + a_2 \langle 0, 1, 0, \ldots, 0 \rangle + a_3 \langle 0, 0, 1, \ldots, 0 \rangle + \ldots + a_n \langle 0, 0, 0, \ldots, 1 \rangle.$$

We conclude that

$$\langle a_1, a_2, a_3, \ldots, a_n \rangle = a_1 \vec{i_1} + a_2 \vec{i_2} + a_3 \vec{i_3} + \ldots + a_n \vec{i_n}.$$

This conclusion is consistent with the remark made earlier that $\langle a, b \rangle = a\vec{i} + b\vec{j}$.

For some general linear transformation $L : \mathbb{R}^n \mapsto \mathbb{R}^m$ such that

$$L(\vec{i_1}) = \vec{v_1},$$
$$L(\vec{i_2}) = \vec{v_2},$$
$$\vdots$$
$$L(\vec{i_n}) = \vec{v_n},$$

we have the linear combination:

$$L\left(\sum_{k=1}^{n} a_k \vec{i_k}\right) = \sum_{k=1}^{n} a_k \vec{v_k}.$$

We now introduce the following new notation for clarity and consistency later on:

Definition 8.2.8. We can express a vector as a **column vector**:

$$\langle a_1, a_2, \ldots, a_n \rangle = \begin{bmatrix} a_1 \\ a_2 \\ \vdots \\ a_n \end{bmatrix}$$

Definition 8.2.9. An $n \times m$ **matrix** is an array of numbers with n rows and m columns.

For instance, a 3×5 matrix can be:

$$\begin{bmatrix} 1 & 2 & 3 & 4 & 5 \\ 6 & 7 & 8 & 9 & 10 \\ 5 & 4 & 3 & 2 & 1 \end{bmatrix}$$

Other examples: $\begin{bmatrix} 117 \end{bmatrix}$ is a 1×1 matrix, and $\begin{bmatrix} 1 & 1 & 7 \end{bmatrix}$ is a 1×3 matrix.

We will call each number inside a matrix an **entry**.

Definition 8.2.10. Let $L : \mathbb{R}^n \mapsto \mathbb{R}^m$ and suppose

$$L(\vec{i_1}) = \vec{v_1},$$
$$L(\vec{i_2}) = \vec{v_2},$$
$$L(\vec{i_3}) = \vec{v_3},$$
$$\vdots$$
$$L(\vec{i_n}) = \vec{v_n},$$

where $\vec{v_1}, \vec{v_2}, \vec{v_3}, \ldots, \vec{v_n}$ are column vectors.

Then the matrix for the linear transformation L will be

$$\begin{bmatrix} \vec{v_1} & \vec{v_2} & \vec{v_3} & \ldots & \vec{v_n} \end{bmatrix}.$$

This would be an $m \times n$ matrix because each of the column vectors $\vec{v_1}, \vec{v_2}, \vec{v_3}, \ldots, \vec{v_n}$ have m vertical entries, as they are in $\mathbb{R}^m$. Thus, an $m \times n$ matrix represents the transformation $\mathbb{R}^n \mapsto \mathbb{R}^m$.

The application of a linear transformation on a column vector is denoted by the *product* of the matrix representing the transformation and that column vector. For instance,

$$\begin{bmatrix} \vec{v_1} & \vec{v_2} & \vec{v_3} & \ldots & \vec{v_n} \end{bmatrix} \begin{bmatrix} a_1 \\ a_2 \\ \vdots \\ a_n \end{bmatrix}$$

is the vector that results from applying a linear transformation on the initial vector $\langle a_1, a_2, \ldots, a_n \rangle$.

In other words, for some vector $\vec{v}$, we have

$$L(\vec{v}) = M\vec{v},$$

where M is the matrix representing the linear transformation L.

Essentially, the matrix serves to represent a transformation in a compact fashion. Later examples will highlight why the matrix is such a valuable and important tool. Every time we want to talk about applying a linear transformation to a vector, we don't want to be dealing with the hassle of defining some transformation $L(\langle a, b \rangle)$ in order to convey what the actual transformation is. Instead, we can simply express our transformation as an organized and condensed matrix.

Let's put this into practice. Consider Problem 8.2.3 where

$$L : \mathbb{R}^2 \mapsto \mathbb{R}^2,$$
$$L(\langle a, b \rangle) = \langle 2a - 3b, 3b + 79a \rangle.$$

We have that $L\left(\begin{bmatrix} 1 \\ 0 \end{bmatrix}\right) = \begin{bmatrix} 2 \\ 79 \end{bmatrix}$ and $L\left(\begin{bmatrix} 0 \\ 1 \end{bmatrix}\right) = \begin{bmatrix} -3 \\ 3 \end{bmatrix}$. Then, to find the matrix that represents the overall linear transformation, we put these column vectors together, as such: $\begin{bmatrix} 2 & -3 \\ 79 & 3 \end{bmatrix}$. If we multiply this matrix by any vector $\begin{bmatrix} a \\ b \end{bmatrix}$, we have

$$\begin{bmatrix} 2 & -3 \\ 79 & 3 \end{bmatrix} \begin{bmatrix} a \\ b \end{bmatrix} = \begin{bmatrix} 2a - 3b \\ 79a + 3b \end{bmatrix},$$

which is consistent with our definition that $L(\langle a,b \rangle) = \langle 2a - 3b, 3b + 79a \rangle$.

Notice that the top entry of the resulting column vector, $2a - 3b$, is the dot product of $\langle 2, -3 \rangle$ with $\langle a, b \rangle$. Similarly, the bottom entry, $\langle 79a + 3b \rangle$ is the dot product of $\langle 79, 3 \rangle$ with $\langle a, b \rangle$.

Problem 8.2.11. Let $L : \mathbb{R}^2 \mapsto \mathbb{R}^3$ satisfy $L(\langle a, b \rangle) = \langle a - 2b, 2a + 3b, -b \rangle$. Determine the matrix for L.

Solution. First, we calculate the linear transformations of the standard basis vectors in $\mathbb{R}^2$:

$$L(\langle 1, 0 \rangle) = \langle 1, 2, 0 \rangle,$$
$$L(\langle 0, 1 \rangle) = \langle -2, 3, -1 \rangle.$$

Therefore our matrix is $\begin{bmatrix} 1 & -2 \\ 2 & 3 \\ 0 & -1 \end{bmatrix}$. Given an arbitrary $\mathbb{R}^2$ vector $\begin{bmatrix} a \\ b \end{bmatrix}$, we have a relationship between the matrix and the vector:

$$\begin{bmatrix} 1 & -2 \\ 2 & 3 \\ 0 & -1 \end{bmatrix} \begin{bmatrix} a \\ b \end{bmatrix} = \begin{bmatrix} a - 2b \\ 2a + 3b \\ -b \end{bmatrix}.$$

Again, notice that the first entry of the resulting column vector, $a - 2b$, is the dot product of $\langle 1, -2 \rangle$ with $\langle a, b \rangle$.

Confirm for yourself that the rest follow the same rule. $\square$

From these past two examples, we can make the conclusion that each entry in the resulting column vector (that is, the vector that results from applying the linear transformation on the initial vector) is the dot product of its corresponding row in the matrix with the initial vector.

Problem 8.2.12. Calculate the following product:

$$\begin{bmatrix} 1 & 2 & 3 & 10 \\ 4 & 5 & 6 & 11 \\ 7 & 8 & 9 & \pi \end{bmatrix} \begin{bmatrix} 1 \\ 2 \\ 3 \\ 4 \end{bmatrix}.$$

Solution. From our observation about the relationship between the dot product and the matrix, it is not hard to see that for each row in the matrix, each number in that row is multiplied to its corresponding number in the column vector (from top to bottom), then the sum of those products becomes the corresponding entry in the final vector:

$$\begin{bmatrix} 1 & 2 & 3 & 10 \\ 4 & 5 & 6 & 11 \\ 7 & 8 & 9 & \pi \end{bmatrix} \begin{bmatrix} 1 \\ 2 \\ 3 \\ 4 \end{bmatrix} = \begin{bmatrix} 1 \cdot 1 + 2 \cdot 2 + 3 \cdot 3 + 10 \cdot 4 \\ 4 \cdot 1 + 5 \cdot 2 + 6 \cdot 3 + 11 \cdot 4 \\ 7 \cdot 1 + 8 \cdot 2 + 9 \cdot 3 + \pi \cdot 4 \end{bmatrix} = \begin{bmatrix} 54 \\ 76 \\ 50 + 4\pi \end{bmatrix}.$$

$\square$

Exercise 8.2.13. Evaluate
$$\begin{bmatrix} 1 & -1 & 2 & 3 \\ 4 & 6 & 1 & 5 \end{bmatrix} \begin{bmatrix} 1 \\ 2 \\ 1 \\ 5 \end{bmatrix}.$$

Definition 8.2.14. Suppose M is an $n \times m$ matrix. Then $M = [a_{ij}]$ denotes all numbers in that matrix where i goes from 1 to n while j goes from 1 to m.

This will help us describe arbitrary matrices of any dimensions without writing out all entries in a cumbersome fashion.

For example, if we had a 2×3 matrix M, the notation $M = [a_{ij}]$ means that
$$M = \begin{bmatrix} a_{11} & a_{12} & a_{13} \\ a_{21} & a_{22} & a_{23} \end{bmatrix}$$
for arbitrary numbers a_{ij}, where $i = 1, 2$, and $j = 1, 2, 3$.

Now, we introduce operations that can be applied to matrices. While we have observed what a matrix applied to a vector results in, we have not assigned any meaning to "adding" or "multiplying" two matrices together. Therefore, in the context of linear transformations, we establish definitions for matrix addition and multiplication.

Definition 8.2.15 (Matrix Addition). Let M_1, M_2 represent linear transformations $T_1 : \mathbb{R}^n \to \mathbb{R}^m$, $T_2 : \mathbb{R}^n \to \mathbb{R}^m$ respectively. Then we will define $M_1 + M_2$, the sum of the matrices, to represent the sum of the linear transformations $(T_1 + T_2) : \mathbb{R}^n \to \mathbb{R}^m$.

By representing a sum of two matrices as the result when two functions (linear transformations) are added together, we may proceed with our theorem which establishes how exactly two matrices can be added together. Keep in mind that the two matrices must have the same dimensions for the addition to be valid.

> **Theorem 8.2.16**
> Suppose M_1, M_2 are matrices, such that $M_1 = [a_{ij}]$ and $M_2 = [b_{ij}]$. Then,
> $$M_1 + M_2 = [a_{ij} + b_{ij}].$$

Intuitively, this states that the sum of two linear transformations is also a linear transformation represented by a matrix. We can obtain each entry of this matrix by adding its corresponding entry in the matrix representing the first linear transformation to its corresponding entry in the matrix representing the second linear transformation.

Proof. Let M_1, M_2 represent two linear transformations. Let $\vec{v} = \begin{bmatrix} r_1 \\ r_2 \\ \vdots \\ r_m \end{bmatrix}$. Since we are able to add functions together, we must have that $M_1\vec{v} + M_2\vec{v} = (M_1 + M_2)\vec{v}$. First, we simplify $M_1\vec{v} + M_2\vec{v}$:

$$M_1\vec{v} + M_2\vec{v} = \begin{bmatrix} a_{11} & a_{12} & \ldots & a_{1m} \\ a_{21} & a_{22} & \ldots & a_{2m} \\ \vdots & & \ddots & \vdots \\ a_{n1} & a_{n2} & \ldots & a_{nm} \end{bmatrix} \begin{bmatrix} r_1 \\ r_2 \\ \vdots \\ r_m \end{bmatrix} + \begin{bmatrix} b_{11} & b_{12} & \ldots & b_{1m} \\ b_{21} & b_{22} & \ldots & b_{2m} \\ \vdots & & \ddots & \vdots \\ b_{n1} & b_{n2} & \ldots & b_{nm} \end{bmatrix} \begin{bmatrix} r_1 \\ r_2 \\ \vdots \\ r_m \end{bmatrix}$$

$$= \begin{bmatrix} a_{11}r_1 + a_{12}r_2 + \ldots + a_{1m}r_m \\ a_{21}r_1 + a_{22}r_2 + \ldots + a_{2m}r_m \\ \vdots \\ a_{n1}r_1 + a_{n2}r_2 + \ldots + a_{nm}r_m \end{bmatrix} + \begin{bmatrix} b_{11}r_1 + b_{12}r_2 + \ldots + b_{1m}r_m \\ b_{21}r_1 + b_{22}r_2 + \ldots + b_{2m}r_m \\ \vdots \\ b_{n1}r_1 + b_{n2}r_2 + \ldots + b_{nm}r_m \end{bmatrix}$$

$$= \begin{bmatrix} \sum_{i=1}^{m}(a_{1i} + b_{1i})r_i \\ \sum_{i=1}^{m}(a_{2i} + b_{2i})r_i \\ \vdots \\ \sum_{i=1}^{m}(a_{ni} + b_{ni})r_i \end{bmatrix}$$

$$= \begin{bmatrix} a_{ij} + b_{ij} \end{bmatrix} \begin{bmatrix} r_1 \\ r_2 \\ \vdots \\ r_m \end{bmatrix}.$$

Therefore, $M_1 + M_2 = \begin{bmatrix} a_{ij} + b_{ij} \end{bmatrix}$. □

Problem 8.2.17. Evaluate the following sum:

$$\begin{bmatrix} 3 & 4 \\ 5 & 6 \end{bmatrix} + \begin{bmatrix} -1 & 8 \\ 16 & -7 \end{bmatrix}.$$

Solution. We simply add each corresponding entry together:

$$\begin{bmatrix} 3 & 4 \\ 5 & 6 \end{bmatrix} + \begin{bmatrix} -1 & 8 \\ 16 & -7 \end{bmatrix} = \begin{bmatrix} 3 + (-1) & 4 + 8 \\ 5 + 16 & 6 + (-7) \end{bmatrix} = \begin{bmatrix} 2 & 12 \\ 21 & -1 \end{bmatrix}.$$ □

Now that we have established the sum of two linear transformations, we now define matrix multiplication to represent the *composition* of those transformations:

Definition 8.2.18 (Matrix Multiplication). Consider two linear transformations T_1, T_2, where $T_1 : \mathbb{R}^l \mapsto \mathbb{R}^m$ and $T_2 : \mathbb{R}^m \mapsto \mathbb{R}^n$. Let matrix M_1 correspond to T_1 and matrix M_2 correspond to T_2. Then the composition $T_2 \circ T_1 : \mathbb{R}^l \to \mathbb{R}^n$ is also a linear transformation, and we define $M_2 M_1$ to represent this composition.

This definition indicates that the order in which the matrices are multiplied matters, since composition of functions is not commutative. Furthermore, we have restrictions on the dimensions involved: in a product $M_2 M_1$, the number of columns in M_2 must be equal to the number of rows in M_1. This follows from the necessary condition that the domain of T_1 must be the same set as the codomain of T_2 for $T_2 \circ T_1$ to be a valid composition.

> **Theorem 8.2.19**
> Suppose M_1 is an $m \times l$ matrix, and M_2 is an $n \times m$ matrix, such that $M_1 = [b_{ij}]$ and $M_2 = [a_{ij}]$. Then, the $n \times l$ matrix $M_2 M_1 = [c_{ij}]$, where $c_{ij} = \sum_{k=1}^{m} a_{ik} b_{kj}$.

Proof. Consider the composition of those two linear transformations:

$$T_2 \circ T_1(\vec{v}) = \vec{w}.$$

As a result of the composition, we consider the relation

$$M_2(M_1 \vec{v}) = (M_2 M_1)\vec{v}.$$

Note that when we take the composition of T_2 and T_1, it is required that the codomain of $T_1 \subseteq$ domain of T_2. then we must have that the product of an (n by m) matrix and an (m by l) matrix results in an (n by l) matrix.

As stated, we let $M_1 = [b_{ij}]$ and $M_2 = [a_{ij}]$. Furthermore, let $\vec{v} = \begin{bmatrix} x_1 \\ x_2 \\ \vdots \\ x_l \end{bmatrix}$, where $\vec{v} \in \mathbb{R}^l$. First, we compute $M_1 \vec{v}$, which is a legal operation because $T_1 : \mathbb{R}^l \mapsto \mathbb{R}^m$:

$$M_1 \vec{v} = \begin{bmatrix} b_{11} & b_{12} & \cdots & b_{1l} \\ b_{21} & b_{22} & \cdots & b_{2l} \\ \vdots & & \ddots & \vdots \\ b_{m1} & b_{m2} & \cdots & b_{ml} \end{bmatrix} \begin{bmatrix} x_1 \\ x_2 \\ \vdots \\ x_l \end{bmatrix} = \begin{bmatrix} \sum_{k=1}^{l} b_{1k} x_k \\ \sum_{k=1}^{l} b_{2k} x_k \\ \vdots \\ \sum_{k=1}^{l} b_{mk} x_k \end{bmatrix}$$

We then compute $M_2(M_1 \vec{v})$:

$$M_2(M_1 \vec{v}) = \begin{bmatrix} a_{11} & a_{12} & \cdots & a_{1m} \\ a_{21} & a_{22} & \cdots & a_{2m} \\ \vdots & & \ddots & \vdots \\ a_{n1} & a_{n2} & \cdots & a_{nm} \end{bmatrix} \begin{bmatrix} \sum_{k=1}^{l} b_{1k} x_k \\ \sum_{k=1}^{l} b_{2k} x_k \\ \vdots \\ \sum_{k=1}^{l} b_{mk} x_k \end{bmatrix}$$

$$= \begin{bmatrix} \sum_{j=1}^{m} \left(a_{1j} \sum_{k=1}^{l} b_{jk} x_k \right) \\ \sum_{j=1}^{m} \left(a_{2j} \sum_{k=1}^{l} b_{jk} x_k \right) \\ \vdots \\ \sum_{j=1}^{m} \left(a_{nj} \sum_{k=1}^{l} b_{jk} x_k \right) \end{bmatrix}$$

Consider the entry, $\sum_{j=1}^{m} \left(a_{pj} \sum_{k=1}^{l} b_{jk} x_k \right)$, for $p = 1, 2, \ldots, n$. Note that

$$\sum_{j=1}^{m} \left(a_{pj} \sum_{k=1}^{l} b_{jk} x_k \right) = \sum_{j=1}^{m} \left(\sum_{k=1}^{l} a_{pj} b_{jk} x_k \right)$$

$$= \sum_{j=1}^{m} \sum_{k=1}^{l} \left(a_{pj} b_{jk} \right) x_k$$

$$= \sum_{j=1}^{m} \left((a_{pj} b_{j1}) x_1 + (a_{pj} b_{j2}) x_2 + \ldots + (a_{pj} b_{jl}) x_l \right)$$

$$= x_1 \sum_{k=1}^{m} a_{pk} b_{k1} + x_2 \sum_{k=1}^{m} a_{pk} b_{k2} + \ldots + x_l \sum_{k=1}^{m} a_{pk} b_{kl}.$$

Given that p goes from 1 to n, we can rewrite the enormous column vector as:

$$M_2(M_1 \vec{v}) = (M_2 M_1) \vec{v} = \begin{bmatrix} \sum_{k=1}^{m} a_{1k} b_{k1} & \sum_{k=1}^{m} a_{1k} b_{k2} & \cdots & \sum_{k=1}^{m} a_{1k} b_{kl} \\ \sum_{k=1}^{m} a_{2k} b_{k1} & \sum_{k=1}^{m} a_{2k} b_{k2} & \cdots & \sum_{k=1}^{m} a_{2k} b_{kl} \\ \vdots & & \ddots & \vdots \\ \sum_{k=1}^{m} a_{nk} b_{k1} & \sum_{k=1}^{m} a_{nk} b_{k2} & \cdots & \sum_{k=1}^{m} a_{nk} b_{kl} \end{bmatrix} \begin{bmatrix} x_1 \\ x_2 \\ \vdots \\ x_l \end{bmatrix}$$

Therefore, $M_2 M_1 = [c_{ij}]$ where $c_{ij} = \sum_{k=1}^{m} a_{ik} b_{kj}$. $\square$

Problem 8.2.20. Evaluate the following products, if possible:

1. $\begin{bmatrix} 1 & 2 & 3 \\ 4 & 5 & 6 \end{bmatrix} \begin{bmatrix} -1 & 1 \\ -2 & 2 \\ -3 & 3 \end{bmatrix}$

2. $\begin{bmatrix} -1 & 1 \\ -2 & 2 \\ -3 & 3 \end{bmatrix} \begin{bmatrix} 1 & 2 & 3 \\ 4 & 5 & 6 \end{bmatrix}$

3. $\begin{bmatrix} 1 & 2 \\ -5 & 6 \end{bmatrix} \begin{bmatrix} 7 & 4 \\ 2 & -1 \\ 0 & 3 \end{bmatrix}$

4. $\begin{bmatrix} 7 & 4 \\ 2 & -1 \\ 0 & 3 \end{bmatrix} \begin{bmatrix} 1 & 2 \\ -5 & 6 \end{bmatrix}$

Solution.

1. $\begin{bmatrix} 1 & 2 & 3 \\ 4 & 5 & 6 \end{bmatrix} \begin{bmatrix} -1 & 1 \\ -2 & 2 \\ -3 & 3 \end{bmatrix} = \begin{bmatrix} 1 \cdot -1 + 2 \cdot -2 + 3 \cdot -3 & 1 \cdot 1 + 2 \cdot 2 + 3 \cdot 3 \\ 4 \cdot -1 + 5 \cdot -2 + 6 \cdot -3 & 4 \cdot 1 + 5 \cdot 2 + 6 \cdot 3 \end{bmatrix} = \begin{bmatrix} -14 & 14 \\ -32 & 32 \end{bmatrix}.$

2. $\begin{bmatrix} -1 & 1 \\ -2 & 2 \\ -3 & 3 \end{bmatrix} \begin{bmatrix} 1 & 2 & 3 \\ 4 & 5 & 6 \end{bmatrix} = \begin{bmatrix} -1 \cdot 1 + 1 \cdot 4 & -1 \cdot 2 + 1 \cdot 5 & -1 \cdot 3 + 1 \cdot 6 \\ -2 \cdot 1 + 2 \cdot 4 & -2 \cdot 2 + 2 \cdot 5 & -2 \cdot 3 + 2 \cdot 6 \\ -3 \cdot 1 + 3 \cdot 4 & -3 \cdot 2 + 3 \cdot 5 & -3 \cdot 3 + 3 \cdot 6 \end{bmatrix} = \begin{bmatrix} 3 & 3 & 3 \\ 6 & 6 & 6 \\ 9 & 9 & 9 \end{bmatrix}.$

3. Taking the product $\begin{bmatrix} 1 & 2 \\ -5 & 6 \end{bmatrix} \begin{bmatrix} 7 & 4 \\ 2 & -1 \\ 0 & 3 \end{bmatrix}$ is not possible because each row of the first matrix is 2 entries long, while each column of the second matrix is 3 entries long. We can only take the product when each row of the first matrix has the same number of entries as each column of the second matrix.

4. $\begin{bmatrix} 7 & 4 \\ 2 & -1 \\ 0 & 3 \end{bmatrix} \begin{bmatrix} 1 & 2 \\ -5 & 6 \end{bmatrix} = \begin{bmatrix} 7 \cdot 1 + 4 \cdot -5 & 7 \cdot 2 + 4 \cdot 6 \\ 2 \cdot 1 + -1 \cdot -5 & 2 \cdot 2 + -1 \cdot 6 \\ 0 \cdot 1 + 3 \cdot -5 & 0 \cdot 2 + 3 \cdot 6 \end{bmatrix} = \begin{bmatrix} -13 & 38 \\ 7 & -2 \\ -15 & 18 \end{bmatrix}.$ □

Recall from the previous chapter that if we rotate a point (x, y) by an angle of θ counter-clockwise about the origin, it goes to

$$(x \cos \theta - y \sin \theta, x \sin \theta + y \cos \theta).$$

We can associate the point (x, y) with a vector whose tail is at the origin and tip at the point (x, y), which is $\langle x, y \rangle$.

Definition 8.2.21. The **rotation matrix** R_θ to be the matrix that transforms the vector $\langle x, y \rangle$ into the vector rotated counter-clockwise by angle θ:

$$\underbrace{\begin{bmatrix} \cos \theta & -\sin \theta \\ \sin \theta & \cos \theta \end{bmatrix}}_{R_\theta} \begin{bmatrix} x \\ y \end{bmatrix} = \begin{bmatrix} x \cos \theta - y \sin \theta \\ x \sin \theta + y \cos \theta \end{bmatrix}.$$

Problem 8.2.22. Prove $R_\alpha R_\theta = R_{\alpha + \theta}$.

Proof. We can directly evaluate the product of the matrices, then apply sum and difference formulas of sine and cosine appropriately.

$$R_\alpha R_\theta = \begin{bmatrix} \cos \alpha & -\sin \alpha \\ \sin \alpha & \cos \alpha \end{bmatrix} \begin{bmatrix} \cos \theta & -\sin \theta \\ \sin \theta & \cos \theta \end{bmatrix}$$

$$= \begin{bmatrix} \cos\alpha\cos\theta - \sin\alpha\sin\theta & -\cos\alpha\sin\theta - \sin\alpha\cos\theta \\ \sin\alpha\cos\theta + \cos\alpha\sin\theta & -\sin\alpha\sin\theta + \cos\alpha\cos\theta \end{bmatrix}$$

$$= \begin{bmatrix} \cos(\alpha+\theta) & -\sin(\alpha+\theta) \\ \sin(\alpha+\theta) & \cos(\alpha+\theta) \end{bmatrix}$$

$$= R_{\alpha+\theta}. \qquad \square$$

Now, what if we multiplied a scalar by some matrix? Intuitively, if M is a matrix and $\vec{v}$ is a vector, then $(kM)\vec{v}$ should equal $k(M\vec{v})$. It is clear that the only matrix that makes this work is $[ka_{ij}]$ for a_{ij} in M. For example,

$$3\begin{bmatrix} 1 & 1 \\ 1 & 1 \end{bmatrix} = \begin{bmatrix} 1\cdot 3 & 1\cdot 3 \\ 1\cdot 3 & 1\cdot 3 \end{bmatrix} = \begin{bmatrix} 3 & 3 \\ 3 & 3 \end{bmatrix}.$$

Furthermore, a convenient property of matrix multiplication is that it is associative. In other words, if M is an $a \times b$ matrix, N is a $b \times c$ matrix, and P is a $c \times d$ matrix, then $(MN)P = M(NP)$. You are welcome to prove this on your own.

One important condition on matrices is that matrix multiplication is not commutative. For example,

$$\begin{bmatrix} 1 & 0 \\ 0 & 0 \end{bmatrix}\begin{bmatrix} 0 & 2 \\ 0 & 0 \end{bmatrix} = \begin{bmatrix} 0 & 2 \\ 0 & 0 \end{bmatrix}.$$

However, if we switch the matrices:

$$\begin{bmatrix} 0 & 2 \\ 0 & 0 \end{bmatrix}\begin{bmatrix} 1 & 0 \\ 0 & 0 \end{bmatrix} = \begin{bmatrix} 0 & 0 \\ 0 & 0 \end{bmatrix},$$

which is different from the first matrix we got. Thus, while matrix multiplication is associative, it is not commutative.

Moving on, we introduce some new vocabulary to describe special matrices and parts of matrices.

Definition 8.2.23. We define $M_n(\mathbb{R})$ to be the set of $n \times n$ matrices with elements in $\mathbb{R}$. A special name for an $n \times n$ matrix is a **square matrix**.

Definition 8.2.24. If M is an $n \times n$ square matrix i.e. $[a_{nn}]$, then the **main diagonal** consists of the entries of the form a_{kk}, where $k = 1, \ldots, n$.

Definition 8.2.25. Consider the linear transformation $T : \mathbb{R}^n \to \mathbb{R}^n$ such that for all elements $\vec{i}_k$ in the standard basis, $T(\vec{i}_k) = \vec{i}_k$. Let $\vec{v}$ be a vector in $\mathbb{R}^n$ which can be written as $\langle a_1, a_2, \ldots, a_n \rangle$. Using the various properties of a linear transformation as well as the observation that $\vec{v}$ can be written as a linear combination of the standard basis vectors, we have

$$T(\vec{v}) = T\left(\sum_{k=1}^{n} a_k \vec{i}_k\right)$$

$$= \sum_{k=1}^{n} T(a_k \vec{i}_k)$$

$$= \sum_{k=1}^{n} a_k T(\vec{i}_k)$$

$$= \sum_{k=1}^{n} a_k \vec{\imath}_k$$
$$= \vec{v}.$$

Therefore, for all $\vec{v} \in \mathbb{R}^n$, $T(\vec{v}) = \vec{v}$. We call T the **identity linear transformation**.

Now, we consider the matrix for this transformation. By looking at the column vectors, we can see that it will look like:
$$\begin{bmatrix} 1 & 0 & 0 & \ldots & 0 & 0 \\ 0 & 1 & 0 & \ldots & 0 & 0 \\ 0 & 0 & 1 & \ldots & 0 & 0 \\ \vdots & & & \ddots & & \vdots \\ 0 & 0 & 0 & \ldots & 1 & 0 \\ 0 & 0 & 0 & \ldots & 0 & 1 \end{bmatrix}$$

Definition 8.2.26. A matrix of this form is called the $n \times n$ **identity matrix**, denoted I_n. It takes a vector to itself. All entries in the main diagonal of I_n have the value of 1, and all other entries have the value of 0.

Problem 8.2.27. Now, let us consider the product $I_n M$ for some $n \times m$ matrix M.

$$\begin{bmatrix} 1 & 0 & \ldots & 0 \\ 0 & 1 & \ldots & 0 \\ \vdots & & \ddots & \vdots \\ 0 & 0 & \ldots & 1 \end{bmatrix} \begin{bmatrix} a_{11} & a_{12} & \ldots & a_{1m} \\ a_{21} & a_{22} & \ldots & a_{2m} \\ \vdots & & \ddots & \vdots \\ a_{n1} & a_{n2} & \ldots & a_{nm} \end{bmatrix}$$

Prove $I_n M = M$.

Proof. If we let $M = [a_{ij}]$ and $I_n = [b_{ij}]$, then
$$I_n M = \left[\sum_{k=1}^{n} b_{ik} a_{kj} \right].$$

However, we know that all of the values of b_{ik} are 0 except for entries of the form b_{ii}, which are all 1. Thus, all of the values of $b_{ik} a_{kj}$ are 0, except for $b_{ii} a_{ij} = a_{ij}$. This implies that
$$\sum_{k=1}^{n} b_{ik} a_{kj} = a_{ij}.$$

Therefore, $I_n M = [a_{ij}] = M$ i.e. $I_n M = M$. $\square$

We have demonstrated that not only does I_n represent the identity linear transformation, it also serves as the identity for matrix multiplication!

Exercise 8.2.28. Using an analogous line of reasoning as shown above, prove $M I_n = M$.

We can observe how the identity matrix has appeared in places we have seen before. Consider R_0, the rotation matrix by an angle of 0. It is clear that rotating a vector by 0 will not change the vector at all. In other words, R_0 should be an identity matrix. This can be easily demonstrated:

$$R_0 = \begin{bmatrix} \cos 0° & -\sin 0° \\ \sin 0° & \cos 0° \end{bmatrix} = \begin{bmatrix} 1 & 0 \\ 0 & 1 \end{bmatrix} = I_2.$$

As with fields, the existence of an identity means that we should look for *inverses* as well.

Definition 8.2.29. The **inverse** of a matrix M is denoted as M^{-1}, such that $M^{-1}M = I$, i.e. the identity matrix.

To get a sense of how matrix inverses can be applied in other parts of mathematics, consider the following system of equations:

$$2x + 3y = m,$$
$$3x + 5y = n.$$

Standard algebraic techniques yield $(x, y) = (5m - 3n, -3m + 2n)$ as the set of possible solutions. However, we can also express this system of equations as a matrix operation:

$$\underbrace{\begin{bmatrix} 2 & 3 \\ 3 & 5 \end{bmatrix}}_{M} \begin{bmatrix} x \\ y \end{bmatrix} = \begin{bmatrix} m \\ n \end{bmatrix}$$

Then our main objective is to find solutions to the equation $M\vec{x} = \vec{v}$, where $\vec{x}, \vec{v}$ are given vectors and M is a matrix of an appropriate dimension. This is where our inverse matrix, denoted as M^{-1}, fulfills its role as a multiplicative inverse to this equation:

$$M^{-1}(M\vec{x}) = M^{-1}\vec{v}$$
$$(M^{-1}M)\vec{x} = M^{-1}\vec{v}$$
$$I\vec{x} = M^{-1}\vec{v}$$
$$\therefore \vec{x} = M^{-1}\vec{v}.$$

Suppose $\vec{x}, \vec{v}$ are in the same dimension, and M is a square matrix. When does M^{-1} exist?

For now, we will deal with the 2×2 square matrix. Let $M = \begin{bmatrix} a & b \\ c & d \end{bmatrix}$, and $M^{-1} = \begin{bmatrix} x & y \\ z & w \end{bmatrix}$. We should figure out what x, y, z, w are in terms of a, b, c, d.

By our definition of the inverse, we must have:

$$\begin{bmatrix} a & b \\ c & d \end{bmatrix} \begin{bmatrix} x & y \\ z & w \end{bmatrix} = \begin{bmatrix} 1 & 0 \\ 0 & 1 \end{bmatrix}.$$

Matrix multiplication yields:

$$\begin{bmatrix} ax + bz & ay + bw \\ cx + dz & cy + dw \end{bmatrix} = \begin{bmatrix} 1 & 0 \\ 0 & 1 \end{bmatrix}.$$

We end up with a system of four equations:

$$ax + bz = 1,$$
$$ay + bw = 0,$$
$$cx + dz = 0,$$
$$cy + dw = 1.$$

Applying our usual algebraic techniques, we eventually find the solutions to x, y, z, w:

$$M^{-1} = \begin{bmatrix} x & y \\ z & w \end{bmatrix} = \begin{bmatrix} \frac{d}{ad-bc} & \frac{-b}{ad-bc} \\ \frac{-c}{ad-bc} & \frac{a}{ad-bc} \end{bmatrix}.$$

Notice that the common denominator is $ad - bc$. Whether this quantity will equal 0 or not will *determine* whether M has an inverse or not. This quantity will serve as an important trait of the matrix.

Definition 8.2.30. Given a 2×2 matrix $M = \begin{bmatrix} a & b \\ c & d \end{bmatrix}$, the **determinant** of M is denoted as $\text{Det}(M) = ad - bc$.

Definition 8.2.31. We will define the determinant of any identity matrix to be 1. In other words, $\text{Det}(I_n) = 1$.

Lastly, we can factor out $\dfrac{1}{ad - bc}$ from M^{-1}:

$$M^{-1} = \begin{bmatrix} \frac{d}{ad-bc} & \frac{-b}{ad-bc} \\ \frac{-c}{ad-bc} & \frac{a}{ad-bc} \end{bmatrix} = \frac{1}{ad - bc} \begin{bmatrix} d & -b \\ -c & a \end{bmatrix}.$$

We can summarize everything we have just shown:

> **Theorem 8.2.32**
>
> Given a 2×2 square matrix M, M has an inverse if and only if $\text{Det}(M) \neq 0$, such that
>
> $$M^{-1} = \frac{1}{\text{Det}(M)} \begin{bmatrix} d & -b \\ -c & a \end{bmatrix}.$$

Going back to our initial example,

$$\begin{bmatrix} 2 & 3 \\ 3 & 5 \end{bmatrix} \begin{bmatrix} x \\ y \end{bmatrix} = \begin{bmatrix} m \\ n \end{bmatrix},$$

we can apply our formula for a 2×2 matrix inverse:

$$\begin{bmatrix} 2 & 3 \\ 3 & 5 \end{bmatrix}^{-1} = \frac{1}{1} \begin{bmatrix} 5 & -3 \\ -3 & 2 \end{bmatrix} = \begin{bmatrix} 5 & -3 \\ -3 & 2 \end{bmatrix}.$$

Therefore,
$$\begin{bmatrix} x \\ y \end{bmatrix} = \begin{bmatrix} 2 & 3 \\ 3 & 5 \end{bmatrix}^{-1} \begin{bmatrix} m \\ n \end{bmatrix} = \begin{bmatrix} 5 & -3 \\ -3 & 2 \end{bmatrix} \begin{bmatrix} m \\ n \end{bmatrix} = \begin{bmatrix} 5m - 3n \\ -3m + 2n \end{bmatrix},$$
which is indeed consistent with the solutions $(x, y) = (5m - 3n, -3m + 2n)$ that we had found for the system of equations using algebraic techniques.

Problem 8.2.33. Compute $\begin{bmatrix} 7 & 5 \\ -1 & 2 \end{bmatrix}^{-1}$. Use this to solve the equation $\begin{bmatrix} 7 & 5 \\ -1 & 2 \end{bmatrix} \begin{bmatrix} x \\ y \end{bmatrix} = \begin{bmatrix} 7 \\ 11 \end{bmatrix}$.

Solution. This is a straight application of our formula:
$$\begin{bmatrix} 7 & 5 \\ -1 & 2 \end{bmatrix}^{-1} = \frac{1}{19} \begin{bmatrix} 2 & -5 \\ 1 & 7 \end{bmatrix} = \begin{bmatrix} \frac{2}{19} & \frac{-5}{19} \\ \frac{1}{19} & \frac{7}{19} \end{bmatrix}.$$

Therefore $\begin{bmatrix} x \\ y \end{bmatrix} = \begin{bmatrix} \frac{2}{19} & \frac{-5}{19} \\ \frac{1}{19} & \frac{7}{19} \end{bmatrix} \begin{bmatrix} 7 \\ 11 \end{bmatrix} = \begin{bmatrix} \frac{-41}{19} \\ \frac{84}{19} \end{bmatrix}$, i.e. the solution $(x, y) = \left(\frac{-41}{19}, \frac{84}{19} \right)$. □

Problem 8.2.34. Using the formula for matrix inverse, find $R_{(-\theta)}$.

Solution. It is obvious that $R_{(-\theta)}$ is the inverse of R_θ, since rotating by θ and then rotating by $-\theta$ will result in no rotation being done to the initial vector at all.

Then, we compute the inverse of R_θ:
$$\begin{bmatrix} \cos \theta & -\sin \theta \\ \sin \theta & \cos \theta \end{bmatrix}^{-1} = \frac{1}{\cos^2 \theta + \sin^2 \theta} \begin{bmatrix} \cos \theta & \sin \theta \\ -\sin \theta & \cos \theta \end{bmatrix}$$
$$= \begin{bmatrix} \cos \theta & \sin \theta \\ -\sin \theta & \cos \theta \end{bmatrix}$$
$$= \begin{bmatrix} \cos(-\theta) & -\sin(-\theta) \\ \sin(-\theta) & \cos(-\theta) \end{bmatrix}$$
$$= R_{(-\theta)}.$$
□

For the following examples, we are assuming that M is a 2×2 square matrix, since we have only discussed the determinant and inverse of that kind of matrix so far.

Problem 8.2.35. Let $k \in \mathbb{R}$. Prove $\text{Det}(kM) = k^2 \text{Det}(M)$ for a 2×2 matrix M.

Proof. Let $M = \begin{bmatrix} a & b \\ c & d \end{bmatrix}$. Then, $\text{Det}(kM) = \text{Det}\left(k \begin{bmatrix} a & b \\ c & d \end{bmatrix} \right) = \text{Det}\left(\begin{bmatrix} ka & kb \\ kc & kd \end{bmatrix} \right) = ka \cdot kd - kb \cdot kc = k^2(ad) - k^2(bc) = k^2(ad - bc) = k^2 \text{Det}(M)$, and we are done. □

Problem 8.2.36. Prove $\text{Det}(MN) = \text{Det}(M) \text{Det}(N)$.

Proof. Let $M = \begin{bmatrix} a & b \\ c & d \end{bmatrix}$ and $N = \begin{bmatrix} e & f \\ g & h \end{bmatrix}$. Then $\text{Det}(M) \text{Det}(N) = (ad - bc)(eh - fg) = adeh - adfg - bceh + bcfg$.

Note that $MN = \begin{bmatrix} a & b \\ c & d \end{bmatrix} \begin{bmatrix} e & f \\ g & h \end{bmatrix} = \begin{bmatrix} ae+bg & af+bh \\ ce+dg & cf+dh \end{bmatrix}$, so $\text{Det}(MN) = (ae+bg)(cf+dh) - (af+bh)(ce+dg)$. Simplifying leaves us with $adeh - adfg - bceh + bcfg$, which equals $\text{Det}(M)\text{Det}(N)$, so we are done. $\square$

Problem 8.2.37. Does $\text{Det}(M+N) = \text{Det}(M) + \text{Det}(N)$?

Solution. Using the same variables for M and N in the previous example, we have that $M+N = \begin{bmatrix} a+e & b+f \\ c+g & d+h \end{bmatrix}$, so $\text{Det}(M+N) = (a+e)(d+h) - (b+f)(c+g) = (ad+ah+de+eh) - (bc+bg+cf+fg)$. This clearly does not equal $\text{Det}(M) + \text{Det}(N) = ad - bc + eh - fg$, so $\text{Det}(M+N) \neq \text{Det}(M) + \text{Det}(N)$. $\square$

Problem 8.2.38. Prove $\text{Det}(M^{-1}) = (\text{Det}(M))^{-1}$.

We could approach this proof algebraically just like our previous examples. However, we can proceed with a much cleaner proof by using previously proven results:

Proof. As previously proven in an example, $\text{Det}(M^{-1}M) = \text{Det}(M^{-1})\text{Det}(M)$. But recall that $M^{-1}M = I$, so we have $\text{Det}(I) = \text{Det}(M^{-1})\text{Det}(M) \implies \text{Det}(M^{-1})\text{Det}(M) = 1$, so therefore $\text{Det}(M^{-1}) = (\text{Det}(M))^{-1}$. $\square$

Now that we have dealt with rotation matrices, we can also consider the transformation of *reflection*. We seek to reflect a vector over some line. To get a notion of how we should define this, take a line through the origin:

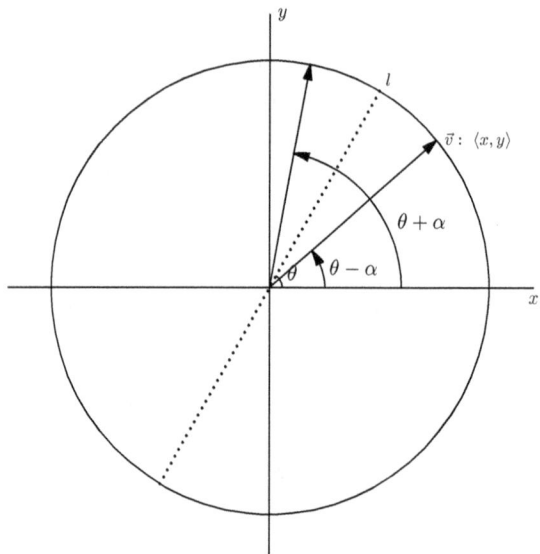

Let the angle of line l with respect to the x-axis be θ. Let T_θ be the linear transformation that reflects a vector across the line making an angle of θ with the x-axis.

Let the angle of the gap between the vector and the line be α. The transformation will take a vector making an angle of $\theta - \alpha$ to one making an angle of $\theta + \alpha$ (since reflection copies the angle).

We wish to express the initial vector as $\langle \cos\beta, \sin\beta \rangle$, so let $\beta = \theta - \alpha$, which implies $\theta + \alpha = 2\theta - \beta$, so therefore, the vector $\langle \cos\beta, \sin\beta \rangle$ will reflect to the vector $\langle \cos(2\theta - \beta), \sin(2\theta - \beta) \rangle$ under T_θ.

We can find the matrix that corresponds to T_θ; denote it H_θ. Under our definition, we must have:
$$H_\theta \cdot \begin{bmatrix} \cos\beta \\ \sin\beta \end{bmatrix} = \begin{bmatrix} \cos(2\theta - \beta) \\ \sin(2\theta - \beta) \end{bmatrix}.$$

But note that
$$\begin{bmatrix} \cos(2\theta - \beta) \\ \sin(2\theta - \beta) \end{bmatrix} = \begin{bmatrix} \cos 2\theta \cos\beta + \sin 2\theta \sin\beta \\ \sin 2\theta \cos\beta - \cos 2\theta \sin\beta \end{bmatrix} = \begin{bmatrix} \cos 2\theta & \sin 2\theta \\ \sin 2\theta & -\cos 2\theta \end{bmatrix} \begin{bmatrix} \cos\beta \\ \sin\beta \end{bmatrix}.$$

Therefore, we have our reflection matrix:
$$H_\theta = \begin{bmatrix} \cos 2\theta & \sin 2\theta \\ \sin 2\theta & -\cos 2\theta \end{bmatrix}.$$

Definition 8.2.39. The **reflection matrix**, denoted by H_θ, reflects a vector over a line given the angle θ between the line and the x-axis.

$$\underbrace{\begin{bmatrix} \cos 2\theta & \sin 2\theta \\ \sin 2\theta & -\cos 2\theta \end{bmatrix}}_{H_\theta} \begin{bmatrix} x \\ y \end{bmatrix} = \begin{bmatrix} x \cos 2\theta + y \sin 2\theta \\ x \sin 2\theta - y \cos 2\theta \end{bmatrix}.$$

Problem 8.2.40. Prove that the product of a reflection matrix and a rotation matrix is a reflection matrix.

Proof. Since matrix multiplication is not commutative, we must consider both cases whether a reflection matrix is being multiplied to a rotation matrix or the other way around.

$$H_\varphi R_\theta = \begin{bmatrix} \cos 2\varphi & \sin 2\varphi \\ \sin 2\varphi & -\cos 2\varphi \end{bmatrix} \begin{bmatrix} \cos\theta & -\sin\theta \\ \sin\theta & \cos\theta \end{bmatrix}$$
$$= \begin{bmatrix} \cos 2\varphi \cos\theta + \sin 2\varphi \sin\theta & -\cos 2\varphi \sin\theta + \sin 2\varphi \cos\theta \\ \sin 2\varphi \cos\theta - \cos 2\varphi \sin\theta & -\sin\theta \sin 2\varphi - \cos 2\varphi \cos\theta \end{bmatrix}$$
$$= \begin{bmatrix} \cos(2\varphi - \theta) & \sin(2\varphi - \theta) \\ \sin(2\varphi - \theta) & -\cos(2\varphi - \theta) \end{bmatrix}$$
$$= H_{2\varphi - \theta}.$$

$$R_\theta H_\varphi = \begin{bmatrix} \cos\theta & -\sin\theta \\ \sin\theta & \cos\theta \end{bmatrix} \begin{bmatrix} \cos 2\varphi & \sin 2\varphi \\ \sin 2\varphi & -\cos 2\varphi \end{bmatrix}$$
$$= \begin{bmatrix} \cos 2\varphi \cos\theta - \sin 2\varphi \sin\theta & \cos\theta \sin 2\varphi + \sin\theta \cos 2\varphi \\ \sin\theta \cos 2\varphi + \cos\theta \sin 2\varphi & \sin\theta \sin 2\varphi - \cos\theta \cos 2\varphi \end{bmatrix}$$
$$= \begin{bmatrix} \cos(2\varphi + \theta) & \sin(2\varphi + \theta) \\ \sin(2\varphi + \theta) & -\cos(2\varphi + \theta) \end{bmatrix}$$
$$= H_{2\varphi + \theta}. \qquad \square$$

Problem 8.2.41. Compute $H_{\frac{\pi}{4}} \cdot \begin{bmatrix} x \\ y \end{bmatrix}$ and $R_{\frac{\pi}{2}} \cdot \begin{bmatrix} x \\ y \end{bmatrix}$.

Solution.
$$H_{\frac{\pi}{4}} \cdot \begin{bmatrix} x \\ y \end{bmatrix} = \begin{bmatrix} \cos \frac{\pi}{2} & \sin \frac{\pi}{2} \\ \sin \frac{\pi}{2} & -\cos \frac{\pi}{2} \end{bmatrix} \begin{bmatrix} x \\ y \end{bmatrix} = \begin{bmatrix} 0 & 1 \\ 1 & 0 \end{bmatrix} \begin{bmatrix} x \\ y \end{bmatrix} = \begin{bmatrix} y \\ x \end{bmatrix}$$
$$R_{\frac{\pi}{2}} \cdot \begin{bmatrix} x \\ y \end{bmatrix} = \begin{bmatrix} \cos \frac{\pi}{2} & -\sin \frac{\pi}{2} \\ \sin \frac{\pi}{2} & \cos \frac{\pi}{2} \end{bmatrix} \begin{bmatrix} x \\ y \end{bmatrix} = \begin{bmatrix} 0 & -1 \\ 1 & 0 \end{bmatrix} \begin{bmatrix} x \\ y \end{bmatrix} = \begin{bmatrix} -y \\ x \end{bmatrix}$$
□

Exercise 8.2.42. Describe what the matrix $\begin{bmatrix} 5 & 0 \\ 0 & 6 \end{bmatrix}$ does to a vector.

Exercise 8.2.43. Find a matrix that takes each vector $\vec{v}$ to $2\vec{v}$.

Problem 8.2.44. Rotate the set of all points of the form $\begin{bmatrix} t \\ t^2 \end{bmatrix}$ by $\frac{\pi}{4}$ radians counter-clockwise, then find the Cartesian equation which represents the set of those rotated points.

Solution. We have,
$$R_{\frac{\pi}{4}} \begin{bmatrix} t \\ t^2 \end{bmatrix} = \begin{bmatrix} \frac{\sqrt{2}}{2} & -\frac{\sqrt{2}}{2} \\ \frac{\sqrt{2}}{2} & \frac{\sqrt{2}}{2} \end{bmatrix} \begin{bmatrix} t \\ t^2 \end{bmatrix} = \begin{bmatrix} \frac{\sqrt{2}}{2}t - \frac{\sqrt{2}}{2}t^2 \\ \frac{\sqrt{2}}{2}t + \frac{\sqrt{2}}{2}t^2 \end{bmatrix}.$$

We now have the parametrization $x = \frac{\sqrt{2}}{2}t - \frac{\sqrt{2}}{2}t^2$, $y = \frac{\sqrt{2}}{2}t + \frac{\sqrt{2}}{2}t^2$, from which we can add these equations together and simplify to get the conic $\boxed{x^2 + 2xy + y^2 + \sqrt{2}x - \sqrt{2}y = 0}$. □

The objective of this problem is to demonstrate that we can use rotation matrices to rotate graphs. In that problem, we expressed the initial Cartesian equation such as $y = x^2$ as a parametrization, through which we can rotate it $\frac{\pi}{4}$ radians counter-clockwise, resulting in the oblique parabola $x^2 + 2xy + y^2 + \sqrt{2}x - \sqrt{2}y = 0$.

Problem 8.2.45. Use a rotation matrix to rotate $x^2 - y^2 = 1$ by $\frac{\pi}{4}$ radians counter-clockwise.

Solution. Recall the identity $\sec^2 \theta = 1 + \tan^2 \theta$, from which we can deduce that the parametrization of this equation is $x = \sec t$, $y = \tan t$. We proceed with our transformation:
$$R_{\frac{\pi}{4}} \begin{bmatrix} \sec t \\ \tan t \end{bmatrix} = \begin{bmatrix} \frac{\sqrt{2}}{2} & -\frac{\sqrt{2}}{2} \\ \frac{\sqrt{2}}{2} & \frac{\sqrt{2}}{2} \end{bmatrix} \begin{bmatrix} \sec t \\ \tan t \end{bmatrix} = \begin{bmatrix} \frac{\sqrt{2}}{2}\sec t - \frac{\sqrt{2}}{2}\tan t \\ \frac{\sqrt{2}}{2}\sec t + \frac{\sqrt{2}}{2}\tan t \end{bmatrix}.$$

We have the parametric equations $x = \frac{\sqrt{2}}{2}\sec t - \frac{\sqrt{2}}{2}\tan t$ and $y = \frac{\sqrt{2}}{2}\sec t + \frac{\sqrt{2}}{2}\tan t$. A particularly clean method to finding the equation in terms of x and y is to multiply x and y together, resulting in a difference-of-squares, which ultimately simplifies to $\boxed{xy = \frac{1}{2}}$. □

We have been going over various transformations, but there is a special situation that we should address. After applying some linear transformation, what if the vector only changes by a scalar factor?

Definition 8.2.46. A matrix M has **eigenvector** non-zero $\vec{v}$ with a scalar **eigenvalue** λ if

$$M\vec{v} = \lambda\vec{v}.$$

Let's investigate this definition with some examples:

$$\begin{bmatrix} 5 & 0 \\ 0 & 6 \end{bmatrix} \begin{bmatrix} 1 \\ 0 \end{bmatrix} = \begin{bmatrix} 5 \\ 0 \end{bmatrix} = \overbrace{5}^{\text{eigenvalue}} \cdot \underbrace{\begin{bmatrix} 1 \\ 0 \end{bmatrix}}_{\text{eigenvector}}$$

When we multiply the eigenvector $\langle 1, 0 \rangle$ by a scalar of 5, the resulting vector is equivalent to taking the matrix transformation of that vector! In other words, the direction of the vector remains the same after a transformation is applied.

Here are some more examples of eigenvectors with their eigenvalues for the given matrix above:

$$\begin{bmatrix} 5 & 0 \\ 0 & 6 \end{bmatrix} \begin{bmatrix} 0 \\ 1 \end{bmatrix} = \begin{bmatrix} 0 \\ 6 \end{bmatrix} = 6 \cdot \begin{bmatrix} 0 \\ 1 \end{bmatrix}$$

$$\begin{bmatrix} 5 & 0 \\ 0 & 6 \end{bmatrix} \begin{bmatrix} k \\ 0 \end{bmatrix} = \begin{bmatrix} 5k \\ 0 \end{bmatrix} = 5 \cdot \begin{bmatrix} k \\ 0 \end{bmatrix}$$

In general, according to our definition, the eigenvector exists iff it is *non-zero*. When do we know this is the case? Consider our equation,

$$M\vec{v} = \lambda\vec{v}$$

This can be rewritten as $M\vec{v} = \lambda I \vec{v}$, i.e. $(M - \lambda I)\vec{v} = \vec{0}$.

For convenience, let $N = M - \lambda I$, so we have $N\vec{v} = \vec{0}$. Assume N has an inverse. Then we can multiply both sides of the equation by that: $N^{-1}(N\vec{v}) = N^{-1}\vec{0}$, i.e. $N^{-1}(N\vec{v}) = \vec{0}$. This rearranges to $(N^{-1}N)\vec{v} = \vec{0} \implies I\vec{v} = \vec{0} \implies \vec{v} = \vec{0}$, which is a contradiction of our definition.

Therefore, $N = M - \lambda I$ does *not* have an inverse. In order for a $\vec{v} \neq 0$ to exist, we would need $M - \lambda I$ not to have an inverse, which happens iff $\text{Det}(M - \lambda I) = 0$.

By evaluating the determinant of $M - \lambda I$, we can determine which values of λ (i.e. eigenvalues) force $M - \lambda I$ not to have an inverse and therefore ensure that the eigenvector exists for that value of λ.

> **Example 8.2.47**
>
> Find all eigenvectors and eigenvalues for the matrix $\begin{bmatrix} 5 & 0 \\ 0 & 6 \end{bmatrix}$.

Solution. Note that $M - \lambda I = \begin{bmatrix} 5-\lambda & 0 \\ 0 & 6-\lambda \end{bmatrix}$, therefore $\text{Det}(M - \lambda I) = (5-\lambda)(6-\lambda)$, so the values of λ which force $\text{Det}(M - \lambda I)$ to equal 0 are $\lambda = 5, 6$. We consider each value separately:

- Consider $\lambda = 5$. As $M\vec{v} = \lambda \vec{v}$, we have:

$$M\vec{v} = \begin{bmatrix} 5 & 0 \\ 0 & 6 \end{bmatrix} \begin{bmatrix} x \\ y \end{bmatrix} = \begin{bmatrix} 5x \\ 6y \end{bmatrix}$$

$$\lambda \vec{v} = 5 \cdot \begin{bmatrix} x \\ y \end{bmatrix} = \begin{bmatrix} 5x \\ 5y \end{bmatrix}$$

We get $\begin{bmatrix} 5x \\ 6y \end{bmatrix} = \begin{bmatrix} 5x \\ 5y \end{bmatrix}$, therefore $y = 0$ for any value of x.

So our eigenvectors of $\lambda = 5$ are of the form $\begin{bmatrix} x \\ 0 \end{bmatrix} = x \begin{bmatrix} 1 \\ 0 \end{bmatrix}$.

- If $\lambda = 6$, we can follow a similar process: $M\vec{v} = \begin{bmatrix} 5 & 0 \\ 0 & 6 \end{bmatrix} \begin{bmatrix} x \\ y \end{bmatrix} = \begin{bmatrix} 5x \\ 6y \end{bmatrix}$ and $\lambda \vec{v} = 6 \cdot \begin{bmatrix} x \\ y \end{bmatrix} = \begin{bmatrix} 6x \\ 6y \end{bmatrix}$, so $\begin{bmatrix} 5x \\ 6y \end{bmatrix} = \begin{bmatrix} 6x \\ 6y \end{bmatrix}$, implying $x = 0$ for any value of y.

Our eigenvectors of $\lambda = 6$ are of the form $\begin{bmatrix} 0 \\ y \end{bmatrix} = y \begin{bmatrix} 0 \\ 1 \end{bmatrix}$. □

Problem 8.2.48. Find eigenvectors and eigenvalues for $M = \begin{bmatrix} 2 & -1 \\ -4 & 5 \end{bmatrix}$.

Solution. Note that $\text{Det}(M - \lambda I) = \text{Det}\left(\begin{bmatrix} 2-\lambda & -1 \\ -4 & 5-\lambda \end{bmatrix}\right) = (2-\lambda)(5-\lambda) - (-1)(-4) = \lambda^2 - 7\lambda + 6 = (\lambda - 1)(\lambda - 6)$.

- Case $\lambda = 1$:

$$\begin{bmatrix} 2 & -1 \\ -4 & 5 \end{bmatrix} \begin{bmatrix} x \\ y \end{bmatrix} = \begin{bmatrix} 2x - y \\ -4x + 5y \end{bmatrix} = 1 \cdot \begin{bmatrix} x \\ y \end{bmatrix}$$

leaving us with the system of equations $2x - y = x$, $-4x + 5y = y$, whose solution is $y = x$.

Eigenvectors of $\lambda = 1$ are of the form $\begin{bmatrix} x \\ x \end{bmatrix}$ i.e. scalar multiples of $\begin{bmatrix} 1 \\ 1 \end{bmatrix}$.

- Case $\lambda = 6$:

$$\begin{bmatrix} 2 & -1 \\ -4 & 5 \end{bmatrix} \begin{bmatrix} x \\ y \end{bmatrix} = \begin{bmatrix} 2x - y \\ -4x + 5y \end{bmatrix} = 6 \cdot \begin{bmatrix} x \\ y \end{bmatrix} = \begin{bmatrix} 6x \\ 6y \end{bmatrix}$$

The system of equations is $2x - y = 6x$ and $-4x + 5y = 6y$, so the solution is $y = -4x$.

Eigenvectors of $\lambda = 6$ are of the form $\begin{bmatrix} x \\ -4x \end{bmatrix}$ i.e scalar multiples of $\begin{bmatrix} 1 \\ -4 \end{bmatrix}$. □

Exercise 8.2.49. Find eigenvectors and eigenvalues of the matrix $\begin{bmatrix} 2 & 1 \\ -4 & -3 \end{bmatrix}$.

Exercise 8.2.50. Find eigenvectors and eigenvalues of the matrix $\begin{bmatrix} 1 & 3 \\ -4 & -6 \end{bmatrix}$.

Problem 8.2.51. Find eigenvalues and eigenvectors for R_θ.

Solution. The determinant of $R_\theta - I\lambda = \begin{bmatrix} \cos\theta - \lambda & -\sin\theta \\ \sin\theta & \cos\theta - \lambda \end{bmatrix}$ must equal 0, i.e. $(\cos\theta - \lambda)^2 + \sin^2\theta = 0$. This rearranges to $\cos\theta - \lambda = \pm\sqrt{-\sin^2\theta} \implies \lambda = \cos\theta \pm i\sin\theta = \text{cis}\pm\theta$.

- Case $\lambda = \cos\theta + i\sin\theta$:
$$\begin{bmatrix} \cos\theta & -\sin\theta \\ \sin\theta & \cos\theta \end{bmatrix} \begin{bmatrix} x \\ y \end{bmatrix} = (\cos\theta + i\sin\theta)\begin{bmatrix} x \\ y \end{bmatrix} = \begin{bmatrix} x\cos\theta + xi\sin\theta \\ y\cos\theta + yi\sin\theta \end{bmatrix}$$

This results in a system of equations:
$$x\cos\theta - y\sin\theta = x\cos\theta + xi\sin\theta,$$
$$x\sin\theta + y\cos\theta = y\cos\theta + yi\sin\theta.$$

After some simplification, we have $y = -ix$ and $x = yi$, we can conclude that all eigenvectors are of the form $\begin{bmatrix} x \\ -xi \end{bmatrix}$, i.e. scalar multiples of $\begin{bmatrix} 1 \\ -i \end{bmatrix}$.

- Case $\lambda = \cos\theta - i\sin\theta$:
$$\begin{bmatrix} \cos\theta & -\sin\theta \\ \sin\theta & \cos\theta \end{bmatrix} \begin{bmatrix} x \\ y \end{bmatrix} = (\cos\theta - i\sin\theta)\begin{bmatrix} x \\ y \end{bmatrix} = \begin{bmatrix} x\cos\theta - xi\sin\theta \\ y\cos\theta - yi\sin\theta \end{bmatrix}$$

We similarly solve a system of equations to get $y = xi$, $x = -yi$, implying that our eigenvectors are of the form $\begin{bmatrix} x \\ xi \end{bmatrix}$, i.e. scalar multiples of $\begin{bmatrix} 1 \\ i \end{bmatrix}$. $\square$

Problem 8.2.52. Find eigenvalues and eigenvectors of H_θ.

Solution. The determinant of $H_\theta - \lambda I = \begin{bmatrix} \cos 2\theta - \lambda & \sin 2\theta \\ \sin 2\theta & -\cos 2\theta - \lambda \end{bmatrix}$ must equal zero, i.e. $-(\cos 2\theta + \lambda)(\cos 2\theta - \lambda) - \sin^2 2\theta = 0$, which rearranges to $\cos^2 2\theta - \lambda^2 + \sin^2 2\theta = 0$, giving solutions $\lambda = \pm 1$.

- Case $\lambda = 1$:
$$\begin{bmatrix} \cos 2\theta & \sin 2\theta \\ \sin 2\theta & -\cos 2\theta \end{bmatrix} \begin{bmatrix} x \\ y \end{bmatrix} = \begin{bmatrix} x \\ y \end{bmatrix}$$

This gives the system of equations
$$x\cos 2\theta + y\sin 2\theta = x,$$
$$x\sin 2\theta - y\cos 2\theta = y.$$

After simplification, we end up with $y = \dfrac{1 - \cos 2\theta}{\sin 2\theta}x$, which resembles the half-angle formula for tangent, from which we can deduce that $y = x\tan\theta$, so our eigenvectors are of the form $\begin{bmatrix} x \\ x\tan\theta \end{bmatrix}$, i.e. $x\begin{bmatrix} 1 \\ \tan\theta \end{bmatrix}$. As x is a scalar which spans over all $\mathbb{R}$, we are allowed to make the substitution $x \longrightarrow x\cos\theta$, so we can express the form of the eigenvector as $x\begin{bmatrix} \cos\theta \\ \sin\theta \end{bmatrix}$ i.e. all scalar multiples of $\begin{bmatrix} \cos\theta \\ \sin\theta \end{bmatrix}$.

- Case $\lambda = -1$:
$$\begin{bmatrix} \cos 2\theta & \sin 2\theta \\ \sin 2\theta & -\cos 2\theta \end{bmatrix} \begin{bmatrix} x \\ y \end{bmatrix} = \begin{bmatrix} -x \\ -y \end{bmatrix}$$

Similarly, we solve a system of equations to get the solution $y = -\dfrac{1 + \cos 2\theta}{\sin 2\theta} x = -x \cot \theta$, so our eigenvectors can be expressed in the form $x \begin{bmatrix} 1 \\ -\cot \theta \end{bmatrix}$, and using the valid substitution $x \longrightarrow x \sin \theta$, we have a cleaner form $x \begin{bmatrix} \sin \theta \\ -\cos \theta \end{bmatrix}$ i.e. all scalar multiples of $\begin{bmatrix} \sin \theta \\ -\cos \theta \end{bmatrix}$. □

Definition 8.2.53. A set of vectors $\vec{v_1}, \vec{v_2}, \ldots, \vec{v_n}$ is **linearly independent** if whenever $a_1 \vec{v_1} + a_2 \vec{v_2} + \ldots + a_n \vec{v_n} = 0$, then $a_1 = a_2 = \ldots = a_n = 0$.

Otherwise, the set of vectors is **linearly dependent**.

Problem 8.2.54. Determine if the vectors $\begin{bmatrix} 1 \\ -1 \end{bmatrix}, \begin{bmatrix} 4 \\ -1 \end{bmatrix}$ are linearly independent or not.

Solution. Consider scalars $a, b \in \mathbb{R}$ such that
$$a \begin{bmatrix} 1 \\ -1 \end{bmatrix} + b \begin{bmatrix} 4 \\ -1 \end{bmatrix} = \begin{bmatrix} 0 \\ 0 \end{bmatrix}.$$

We have the system of equations $a + 4b = 0$ and $-a - b = 0$, which imply $a = b = 0$, so these vectors are indeed linearly independent. □

Problem 8.2.55. Are the vectors $\begin{bmatrix} 1 \\ 2 \end{bmatrix}$ and $\begin{bmatrix} 2 \\ 4 \end{bmatrix}$ linearly independent?

Solution. Note that
$$-2 \begin{bmatrix} 1 \\ 2 \end{bmatrix} + 1 \begin{bmatrix} 2 \\ 4 \end{bmatrix} = \begin{bmatrix} 0 \\ 0 \end{bmatrix}.$$

Since $-2, 1 \neq 0$, $\begin{bmatrix} 1 \\ 2 \end{bmatrix}$ and $\begin{bmatrix} 2 \\ 4 \end{bmatrix}$ are linearly dependent. □

Exercise 8.2.56. Prove that $\vec{v}, \vec{w}$ are linearly independent if and only if one is a scalar multiple of the other.

> **Theorem 8.2.57**
> Any three vectors in $\mathbb{R}^2$ are linearly dependent.

Proof. Let our three vectors be
$$\begin{bmatrix} a \\ b \end{bmatrix}, \begin{bmatrix} c \\ d \end{bmatrix}, \begin{bmatrix} e \\ f \end{bmatrix}.$$

Suppose we try to solve the equation
$$x \begin{bmatrix} a \\ b \end{bmatrix} + y \begin{bmatrix} c \\ d \end{bmatrix} = \begin{bmatrix} e \\ f \end{bmatrix}.$$

Note that this equation can be rewritten as

$$\begin{bmatrix} a & c \\ b & d \end{bmatrix} \begin{bmatrix} x \\ y \end{bmatrix} = \begin{bmatrix} e \\ f \end{bmatrix}.$$

There exists a solution to this whenever the matrix $\begin{bmatrix} a & c \\ b & d \end{bmatrix}$ has an inverse, i.e. the determinant $ad - bc \neq 0$. If we have a solution to this equation, then we're done, since the sum of some scalar multiples of the first two vectors will indeed result in the third vector.

Otherwise, assume that $ad - bc = 0$. Without loss of generality, let $a \neq 0$. Then we have $a = \frac{bc}{d}$, so $d = \frac{bc}{a}$, so our first two vectors are

$$\begin{bmatrix} a \\ b \end{bmatrix}, \begin{bmatrix} c \\ \frac{bc}{a} \end{bmatrix}.$$

But note that

$$\frac{c}{a} \begin{bmatrix} a \\ b \end{bmatrix} + -1 \begin{bmatrix} c \\ \frac{bc}{a} \end{bmatrix} = \begin{bmatrix} 0 \\ 0 \end{bmatrix}.$$

We have shown that the three vectors are linearly dependent in either case, and so we are done. □

It turns out that this theorem is true in general (i.e. that any $n + 1$ vectors in $\mathbb{R}^n$ are linearly dependent).

Any n linearly independent vector in $\mathbb{R}^n$ is called a **basis** for $\mathbb{R}^n$. This is a generalization of the standard basis vectors that we had defined earlier in the chapter.

Recall that we were able to express any vector as a linear combination of the standard basis vectors: $\langle a_1, a_2, a_3, \ldots, a_n \rangle = a_1 \vec{i_1} + a_2 \vec{i_2} + a_3 \vec{i_3} + \ldots + a_n \vec{i_n}$.

This can be extended to any basis in general; any vector in $\mathbb{R}^n$ can be written as a linear combination of vectors in the basis.

Problem 8.2.58. Why can't $\begin{bmatrix} 1 \\ 0 \\ 0 \end{bmatrix}, \begin{bmatrix} 0 \\ 1 \\ 0 \end{bmatrix}$, and $\begin{bmatrix} 1 \\ 1 \\ 0 \end{bmatrix}$ be a basis in $\mathbb{R}^3$?

Solution. First, it is easy to observe that $\begin{bmatrix} 1 \\ 0 \\ 0 \end{bmatrix} + \begin{bmatrix} 0 \\ 1 \\ 0 \end{bmatrix} = \begin{bmatrix} 1 \\ 1 \\ 0 \end{bmatrix}$, so they are not linearly independent.

Furthermore, we cannot express the vector $\begin{bmatrix} 0 \\ 0 \\ 1 \end{bmatrix}$ as any linear combination of these vectors because their third entries are all 0. This fails the fact that any vector in $\mathbb{R}^3$ can be written as a linear combination of vectors in the basis for $\mathbb{R}^3$. □

We shift our discussion of matrices back to the determinant. It turns out that it has far greater significance than one may initially conceive. Consider a triangle made up of vectors:

Any vector in $\mathbb{R}^n$ can be written as a linear combination of vectors in the basis.

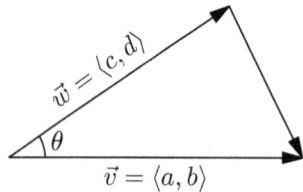

Theorem 8.2.59

The area of a triangle defined by the vectors $\vec{w} = \langle a, b \rangle$ and $\vec{v} = \langle c, d \rangle$ is:
$$\frac{1}{2}|ad - bc| = \frac{1}{2}\left|\text{Det}\left(\begin{bmatrix} a & c \\ b & d \end{bmatrix}\right)\right|.$$

Proof. Let θ be the angle between $\vec{v}$ and $\vec{w}$. Then $\cos\theta = \dfrac{\vec{v} \cdot \vec{w}}{\|\vec{v}\|\|\vec{w}\|}$. From this, we can derive that $\sin\theta = \sqrt{1 - \left(\dfrac{\vec{v} \cdot \vec{w}}{\|\vec{v}\|\|\vec{w}\|}\right)^2}$. By Theorem 6.6.1, we can apply the area formula $\dfrac{1}{2}ab\sin C$ (for any two sides a, b with included angle C) to our vectors which make up the triangle to get our desired expression. Instead of sides a and b, we have $\|\vec{v}\|$ and $\|\vec{w}\|$, and replace C by θ in the context of this proof.

$$\begin{aligned}
\textbf{Area} &= \frac{1}{2}\|\vec{v}\|\|\vec{w}\|\sin\theta \\
&= \frac{1}{2}\sqrt{\|\vec{v}\|^2\|\vec{w}\|^2 - (\vec{v}\cdot\vec{w})^2} \\
&= \frac{1}{2}\sqrt{(a^2+b^2)(c^2+d^2) - (ac+bd)^2} \\
&= \frac{1}{2}\sqrt{(ac)^2 + (ad)^2 + (bc)^2 + (bd)^2 - (ac)^2 - 2(ac)(bd) - (bd)^2} \\
&= \frac{1}{2}\sqrt{(ad)^2 + (bc)^2 - 2(ad)(bc)} \\
&= \frac{1}{2}\sqrt{(ad-bc)^2} \\
&= \frac{1}{2}|ad - bc| \\
&= \frac{1}{2}\left|\text{Det}\left(\begin{bmatrix} a & c \\ b & d \end{bmatrix}\right)\right|.
\end{aligned}$$
□

Now, we can easily derive the area of a parallelogram:

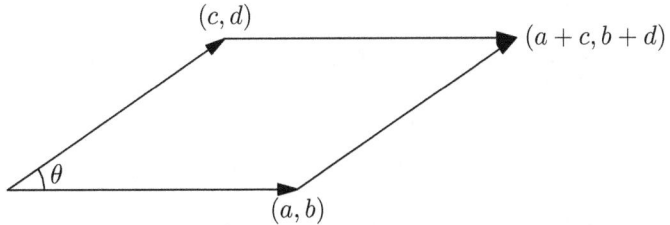

Theorem 8.2.60

The area of a parallelogram formed by vectors $\langle a, b \rangle$ and $\langle c, d \rangle$ is

$$\left| \text{Det} \left(\begin{bmatrix} a & c \\ b & d \end{bmatrix} \right) \right|.$$

What if we place the triangle on a general coordinate system?

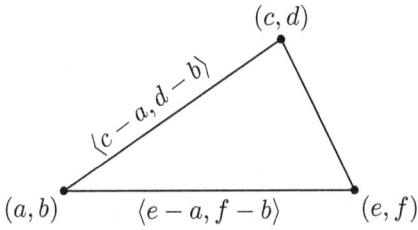

Theorem 8.2.61 (Shoelace Theorem)

Consider a triangle with general coordinates (a, b), (c, d), and (e, f). Then the area of this triangle is

$$\frac{1}{2} |(ad + cf + eb) - (bc + de + fa)|.$$

Proof. Based on our coordinates (a, b), (c, d), and (e, f), the two vectors with common tail on (a, b) are $\langle c - a, d - b \rangle$ and $\langle e - a, f - b \rangle$. We can then apply Theorem 8.2.59:

$$\begin{aligned}
\textbf{Area} &= \frac{1}{2} \left| \text{Det} \left(\begin{bmatrix} c - a & e - a \\ d - b & f - b \end{bmatrix} \right) \right| \\
&= \frac{1}{2} |(c - a)(f - b) - (e - a)(d - b)| \\
&= \frac{1}{2} |cf - ab - af + ab - ed + eb + ad - ab| \\
&= \frac{1}{2} |(ad + cf + eb) - (bc + de + fa)|.
\end{aligned}$$

□

This theorem seems quite complex, but it is actually quite simple once you see the pattern.

What we do is list out the coordinates, and repeat the first point (which would be (a, b) in this example) at the end as well:

$$\begin{array}{cc} a & b \\ c & d \\ e & f \\ a & b \end{array}$$

Then, draw diagonal lines from a to d, c to f, and e to b, as such:

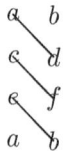

Take the product of each diagonal pair and add them all up. Here, we would have $ad + cf + eb$. Then, draw diagonal lines from b to c, d to e, and f to a:

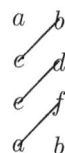

Do the same thing as last time: take the product of each diagonal pair and add all the products. So we have the quantity $bc + de + fa$.

We have found the two quantities used in the formula $\frac{1}{2}|(ad + cf + eb) - (bc + de + fa)|$ we discovered, so we can compute the area now.

This method of listing out the coordinates and taking diagonals is very helpful for applying Shoelace Theorem correctly without having to completely memorize it.

> **Theorem 8.2.62** (Generalized Shoelace Theorem)
> The area of a polygon defined by the points (x_i, y_i) for $1 \leq i \leq n$ (in counterclockwise order) is
> $$\frac{1}{2}((x_1y_2 + x_2y_3 + \cdots + x_{n-1}y_n + x_ny_1) - (y_1x_2 + y_2x_3 + \cdots + y_{n-1}x_n + y_nx_1)).$$

This theorem can be proved by induction on the n-sided polygon. At the inductive step, we add one more point outside the n-sided polygon. If we connect the two closest points on the polygon to this new point, we end up with an $n+1$-sided polygon.

We can then compute the area of this by adding the existing area of the n-sided polygon (which would be the assumption made by the inductive hypothesis) to the area of the triangle formed by the new point and the two closest points.

In general, to use the generalized Shoelace Theorem properly, we must list out the coordinates in either clockwise or counter-clockwise order (the direction doesn't matter, as long as the coordinates are in order). Do not forget to repeat the first pair of coordinates at the end too.

We can then apply our method of drawing diagonal lines to arrive at the expression given by the theorem.

Problem 8.2.63. Find the area of the quadrilateral with points at $(1,1)$, $(9,0)$, $(2,4)$, and $(7,6)$.

Solution. We set up our list of coordinates in clockwise order (or counter-clockwise order; it doesn't matter because of the absolute value sign):

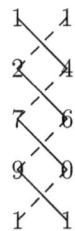

From the solid diagonal lines, we end up with the quantity $1 \cdot 4 + 2 \cdot 6 + 7 \cdot 0 + 9 \cdot 1 = 25$.

From the dashed diagonal lines, we have $1 \cdot 2 + 4 \cdot 7 + 6 \cdot 9 + 0 \cdot 1 = 84$.

Thus, our area is $\frac{1}{2}|25 - 84| = \boxed{\frac{59}{2}}$.

Note that drawing these diagonal lines makes the diagram resemble shoelaces - hence, the name of the theorem. □

Lastly, we move on to row and column operations on matrices. This will enable us to compute the determinant of a 3×3 matrix.

Consider the following matrices:

$$A = \begin{bmatrix} a & 0 \\ 0 & 1 \end{bmatrix} \quad B = \begin{bmatrix} 1 & 0 \\ 0 & b \end{bmatrix} \quad C = \begin{bmatrix} 1 & c \\ 0 & 1 \end{bmatrix} \quad D = \begin{bmatrix} 1 & 0 \\ d & 1 \end{bmatrix} \quad E = \begin{bmatrix} 0 & 1 \\ 1 & 0 \end{bmatrix}$$

for any $a, b, c, d \in \mathbb{R}$. Let $M = \begin{bmatrix} r & s \\ t & u \end{bmatrix}$ represent a general 2×2 matrix.

- If we multiply the matrix A to the left of matrix M, we get

$$AM = \begin{bmatrix} a & 0 \\ 0 & 1 \end{bmatrix} \begin{bmatrix} r & s \\ t & u \end{bmatrix} = \begin{bmatrix} ar & as \\ t & u \end{bmatrix}.$$

The top row of M is multiplied by scalar a.

- If we multiply the matrix A to the right of matrix M, we get

$$MA = \begin{bmatrix} r & s \\ t & u \end{bmatrix} \begin{bmatrix} a & 0 \\ 0 & 1 \end{bmatrix} = \begin{bmatrix} ar & s \\ at & u \end{bmatrix}.$$

The left column of M is multiplied by scalar a.

- If we multiply the matrix B to the left of matrix M, we get

$$BM = \begin{bmatrix} 1 & 0 \\ 0 & b \end{bmatrix} \begin{bmatrix} r & s \\ t & u \end{bmatrix} = \begin{bmatrix} r & s \\ bt & bu \end{bmatrix}.$$

  The bottom row of M is multiplied by scalar b.

- If we multiply the matrix B to the right of matrix M, we get

$$MB = \begin{bmatrix} r & s \\ t & u \end{bmatrix} \begin{bmatrix} 1 & 0 \\ 0 & b \end{bmatrix} = \begin{bmatrix} r & bs \\ t & bu \end{bmatrix}.$$

  The right column of M is multiplied by scalar b.

- If we multiply the matrix C to the left of matrix M, we get

$$CM = \begin{bmatrix} 1 & c \\ 0 & 1 \end{bmatrix} \begin{bmatrix} r & s \\ t & u \end{bmatrix} = \begin{bmatrix} r+ct & s+cu \\ t & u \end{bmatrix}.$$

  Then, c times the bottom row is added to the top row of M.

- If we multiply the matrix C to the right of matrix M, we get

$$MC = \begin{bmatrix} r & s \\ t & u \end{bmatrix} \begin{bmatrix} 1 & c \\ 0 & 1 \end{bmatrix} = \begin{bmatrix} r & s+cr \\ t & u+ct \end{bmatrix}.$$

  Then, c times the left column is added to the right column of M.

- If we multiply the matrix D to the left of matrix M, we get

$$DM = \begin{bmatrix} 1 & 0 \\ d & 1 \end{bmatrix} \begin{bmatrix} r & s \\ t & u \end{bmatrix} = \begin{bmatrix} r & s \\ t+dr & u+ds \end{bmatrix}.$$

  Then, d times the top row is added to the bottom row of M.

- If we multiply the matrix D to the right of matrix M, we get

$$MD = \begin{bmatrix} r & s \\ t & u \end{bmatrix} \begin{bmatrix} 1 & 0 \\ d & 1 \end{bmatrix} = \begin{bmatrix} r+ds & s \\ t+du & u \end{bmatrix}.$$

  Then, d times the right column is added to the left column of M.

- If we multiply the matrix E to the left of matrix M, we get

$$EM = \begin{bmatrix} 0 & 1 \\ 1 & 0 \end{bmatrix} \begin{bmatrix} r & s \\ t & u \end{bmatrix} = \begin{bmatrix} t & u \\ r & s \end{bmatrix}.$$

  The rows of M are swapped.

- If we multiply the matrix E to the right of matrix M, we get

$$ME = \begin{bmatrix} r & s \\ t & u \end{bmatrix} \begin{bmatrix} 0 & 1 \\ 1 & 0 \end{bmatrix} = \begin{bmatrix} s & r \\ u & t \end{bmatrix}.$$

The columns of M are swapped.

Note that $\text{Det}(A) = a$ and $\text{Det}(B) = b$, which implies that $\text{Det}(AM) = \text{Det}(MA) = a \cdot \text{Det}(M)$ and $\text{Det}(BM) = \text{Det}(MB) = b \cdot \text{Det}(M)$. Therefore, if we multiply a row or column of a matrix M by some scalar, then the determinant of M is also multiplied by that scalar.

Furthermore, $\text{Det}(C) = \text{Det}(D) = 1$, so $\text{Det}(CM) = \text{Det}(MC) = \text{Det}(DM) = \text{Det}(MD) = 1 \cdot \text{Det}(M) = \text{Det}(M)$. This means that adding a multiple of some row to another row or adding a multiple of some column to another column does not affect the determinant.

Lastly, $\text{Det}(E) = -1$, which means that swapping a pair of rows or a pair of columns also flips the sign of the determinant.

This result can be generalized to higher $n \times n$ matrices. However, without proof, we shall summarize the information above in a general fashion:

> **Theorem 8.2.64 (Row and Column Operations)**
>
> Consider an $n \times n$ matrix M. We are allowed the following row and column operations:
>
> 1. When any row or any column is multiplied by some scalar k, the determinant of M is also multiplied by k.
>
> 2. A multiple of some row added to another row, or a multiple of some column added to another column, does not change the determinant of M.
>
> 3. When a pair of rows or a pair of columns is swapped, the sign of the determinant is flipped (positive to negative, and vice-versa).

> **Theorem 8.2.65**
>
> Consider a 3×3 matrix with arbitrary entries, as shown:
>
> $$\begin{bmatrix} a & b & c \\ d & e & f \\ g & h & i \end{bmatrix}$$
>
> The determinant of this matrix is:
>
> $$aei - bdi - ceg - ahf + cdh + bfg.$$

To prove the theorem, we will first need a definition and a lemma:

Definition 8.2.66. Consider a matrix M in this particular form:
$$M = \begin{bmatrix} r & s & t \\ 0 & u & v \\ 0 & 0 & w \end{bmatrix}.$$

We call this **upper triangular form**, where all entries below the non-zero main diagonal are zeroes.

> **Lemma 8.2.67**
>
> If matrix M is in upper triangular form, then $\text{Det}(M) = ruw$.

Proof. Note that
$$\begin{bmatrix} r & s & t \\ 0 & u & v \\ 0 & 0 & w \end{bmatrix} = \begin{bmatrix} r & 0 & 0 \\ 0 & u & 0 \\ 0 & 0 & w \end{bmatrix} \begin{bmatrix} 1 & r^{-1}s & r^{-1}t \\ 0 & 1 & u^{-1}v \\ 0 & 0 & 1 \end{bmatrix}.$$

Observe the following:
$$\text{Det}\left(\begin{bmatrix} r & 0 & 0 \\ 0 & u & 0 \\ 0 & 0 & w \end{bmatrix}\right) = \text{Det}\left(\begin{bmatrix} r & 0 & 0 \\ 0 & 1 & 0 \\ 0 & 0 & 1 \end{bmatrix} \begin{bmatrix} 1 & 0 & 0 \\ 0 & u & 0 \\ 0 & 0 & 1 \end{bmatrix} \begin{bmatrix} 1 & 0 & 0 \\ 0 & 1 & 0 \\ 0 & 0 & w \end{bmatrix}\right) = ruw.$$

But notice that $\begin{bmatrix} r & 0 & 0 \\ 0 & 1 & 0 \\ 0 & 0 & 1 \end{bmatrix}$ is the result of multiplying the first row of I_3 by r. Since the determinant of I_3 is 1, the determinant of $\begin{bmatrix} r & 0 & 0 \\ 0 & 1 & 0 \\ 0 & 0 & 1 \end{bmatrix}$ is r. Likewise, $\begin{bmatrix} 1 & 0 & 0 \\ 0 & u & 0 \\ 0 & 0 & 1 \end{bmatrix}$ and $\begin{bmatrix} 1 & 0 & 0 \\ 0 & 1 & 0 \\ 0 & 0 & w \end{bmatrix}$ have determinants of u and w respectively. Thus,
$$\text{Det}\left(\begin{bmatrix} r & 0 & 0 \\ 0 & u & 0 \\ 0 & 0 & w \end{bmatrix}\right) = \text{Det}\left(\begin{bmatrix} r & 0 & 0 \\ 0 & 1 & 0 \\ 0 & 0 & 1 \end{bmatrix} \begin{bmatrix} 1 & 0 & 0 \\ 0 & u & 0 \\ 0 & 0 & 1 \end{bmatrix} \begin{bmatrix} 1 & 0 & 0 \\ 0 & 1 & 0 \\ 0 & 0 & w \end{bmatrix}\right) = ruw.$$

Now take a look at the matrix
$$\begin{bmatrix} 1 & r^{-1}s & r^{-1}t \\ 0 & 1 & u^{-1}v \\ 0 & 0 & 1 \end{bmatrix}.$$

Denoting the first row, second row, and third row as R_1, R_2, and R_3 respectively, note that we can perform the row operation $-(u^{-1}v)R_3 + R_2 \longrightarrow R_2$ to eliminate only the $u^{-1}v$ term from the second row, and the row operation $-(r^{-1}t)R_3 + R_1 \longrightarrow R_1$ to eliminate only the $r^{-1}t$ term from the first row. Finally, we can do a row operation $-(r^{-1}s)R_2 + R_1 \longrightarrow R_1$ to eliminate only the $r^{-1}s$ term from the first row. We are left with the identity matrix I_3. We have established that
$$\text{Det}\left(\begin{bmatrix} 1 & r^{-1}s & r^{-1}t \\ 0 & 1 & u^{-1}v \\ 0 & 0 & 1 \end{bmatrix}\right) = \text{Det}(I_3),$$

since these row operations do not affect the overall determinant of the matrix. Thus we can conclude the proof of this lemma:

$$\text{Det}\left(\begin{bmatrix} r & s & t \\ 0 & u & v \\ 0 & 0 & w \end{bmatrix}\right) = \text{Det}\left(\begin{bmatrix} r & 0 & 0 \\ 0 & u & 0 \\ 0 & 0 & w \end{bmatrix}\right) \text{Det}\left(\begin{bmatrix} 1 & r^{-1}s & r^{-1}t \\ 0 & 1 & u^{-1}v \\ 0 & 0 & 1 \end{bmatrix}\right)$$

$$= \text{Det}\left(\begin{bmatrix} r & 0 & 0 \\ 0 & u & 0 \\ 0 & 0 & w \end{bmatrix}\right) \text{Det}(I_3) = \text{Det}\left(\begin{bmatrix} r & 0 & 0 \\ 0 & u & 0 \\ 0 & 0 & w \end{bmatrix} \cdot I_3\right)$$

$$= \text{Det}\left(\begin{bmatrix} r & 0 & 0 \\ 0 & u & 0 \\ 0 & 0 & w \end{bmatrix}\right) = ruw. \qquad \square$$

Now, we proceed to prove the actual theorem of the 3×3 matrix determinant.

Proof. We intend to take advantage of row operations to find our determinant.

To use Lemma 8.2.67 to our advantage, we must convert our initial matrix

$$\begin{bmatrix} a & b & c \\ d & e & f \\ g & h & i \end{bmatrix},$$

to upper triangular form, through row operations. We use the same notation as used in the proof of Lemma 8.2.67. First we eliminate the d term:

$$\begin{bmatrix} a & b & c \\ d & e & f \\ g & h & i \end{bmatrix} \xrightarrow{-\frac{d}{a}R_1 + R_2 \to R_2} \begin{bmatrix} a & b & c \\ 0 & e - \frac{bd}{a} & f - \frac{cd}{a} \\ g & h & i \end{bmatrix}$$

Then we eliminate the g term:

$$\begin{bmatrix} a & b & c \\ 0 & e - \frac{bd}{a} & f - \frac{cd}{a} \\ g & h & i \end{bmatrix} \xrightarrow{-\frac{g}{a}R_1 + R_3 \to R_3} \begin{bmatrix} a & b & c \\ 0 & e - \frac{bd}{a} & f - \frac{cd}{a} \\ 0 & h - \frac{bg}{a} & i - \frac{cg}{a} \end{bmatrix}$$

And lastly, we eliminate the h term:

$$\begin{bmatrix} a & b & c \\ 0 & e - \frac{bd}{a} & f - \frac{cd}{a} \\ 0 & h - \frac{bg}{a} & i - \frac{cg}{a} \end{bmatrix} \xrightarrow{-\frac{\left(h - \frac{bg}{a}\right)}{\left(e - \frac{bd}{a}\right)} R_2 + R_3 \to R_3} \begin{bmatrix} a & b & c \\ 0 & e - \frac{bd}{a} & f - \frac{cd}{a} \\ 0 & 0 & \left(i - \frac{cg}{a} - \frac{\left(h - \frac{bg}{a}\right)}{\left(e - \frac{bd}{a}\right)}\left(f - \frac{cd}{a}\right)\right) \end{bmatrix}$$

By Lemma 8.2.67, the determinant is

$$a\left(e - \frac{bd}{a}\right)\left(i - \frac{cg}{a} - \frac{\left(h - \frac{bg}{a}\right)}{\left(e - \frac{bd}{a}\right)}\left(f - \frac{cd}{a}\right)\right) = a\left(\left(i - \frac{cg}{a}\right)\left(e - \frac{bd}{a}\right) - \left(h - \frac{bg}{a}\right)\left(f - \frac{cd}{a}\right)\right)$$

$$= \frac{1}{a}\left((ai - cg)(ae - bd) - (ah - bg)(af - cd)\right).$$

This simplifies to

$$\frac{1}{a}\left(a^2ei - abdi - aceg + bdcg - a^2hf + acdh + abfg - bcdg\right) = aei - bdi - ceg - ahf + cdh + bfg. \quad \square$$

This formula is certainly intimidating, but there is a visual memorization technique that is similar to the method we used to invoke the Shoelace theorem.

First, consider this **augmented matrix** with the first two columns appended at the end.

$$\left[\begin{array}{ccc|cc} a & b & c & a & b \\ d & e & f & d & e \\ g & h & i & g & h \end{array}\right]$$

Consider the three diagonals going from top-left to bottom-right, and take the sum of the products of the three entries in each of the diagonals, i.e. $aei + bfg + cdh$, as shown:

$$\left[\begin{array}{ccc|cc} \boxed{a} & b & c & a & b \\ d & \boxed{e} & f & d & e \\ g & h & \boxed{i} & g & h \end{array}\right], \left[\begin{array}{ccc|cc} a & \boxed{b} & c & a & b \\ d & e & \boxed{f} & d & e \\ g & h & i & \boxed{g} & h \end{array}\right], \left[\begin{array}{ccc|cc} a & b & \boxed{c} & a & b \\ d & e & f & \boxed{d} & e \\ g & h & i & g & \boxed{h} \end{array}\right]$$

Then consider the three diagonals going the other way, i.e. going from top-right to bottom-left, and, like above, take the sum of the products of the three entries in each of the diagonals, i.e. $ceg + afh + bdi$, as shown:

$$\left[\begin{array}{ccc|cc} a & b & \boxed{c} & a & b \\ d & \boxed{e} & f & d & e \\ \boxed{g} & h & i & g & h \end{array}\right], \left[\begin{array}{ccc|cc} a & b & c & \boxed{a} & b \\ d & e & \boxed{f} & d & e \\ g & \boxed{h} & i & g & h \end{array}\right], \left[\begin{array}{ccc|cc} a & b & c & a & \boxed{b} \\ d & e & f & \boxed{d} & e \\ g & h & \boxed{i} & g & h \end{array}\right]$$

Then our determinant is simply the first sum minus the second sum, i.e. $aei + bfg + cdh - (ceg + afh + bdi)$, which is what the theorem states.

Problem 8.2.68. Compute the determinant of $\begin{bmatrix} 2 & 3 & 6 \\ 1 & -4 & 3 \\ 2 & 5 & 9 \end{bmatrix}$ using the method shown above.

Solution. The Shoelace technique gives us $(2)(-4)(9)+(3)(3)(2)+(6)(1)(5)-(6)(-4)(2)-(2)(3)(5)-(3)(1)(9) = -72 + 18 + 30 - (-48) - 30 - 27 = \boxed{-33}$. $\quad \square$

There is also another way to evaluate the 3×3 determinant. With the matrix

$$\begin{bmatrix} a & b & c \\ d & e & f \\ g & h & i \end{bmatrix},$$

consider the first row, which is a, b, and c. For each entry, imagine that you delete the row and column of the matrix which contains that entry you are considering. You will have exactly four entries left that have not been deleted. Form a 2 × 2 matrix out of those four entries in the exact same order. The determinant of this resulting 2 × 2 matrix is called a **minor**.

For example, the minor for a would be:

$$\text{Det}\left(\begin{bmatrix} \not{a} & \not{b} & \not{c} \\ \not{d} & e & f \\ \not{g} & h & i \end{bmatrix}\right) \implies \text{Det}\left(\begin{bmatrix} e & f \\ h & i \end{bmatrix}\right).$$

The minor for e would be:

$$\text{Det}\left(\begin{bmatrix} a & \not{b} & c \\ \not{d} & \not{e} & \not{f} \\ g & \not{h} & i \end{bmatrix}\right) \implies \text{Det}\left(\begin{bmatrix} a & c \\ g & i \end{bmatrix}\right).$$

We can find the determinant of the 3 × 3 matrix by considering one whole row or column, and for each entry, find the product of that entry and its minor. The determinant would then be the *alternating sum* of those products, based on the following sign pattern for 3 × 3 determinants:

$$\begin{bmatrix} + & - & + \\ - & + & - \\ + & - & + \end{bmatrix}$$

For example, we can evaluate the minors on the first row to get:

$$\text{Det}\left(\begin{bmatrix} a & b & c \\ d & e & f \\ g & h & i \end{bmatrix}\right) = a \cdot \text{Det}\left(\begin{bmatrix} e & f \\ h & i \end{bmatrix}\right) - b \cdot \text{Det}\left(\begin{bmatrix} d & f \\ g & i \end{bmatrix}\right) + c \cdot \text{Det}\left(\begin{bmatrix} d & e \\ g & h \end{bmatrix}\right).$$

We can also find the same determinant by evaluating minors on the second column:

$$\text{Det}\left(\begin{bmatrix} a & b & c \\ d & e & f \\ g & h & i \end{bmatrix}\right) = -b \cdot \text{Det}\left(\begin{bmatrix} d & f \\ g & i \end{bmatrix}\right) + e \cdot \text{Det}\left(\begin{bmatrix} a & c \\ g & i \end{bmatrix}\right) - h \cdot \text{Det}\left(\begin{bmatrix} a & c \\ d & f \end{bmatrix}\right).$$

Problem 8.2.69. Solve Problem 8.2.68 using the minors method and confirm that you get the same answer.

Example 8.2.70

Use matrices to solve the following system of equations:

$$2x + 3y + 4z = 4,$$
$$x - 2y + 5z = 1,$$
$$3x + 6y - z = 2.$$

Solution. We read off the coefficients of x, y, and z from each of the three equations into a 3×3 matrix. However, we also read the constants 4, 1, and 2 into a separate column appended at the end of the matrix; this addition of an 'extra column' results in an augmented matrix, as shown:

$$\begin{bmatrix} 2 & 3 & 4 & | & 4 \\ 1 & -2 & 5 & | & 1 \\ 3 & 6 & -1 & | & 2 \end{bmatrix}$$

If we convert this to upper triangular form, then we have a matrix in the form

$$\begin{bmatrix} a & b & c & | & r \\ 0 & d & e & | & s \\ 0 & 0 & f & | & u \end{bmatrix},$$

from which we read off the equations as $fz = u$, $dy + ez = s$, and $ax + by + cz = r$. Using the equation $fz = u$, we can find the value of z, from which we can substitute it into $dy + ez = s$ to find y, and substitute in y for $ax + by + cz = r$ to find x. This process is called *back substitution*.

We can use row operations, as follows (keep in mind that we treat the fourth augmented column the same as others!):

$$\begin{bmatrix} 2 & 3 & 4 & | & 4 \\ 1 & -2 & 5 & | & 1 \\ 3 & 6 & -1 & | & 2 \end{bmatrix} \xrightarrow{R_1 \leftrightarrow R_2} \begin{bmatrix} 1 & -2 & 5 & | & 1 \\ 2 & 3 & 4 & | & 4 \\ 3 & 6 & -1 & | & 2 \end{bmatrix}$$

$$\begin{bmatrix} 1 & -2 & 5 & | & 1 \\ 2 & 3 & 4 & | & 4 \\ 3 & 6 & -1 & | & 2 \end{bmatrix} \xrightarrow[-3R_1+R_3 \to R_3]{-2R_1+R_2 \to R_2} \begin{bmatrix} 1 & -2 & 5 & | & 1 \\ 0 & 7 & -6 & | & 2 \\ 0 & 12 & -16 & | & -1 \end{bmatrix}$$

$$\begin{bmatrix} 1 & -2 & 5 & | & 1 \\ 0 & 7 & -6 & | & 2 \\ 0 & 12 & -16 & | & -1 \end{bmatrix} \xrightarrow{7R_3 \to R_3} \begin{bmatrix} 1 & -2 & 5 & | & 1 \\ 0 & 7 & -6 & | & 2 \\ 0 & 84 & -112 & | & -7 \end{bmatrix}$$

$$\begin{bmatrix} 1 & -2 & 5 & | & 1 \\ 0 & 7 & -6 & | & 2 \\ 0 & 84 & -112 & | & -7 \end{bmatrix} \xrightarrow{-12R_2+R_3 \to R_3} \begin{bmatrix} 1 & -2 & 5 & | & 1 \\ 0 & 7 & -6 & | & 2 \\ 0 & 0 & -40 & | & -31 \end{bmatrix}$$

At this point, we have that $-40z = 31 \implies z = \dfrac{31}{40}$ from the last row. We then plug in this value to $7y - 6z = 2$ (second row), yielding $y = \dfrac{19}{20}$. Lastly, we have $x - 2y + 5z = 1$ from the first row, and plugging in respective values of y and z give $x = -\dfrac{39}{40}$. Therefore our solution is $(x, y, z) = \boxed{\left(-\dfrac{39}{40}, \dfrac{19}{20}, \dfrac{31}{40}\right)}$.

Alternatively, we could keep applying our row operations until we get to a form

$$\begin{bmatrix} 1 & 0 & 0 & | & a \\ 0 & 1 & 0 & | & b \\ 0 & 0 & 1 & | & c \end{bmatrix}$$

for arbitrary $a, b, c \in \mathbb{R}$, from which we can directly read off our values for x, y, z. □

We now generalize the concept of eigenvectors and eigenvalues to 3×3 matrices. This is very complicated for general matrices, so we limit our discussion of eigenvalues and eigenvectors to 3×3 matrices in upper triangular form.

Example 8.2.71

Find eigenvectors and eigenvalues for

$$M = \begin{bmatrix} 1 & 2 & 3 \\ 0 & 4 & 5 \\ 0 & 0 & 6 \end{bmatrix}.$$

Solution. If λ is an eigenvalue of this matrix, then $\text{Det}(M - \lambda I) = 0$. By Lemma 8.2.67, we can evaluate this as

$$\text{Det}\left(\begin{bmatrix} 1-\lambda & 2 & 3 \\ 0 & 4-\lambda & 5 \\ 0 & 0 & 6-\lambda \end{bmatrix}\right) = (1-\lambda)(4-\lambda)(6-\lambda) = 0.$$

Thus, the only possible roots of this polynomial are λ are $1, 4, 6$.

- Case $\lambda = 1$:

    Writing the equation out, we have

    $$\begin{bmatrix} 1 & 2 & 3 \\ 0 & 4 & 5 \\ 0 & 0 & 6 \end{bmatrix} \begin{bmatrix} a \\ b \\ c \end{bmatrix} = \begin{bmatrix} a + 2b + 3c \\ 4b + 5c \\ 6c \end{bmatrix} = \begin{bmatrix} a \\ b \\ c \end{bmatrix}.$$

    We now have 3 equations:

    $$a + 2b + 3c = a,$$
    $$4b + 5c = b,$$
    $$6c = c.$$

    The third equation gives us $c = 0$. Back-substituting, we also get $b = 0$. Then, $a = a$, which is true for any a. Thus, the eigenvectors for $\lambda = 1$ are of the form $\begin{bmatrix} a \\ 0 \\ 0 \end{bmatrix} = a \begin{bmatrix} 1 \\ 0 \\ 0 \end{bmatrix}$ i.e. scalar multiples of $\begin{bmatrix} 1 \\ 0 \\ 0 \end{bmatrix}$.

- Case $\lambda = 4$:

    Similarly, we have the equations

    $$a + 2b + 3c = 4a,$$
    $$4b + 5c = 4b,$$

$$6c = 4c.$$

Like before, the third equations implies $c = 0$. Then the second equation simplifies to $4b = 4b$ i.e. $b = b$, which is true for any value of b.

Furthermore, since $c = 0$, the first equation $a + 2b + 3c = 4a$ reduces to $2b = 3a$ i.e. $a = \frac{3}{2}b$, therefore the eigenvectors are of the form $\begin{bmatrix} \frac{2}{3}b \\ b \\ 0 \end{bmatrix} = b \begin{bmatrix} \frac{2}{3} \\ 1 \\ 0 \end{bmatrix}$, from which we can make the valid substitution $b \longrightarrow 3b$ to get the cleaner form: $b \begin{bmatrix} 2 \\ 3 \\ 0 \end{bmatrix}$ i.e. scalar multiples of $\begin{bmatrix} 2 \\ 3 \\ 0 \end{bmatrix}$.

- Case $\lambda = 6$:

$$a + 2b + 3c = 6a,$$
$$4b + 5c = 6b,$$
$$6c = 6c.$$

The third equation implies $c = c$ for any value of c. The second equation simplifies to $b = \frac{5}{2}c$ and the first equation simplifies to $a = \frac{8}{5}c$, therefore our eigenvectors are of the form $\begin{bmatrix} \frac{8}{5}c \\ \frac{5}{2}c \\ c \end{bmatrix} = c \begin{bmatrix} \frac{8}{5} \\ \frac{5}{2} \\ 1 \end{bmatrix}$.

Then we can substitute $c \longrightarrow 10c$ to get $c \begin{bmatrix} 16 \\ 25 \\ 10 \end{bmatrix}$ i.e. scalar multiples of $\begin{bmatrix} 16 \\ 25 \\ 10 \end{bmatrix}$. □

Problem 8.2.72. Find eigenvalues and eigenvectors for the matrix
$$\begin{bmatrix} 2 & 1 & 4 \\ 0 & -3 & 2 \\ 0 & 0 & 1 \end{bmatrix}.$$

Solution. We know that $\text{Det}(M - \lambda I) = 0$ for given matrix M and possible eigenvalues λ. Then, we have

$$\text{Det}\left(\begin{bmatrix} 2-\lambda & 1 & 4 \\ 0 & -3-\lambda & 2 \\ 0 & 0 & 1-\lambda \end{bmatrix} \right) = (2-\lambda)(-3-\lambda)(1-\lambda) = 0.$$

We have the roots $\lambda = 2, -3, 1$. We check each case:

1. For $\lambda = 2$, we have
$$\begin{bmatrix} 2 & 1 & 4 \\ 0 & -3 & 2 \\ 0 & 0 & 1 \end{bmatrix} \begin{bmatrix} x \\ y \\ z \end{bmatrix} = 2 \begin{bmatrix} x \\ y \\ z \end{bmatrix}.$$

We are left with the system of equations
$$2x + y + 4z = 2x,$$

$$-3y + 2z = 2y,$$
$$z = 2z.$$

The last equation implies $z = 0$, from which we determine $y = 0$ as well (from the second equation), and in the first equation we find $x = x$ for any x, therefore our eigenvectors for $\lambda = 2$ are of the form $\begin{bmatrix} x \\ 0 \\ 0 \end{bmatrix}$ i.e. scalar multiples of $\begin{bmatrix} 1 \\ 0 \\ 0 \end{bmatrix}$.

2. For $\lambda = -3$, we similarly set up a system of equations:
$$2x + y + 4z = -3x,$$
$$-3y + 2z = -3y,$$
$$z = -3z.$$

We find $z = 0$, $y = y$, and $x = -\frac{1}{5}y$, therefore our eigenvectors are $\begin{bmatrix} -\frac{1}{5}y \\ y \\ 0 \end{bmatrix}$ i.e. scalar multiples of $\begin{bmatrix} -1 \\ 5 \\ 0 \end{bmatrix}$.

3. For $\lambda = 1$, we have the system of equations
$$2x + y + 4z = x,$$
$$-3y + 2z = y,$$
$$z = z.$$

We find $z = z$, $z = 2y$, and $x = -9y$, therefore our eigenvectors are $\begin{bmatrix} -9y \\ y \\ 2y \end{bmatrix}$ i.e. scalar multiples of $\begin{bmatrix} -9 \\ 1 \\ 2 \end{bmatrix}$. $\square$

Sometimes, an eigenvalue can be a double root when the determinant equation is written out, as presented in the following problem:

Problem 8.2.73. Find eigenvectors and eigenvalues for
$$M = \begin{bmatrix} 1 & 0 & 0 \\ 0 & 4 & 0 \\ 0 & 0 & 4 \end{bmatrix}.$$

Solution. If λ is an eigenvalue of this matrix, then $\text{Det}(M - \lambda I) = 0$. Writing this out,
$$\text{Det}\left(\begin{bmatrix} 1-\lambda & 0 & 0 \\ 0 & 4-\lambda & 0 \\ 0 & 0 & 4-\lambda \end{bmatrix}\right) = (1-\lambda)(4-\lambda)^2 = 0.$$

Thus, the only possible values of λ are $1, 4$, where 4 is a double root:

- Case $\lambda = 1$:

    Write the equation out:
    $$\begin{bmatrix} 1 & 0 & 0 \\ 0 & 4 & 0 \\ 0 & 0 & 4 \end{bmatrix} \begin{bmatrix} a \\ b \\ c \end{bmatrix} = \begin{bmatrix} a \\ 4b \\ 4c \end{bmatrix} = \begin{bmatrix} a \\ b \\ c \end{bmatrix}.$$

    We now have 3 equations:
    $$a = a,$$
    $$4b = b,$$
    $$4c = c.$$

    The third equation gives us $c = 0$. Similarly, $b = 0$. Then, $a = a$, which is true for any a. Thus, the solution for $\lambda = 1$ is $\begin{bmatrix} a \\ 0 \\ 0 \end{bmatrix} = a \begin{bmatrix} 1 \\ 0 \\ 0 \end{bmatrix}$ i.e. scalar multiples of $\begin{bmatrix} 1 \\ 0 \\ 0 \end{bmatrix}$.

- Case $\lambda = 4$:

    Similar to what we did previously, we have
    $$a = 4a,$$
    $$4b = 4b,$$
    $$4c = 4c.$$

    The last two equations give us $c = c$ and $b = b$, which are always true. Finally, the first equation gives us $a = 0$. Thus, the solutions are of the form $\begin{bmatrix} 0 \\ b \\ c \end{bmatrix}$. □

Unlike the previous example, this eigenvector has two different variables. In general, when an eigenvalue is a double root, there will be an eigenvector with two different *degrees of freedom* (i.e. the vector is defined by 2 variables).

Problem 8.2.74. What are the determinants of the following matrices?
$$\begin{bmatrix} 1 & 2 & 3 \\ 2 & 4 & 6 \\ 7 & 7 & 7 \end{bmatrix}, \quad \begin{bmatrix} 1 & 2 & 4 \\ 3 & 7 & 8 \\ 4 & 9 & 12 \end{bmatrix}$$

Solution. For the first one, note that we can completely eliminate the second row by a row operation:
$$\begin{bmatrix} 1 & 2 & 3 \\ 2 & 4 & 6 \\ 7 & 7 & 7 \end{bmatrix} \xrightarrow{-2R_1 + R_2 \to R_2} \begin{bmatrix} 1 & 2 & 3 \\ 0 & 0 & 0 \\ 7 & 7 & 7 \end{bmatrix}.$$

As the Shoelace technique is applied, notice that all terms in the expression for the determinant (i.e. $aei - bdi - ceg - ahf + cdh + bfg$) include a term from the second row. If all the entries in the second row are zeroes, all the terms in the determinant are zeroes, and therefore the determinant is zero.

Therefore, the determinant of the first matrix is 0.

We can make this same argument about any row or column. Thus, we conclude that if any row or column is all zeroes, then the determinant is necessarily 0.

Similarly, for the second matrix, we can eliminate the third row by two special row operations:

$$\begin{bmatrix} 1 & 2 & 4 \\ 3 & 7 & 8 \\ 4 & 9 & 12 \end{bmatrix} \xrightarrow[-R_2+R_3 \to R_3]{-R_1+R_3 \to R_3} \begin{bmatrix} 1 & 2 & 4 \\ 3 & 7 & 8 \\ 0 & 0 & 0 \end{bmatrix}.$$

The determinant is clearly 0. From this, we can conclude in general that if some rows sum up to another row, then the determinant is necessarily 0. $\square$

From these two examples of matrices, we can even make a broader conclusion: if the rows (taken as vectors) are not *linearly independent*, then the determinant is 0. This is because our row operations allow us to replace a row with any linear combination of the rows, i.e. we can do $aR_1 + bR_2 + cR_3 \to R_1$ for any integer a, b, and c (as long as they aren't all 0). Therefore, if the rows are linearly dependent, then we can find $a, b, c \neq 0$ such that $aR_1 + bR_2 + cR_3 = 0$. Then, we can apply row operations to get a row equal to 0, and thereby conclude that the determinant is 0.

8.3 3-D Geometry

Although we have had experience with the two dimensional Cartesian plane (plotting points and lines), it is not until knowledge of parametric equations, vectors, and matrices are needed to establish some foundation for developing ways to represent lines and planes.

First, we discuss how to represent lines in 3D space, through vectors.

$$\underset{(x_0, y_0, z_0)}{\overset{P}{\bullet}} \longrightarrow \underset{(x_1, y_1, z_1)}{\overset{Q}{\bullet}}$$

Consider a point R on the line $\overleftrightarrow{PQ}$. Then $\overrightarrow{PR}$ will be a scalar multiple of $\overrightarrow{PQ}$. This results in the parameterization

$$\overrightarrow{PR} = t\overrightarrow{PQ}.$$

Denote $P = (x_0, y_0, z_0)$ and $Q = (x_1, y_1, z_1)$. Then $\overrightarrow{PQ} = \langle x_1 - x_0, y_1 - y_0, z_1 - z_0 \rangle$, therefore

$$\overrightarrow{PR} = t \langle x_1 - x_0, y_1 - y_0, z_1 - z_0 \rangle.$$

from which we can conclude

$$R = (x_0 + t(x_1 - x_0), y_0 + t(y_1 - y_0), z_0 + t(z_1 - z_0)).$$

Since R is an arbitrary point that lies on the line $\overleftrightarrow{PQ}$, we can establish the following:

Definition 8.3.1. A line in three-dimensional space can be expressed in **parametric form** with the following:

$$x = x_0 + t(x_1 - x_0),$$
$$y = y_0 + t(y_1 - y_0),$$
$$z = z_0 + t(z_1 - z_0).$$

Problem 8.3.2. Give a parametric representation for a line containing $(1, 2, 3)$ and $(-3, -2, 7)$.

Solution. Applying our definition, we have

$$x = 1 + t(-3 - 1) = 1 - 4t,$$
$$y = 2 + t(-2 - 2) = 2 - 4t,$$
$$z = 3 + t(7 - 3) = 3 + 4t.$$

Since each contains $4t$, we can make the substitution $4t \longrightarrow t$ to simplify our parameterization:

$$x = 1 - t,$$
$$y = 2 - t,$$
$$z = 3 + t.$$
□

Problem 8.3.3. Does the line from Problem 8.3.2 intersect the line containing $(0, 0, 0)$ and $(1, 4, 9)$?

Solution. Our second line has the parameterization

$$x = u,$$
$$y = 4u,$$
$$z = 9u.$$

We use u as the parameter here because since we will use t as the parameter for the line from Problem 8.3.2. The parameters for the two lines are not necessarily the same.

To find the intersection, simply set the two parameterizations equal to each other:

$$1 - t = u,$$
$$2 - t = 4u,$$
$$3 + t = 9u.$$

Substituting the first equation into the second equation, we have $4(1-t) = 2 - t$ which yields $t = \dfrac{2}{3}$ and $u = \dfrac{1}{3}$. However, these values fail the third equation, thus there is no solution, and the lines do not intersect. □

Problem 8.3.4. Find the parametric equation of the line containing $(1, -2, 3)$ and $(2, 1, -5)$.

Solution.
$$x = 1 + (2 - 1)t = 1 + t,$$
$$y = -2 + (1 - (-2))t = -2 + 3t,$$
$$z = 3 + (-5 - 3)t = 3 - 8t.$$
□

Now we seek to come up with a proper definition for planes in space. The following diagram will motivate us to define a plane in the following fashion:

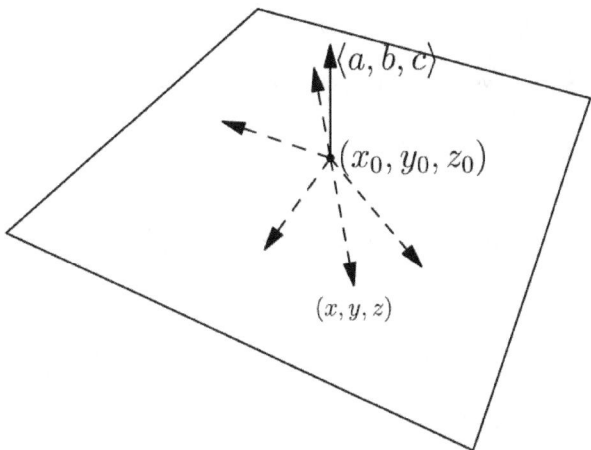

For any point (x, y, z) that is on the plane, notice that the vector $\langle a, b, c \rangle$ is orthogonal to the vector containing points (x_0, y_0, z_0) and (x, y, z).

Definition 8.3.5. A **plane** in three-dimensional space is the set of points (x, y, z) such that the vector containing (x, y, z) and (x_0, y_0, z_0) is orthogonal to $\langle a, b, c \rangle$. We can then find the equation for a plane:

$$\langle a, b, c \rangle \cdot \langle x - x_0, y - y_0, z - z_0 \rangle = 0,$$
$$ax - ax_0 + by - by_0 + cy - cy_0 = 0.$$

Let d be some constant equal to $ax_0 + by_0 + cz_0$, therefore our general equation for a plane (after some rearranging) is

$$ax + by + cz = d.$$

Definition 8.3.6. A vector or line is called **normal** to some plane when it is perpendicular to that plane.

Problem 8.3.7. Find the point on the line from Problem 8.3.4 closest to the origin $(0, 0, 0)$.

Solution. We find a vector that contains the points $(1, -2, 3)$ and $(2, 1, -5)$ is

$$\langle 2 - 1, 1 - (-2), -5 - 3 \rangle = \langle 1, 3, -8 \rangle.$$

Furthermore, the line from the origin to the closest point should be perpendicular to the line (the shortest distance from a point to a line is the perpendicular).

If we let that closest point on the line be $(1 + t, -2 + 3t, 3 - 8t)$ using the parametric equations of the line, then the vector starting from $(0, 0, 0)$ and ending at $(1 + t, -2 + 3t, 3 - 8t)$ is simply $\langle 1 + t, -2 + 3t, 3 - 8t \rangle$. This vector must be orthogonal to the vector $\langle 1, 3, -8 \rangle$, therefore we have

$$\langle 1 + t, -2 + 3t, 3 - 8t \rangle \cdot \langle 1, 3, -8 \rangle = 0.$$

Evaluating the dot product gives

$$(1+t) \cdot 1 + (-2+3t) \cdot 3 + (3-8t) \cdot -8 = 0.$$

The solution is $t = \dfrac{29}{74}$. Now, we can plug this value into our parametric equations of the line to get the point $\boxed{\left(\dfrac{103}{74}, -\dfrac{61}{74}, -\dfrac{10}{74}\right)}$. □

Problem 8.3.8. Find the intersection of the line from Problem 8.3.4 with the plane whose equation is $x + y + 4z = 11$.

Solution. Plugging in our parametric equations for the line, we have

$$1 + t + -2 + 3t + 4(3-8t) = 11.$$

This simplifies to $t = 0$, and so we plug this back into our parameterization for the line, resulting in the point $(1+0, -2+3(0), 3-8(0)) = \boxed{(1,-2,3)}$. □

Problem 8.3.9. Find the intersection of planes $x + y + 4z = 11$ and $x + y + 3z = 11$.

Solution. As we have to find the intersection, we simply substitute $x + y + 4z$ into the second equation, as such:

$$x + y + 4z = x + y + 3z.$$

This results in the solutions $z = 0$ and $x + y = 11$, which is a line with a parameterization of

$$x = 1 + t,$$
$$y = 10 - t,$$
$$z = 0.$$

The intersection of the given planes is a line with that parameterization.

Note that we could also have done $x = 2 + t$, $y = 9 - t$ or $x = 6 + t$, $y = 5 - t$, etc. It does not matter as long as x and y add up to 11 with parameter t. □

Problem 8.3.10. Find the acute angle between the planes given in the previous example.

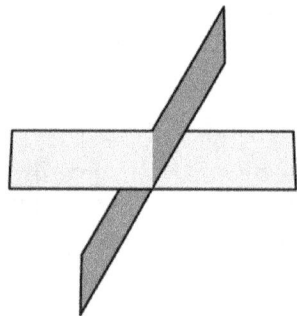

Solution. Denote the acute angle as θ. The equations $x + y + 4z = 11$ and $x + y + 3z = 11$ suggest that their normal vectors are $\langle 1, 1, 4 \rangle$ and $\langle 1, 1, 3 \rangle$ respectively. We can take representations of these vectors such that their tips meet each other while their tails meet at the planes. Then a 'cyclic quadrilateral' is formed with θ such that the angle between the two vectors at their tips is $180 - \theta$ (the other two angles are $90°$ each due to the normal vectors).

We can calculate the cosine of the angle $180 - \theta$ between the tips of the vectors $\langle 1, 1, 4 \rangle$ and $\langle 1, 1, 3 \rangle$, from which we can get $\cos \theta$:

$$\cos(180 - \theta) = \frac{\langle 1,1,4 \rangle \cdot \langle 1,1,3 \rangle}{\|\langle 1,1,4 \rangle\|\|\langle 1,1,3 \rangle\|} = \frac{14}{3\sqrt{22}} = -\cos\theta$$

One may conclude that the angle is $\cos^{-1}\left(-\dfrac{14}{3\sqrt{22}}\right)$, however this is incorrect because the cosine of an acute angle is always positive. To remedy this, we usually take the absolute value of the angle between the two normal vectors. This is our general expression to find the acute angle:

$$\cos\theta = \left|\frac{\vec{v} \cdot \vec{w}}{\|\vec{v}\|\|\vec{w}\|}\right|$$

where $\vec{v}, \vec{w}$ are the vectors normal to the two planes, which in this case would be $\langle 1, 1, 4 \rangle$ and $\langle 1, 1, 3 \rangle$.

The answer is therefore $\theta = \boxed{\cos^{-1}\left(\dfrac{14}{3\sqrt{22}}\right)}$. $\square$

Theorem 8.3.11

The distance from a point (x_0, y_0, z_0) to a plane $ax + by + cz = d$ is

$$\frac{|ax_0 + by_0 + cz_0 - d|}{\sqrt{a^2 + b^2 + c^2}}.$$

Proof. By our definition of a plane, the vector that is normal to $ax + by + cz = d$ is $\langle a, b, c \rangle$. Let a representation of this vector go through the point (x_0, y_0, z_0), as shown:

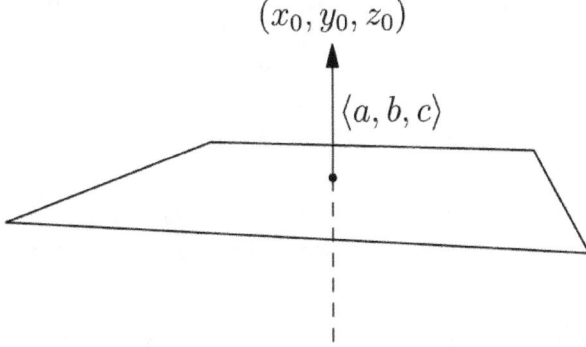

Consider the line that goes through (x_0, y_0, z_0) and contains $\langle a, b, c \rangle$. The parameterization for this line would be

$$x = x_0 + at,$$

$$y = y_0 + bt,$$
$$z = z_0 + ct.$$

To find the intersection of this line and the plane, substitute the parameters into the equation for the plane:
$$a(x_0 + at) + b(y_0 + bt) + c(z_0 + ct) = d.$$

This rearranges to
$$ax_0 + by_0 + cz_0 - d = -t(a^2 + b^2 + c^2).$$

Solving for parameter t, we get
$$t = -\left(\frac{ax_0 + by_0 + cz_0 - d}{a^2 + b^2 + c^2}\right).$$

The shortest distance from the plane to (x_0, y_0, z_0) would be $|t|\|\langle a, b, c\rangle\| = |t|\sqrt{a^2 + b^2 + c^2}$, so we substitute in our value of t to get
$$\left|-\left(\frac{ax_0 + by_0 + cz_0 - d}{a^2 + b^2 + c^2}\right)\right|\sqrt{a^2 + b^2 + c^2} = \frac{|ax_0 + by_0 + cz_0 - d|}{\sqrt{a^2 + b^2 + c^2}},$$

as desired. $\square$

Problem 8.3.12. Find $\left(a\vec{\imath} + b\vec{\jmath} + c\vec{k}\right) \cdot \left(d\vec{\imath} + e\vec{\jmath} + f\vec{k}\right)$.

Solution. The dot product is distributive over addition:
$$\left(a\vec{\imath} + b\vec{\jmath} + c\vec{k}\right) \cdot \left(d\vec{\imath} + e\vec{\jmath} + f\vec{k}\right)$$
$$= ad(\vec{\imath} \cdot \vec{\imath}) + ae(\vec{\imath} \cdot \vec{\jmath}) + af(\vec{\imath} \cdot \vec{k}) + bd(\vec{\jmath} \cdot \vec{\imath}) + be(\vec{\jmath} \cdot \vec{\jmath}) + bf(\vec{\jmath} \cdot \vec{k}) + cd(\vec{k} \cdot \vec{\imath}) + ce(\vec{k} \cdot \vec{\jmath}) + cf(\vec{k} \cdot \vec{k})$$
$$= \boxed{ad + be + cf}.$$
$\square$

Now that we are dealing with three dimensional vectors, we can find a vector that is orthogonal to two other given vectors simultaneously. Consider the following matrix:
$$\begin{bmatrix} \vec{\imath} & \vec{\jmath} & \vec{k} \\ a & b & c \\ d & e & f \end{bmatrix}.$$

This matrix is unlike any other matrix we have considered before. Although we have initially defined matrices to be an array of numbers, we can extend this definition to include vectors as possible entries as well.

The top row consist of the standard basis vectors for $\mathbb{R}^3$. Then, the determinant of this matrix is of the form
$$\vec{\imath}\gamma_1 + \vec{\jmath}\gamma_2 + \vec{k}\gamma_3,$$

where $\gamma_1, \gamma_2, \gamma_3$ are placeholders for the remaining terms. Notice that the determinant itself is a vector.

Now suppose we take the dot product of this with the vector $a\vec{i} + b\vec{j} + c\vec{k}$. By Problem 8.3.12,

$$\left(\vec{i}\gamma_1 + \vec{j}\gamma_2 + \vec{k}\gamma_3\right) \cdot \left(a\vec{i} + b\vec{j} + c\vec{k}\right) = \gamma_1 a + \gamma_2 b + \gamma_3 c.$$

But $\gamma_1 a + \gamma_2 b + \gamma_3 c$ is actually the determinant for the matrix,

$$\begin{bmatrix} a & b & c \\ a & b & c \\ d & e & f \end{bmatrix}$$

(where we have replaced the entries $\vec{i}$, $\vec{j}$, $\vec{k}$ with a, b, c).

For the matrix above, we can perform the row operation $-R_1 + R_2 \to R_2$ reduce the second row to all zeroes. Thus, the determinant of this matrix, which is $\gamma_1 a + \gamma_2 b + \gamma_3 c$, is equal to 0.

Then $\left(\vec{i}\gamma_1 + \vec{j}\gamma_2 + \vec{k}\gamma_3\right) \cdot \left(a\vec{i} + b\vec{j} + c\vec{k}\right) = 0$, indicating that $\vec{i}\gamma_1 + \vec{j}\gamma_2 + \vec{k}\gamma_3$ and $a\vec{i} + b\vec{j} + c\vec{k}$ are orthogonal.

By the same reasoning, we can take the dot product of $\vec{i}\gamma_1 + \vec{j}\gamma_2 + \vec{k}\gamma_3$ and $d\vec{i} + e\vec{j} + f\vec{k}$, which would be $\gamma_1 d + \gamma_2 e + \gamma_3 f$. Then this would be the determinant for the matrix,

$$\begin{bmatrix} d & e & f \\ a & b & c \\ d & e & f \end{bmatrix},$$

and the row operation $-R_1 + R_3 \to R_3$ would indicate that the determinant is 0. Hence, we can likewise conclude that $\vec{i}\gamma_1 + \vec{j}\gamma_2 + \vec{k}\gamma_3$ and $d\vec{i} + e\vec{j} + f\vec{k}$ are orthogonal.

Thus, we have found that $\vec{i}\gamma_1 + \vec{j}\gamma_2 + \vec{k}\gamma_3$ is orthogonal to both $a\vec{i} + b\vec{j} + c\vec{k}$ and $d\vec{i} + e\vec{j} + f\vec{k}$. This is the vector that we have been looking for.

This special vector will be so signficant in 3D geometry that we will define it with a special name:

Definition 8.3.13. The **cross product** is defined as follows:

$$\left(a\vec{i} + b\vec{j} + c\vec{k}\right) \times \left(d\vec{i} + e\vec{j} + f\vec{k}\right) = \text{Det}\left(\begin{bmatrix} \vec{i} & \vec{j} & \vec{k} \\ a & b & c \\ d & e & f \end{bmatrix}\right).$$

This results in a vector that is orthogonal to both $\left(a\vec{i} + b\vec{j} + c\vec{k}\right)$ and $\left(d\vec{i} + e\vec{j} + f\vec{k}\right)$.

Problem 8.3.14. Find $\langle 1, 1, 4 \rangle \times \langle 1, 1, 3 \rangle$.

Solution.
$$\langle 1, 1, 4 \rangle \times \langle 1, 1, 3 \rangle = \text{Det}\left(\begin{bmatrix} \vec{i} & \vec{j} & \vec{k} \\ 1 & 1 & 4 \\ 1 & 1 & 3 \end{bmatrix}\right)$$
$$= 3\vec{i} + 4\vec{j} + \vec{k} - 4\vec{i} - 3\vec{j} - \vec{k}$$
$$= -\vec{i} + \vec{j}$$
$$= \boxed{\langle -1, 1, 0 \rangle}.$$

Properties of the cross product:

1. $\vec{w} \times \vec{v} = -(\vec{v} \times \vec{w})$ (this is also known as *anticommutativity*).

   Proof. Let $\vec{v} = a\vec{i} + b\vec{j} + c\vec{k}$ and $\vec{w} = d\vec{i} + e\vec{j} + f\vec{k}$. Then

   $$\vec{v} \times \vec{w} = \text{Det}\left(\begin{bmatrix} \vec{i} & \vec{j} & \vec{k} \\ a & b & c \\ d & e & f \end{bmatrix}\right),$$

   $$\vec{w} \times \vec{v} = \text{Det}\left(\begin{bmatrix} \vec{i} & \vec{j} & \vec{k} \\ d & e & f \\ a & b & c \end{bmatrix}\right).$$

   For $\vec{w} \times \vec{v}$, rows 2 and 3 of the matrix have been swapped, so its determinant is the negative of the determinant of the matrix for $\vec{v} \times \vec{w}$. Therefore $\vec{w} \times \vec{v} = -(\vec{v} \times \vec{w})$. □

2. $\vec{v} \times \vec{v} = \vec{0}$.

   Proof. From the first property, $\vec{v} \times \vec{v} = -(\vec{v} \times \vec{v})$, from which the result follows. □

3. The cross product is distributive.

4. The standard basis vectors satisfy the following equations:

   $$\vec{i} \times \vec{j} = \vec{k},$$
   $$\vec{j} \times \vec{k} = \vec{i},$$
   $$\vec{k} \times \vec{i} = \vec{j}.$$

5. $(a\vec{v}) \times \vec{w} = a(\vec{v} \times \vec{w})$.

> **Example 8.3.15**
> Find the equation of the plane containing the points $(2, 3, 7)$, $(1, 5, 6)$, and $(-4, 0, 1)$.

Solution. Let $R = (2, 3, 7)$, $M = (1, 5, 6)$, and $J = (-4, 0, 1)$. Then $\overrightarrow{RM} = \langle -1, 2, -1 \rangle$ and $\overrightarrow{MJ} = \langle -5, -5, -5 \rangle$. Taking the cross-product of this gives a vector normal to the plane, so we evaluate with minors:

$$\overrightarrow{RM} \times \overrightarrow{MJ} = \text{Det}\left(\begin{bmatrix} \vec{i} & \vec{j} & \vec{k} \\ -1 & 2 & -1 \\ -5 & -5 & -5 \end{bmatrix}\right)$$

$$= \vec{i} \cdot \text{Det}\left(\begin{bmatrix} 2 & -1 \\ -5 & -5 \end{bmatrix}\right) - \vec{j} \cdot \text{Det}\left(\begin{bmatrix} -1 & -1 \\ -5 & -5 \end{bmatrix}\right) + \vec{k} \cdot \text{Det}\left(\begin{bmatrix} -1 & 2 \\ -5 & -5 \end{bmatrix}\right)$$

$$= -15\vec{i} + 15\vec{k}.$$

The normal vector is $\langle -15, 0, 15 \rangle$, so our equation for the plane is of the form $-15x + 15z = d$. Now we plug in one of our three given points to find the value of d, i.e. plugging in point J we get $-15(-4) + 15(1) = d = 75$, therefore our equation for the plane is $-15x + 15z = 75 \implies$ $\boxed{-x + z = 5}$. □

Problem 8.3.16. Find the equation of the plane containing the points $(1, 2, 4)$, $(2, -1, 1)$, and $(4, 0, 5)$.

Solution. Similarly, we find two vectors given the three points $(1, 2, 4)$, $(2, -1, 1)$, and $(4, 0, 5)$, which are $\langle 1, -3, -3 \rangle$ and $\langle 2, 1, 4 \rangle$. We then take the cross product to find the normal vector of the plane:

$$\langle 1, -3, -3 \rangle \times \langle 2, 1, 4 \rangle = \text{Det}\left(\begin{bmatrix} \vec{i} & \vec{j} & \vec{k} \\ 1 & -3 & -3 \\ 2 & 1 & 4 \end{bmatrix}\right)$$

$$= \vec{i} \cdot \text{Det}\left(\begin{bmatrix} -3 & -3 \\ 1 & 4 \end{bmatrix}\right) - \vec{j} \cdot \text{Det}\left(\begin{bmatrix} 1 & -3 \\ 2 & 4 \end{bmatrix}\right) + \vec{k} \cdot \text{Det}\left(\begin{bmatrix} 1 & -3 \\ 2 & 1 \end{bmatrix}\right)$$

$$= -9\vec{i} - 10\vec{j} + 7\vec{k}.$$

So our equation for the plane is of the form $-9x - 10y + 7z = d$, then we plug in $J = (-4, 0, 1)$ to get $-9(-4) - 10(0) + 7(5) = d = -1$, which simplifies to $\boxed{-9x - 10y + 7z = -1}$. □

Problem 8.3.17. Find the intersection of the plane from Problem 8.3.16 with the plane $x + y + z = 0$.

Solution. We have the following equations:

$$-9x - 10y + 7z = -1, \tag{1}$$
$$x + y + z = 0. \tag{2}$$

Multiplying 7 times equation (2) then adding to equation (1) gives

$$16x + 17y = 1,$$

and multiplying 9 times equation (2) then adding to equation (1) gives

$$-y + 16z = -1.$$

We can use these equations to find two points which lie on the intersection of the two planes, then determining the parameterization of the line using those two points.

Plugging in $y = 1$ gives the solutions $(-1, 1, 0)$, and plugging in $z = 1$ gives the solutions $(-18, 17, 1)$. Therefore the parameterization of the line is

$$x = -1 - 17t,$$
$$y = 1 + 16t,$$
$$z = t.$$

□

Problem 8.3.18. Find the intersection of the plane from Problem 8.3.16 with the line that contains $(3, 4, 5)$ and $(5, 12, 13)$.

Solution. The parameterization for the line with points $(3, 4, 5)$ and $(5, 12, 13)$ is:
$$x = 3 + 2t,$$
$$y = 4 + 8t,$$
$$z = 5 + 8t.$$

Note that we can divide coefficients of parameter t by 2, so our simplified parameterization is
$$x = 3 + t,$$
$$y = 4 + 4t,$$
$$z = 5 + 4t.$$

To find the intersection, we simply substitute in the parametric definitions into the equation of the plane, which is $-9x - 10y + 7z = -1$, so we get
$$-9(3 + t) - 10(4 + 4t) + 7(5 + 4t) = -1.$$

Solving this gives $t = -\dfrac{31}{21}$. We plug this back into the parameterization of the line to get the point $\boxed{\left(\dfrac{32}{21}, -\dfrac{40}{21}, -\dfrac{19}{21}\right)}$. □

Problem 8.3.19. Determine the distance from the origin to the line in Problem 8.3.18.

Solution. Recall that the line in discussion has the parameterization
$$x = 3 + t,$$
$$y = 4 + 4t,$$
$$z = 5 + 4t.$$

Consider the vector from $(0, 0, 0)$ to an arbitrary point on the line, which can be represented as $(3+t, 4+4t, 5+4t)$. The vector going from the origin to this arbitrary point is just $\langle 3+t, 4+4t, 5+4t \rangle$. We can determine a vector in the line by taking two points on the line, i.e. $(3, 4, 5)$ and $(5, 12, 13)$, which yields $\langle 2, 8, 8 \rangle$. By Theorem 8.1.23, $\vec{v}$ and $\vec{w}$ are orthogonal if and only if $\vec{v} \cdot \vec{w} = 0$. So we have
$$\langle 3+t, 4+4t, 5+4t \rangle \cdot \langle 2, 8, 8 \rangle = 0.$$

This evaluates to
$$6 + 2t + 32 + 32t + 40 + 32t = 0,$$
and solving gives $t = -\dfrac{13}{11}$. Therefore the distance is just the magnitude of the vector
$$\langle 3+t, 4+4t, 5+4t \rangle,$$
which is
$$\sqrt{\left(\dfrac{20}{11}\right)^2 + \left(\dfrac{8}{11}\right)^2 + \left(\dfrac{3}{11}\right)^2} = \boxed{\dfrac{\sqrt{473}}{11}}.$$
□

Theorem 8.3.20

Let θ is the included angle between $\vec{v}$ and $\vec{w}$ if their tails were placed on each other. Then we have
$$\|\vec{v} \times \vec{w}\| = \|\vec{v}\|\|\vec{w}\| \sin \theta.$$

Proof. Since $\cos \theta = \dfrac{\vec{v} \cdot \vec{w}}{\|\vec{v}\|\|\vec{w}\|}$, we get $\sin \theta = \sqrt{1 - \left(\dfrac{\vec{v} \cdot \vec{w}}{\|\vec{v}\|\|\vec{w}\|}\right)^2}$. Let $\vec{v} = \langle a, b, c \rangle$ and $\vec{w} = \langle d, e, f \rangle$. Then,

$$\|\vec{v}\|\|\vec{w}\| \sin \theta = \sqrt{\|\vec{v}\|^2 \|\vec{w}\|^2 - (\vec{v} \cdot \vec{w})^2}$$
$$= \sqrt{(a^2 + b^2 + c^2)(d^2 + e^2 + f^2) - (ad + be + cf)^2}.$$

After much algebraic manipulation, we see that this rearranges to

$$\sqrt{(bf - ce)^2 + (cd - af)^2 + (ae - bd)^2}.$$

Given $\vec{v} = \langle a, b, c \rangle$ and $\vec{w} = \langle d, e, f \rangle$, we can find $\vec{v} \times \vec{w}$:

$$\mathrm{Det}\left(\begin{bmatrix} \vec{i} & \vec{j} & \vec{k} \\ a & b & c \\ d & e & f \end{bmatrix}\right) = \vec{i}(bf - ae) + \vec{j}(cd - af) + \vec{k}(ae - bd),$$

and therefore $\|\vec{v} \times \vec{w}\| = \sqrt{(bf - ce)^2 + (cd - af)^2 + (ae - bd)^2}$, which we have found to be equal to $\|\vec{v}\|\|\vec{w}\| \sin \theta$. So, we are done. $\square$

This allows us to compute either the dot product or $\sin \theta$ if we have the other.

Now, recall the formula based on Theorem 6.6.1 which states that the area of the triangle formed by $\vec{v}$ and $\vec{w}$ with their tails placed on each other, and included angle θ, would be $\dfrac{1}{2}\|\vec{v}\|\|\vec{w}\| \sin \theta$. As a result of Theorem 8.3.20, we conclude that the area of such a triangle is $\dfrac{1}{2}\|\vec{v} \times \vec{w}\|$.

Then $\|\vec{v}\|\|\vec{w}\| \sin \theta = \|\vec{v} \times \vec{w}\|$ is the area of the parallelogram (since it is twice the area of the triangle):

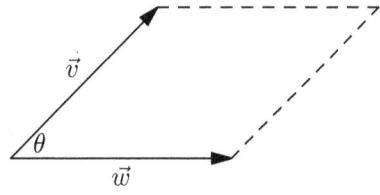

Chapter 9

Limits

We are finally at the gates of calculus, and to begin, we must revisit the concept of limits.

I strongly recommend that you review the section on the limits of sequences, as we will be taking it a step further when considering the limits of functions.

Note that we will only be covering an introduction of calculus, mainly limits (this chapter) and derivatives (next chapter). It is essential that you come to truly understand the concept of the limit, as this is the underlying, fundamental principle of calculus.

The Definition

Recall the definition for the limit of a sequence, i.e. $\lim_{n \to \infty} a_n = L$:

$$\forall \varepsilon > 0 \; \exists N \text{ s.t. } \forall n > N, \; |a_n - L| < \varepsilon.$$

We could also write it as

$$\forall \varepsilon > 0 \; \exists N \text{ s.t. } n > N \longrightarrow |a_n - L| < \varepsilon,$$

after replacing the universal quantifier with an implication.

In this section, we will discuss the finite limit of a function, which will be denoted by $\lim_{x \to a} f(x) = L$. This is read as "the limit as x approaches a of $f(x)$ is L." Its definition will be similar to that of the limit for a sequence.

In order to get a sense of how we can approach forming a definition for this, we keep in mind the following idea:

> We can make $f(x)$ as close as we want to L by making x sufficiently close to a.

Keeping this principle in mind, here is the $\varepsilon - \delta$ ("epsilon-delta") definition of the limit:

Definition 9.0.1. The **limit** of $f(x)$ as x approaches a is L, i.e. $\lim_{x \to a} f(x) = L$, iff

$$\forall \varepsilon > 0 \; \exists \delta > 0 \; \forall x, \; 0 < |x - a| < \delta \to |f(x) - L| < \varepsilon.$$

Essentially, this definition is a slight modification of what we had for sequences.

For sequences, we were able to make a_n arbitrarily close to L by going sufficiently down the terms of the sequence.

However, for a function, we need to consider what it means for x to "approach" the value a. Here, we mean that the distance between x and a, which is $|x - a|$, is getting smaller.

Given some positive number $\varepsilon > 0$, we can find a positive number δ such that the distance between x and a is less than δ. Similar to the limit of a sequence, the value ε serves as a threshold for $f(x)$ to be close to L, via the condition $|f(x) - L| < \varepsilon$.

Since ε can be ANY positive number, it serves as the "make $f(x)$ as close as we want to L" part of the principle.

We can find a sufficiently small distance between x and a (i.e. find some δ) in order to satisfy this condition that $f(x)$ must be within ε of L.

To prove that the limit is some particular value, we need to find an expression for δ in terms of ε such that if $|x - a| < \delta$, then $|f(x) - L| < \varepsilon$.

9.1 Linear Functions

For the following few problems, we will introduce proving limits of linear functions, as they are the most basic and straightforward.

> **Example 9.1.1**
> Find and prove $\lim\limits_{x \to 3} 3x + 5$.

We can expect the limit of $3x + 5$ where x approaches 3 to be 14 (we can simply plug in 3 into the given function). To rigorously prove this limit, the existence quantifier of the definition suggests that we must find an expression for δ in terms of ε such that the implication

$$0 < |x - 3| < \delta \longrightarrow |(3x + 5) - 14| < \varepsilon$$

is satisfied. Let's take a closer look at $|(3x + 5) - 14| < \varepsilon$. We perform a series of algebraic manipulations:

$$|(3x + 5) - 14| < \varepsilon$$
$$|3x - 9| < \varepsilon$$
$$|3(x - 3)| < \varepsilon$$
$$|3||x - 3| < \varepsilon$$
$$3|x - 3| < \varepsilon$$
$$|x - 3| < \frac{\varepsilon}{3}$$

Note that all of these steps are reversible, therefore we can rewrite our implication as

$$0 < |x - 3| < \delta \longrightarrow |x - 3| < \frac{\varepsilon}{3}.$$

From here, it is obvious that our implication can only be satisfied if we let $\delta = \dfrac{\varepsilon}{3}$. However, even though we have essentially 'solved' the proof going backwards, we must write the proof going forwards, as shown:

Proof. For a given $\varepsilon > 0$, let $\delta = \dfrac{\varepsilon}{3}$. Then,

$$0 < |x - 3| < \delta$$
$$|x - 3| < \frac{\varepsilon}{3}$$
$$3|x - 3| < \varepsilon$$
$$|3||x - 3| < \varepsilon$$
$$|3(x - 3)| < \varepsilon$$
$$|3x - 9| < \varepsilon$$
$$|(3x + 5) - 14| < \varepsilon$$

Therefore, for any given $\varepsilon > 0$, we have found a δ which satisfies

$$0 < |x - 3| < \delta \longrightarrow |(3x + 5) - 14| < \varepsilon$$

which is the definition of $\lim\limits_{x \to 3} 3x + 15 = 14$, so we're done. $\square$

The proofs for the rest will be written forward, but for each problem, make sure you attempt the proof and find an expression for δ in terms of ε first before looking at the solution.

Problem 9.1.2. Prove $\lim\limits_{x \to 2} 2x + 3 = 7$.

Proof. For a given $\varepsilon > 0$, let $\delta = \dfrac{\varepsilon}{2}$. Then,

$$0 < |x - 2| < \delta$$
$$|x - 2| < \frac{\varepsilon}{2}$$
$$2|x - 2| < \varepsilon$$
$$|2||x - 2| < \varepsilon$$
$$|2(x - 2)| < \varepsilon$$
$$|2x - 4| < \varepsilon$$
$$|(2x + 3) - 7| < \varepsilon$$

Therefore, for any given $\varepsilon > 0$, we have found a δ which satisfies

$$0 < |x - 2| < \delta \longrightarrow |(2x + 3) - 7| < \varepsilon$$

which is the definition for $\lim\limits_{x \to 2} 2x + 3 = 7$, and we are done. $\square$

Problem 9.1.3. Prove $\lim\limits_{x \to -2} 8 - 7x = 22$.

Proof. For a given $\varepsilon > 0$, let $\delta = \dfrac{\varepsilon}{7}$. Then,

$$0 < |x - (-2)| < \delta$$
$$|x - (-2)| < \frac{\varepsilon}{7}$$
$$7|x - (-2)| < \varepsilon$$
$$|-7||x - (-2)| < \varepsilon$$
$$|-7(x - (-2))| < \varepsilon$$
$$|-7(x + 2)| < \varepsilon$$
$$|-7x - 14| < \varepsilon$$
$$|(8 - 7x) - 22| < \varepsilon$$

Therefore, for any given $\varepsilon > 0$, we have found a δ which satisfies

$$0 < |x - (-2)| < \delta \longrightarrow |(8 - 7x) - 22| < \varepsilon$$

which is the definition for $\lim_{x \to -2} 8 - 7x = 22$, so we are done. $\square$

Exercise 9.1.4. Prove $\lim_{x \to 2} 3x + 5555 = 5561$.

Example 9.1.5

Let $f(x) = \begin{cases} 7 & x \leq 4 \\ 5 & x > 4 \end{cases}$. Prove that $\lim_{x \to 4} f(x)$ does not exist.

Proof. We proceed with proof by contradiction. Assume that $\lim_{x \to 4} f(x) = L$. Then,

$$\forall \varepsilon > 0 \; \exists \delta > 0 \; \forall x, \; 0 < |x - 4| < \delta \to |f(x) - L| < \varepsilon.$$

Consider the negation of this statement:

$$\exists \varepsilon > 0 \; \forall \delta > 0 \; \exists x, \; 0 < |x - 4| < \delta \land |f(x) - L| \geq \varepsilon.$$

As long as we can find a single value of ε such that the implication is false for any δ, then we will have shown that the limit does not exist.

First, we rewrite the implication to get

$$4 - \delta < x < 4 + \delta \to L - \varepsilon < f(x) < L + \varepsilon.$$

Assume $\varepsilon = \dfrac{1}{2}$ (in fact, any value of $\varepsilon \in (0, 1)$ can be used to demonstrate a contradiction). Then we have

$$4 - \delta < x < 4 + \delta \to L - \frac{1}{2} < f(x) < L + \frac{1}{2},$$

which can be represented as

$$x \in (4 - \delta, 4 + \delta) \to f(x) \in \left(L - \frac{1}{2}, L + \frac{1}{2}\right).$$

For any $\delta > 0$, there are values of x in the interval $(4 - \delta, 4 + \delta)$ such that $x < 4$ and $x > 4$, which imply $f(x) = 5$ and $f(x) = 7$ respectively. However, the interval $\left(L - \frac{1}{2}, L + \frac{1}{2}\right)$ has a length of 1; it is impossible that 5 and 7 are both contained within this interval, so we have a contradiction. Therefore the limit does not exist. □

Problem 9.1.6. Given the following function,

$$f(x) = \begin{cases} 0 & x \leq 0 \\ 1 & x > 0 \end{cases}$$

prove that $\lim_{x \to 0} f(x)$ either exists and is equal to some value, or does not exist.

Proof. We shall show that there exists no limit for this function. First, assume that the limit is L. Writing out the definition, we have

$$\forall \varepsilon > 0 \; \exists \delta > 0 \; \forall x, \; 0 < |x - 0| < \delta \longrightarrow |f(x) - L| < \varepsilon.$$

As long as we find a ε that fails this definition, then we will have disproved the limit. Consider $\varepsilon = \frac{1}{4}$. When we take a closer look at the implication,

$$0 < |x - 0| < \delta \longrightarrow |f(x) - L| < \frac{1}{4},$$

we see that $|f(x) - L| < \frac{1}{4}$ implies that $f(x) \in \left(L - \frac{1}{4}, L + \frac{1}{4}\right)$.

Let $x = \frac{\delta}{2}$ and $x = -\frac{\delta}{2}$, which are allowed because these values satisfy $0 < |x - 0| < \delta$. Since $\delta > 0$, we know that $f\left(\frac{\delta}{2}\right) = 1$ and $f\left(-\frac{\delta}{2}\right) = 0$, based on the given definition of the function. However, it has been demonstrated that $f(x) \in \left(L - \frac{1}{4}, L + \frac{1}{4}\right)$, and this interval clearly cannot contain both 0 and 1 for any value of L. Therefore, we have a contradiction for $\varepsilon = \frac{1}{4}$, so the limit does not exist. □

Exercise 9.1.7. Prove $\lim_{x \to 0} \frac{|x|}{x}$ does not exist.

9.2 Non-linear Functions

Before we tackle some harder proofs, we first make the following key observation:

Remark 9.2.1. If the definition is true for a specific ε_0, then it is also true for any $\widetilde{\varepsilon_0} > \varepsilon_0$.

If a particular δ_0 works, then any $\widetilde{\delta_0} < \delta_0$ will also work.

To see why, write out the implication part of the definition:

$$|x - a| < \delta_0 \rightarrow |f(x) - L| < \varepsilon_0.$$

Assume that this implication is true for δ_0. Then as long as x and a are within δ_0 apart, then they will be "sufficiently close" such that $f(x)$ is within ε of L.

If $\widetilde{\delta_0} < \delta_0$, then x and a are even closer to each other. They are more than sufficiently close in order to satisfy that $f(x)$ is within ε of L. Therefore, the implication

$$|x - a| < \widetilde{\delta_0} \rightarrow |f(x) - L| < \varepsilon_0$$

would also be true.

Likewise, if the implication is true for ε_0, then we have the result $|f(x) - L| < \varepsilon_0$. For $\widetilde{\varepsilon_0} > \varepsilon_0$, we have $|f(x) - L| < \varepsilon_0 < \widetilde{\varepsilon_0}$, i.e. $|f(x) - L| < \widetilde{\varepsilon_0}$, and thus this result must also be true.

Furthermore, we need to establish one more key point.

Lemma 9.2.2

Define non-strict intervals $P = (a, b)$ and $Q = (c, d)$ for $a, b, c, d \in \mathbb{R}$. For any $x \in \mathbb{R}$, if we have $x \in P \longrightarrow x \in Q$, then $P \subseteq Q$ i.e. $(a, b) \subseteq (c, d)$, and subsequently,

$$c \leq a < b \leq d.$$

This lemma should be intuitive and does not need proof: if one interval is contained inside another, then the bounds of the smaller interval must be between the bounds of the larger interval.

Note that for the following examples, I will be explaining the work that one must do before writing a proper limit proof. Therefore these 'proofs' are written backwards, and it is left as exercises to the reader to properly and formally write these proofs forward.

Example 9.2.3

Prove $\lim\limits_{x \to 3} x^2 = 9$.

Proof. Focus on the implication:

$$|x - 3| < \delta \longrightarrow |x^2 - 9| < \varepsilon$$

Replace the absolute value signs by compound inequalities, and rearrange:

$$3 - \delta < x < 3 + \delta \longrightarrow 9 - \varepsilon < x^2 < 9 + \varepsilon$$

At this point, we need to figure out a way to rewrite $9 - \varepsilon < x^2 < 9 + \varepsilon$ as an inequality on x, so we can compare the two inequalities and determine what value of δ in terms of ε is required to satisfy the definition.

The key point of this proof is to assume $\varepsilon < 9$. As long as we can prove that the limit exists for $\varepsilon < 9$, then it will automatically follow for $\varepsilon \geq 9$, as explained in Remark 9.2.1.

Because we conveniently set $\varepsilon < 9$, we can take the square root of $9 - \varepsilon < x^2 < 9 + \varepsilon$, i.e. $\sqrt{9 - \varepsilon} < x < \sqrt{9 + \varepsilon}$.

NOTE: Here is a caveat of this proof: we are assuming that the square root function is increasing in order to take the square root of that inequality. For now, we will take it for granted.

Our implication in discussion is now

$$3 - \delta < x < 3 + \delta \longrightarrow \sqrt{9 - \varepsilon} < x < \sqrt{9 + \varepsilon}$$

We want to pick a δ such that $x \in (3 - \delta, 3 + \delta) \longrightarrow x \in (\sqrt{9 - \varepsilon}, \sqrt{9 + \varepsilon})$. By Lemma 9.2.2, it is sufficient if

$$\sqrt{9 - \varepsilon} \leq 3 - \delta, \quad 3 + \delta \leq \sqrt{9 + \varepsilon}$$

Rearranging, we have

$$\delta \leq 3 - \sqrt{9 - \varepsilon}$$
$$\delta \leq \sqrt{9 + \varepsilon} - 3$$

But now we have two inequalities for δ. How do we know which one to choose?

In fact, we don't need to choose. We can define

$$\delta = \min\{3 - \sqrt{9 - \varepsilon}, \sqrt{9 + \varepsilon} - 3\}$$

so that both inequalities become true. This guarantees that our choice of δ will satisfy the definition of the given limit. $\square$

Alternative Proof. We can proceed with a slightly easier proof. First, write out the implication:

$$|x - 3| < \delta \longrightarrow |x^2 - 9| < \varepsilon$$

Then we have $|x^2 - 9| = |(x - 3)(x + 3)| = |x - 3| \, |x + 3|$. So we want to find a δ such that

$$|x - 3| < \delta \longrightarrow |x - 3| \, |x + 3| < \varepsilon.$$

Now, assume $\delta < 1$. We arbitrarily choose 1 since it is small and relatively straightforward to deal with, but the proof would have been fine if we choose 2, 10, or any other positive number instead.

Then, $|x - 3| < \delta$ means that $|x - 3| < 1$. By the Triangle Inequality,

$$|x| = |x - 3 + 3| \leq |x - 3| + |3| < 1 + 3 = 4.$$

We can then apply Triangle Inequality again to find a bound on $|x+3|$.

$$|x+3| \leq |x| + |3| < 4 + 3 = 7.$$

Now, we use the facts that $|x-3| < \delta$ and $|x+3| < 7$ to conclude that

$$|x-3||x+3| < 7\delta,$$

which in turn we want to be less than ε. To accomplish this, we realize that we want $\delta < \dfrac{\varepsilon}{7}$.

However, we had assumed earlier that $\delta < 1$. Thus, we simply have to find a δ such that it is both less than $\dfrac{\varepsilon}{7}$ and 1. This can be done by defining

$$\delta < \min\left\{1, \frac{\varepsilon}{7}\right\},$$

guaranteeing that our definition of the limit will be satisfied. $\square$

Problem 9.2.4. Prove $\lim\limits_{x \to 99} x^2 = 9801$.

Solution. We must prove that

$$\forall \varepsilon > 0 \ \exists \delta > 0 \ \forall x, \ 0 < |x - 99| < \delta \to \left|x^2 - 9801\right| < \varepsilon.$$

We rewrite $0 < |x - 99| < \delta$ as $99 - \delta < x < 99 + \delta$, and $\left|x^2 - 9801\right| < \varepsilon$ as $9801 - \varepsilon < x^2 < 9801 + \varepsilon$. We want to take the square root of the latter inequality, but this is not possible if $9801 - \varepsilon$ is negative. Therefore, we assume $\varepsilon < 9801$ (remember, as long as ε works, any $\widetilde{\varepsilon} > \varepsilon$ will also work!). Then, $9801 - \varepsilon$ is definitely positive, so we can take the square root to get $\sqrt{9801 - \varepsilon} < x < \sqrt{9801 + \varepsilon}$.

Therefore our goal is to show that

$$99 - \delta < x < 99 + \delta \to \sqrt{9801 - \varepsilon} < x < \sqrt{9801 + \varepsilon}.$$

With interval notation, we want to show that the interval $(99 - \delta, 99 + \delta)$ is contained in the interval $(\sqrt{9801 - \varepsilon}, \sqrt{9801 + \varepsilon})$ (Lemma 9.2.2). It is sufficient that

$$\sqrt{9801 - \varepsilon} < 99 - \delta,$$
$$99 + \delta < \sqrt{9801 + \varepsilon}.$$

These rearrange to

$$\delta < 99 - \sqrt{9801 - \varepsilon},$$
$$\delta < \sqrt{9801 + \varepsilon} - 99.$$

We want both of these inequalities to be true, so we let

$$\delta < \min\left\{99 - \sqrt{9801 - \varepsilon}, \sqrt{9801 + \varepsilon} - 99\right\},$$

so the implication $\forall \varepsilon > 0 \ \exists \delta > 0 \ \forall x, \ 0 < |x - 99| < \delta \to \left|x^2 - 9801\right| < \varepsilon$ is true. $\square$

Problem 9.2.5. Prove $\lim_{x \to 1} \dfrac{1}{x} = 1$.

Proof. We must have
$$|x - 1| < \delta \longrightarrow \left|\frac{1}{x} - 1\right| < \varepsilon$$
which we rewrite as
$$1 - \delta < x < 1 + \delta \longrightarrow 1 - \varepsilon < \frac{1}{x} < 1 + \varepsilon$$

We assume $\varepsilon < 1$. Then we can take the reciprocal of $1 - \varepsilon < \dfrac{1}{x} < 1 + \varepsilon$ to get $\dfrac{1}{1+\varepsilon} < x < \dfrac{1}{1-\varepsilon}$, so we have
$$1 - \delta < x < 1 + \delta \longrightarrow \frac{1}{1+\varepsilon} < x < \frac{1}{1-\varepsilon},$$
which is essentially
$$x \in (1 - \delta, 1 + \delta) \longrightarrow x \in \left(\frac{1}{1+\varepsilon}, \frac{1}{1-\varepsilon}\right).$$

By Lemma 9.2.2, we have
$$\frac{1}{1+\varepsilon} \leq 1 - \delta$$
$$1 + \delta \leq \frac{1}{1-\varepsilon}$$
which rearrange to
$$\delta \leq 1 - \frac{1}{1+\varepsilon}$$
$$\delta \leq \frac{1}{1-\varepsilon} - 1$$

Therefore we choose
$$\delta = \min\left\{1 - \frac{1}{1+\varepsilon}, \frac{1}{1-\varepsilon} - 1\right\}$$
which satisfies the definition of our limit. $\square$

Problem 9.2.6. Prove $\lim_{x \to 3} \dfrac{1}{x} = \dfrac{1}{3}$.

Proof. Consider the implication $|x - 3| < \delta \to \left|\dfrac{1}{x} - \dfrac{1}{3}\right| < \varepsilon$. We break up the absolute value signs to get
$$3 - \delta < x < 3 + \delta \to \frac{1}{3} - \varepsilon < \frac{1}{x} < \frac{1}{3} + \varepsilon.$$

Assume $\varepsilon < \dfrac{1}{3}$, which allows us to take the reciprocal of the latter inequality to get
$$3 - \delta < x < 3 + \delta \to \frac{1}{\frac{1}{3}+\varepsilon} < x < \frac{1}{\frac{1}{3}-\varepsilon}.$$

We want to show that the interval $(3-\delta, 3+\delta)$ is contained inside $\left(\dfrac{1}{\frac{1}{3}+\varepsilon}, \dfrac{1}{\frac{1}{3}-\varepsilon}\right)$. It is sufficient that

$$\frac{1}{\frac{1}{3}+\varepsilon} < 3-\delta,$$

$$3+\delta < \frac{1}{\frac{1}{3}-\varepsilon}.$$

These rearrange to

$$\delta < 3 - \frac{1}{\frac{1}{3}+\varepsilon},$$

$$\delta < \frac{1}{\frac{1}{3}-\varepsilon} - 3.$$

Therefore we take

$$\delta < \min\left\{3 - \frac{1}{\frac{1}{3}+\varepsilon}, \frac{1}{\frac{1}{3}-\varepsilon} - 3\right\}$$

to satisfy both inequalities. □

Alternative Proof. We want to prove that

$$\forall \varepsilon > 0 \; \exists \delta > 0 \; \forall x, \; 0 < |x-3| < \delta \to \left|\frac{1}{x} - \frac{1}{3}\right| < \varepsilon.$$

Assume $\delta < 1$, so $0 < |x-3| < \delta < 1$. Then by the Triangle Inequality, $|3| \leq |3-x| + |x| = |x-3| + |x| < 1 + |x|$, which rearranges to $|x| > 3 - 1 = 2$. Clearly $|x|$ is greater than zero, so we can take the reciprocal of this inequality to get $\dfrac{1}{|x|} < \dfrac{1}{2}$.

Now note that

$$\left|\frac{1}{x} - \frac{1}{3}\right| = \left|\frac{3-x}{3x}\right| = \frac{|3-x|}{|3x|} = \frac{|x-3|}{3|x|} = \frac{1}{3} \cdot \frac{1}{|x|} \cdot |x-3| < \frac{1}{3} \cdot \frac{1}{2} \cdot \delta = \frac{\delta}{6}.$$

We want $\left|\dfrac{1}{x} - \dfrac{1}{3}\right|$ to be less than a given ε, so we should take $\delta < 6\varepsilon$. However, we have also assumed $\delta < 1$, so it is sufficient to take $\delta < \min\{1, 6\varepsilon\}$ to satisfy both inequalities. □

Problem 9.2.7. Prove $\lim\limits_{x \to 1} \dfrac{x}{x+1} = \dfrac{1}{2}$.

Proof. Again, we focus on the implication:

$$|x-1| < \delta \longrightarrow \left|\frac{x}{x+1} - \frac{1}{2}\right| < \varepsilon$$

Note that $|x-1| < \delta$ rearranges to $1 - \delta < x < 1 + \delta$, and $\left|\dfrac{x}{x+1} - \dfrac{1}{2}\right| < \varepsilon$ rearranges to:

$$\frac{1}{2} - \varepsilon < \frac{x}{x+1} < \frac{1}{2} + \varepsilon$$
$$-\frac{1}{2} + \varepsilon > -\frac{x}{x+1} > -\frac{1}{2} - \varepsilon$$
$$1 - \frac{1}{2} + \varepsilon > 1 - \frac{x}{x+1} > 1 - \frac{1}{2} - \varepsilon$$
$$\frac{1}{2} + \varepsilon > \frac{1}{x+1} > \frac{1}{2} - \varepsilon$$
$$\frac{1}{2} - \varepsilon < \frac{1}{x+1} < \frac{1}{2} + \varepsilon$$

Assume $\varepsilon < \dfrac{1}{2}$. Then, we can take the reciprocal of $\dfrac{1}{2} - \varepsilon < \dfrac{1}{x+1} < \dfrac{1}{2} + \varepsilon$, i.e. $\dfrac{1}{\frac{1}{2} - \varepsilon} > x + 1 > \dfrac{1}{\frac{1}{2} + \varepsilon}$, which rearranges to $\dfrac{\frac{1}{2} - \varepsilon}{\frac{1}{2} + \varepsilon} < x < \dfrac{\frac{1}{2} + \varepsilon}{\frac{1}{2} - \varepsilon}$. Therefore our implication is

$$1 - \delta < x < 1 + \delta \longrightarrow \frac{\frac{1}{2} - \varepsilon}{\frac{1}{2} + \varepsilon} < x < \frac{\frac{1}{2} + \varepsilon}{\frac{1}{2} - \varepsilon}$$

which can be rewritten as

$$x \in (1 - \delta, 1 + \delta) \longrightarrow x \in \left(\frac{\frac{1}{2} - \varepsilon}{\frac{1}{2} + \varepsilon}, \frac{\frac{1}{2} + \varepsilon}{\frac{1}{2} - \varepsilon} \right)$$

It is sufficient that

$$\frac{\frac{1}{2} - \varepsilon}{\frac{1}{2} + \varepsilon} \leq 1 - \delta$$
$$1 + \delta \leq \frac{\frac{1}{2} + \varepsilon}{\frac{1}{2} - \varepsilon}$$

so we have $\delta \leq \dfrac{2\varepsilon}{\frac{1}{2} - \varepsilon}$ and $\delta \leq \dfrac{2\varepsilon}{\frac{1}{2} + \varepsilon}$. Therefore, we take

$$\delta = \min\left\{ \frac{2\varepsilon}{\frac{1}{2} - \varepsilon}, \frac{2\varepsilon}{\frac{1}{2} + \varepsilon} \right\}$$

to satisfy the definition of our limit. $\square$

Example 9.2.8
Prove $\lim\limits_{x \to 4} x^2 - 3x + 2 = 6$.

First, noticing that the quadratic $x^2 - 3x + 2 - 6$ is factorable, we rewrite the second part of the implication:

$$|x - 4| < \delta \longrightarrow |x^2 - 3x + 2 - 6| < \varepsilon$$
$$|x^2 - 3x - 4| < \varepsilon$$
$$|(x - 4)(x + 1)| < \varepsilon$$

i.e. $|x - 4| < \delta \longrightarrow |x - 4||x + 1| < \varepsilon$.

Assume $\delta < 1$, therefore $|x - 4| < 1$.

By the Triangle Inequality, note that

$$|x + 1| \leq |x - 4| + |5| < 1 + 5 = 6.$$

We combine the facts $|x - 4| < \delta$ and $|x + 1| < 6$ to get that $|x - 4||x + 1| < 6\delta$.

This suggests that we let $\delta < \frac{\varepsilon}{6}$, but we have also assumed that $\delta < 1$, therefore we take the minimum of those two, i.e. let

$$\delta < \min\left\{1, \frac{\varepsilon}{6}\right\}$$

which will satisfy our definition. However, all of this work was done backwards, and cannot be considered a proper, formal proof. Instead, when we write up the proof, we write it up *forwards*, as shown:

Proof. Given a $\varepsilon > 0$, choose $\delta < \min\left\{1, \frac{\varepsilon}{6}\right\}$. Note that

$$|x - 4| < \delta \longrightarrow |x - 4| < 1 \longrightarrow |x + 1| \leq |x - 4| + |5| < 6$$

by the Triangle Inequality. Therefore,

$$|x-4| < \delta \longrightarrow |x^2-3x+2-6| = |x^2-3x-4| = |(x-4)(x+1)| = |x-4||x+1| < 6|x-4| < 6\cdot\frac{\varepsilon}{6} = \varepsilon.$$

Given a ε, we have found δ such that

$$|x - 4| < \delta \longrightarrow |x^2 - 3x + 2 - 6| < \varepsilon$$

i.e. $\lim_{x \to 4} x^2 - 3x + 2 = 6$. □

9.3 Limit Properties

Up to now, we have been proving limits of various functions. To make our lives easier, we will prove some properties of limits that will allow us to take limits of many more kinds of functions.

Theorem 9.3.1 (Uniqueness of Limits)
If $\lim_{x \to a} f(x) = L$ and $\lim_{x \to a} f(x) = M$, then $L = M$.

Proof. For the sake of contradiction, assume $L \neq M$. Then it follows that $|L - M| > 0$. Now consider

$$\lim_{x \to a} f(x) = L \longleftrightarrow \forall \varepsilon > 0 \; \exists \delta_1 > 0 \; \forall x, \; 0 < |x - a| < \delta_1 \to |f(x) - L| < \varepsilon,$$

$$\lim_{x \to a} f(x) = M \longleftrightarrow \forall \varepsilon > 0 \; \exists \delta_2 > 0 \; \forall x, \; 0 < |x - a| < \delta_2 \to |f(x) - M| < \varepsilon.$$

Choose $\delta = \min\{\delta_1, \delta_2\}$, so we have

$$\forall \varepsilon > 0 \; \exists \delta > 0 \; \forall x, \; 0 < |x - a| < \delta \to |f(x) - L| < \varepsilon \land |f(x) - M| < \varepsilon.$$

Now consider $\varepsilon = \dfrac{|L - M|}{2}$ (since $\dfrac{|L - M|}{2} > 0$). It becomes true that

$$0 < |x - a| < \delta \to |f(x) - L| < \frac{|L - M|}{2} \land |f(x) - M| < \frac{|L - M|}{2}.$$

Then for this chosen value of ε, note that

$$\begin{aligned}
|L - M| &= |L - f(x) + f(x) - M| \\
&\leq |L - f(x)| + |f(x) - M| \\
&= |f(x) - L| + |f(x) - M| \\
&< \frac{|L - M|}{2} + \frac{|L - M|}{2} = |L - M|.
\end{aligned}$$

We have $|L - M| < |L - M|$, a contradiction. Therefore $L = M$. $\square$

Problem 9.3.2. Prove that if $f(x) \geq 0 \; \forall x$ and $\lim_{x \to a} f(x) = L$, then $L \geq 0$.

Proof. Assume for the sake of contradiction that $L < 0$. We are given the definition

$$\lim_{x \to a} f(x) = L \longleftrightarrow \forall \varepsilon > 0 \; \exists \delta > 0 \; \forall x, \; 0 < |x - a| < \delta \to |f(x) - L| < \varepsilon.$$

As $f(x) \geq 0$ is given, $f(x) > L$, i.e. $f(x) - L > 0$. Therefore $|f(x) - L| = f(x) - L$. Consider $\varepsilon = -L$, which is valid because $-L > 0$. We can also choose $\varepsilon = -\dfrac{L}{2}$, or any other value in terms of L that would be positive. It follows that $\exists \delta > 0 \; \forall x, \; 0 < |x - a| < \delta \to f(x) - L < -L$. But $f(x) - L < -L$ rearranges to $f(x) < 0$, which contradicts the given $f(x) \geq 0 \; \forall x$. Therefore $L \geq 0$. $\square$

Theorem 9.3.3 (Limit of the Identity Function)

$\lim_{x \to a} x = a.$

Proof. It is sufficient to let $\delta = \varepsilon$. Then it is obvious that $0 < |x - a| < \delta \longleftrightarrow 0 < |x - a| < \varepsilon \to |x - a| < \varepsilon$. $\square$

> **Theorem 9.3.4** (Limit of a Constant)
> $\lim_{x \to a} c = c$ for some constant c.

Proof. Any δ is valid, since $\forall \varepsilon > 0$ we have $|c - c| = 0 < \varepsilon$ which is always true. $\square$

> **Theorem 9.3.5** (Sum and Product of Limits)
> Suppose $\lim_{x \to a} f(x) = L$ and $\lim_{x \to a} g(x) = M$. Then
>
> a) $\lim_{x \to a} (f(x) + g(x)) = L + M$.
>
> b) $\lim_{x \to a} (f(x)g(x)) = LM$.

Proof. a) We are given $\lim_{x \to a} f(x) = L$ and $\lim_{x \to a} g(x) = M$, therefore

$$\forall \varepsilon > 0 \; \exists \delta_1 > 0 \; \forall x, \; 0 < |x - a| < \delta_1 \longrightarrow |f(x) - L| < \frac{\varepsilon}{2},$$

$$\exists \delta_2 > 0 \; \forall x, \; 0 < |x - a| < \delta_2 \longrightarrow |g(x) - M| < \frac{\varepsilon}{2}.$$

This is allowed because we can always choose a δ_1 or δ_2 that is small enough to make each $|f(x) - L|$ and $|g(x) - M|$ smaller than $\frac{\varepsilon}{2}$.

Let $\delta = \min\{\delta_1, \delta_2\}$. This is because we want to be able to use the same δ for both definitions. Then,

$$\forall \varepsilon > 0 \; \exists \delta > 0 \; \forall x, \; 0 < |x - a| < \delta \longrightarrow |f(x) - L| < \frac{\varepsilon}{2} \wedge |g(x) - M| < \frac{\varepsilon}{2}.$$

Note that $|f(x) + g(x) - (L + M)| = |(f(x) - L) + (g(x) - M)| \leq |f(x) - L| + |g(x) + M|$ by the Triangle Inequality. Therefore, given $\varepsilon > 0$, we have found a δ such that

$$|x - a| < \delta \longrightarrow |f(x) + g(x) - (L + M)| \leq |f(x) - L| + |g(x) + M| < \frac{\varepsilon}{2} + \frac{\varepsilon}{2} = \varepsilon,$$

i.e. $\lim_{x \to a} (f(x) + g(x)) = L + M$, as desired.

b) Let $\widetilde{\varepsilon}$ represent some quantity in terms of ε. Eventually we will figure out exactly what expression we should set $\widetilde{\varepsilon}$ equal to, by doing the proof 'backwards,' to demonstrate the motivation and intuition behind the choice of $\widetilde{\varepsilon}$. After we find out what $\widetilde{\varepsilon}$ exactly is, we will write the proof forwards.

As we are given $\lim_{x \to a} f(x) = L$ and $\lim_{x \to a} g(x) = M$,

$$\forall \varepsilon > 0 \; \exists \delta_1 > 0 \; \forall x, \; 0 < |x - a| < \delta_1 \longrightarrow |f(x) - L| < \widetilde{\varepsilon},$$

$$\exists \delta_2 > 0 \; \forall x, \; 0 < |x - a| < \delta_2 \longrightarrow |g(x) - M| < \widetilde{\varepsilon}.$$

Like before, let $\delta = \min\{\delta_1, \delta_2\}$. Then we can cover both cases:
$$\forall \varepsilon > 0 \ \exists \delta > 0 \ \forall x, \ 0 < |x - a| < \delta \longrightarrow |f(x) - L| < \widetilde{\varepsilon} \land |g(x) - M| < \widetilde{\varepsilon}.$$

Now we apply the Triangle Inequality based on what we are trying to prove:
$$\begin{aligned}|f(x)g(x) - LM| &= |f(x)g(x) - f(x)M + f(x)M - LM| \\ &= |f(x)(g(x) - M) + M(f(x) - L)| \\ &\leq |f(x)||g(x) - M| + |M||f(x) - L|.\end{aligned}$$

Now we should introduce a bound on $|f(x)|$. Therefore we should assume $\varepsilon < 1$. Then it follows that $|f(x) - L| < 1$. By another application of the Triangle Inequality,
$$|f(x)| \leq |f(x) - L| + |L| < 1 + |L|.$$

We can now conclude that
$$\begin{aligned}|f(x)g(x) - LM| &\leq |f(x)||g(x) - M| + |M||f(x) - L| \\ &< (1 + |L|)\widetilde{\varepsilon} + |M|\widetilde{\varepsilon} \\ &= (1 + |L| + |M|)\widetilde{\varepsilon}.\end{aligned}$$

It would be sufficient to let $\widetilde{\varepsilon} = \dfrac{\varepsilon}{1 + |L| + |M|}$, so $|f(x)g(x) - LM| < \widetilde{\varepsilon}(1 + |L| + |M|) < \varepsilon$, as desired.

Now we should write the proof forwards:

As we are given $\lim\limits_{x \to a} f(x) = L$ and $\lim\limits_{x \to a} g(x) = M$,
$$\forall \varepsilon > 0 \ \exists \delta_1 > 0 \ \forall x, \ 0 < |x - a| < \delta_1 \longrightarrow |f(x) - L| < \frac{\varepsilon}{1 + |L| + |M|},$$
$$\exists \delta_2 > 0 \ \forall x, \ 0 < |x - a| < \delta_2 \longrightarrow |g(x) - M| < \frac{\varepsilon}{1 + |L| + |M|}.$$

Let $\delta = \min\{\delta_1, \delta_2\}$. Then $\exists \delta > 0$ such that
$$0 < |x - a| < \delta \longrightarrow |f(x) - L| < \frac{\varepsilon}{1 + |L| + |M|} \land |g(x) - M| < \frac{\varepsilon}{1 + |L| + |M|}.$$

Assume $\varepsilon < 1$, so that $|f(x) - L| < 1$. Then $|f(x)| \leq |f(x) - L| + |L| < 1 + |L|$. Therefore, we conclude that
$$\begin{aligned}|f(x)g(x) - LM| &= |f(x)g(x) - f(x)M + f(x)M - LM| \\ &= |f(x)(g(x) - M) + M(f(x) - L)| \\ &\leq |f(x)||g(x) - M| + |M||f(x) - L| \\ &< (1 + |L|)\frac{\varepsilon}{1 + |L| + |M|} + |M|\frac{\varepsilon}{1 + |L| + |M|} \\ &= (1 + |L| + |M|)\frac{\varepsilon}{1 + |L| + |M|} \\ &= \varepsilon.\end{aligned}$$
$\square$

> **Corollary 9.3.6** (Difference of Limits)
> $$\lim_{x \to a}(f(x) - g(x)) = \lim_{x \to a} f(x) - \lim_{x \to a} g(x).$$

Proof. It follows from Theorem 9.3.4 and Theorem 9.3.5 that $\lim_{x \to a}(f(x) - g(x)) = \lim_{x \to a} f(x) + \lim_{x \to a}(-g(x)) = \lim_{x \to a} f(x) + \lim_{x \to a}(-1) \lim_{x \to a} g(x) = \lim_{x \to a} f(x) - \lim_{x \to a} g(x).$ $\square$

Problem 9.3.7. Prove $\lim_{x \to 5} 2x^3 - x^2 = 225$ using the limit properties we have just established.

Proof. We can 'break up' the polynomial into smaller 'pieces,' by applying sum, difference, and product rules of limits.

$$\begin{aligned}
\lim_{x \to 5} 2x^3 - x^2 &= \lim_{x \to 5} 2x^3 - \lim_{x \to 5} x^2 \\
&= \lim_{x \to 5} 2 \cdot \lim_{x \to 5} x \cdot \lim_{x \to 5} x \cdot \lim_{x \to 5} x - \lim_{x \to 5} x \cdot \lim_{x \to 5} x \\
&= 2 \cdot 5 \cdot 5 \cdot 5 - 5 \cdot 5 \\
&= 255.
\end{aligned}$$
$\square$

> **Lemma 9.3.8**
> If $0 \leq j(x) \leq k(x) \; \forall x$ and $\lim_{x \to a} k(x) = 0$, then $\lim_{x \to a} j(x) = 0$.

Proof. It follows that $k(x) - j(x) \geq 0 \; \forall x$. By Problem 9.3.2, $\lim_{x \to a} k(x) - j(x) \geq 0$. But note that $\lim_{x \to a} k(x) - j(x) = \lim_{x \to a} k(x) - \lim_{x \to a} j(x) = -\lim_{x \to a} j(x)$, therefore $\lim_{x \to a} j(x) \leq 0$. However, as we are also given $j(x) \geq 0 \; \forall x$, so by Problem 9.3.2, $\lim_{x \to a} j(x) \geq 0$. Thus we can only conclude $\lim_{x \to a} j(x) = 0$. $\square$

> **Theorem 9.3.9** (Squeeze Theorem)
> Suppose $f(x) \leq g(x) \leq h(x) \; \forall x$ and $\lim_{x \to a} f(x) = \lim_{x \to a} h(x) = L$. Then $\lim_{x \to a} g(x) = L$.

Proof. The given inequality rearranges to $0 \leq g(x) - f(x) \leq h(x) - f(x)$. Note that $\lim_{x \to a}(h(x) - f(x)) = \lim_{x \to a} h(x) - \lim_{x \to a} f(x) = L - L = 0$. By Lemma 9.3.8, $\lim_{x \to a}(g(x) - f(x)) = 0$, i.e. $\lim_{x \to a} g(x) = \lim_{x \to a} f(x) = L$, as desired. $\square$

Alternative Proof. In fact, we could prove this theorem from scratch, without using previous lemmas.

By definition of limits, there exist δ_1, δ_2 such that

$$0 < |x - a| < \delta_1 \to |f(x) - L| < \varepsilon,$$
$$0 < |x - a| < \delta_2 \to |h(x) - L| < \varepsilon.$$

Let $\delta = \min\{\delta_1, \delta_2\}$, it follows that

$$|x - a| < \delta \to L - \varepsilon < f(x), h(x) < L + \varepsilon.$$

Then

$$L - \varepsilon < f(x) \leq g(x) \leq h(x) < L + \varepsilon \implies |g(x) - L| < \varepsilon,$$

so this choice of δ establishes that $\lim_{x \to a} g(x) = L$. $\square$

Theorem 9.3.10 (Reciprocal of Limits)
Suppose $\lim_{x \to a} g(x) = L$, and $L \neq 0$. Then $\lim_{x \to a} \frac{1}{g(x)} = \frac{1}{L}$.

Proof. Given $\varepsilon > 0$, there exists δ_1 such that $0 < |x - a| < \delta_1 \to |g(x) - L| < \frac{|L|}{2}$, since $\frac{|L|}{2}$ is a number greater than 0. Likewise, there exists δ_2 such that $0 < |x - a| < \delta_2 \to |g(x) - L| < \frac{\varepsilon |L|^2}{2}$. Then take $\delta = \min\{\delta_1, \delta_2\}$, such that

$$0 < |x - a| < \delta \to |g(x) - L| < \frac{|L|}{2} \wedge |g(x) - L| < \frac{\varepsilon |L|^2}{2}.$$

By the Triangle Inequality, $|L| \leq |L - g(x)| + |g(x)| = |g(x) - L| + |g(x)| < \frac{|L|}{2} + |g(x)|$, therefore $|g(x)| > \frac{|L|}{2}$. As both quantities are positive, we can take the reciprocal to get $\frac{1}{|g(x)|} < \frac{2}{|L|}$. Note that we applied the Triangle Inequality on $|L|$ because we seek a lower bound for $|g(x)|$, such that we have an upper bound for $\frac{1}{|g(x)|}$, which is needed to finish the proof.

Therefore, we have found a δ such that

$$\left|\frac{1}{g(x)} - \frac{1}{L}\right| = \left|\frac{L - g(x)}{g(x)L}\right| = \frac{|g(x) - L|}{|g(x)||L|} < \frac{2}{|L|} \cdot \frac{1}{|L|} \cdot \frac{\varepsilon |L|^2}{2} = \varepsilon,$$

given $\varepsilon > 0$, and we can conclude that $\lim_{x \to a} \frac{1}{g(x)} = \frac{1}{L}$. $\square$

Corollary 9.3.11 (Quotient of Limits)
Provided $\lim_{x \to a} g(x) \neq 0$, $\lim_{x \to a} \frac{f(x)}{g(x)} = \frac{\lim_{x \to a} f(x)}{\lim_{x \to a} g(x)}$.

Proof. This follows from application of the reciprocal rule with the product rule. $\square$

Lemma 9.3.12 (Continuity of Polynomials)
Let $P(x)$ be a polynomial. Then $\lim_{x \to a} P(x) = P(a)$.

Proof. Let $P(x) = \sum_{k=0}^{n} b_k x^k$. Then,

$$\lim_{x \to a} P(x) = \lim_{x \to a} \sum_{k=0}^{n} b_k x^k$$
$$= \sum_{k=0}^{n} \lim_{x \to a} b_k \cdot (\lim_{x \to a} x)^k$$
$$= \sum_{k=0}^{n} b_k (a)^k$$
$$= P(a). \qquad \square$$

This theorem officially establishes that we can find the limit of any polynomial by simply plugging in the number and computing the answer.

Lemma 9.3.13 (Continuity of Rational Functions)
Let $P(x)$, $Q(x)$ be polynomials. If $Q(x) \neq 0 \; \forall x$, then

$$\lim_{x \to a} \frac{P(x)}{Q(x)} = \frac{P(a)}{Q(a)}.$$

Proof. We combine the results of Corollary 9.3.11 with Lemma 9.3.12. $\qquad \square$

Problem 9.3.14. Compute the following limits:

1. $\lim\limits_{x \to 2} \dfrac{x^2 - 5}{x^2 + 3x + 1}$

2. $\lim\limits_{x \to 2} \dfrac{x^2 - 4}{x^2 - 3x + 2}$

3. $\lim\limits_{x \to 2} \dfrac{x^3 - 8}{x^2 - 5x + 6}$

4. $\lim\limits_{x \to -3} \dfrac{x^3 + 27}{x^4 - 81}$

Proof.

1. $\lim\limits_{x \to 2} \dfrac{x^2 - 5}{x^2 + 3x + 1} = \dfrac{2^2 - 5}{2^2 + 3 \cdot 2 + 1} = \boxed{-\dfrac{1}{11}}.$

2. We cannot directly plug in $x = 2$, since the denominator becomes 0. However, the polynomials in the numerator and denominator both share $x - 2$ as a common factor, so we cancel those out, leaving us with an expression for which we can plug in $x = 2$ without issues:
$$\lim_{x \to 2} \frac{x^2 - 4}{x^2 - 3x + 2} = \lim_{x \to 2} \frac{(x+2)(x-2)}{(x-2)(x-1)} = \lim_{x \to 2} \frac{x+2}{x-1} = \boxed{4}.$$

3. $\lim_{x \to 2} \dfrac{x^3 - 8}{x^2 - 5x + 6} = \lim_{x \to 2} \dfrac{(x-2)(x^2 + x + 4)}{(x-2)(x-3)} = \lim_{x \to 2} \dfrac{x^2 + 2x + 4}{x - 3} = \boxed{-12}.$

4. $\lim_{x \to -3} \dfrac{x^3 + 27}{x^4 - 81} = \lim_{x \to -3} \dfrac{(x+3)(x^2 - 3x + 9)}{(x^2 + 9)(x^2 - 9)}$
$= \lim_{x \to -3} \dfrac{(x+3)(x^2 - 3x + 9)}{(x^2 + 9)(x+3)(x-3)}$
$= \lim_{x \to -3} \dfrac{x^2 - 3x + 9}{(x^2 + 9)(x-3)}$
$= \dfrac{(-3)^2 - 3(-3) + 9}{((-3)^2 + 9)(-3 - 3)}$
$= \boxed{-\dfrac{1}{4}}.$ □

9.4 Other Limits

When we say "x approaches a," it can either indicate that x is greater than a so x would be decreasing to get closer to a, or x is less than a and x would be increasing to get closer to a.

In our definition of the limit so far, we dealt with this by taking the absolute value of $x - a$ to get the distance between them. However, we can also specify whether $x > a$ or $x < a$, through two types of limits:

Definition 9.4.1. The **right-hand limit** as $x \to a$ of $f(x)$ is L when
$$\lim_{x \to a^+} f(x) = L \longleftrightarrow \forall \varepsilon > 0 \; \exists \delta > 0 \; \forall x, \; 0 < x - a < \delta \to |f(x) - L| < \varepsilon.$$

Definition 9.4.2. The **left-hand limit** as $x \to a$ of $f(x)$ is L when
$$\lim_{x \to a^-} f(x) = L \longleftrightarrow \forall \varepsilon > 0 \; \exists \delta > 0 \; \forall x, \; 0 < a - x < \delta \to |f(x) - L| < \varepsilon.$$

The right-hand limit deals with x approaching a from the right, while the left-hand limit deals with x approaching a from the left.

Notice that the only difference between their definitions and the original definition is the replacement of $|x - a|$ with either $x - a$ or $a - x$. These conditions indicate $x > a$ and $x < a$ respectively.

Since $|x - a|$ can only be one of these two expressions, we have an obvious result that you should attempt to prove.

Exercise 9.4.3. Given $\lim_{x \to a^+} f(x)$ and $\lim_{x \to a^-} f(x)$ exist, prove that $\lim_{x \to a^+} f(x) = \lim_{x \to a^-} f(x) = L \longleftrightarrow \lim_{x \to a} f(x) = L$.

Problem 9.4.4. Let $f(x)$ be the function considered in Example 9.1.5. Evaluate $\lim_{x \to 4^+} f(x)$ and $\lim_{x \to 4^-} f(x)$.

Solution. For $\lim_{x \to 4^+} f(x)$, we are considering $x > 4$. By the piecewise definition, we must have $\lim_{x \to 4^+} f(x) = 5$.

Likewise, for $\lim_{x \to 4^-} f(x)$, $x < 4$ in this context, so $\lim_{x \to 4^-} f(x) = 7$. $\square$

Problem 9.4.5. Prove $\lim_{x \to 0^+} \frac{|x|}{x} = 1$.

Proof. Based on the definition of the right-hand limit, we must prove
$$0 < x - 0 < \delta \longrightarrow \left| \frac{|x|}{x} - 1 \right| < \varepsilon.$$

Since $x > 0$, we know that $\frac{|x|}{x} = \frac{x}{x} = 1$, i.e. $\left| \frac{|x|}{x} - 1 \right| = 0 < \varepsilon$ which is true. $\square$

Problem 9.4.6. Prove $\lim_{x \to 0^-} \frac{|x|}{x} = -1$.

Proof. Based on the definition of the left-hand limit, we must prove
$$0 < 0 - x < \delta \longrightarrow \left| \frac{|x|}{x} - (-1) \right| < \varepsilon.$$

Since $-\delta < x < 0$, we know that $\frac{|x|}{x} = \frac{-x}{x} = -1$. Then,
$$\left| \frac{|x|}{x} - (-1) \right| = |-1 - (-1)| = 0,$$
which is always less than ε since ε is any positive number. $\square$

Problem 9.4.7. Consider the function
$$f(x) = \begin{cases} x^2 - 1 & x \geq 5 \\ 7x - 11 & x < 5 \end{cases}$$

Prove or disprove that $\lim_{x \to 5} f(x)$ exists.

Proof. We use the result of Exercise 9.4.3. Note that $\lim_{x \to 5^+} f(x) = \lim_{x \to 5^+} x^2 - 1 = 24$, and $\lim_{x \to 5^-} f(x) = \lim_{x \to 5^-} 7x - 11 = 24$. As $\lim_{x \to 5^+} f(x) = \lim_{x \to 5^-} f(x) = 24$, $\lim_{x \to 5} f(x) = 24$. $\square$

Problem 9.4.8. Find $\lim\limits_{x \to 4} \dfrac{|x^2 - 16|}{x - 4}$.

Solution. First, we factor: $\lim\limits_{x \to 4} \dfrac{|x^2 - 16|}{x - 4} = \lim\limits_{x \to 4} \dfrac{|x - 4|\,|x + 4|}{x - 4}$.

Now, we consider the right-hand and left-hand limits separately.

For the right-hand limit, $\lim\limits_{x \to 4^+} \dfrac{|x - 4|\,|x + 4|}{x - 4}$, note that $x > 4$ in this case. Then, $|x - 4| = x - 4$. Thus,
$$\lim_{x \to 4^+} \frac{|x - 4|\,|x + 4|}{x - 4} = \lim_{x \to 4^+} \frac{(x - 4)\,|x + 4|}{x - 4} = \lim_{x \to 4^+} |x + 4| = 8.$$

For the left-hand limit, $\lim\limits_{x \to 4^-} \dfrac{|x - 4|\,|x + 4|}{x - 4}$, we must have $x < 4$. Thus, $|x - 4| = 4 - x$, and we have
$$\lim_{x \to 4^-} \frac{|x - 4|\,|x + 4|}{x - 4} = \lim_{x \to 4^-} \frac{(4 - x)\,|x + 4|}{x - 4} = \lim_{x \to 4^-} -|x + 4| = -8.$$

Since $\lim\limits_{x \to 4^+} \dfrac{|x - 4|\,|x + 4|}{x - 4} \neq \lim\limits_{x \to 4^-} \dfrac{|x - 4|\,|x + 4|}{x - 4}$, $\lim\limits_{x \to 4} \dfrac{|x - 4|\,|x + 4|}{x - 4}$ i.e. $\lim\limits_{x \to 4} \dfrac{|x^2 - 16|}{x - 4}$ does not exist. $\square$

Up to now, we have been dealing with x approaching some finite number a. However, as we did for sequences, we can define x going to infinity as well. In fact, since we are dealing with functions, it is possible for x to go to negative infinity as well!

As the Cartesian plane extends infinitely in both dimensions, we could also have $f(x)$ going to infinity or negative infinity for some function f.

Keeping these possibilities in mind, we define a new kind of limits for these:

Definition 9.4.9 (Infinite Limits). We introduce new variables N and M to deal with cases when x or $f(x)$ go to ∞ or $-\infty$. Then,

- $\lim\limits_{x \to \infty} f(x) = L \longleftrightarrow \forall \varepsilon > 0 \; \exists N \; \forall x, \; x > N \to |f(x) - L| < \varepsilon$.

- $\lim\limits_{x \to -\infty} f(x) = L \longleftrightarrow \forall \varepsilon > 0 \; \exists N \; \forall x, \; x < N \to |f(x) - L| < \varepsilon$.

- $\lim\limits_{x \to \infty} f(x) = \infty \longleftrightarrow \forall M \; \exists N \; \forall x, \; x > N \to f(x) > M$.

- $\lim\limits_{x \to -\infty} f(x) = \infty \longleftrightarrow \forall M \; \exists N \; \forall x, \; x < N \to f(x) > M$.

- $\lim\limits_{x \to \infty} f(x) = -\infty \longleftrightarrow \forall M \; \exists N \; \forall x, \; x > N \to f(x) < M$.

- $\lim\limits_{x \to -\infty} f(x) = -\infty \longleftrightarrow \forall M \; \exists N \; \forall x, \; x < N \to f(x) < M$.

- $\lim\limits_{x \to a} f(x) = \infty \longleftrightarrow \forall M \; \exists \delta > 0 \; \forall x, \; 0 < |x - a| < \delta \to f(x) > M$.

- $\lim\limits_{x \to a} f(x) = -\infty \longleftrightarrow \forall M \; \exists \delta > 0 \; \forall x, \; 0 < |x - a| < \delta \to f(x) < M$.

How did we even come up with these definitions? Well, if we have x or $f(x)$ approaching some finite value, then we NEED to signify that the distance between the two is less than some chosen positive number: we use δ for x approaching a and ε for $f(x)$ approaching the limit L. Of course, the "distance" is represented by taking the absolute value of the difference between the two.

Otherwise, if we have ∞ or $-\infty$ involved, then we need to indicate that the value in question (x or $f(x)$) increases or decreases without bound.

For example, if we wanted to show $x \to \infty$, then we would use the idea that for ANY real number N you choose (even when N is an incredibly large number), x would always be greater than that number. This fits with the notion of infinity - x cannot be less than any number since it is always increasing.

Likewise, if we had $x \to -\infty$, then x would always be less than any real number we choose, since it is decreasing.

The exact reasoning applies to $f(x)$ as well.

Thus, whenever we have $f(x)$ going to some finite limit L, then we would include $\forall \varepsilon > 0$ and $|f(x) - L| < \varepsilon$.

However, if $f(x)$ went to ∞ or $-\infty$, then we would have $\forall M$ and $f(x) > M$ or $f(x) < M$ respectively.

If x went to some finite number a, then we would say $\exists \delta > 0$ and $0 < |x - a| < \delta$.

If x went to ∞ or $-\infty$, then we would define $\exists N$ and $x > N$ or $x < N$ respectively.

Then, when we consider the right-hand or left-hand limits as $f(x)$ goes to ∞ or $-\infty$, we can just replace $0 < |x - a| < \delta$ (in the original definition) with $0 < x - a < \delta$ or $0 < a - x < \delta$ respectively.

Problem 9.4.10. Prove $\lim\limits_{x \to \infty} \dfrac{1}{x} = 0$.

Proof. We want to prove that

$$\forall \varepsilon > 0 \ \exists N \ \forall x, \ x > N \to \left| \frac{1}{x} - 0 \right| < \varepsilon.$$

Assume $N > 0$ (we have the same freedom in choosing N as we had with δ). Then $x > N > 0 \to \dfrac{1}{x} < \dfrac{1}{N}$. Since $x > 0$ by assumption, $x = |x|$, so we have $\dfrac{1}{|x|} < \dfrac{1}{N}$, i.e. $\left| \dfrac{1}{x} - 0 \right| < \dfrac{1}{N}$. We want $\left| \dfrac{1}{x} - 0 \right|$ to be less than a given ε, which suggests that $\dfrac{1}{N} < \varepsilon$. Therefore it is sufficient to take $N > \dfrac{1}{\varepsilon}$. $\square$

Problem 9.4.11. Prove $\lim\limits_{x \to 0^-} \dfrac{1}{x} = -\infty$.

Proof. Consider the corresponding definition

$$\forall M \ \exists \delta > 0 \ \forall x, \ 0 < 0 - x < \delta \to \frac{1}{x} < M.$$

We rewrite the former inequality as $0 > x > -\delta$. Since x and $-\delta$ are both negative, we can take the reciprocal to get $\frac{1}{x} < -\frac{1}{\delta}$. However, we want $\frac{1}{x}$ to be less than a given M, so it is sufficient to take $-\frac{1}{\delta} < M$, i.e. $\delta < -\frac{1}{M}$. □

Problem 9.4.12. Prove $\lim\limits_{x \to 3^-} \frac{1}{x-3} = -\infty$.

Proof. Writing out the definition,

$$\forall N \; \exists \delta > 0 \; \forall x, \; 0 < 3 - x < \delta \longrightarrow \frac{1}{x-3} < N.$$

First, note that $0 < 3 - x < \delta$ can be rewritten as $0 > x - 3 > -\delta$.

If some value of N works, then any value greater than it must also work. Therefore, we can assume that $N < 0$. Now, we can reciprocate the inequality $\frac{1}{x-3} < N$ to get $x - 3 > \frac{1}{N}$. Now, it becomes clear that we want $-\delta = \frac{1}{N}$, or $\delta = -\frac{1}{N}$. Then, $0 > x - 3 > \frac{1}{N} \longrightarrow \frac{1}{x-3} < N$ as desired. □

Problem 9.4.13. Prove $\lim\limits_{x \to \infty} \frac{\sin x}{x} = 0$.

Proof. Consider the definition of the limit:

$$\forall \varepsilon > 0 \; \exists N \; \forall x, \; x > N \longrightarrow \left|\frac{\sin x}{x}\right| < \varepsilon.$$

Rewrite $\left|\frac{\sin x}{x}\right|$ as $\frac{|\sin x|}{|x|}$. Note that $-1 \leq \sin x \leq 1$, so $|\sin x| \leq 1$. Therefore, $\frac{|\sin x|}{|x|} \leq \frac{1}{|x|}$. As before, we can assume $N > 0$ so that $x > N \longrightarrow x > 0 \longrightarrow |x| = x$, and $\frac{1}{|x|} = \frac{1}{x}$. Putting all of this together, we need

$$\left|\frac{\sin x}{x}\right| = \frac{|\sin x|}{|x|} \leq \frac{1}{|x|} = \frac{1}{x} < \varepsilon$$

to be true. It then suffices to prove that

$$\forall \varepsilon > 0 \; \exists N \; \forall x, \; x > N \longrightarrow \frac{1}{x} < \varepsilon.$$

However, this is just the definition of $\lim\limits_{x \to \infty} \frac{1}{x} = 0$, and we have already proven this in Problem 9.4.10. □

Problem 9.4.14. Prove $\lim\limits_{n \to \infty} \sin x$ does not exist.

Proof. Assume by contradiction that the limit L exists. The definition for $\lim\limits_{n \to \infty} \sin x = L$ is:

$$\forall \varepsilon > 0 \; \exists N \; \forall x, \; x > N \longrightarrow |\sin x - L| < \varepsilon.$$

Consider the negation of this statement:

$$\exists \varepsilon > 0 \ \forall N \ \exists x, \ x > N \wedge |\sin x - L| \geq \varepsilon.$$

If we can choose a value of ε such that no value of N works, then there will be no limit L that exists. I claim that $\varepsilon = \dfrac{1}{4}$ fails the definition (as a note, we can choose any ε less than 1 and greater than 0 to demonstrate a contradiction).

For any N, there is a multiple of 2π that is larger than N (in particular, it would be $2\pi \left\lceil \dfrac{N}{2\pi} \right\rceil$, but that is not important in this proof). Let T be this multiple of 2π. Then $\sin\left(T + \dfrac{\pi}{2}\right) = 1$ and $\sin\left(T + \dfrac{3\pi}{2}\right) = -1$.

Our definition of the limit suggests $|\sin x - L| < \varepsilon$ i.e. $L - \varepsilon < \sin x < L + \varepsilon$. This implies $\sin x \in (L - \varepsilon, L + \varepsilon)$. Noting that we chose $\varepsilon = \dfrac{1}{4}$, we see that this is an interval of size $\dfrac{1}{2}$. This interval cannot possibly contain both -1 and 1, and so no value of N could possibly work for $\varepsilon = \dfrac{1}{4}$. We have arrived at a contradiction, thus, no value of L works, and the limit does not exist. $\square$

9.5 Trigonometric Limits

We define sine, cosine via the unit circle.

> **Example 9.5.1**
> Prove that $\lim\limits_{\theta \to 0} \sin \theta = 0$ and $\lim\limits_{\theta \to 0} \cos \theta = 1$.

Proof. Assume $0 < \theta < \dfrac{\pi}{2}$, where θ is in radians. We only care about θ being close to 0, which is why we restrict θ to be less than $\dfrac{\pi}{2}$ radians. Consider the unit circle:

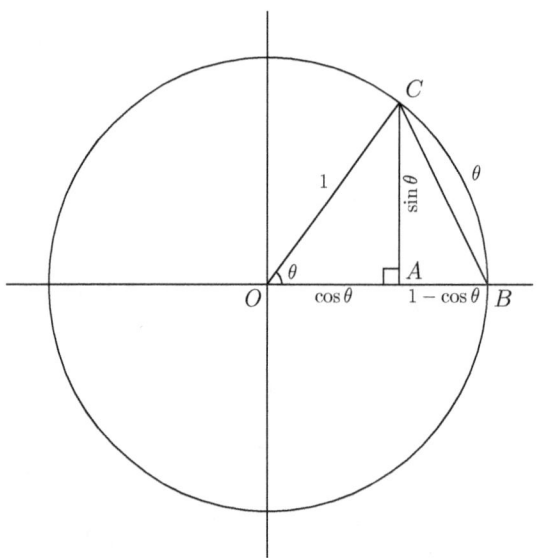

We will take for granted that $\widehat{BC} > \overline{BC}$ (we will glance over the rigorous proof for this), and since $\overline{BC}$ is the hypotenuse of $\triangle ABC$, $\overline{BC} > \overline{AC}$ and $\overline{BC} > \overline{AB}$. Therefore, $\widehat{BC} > \overline{AC}$ and $\widehat{BC} > \overline{AB}$. Since θ is in radians, the length of $\widehat{BC}$ is θ. Note that $\overline{AC} = \sin\theta$ and $\overline{AB} = 1 - \cos\theta$. We have the inequalities:

$$0 < \sin\theta < \theta,$$
$$0 < 1 - \cos\theta < \theta.$$

As $\lim_{\theta \to 0^+} 0 = \lim_{\theta \to 0^+} \theta = 0$, by Theorem 9.3.9, $\lim_{\theta \to 0^+} \sin\theta = \lim_{\theta \to 0^+} 1 - \cos\theta = 0$; the latter rearranges to $\lim_{\theta \to 0^+} \cos\theta = 1$.

Lemma 9.5.2

Assuming both limits exist, $\lim_{x \to a^+} f(x) = \lim_{x \to -a^-} f(-x)$.

Proof. Consider the definition of $\lim_{x \to a^+} f(x) = L$,

$$\forall \varepsilon > 0 \ \exists \delta > 0 \ \forall x, \ 0 < x - a < \delta \to |f(x) - L| < \varepsilon.$$

Substitute $x \to -x$. Then,

$$0 < (-x) - a < \delta \to |f(-x) - L| < \varepsilon$$
$$0 < -a - x < \delta \to |f(-x) - L| < \varepsilon$$

which is the definition of $\lim_{x \to -a^-} f(-x) = L$. Therefore the definitions are equivalent, i.e. $\lim_{x \to a^+} f(x) = \lim_{x \to -a^-} f(-x)$. □

By Lemma 9.5.2, it follows that $\lim_{\theta \to 0^+} \sin\theta = \lim_{\theta \to -0^-} \sin(-\theta) = -\lim_{\theta \to -0^-} \sin\theta = -\lim_{\theta \to 0^-} \sin\theta$. Since $\lim_{\theta \to 0^+} \sin\theta = 0$, $-\lim_{\theta \to 0^-} \sin\theta = 0$, i.e. $\lim_{\theta \to 0^-} \sin\theta = 0$. By Exercise 9.4.3, we conclude that $\lim_{\theta \to 0} \sin\theta = 0$.

Similarly, we note that $\lim_{\theta \to 0^+} \cos\theta = \lim_{\theta \to -0^-} \cos(-\theta) = \lim_{\theta \to -0^-} \cos\theta = \lim_{\theta \to 0^-} \cos\theta$ by Lemma 9.5.2. Since $\lim_{\theta \to 0^+} \cos\theta = 1$, we have $\lim_{\theta \to 0^-} \cos\theta = 1$. By Exercise 9.4.3, we conclude that $\lim_{\theta \to 0} \cos\theta = 1$. □

Lemma 9.5.3

$\lim_{x \to a} f(x) = L \longleftrightarrow \lim_{h \to 0} f(a + h) = L.$

Proof. The definition of $\lim_{x \to a} f(x) = L$ is

$$\forall \varepsilon > 0 \ \exists \delta > 0 \ \forall x, \ 0 < |x - a| < \delta \to |f(x) - L| < \varepsilon.$$

Substitute $x \to a+h$. Then,

$$\forall \varepsilon > 0 \; \exists \delta > 0 \; \forall h, \; 0 < |a+h-a| < \delta \to |f(a+h) - L| < \varepsilon,$$

which simplifies to

$$\forall \varepsilon > 0 \; \exists \delta > 0 \; \forall h, \; 0 < |h-0| < \delta \to |f(a+h) - L| < \varepsilon,$$

i.e. the definition of $\lim_{h \to 0} f(a+h) = L$. Since the definitions are equivalent, $\lim_{x \to a} f(x) = L \longleftrightarrow \lim_{h \to 0} f(a+h) = L$. □

> **Theorem 9.5.4** (Continuity of Trigonometric Functions)
> If a is in the domain, then $\lim_{x \to a} \text{Trig}(x) = \text{Trig}(a)$, where $\text{Trig} = \sin, \cos, \tan, \csc, \sec, \cot$.

Proof. We will prove this for $\sin x$ and $\cos x$, and the rest will follow by Theorem 9.3.10.

We proceed by Lemma 9.5.3 on $\sin x$ and $\cos x$.

$$\begin{aligned}
\lim_{x \to a} \sin x &= \lim_{h \to 0} \sin(a+h) \\
&= \lim_{h \to 0} (\sin a \cos h + \cos a \sin h) \\
&= \lim_{h \to 0} \sin a \cdot \lim_{h \to 0} \cos h + \lim_{h \to 0} \cos a \cdot \lim_{h \to 0} \sin h \\
&= \sin a \cdot 1 + \cos a \cdot 0 \\
&= \sin a.
\end{aligned}$$

$$\begin{aligned}
\lim_{x \to a} \cos x &= \lim_{h \to 0} \cos(a+h) \\
&= \lim_{h \to 0} (\cos a \cos h - \sin a \sin h) \\
&= \lim_{h \to 0} \cos a \cdot \lim_{h \to 0} \cos h - \lim_{h \to 0} \sin a \cdot \lim_{h \to 0} \sin h \\
&= \cos a \cdot 1 + \sin a \cdot 0 \\
&= \cos a.
\end{aligned}$$
□

> **Theorem 9.5.5**
> $$\lim_{\theta \to 0} \frac{\sin \theta}{\theta} = 1.$$

Proof. Assume $0 < \theta < \dfrac{\pi}{2}$, where θ is in radians. Consider the following diagram:

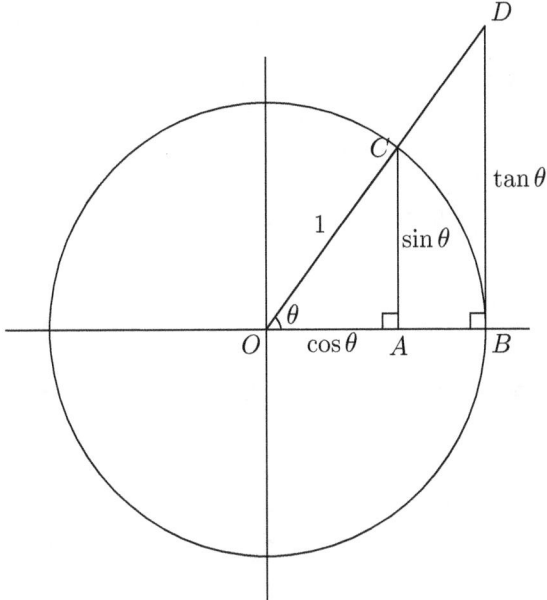

It is clear that we have the following inequality:

$$\text{Area of } \triangle OAC < \text{Area of sector } OBC < \text{Area of } \triangle OBD.$$

We find our respective areas:
$$\frac{\sin\theta\cos\theta}{2} < \frac{\theta}{2} < \frac{\tan\theta}{2}.$$

This rearranges to
$$\frac{1}{\cos\theta} > \frac{\sin\theta}{\theta} > \cos\theta.$$

Note that $\lim_{\theta\to 0^+} \frac{1}{\cos\theta} = 1$ and $\lim_{\theta\to 0^+} \cos\theta = 1$, therefore by Theorem 9.3.9, we have that $\lim_{\theta\to 0^+} \frac{\sin\theta}{\theta} = 1$.

We can then proceed with Lemma 9.5.2, and eventually conclude that $\lim_{\theta\to 0^-} \frac{\sin\theta}{\theta} = 1$, so therefore $\lim_{\theta\to 0} \frac{\sin\theta}{\theta} = 1$. □

Lemma 9.5.6
$\lim_{x\to 0} f(x) = L \longleftrightarrow \lim_{x\to 0} f(kx) = L$ provided $k \neq 0$.

Proof. The definition of $\lim_{x\to 0} f(x) = L$ is

$$\forall \varepsilon > 0\ \exists \delta_1 > 0\ \forall x,\ 0 < |x - 0| < \delta_1 \to |f(x) - L| < \varepsilon.$$

Substitute $x \to kx$. Then we have,

$$\forall \varepsilon > 0 \; \exists \delta_1 > 0 \; \forall x, \; 0 < |kx - 0| < \delta_1 \to |f(kx) - L| < \varepsilon,$$

which rearranges to

$$\forall \varepsilon > 0 \; \exists \delta_1 > 0 \; \forall x, \; 0 < |k| \, |x| < \delta_1 \to |f(kx) - L| < \varepsilon.$$

Choose $\delta_2 = \dfrac{\delta_1}{|k|}$. It follows that

$$\forall \varepsilon > 0 \; \exists \delta_2 > 0 \; \forall x, \; 0 < |x - 0| < \delta_2 \to |f(kx) - L| < \varepsilon,$$

which is just the definition of $\lim\limits_{x \to 0} f(kx) = L$. □

> **Lemma 9.5.7**
>
> $\lim\limits_{x \to a} f(x) = L \longleftrightarrow \lim\limits_{x \to \frac{a}{k}} f(kx) = L$ provided $k \neq 0$.

The proof is very similar to that of the previous lemma.

Proof. The definition of $\lim\limits_{x \to a} f(x) = L$ is

$$\forall \varepsilon > 0 \; \exists \delta_1 > 0 \; \forall x, \; 0 < |x - a| < \delta_1 \to |f(x) - L| < \varepsilon.$$

Substitute $x \to kx$. Then we have,

$$\forall \varepsilon > 0 \; \exists \delta_1 > 0 \; \forall x, \; 0 < |kx - a| < \delta_1 \to |f(kx) - L| < \varepsilon,$$

which rearranges to

$$\forall \varepsilon > 0 \; \exists \delta_1 > 0 \; \forall x, \; 0 < |k| \left| x - \frac{a}{k} \right| < \delta_1 \to |f(kx) - L| < \varepsilon.$$

Choose $\delta_2 = \dfrac{\delta_1}{|k|}$. It follows that

$$\forall \varepsilon > 0 \; \exists \delta_2 > 0 \; \forall x, \; 0 < \left| x - \frac{a}{k} \right| < \delta_2 \to |f(kx) - L| < \varepsilon,$$

which is just the definition of $\lim\limits_{x \to 0} f(kx) = L$. □

Problem 9.5.8. Find and justify the following limits:

1. $\lim\limits_{x \to 0} \cos 2x$

2. $\lim\limits_{x \to 0} \dfrac{\sin 2x}{2x}$

3. $\lim_{x \to 0} \dfrac{\sin 2x}{3x}$

4. $\lim_{x \to 0} \dfrac{\sin 6x}{\sin 5x}$

5. $\lim_{x \to 0} \dfrac{\tan 3x}{x}$

6. $\lim_{x \to 0} \dfrac{1 - \cos x}{x}$

Solution. We apply the results of Example 9.5.1, Theorem 9.5.5 with Lemma 9.5.6 after some clever algebraic manipulations.

1. $\lim_{x \to 0} \cos 2x = \boxed{1}$.

2. $\lim_{x \to 0} \dfrac{\sin 2x}{2x} = \boxed{1}$.

3. $\lim_{x \to 0} \dfrac{\sin 2x}{3x} = \lim_{x \to 0} \dfrac{\sin 2x}{2x} \cdot \dfrac{2}{3} = \boxed{\dfrac{2}{3}}$.

4. $\lim_{x \to 0} \dfrac{\sin 6x}{\sin 5x} = \lim_{x \to 0} \dfrac{\frac{\sin 6x}{x}}{\frac{\sin 5x}{x}} = \lim_{x \to 0} \dfrac{\frac{\sin 6x}{6x} \cdot 6}{\frac{\sin 5x}{5x} \cdot 5} = \dfrac{6}{5} \lim_{x \to 0} \dfrac{\frac{\sin 6x}{6x}}{\frac{\sin 5x}{5x}} = \dfrac{6}{5} \cdot \dfrac{1}{1} = \boxed{\dfrac{6}{5}}$.

5. $\lim_{x \to 0} \dfrac{\tan 3x}{x} = \lim_{x \to 0} \dfrac{\sin 3x}{x \cos 3x} = \lim_{x \to 0} \dfrac{\frac{\sin 3x}{3x}}{x \cdot \frac{\cos 3x}{3x}} = \lim_{x \to 0} \dfrac{\frac{\sin 3x}{3x}}{\frac{\cos 3x}{3}} = \dfrac{\lim_{x \to 0} \frac{\sin 3x}{3x}}{\frac{1}{3} \lim_{x \to 0} \cos 3x} = \dfrac{1}{\frac{1}{3} \cdot 1} = \boxed{3}$.

6. $\lim_{x \to 0} \dfrac{1 - \cos x}{x} = \lim_{x \to 0} \dfrac{1 - \cos x}{x} \cdot \dfrac{1 + \cos x}{1 + \cos x} = \lim_{x \to 0} \dfrac{1 - \cos^2 x}{x(1 + \cos x)} = \lim_{x \to 0} \dfrac{\sin^2 x}{x(1 + \cos x)} = \lim_{x \to 0} \dfrac{\sin x}{x} \cdot \lim_{x \to 0} \sin x \cdot \lim_{x \to 0} \dfrac{1}{1 + \cos x} = 1 \cdot 0 \cdot \dfrac{1}{2} = \boxed{0}$. $\square$

Exercise 9.5.9. Find and justify $\lim_{x \to 0} \dfrac{\tan^2 x + 2x}{x + x^2}$ and $\lim_{x \to 0} \dfrac{x^2(3 + \sin x)}{(x + \sin x)^2}$.

9.6 Advanced Concepts

Theorem 9.6.1

Let $P(x)$, $Q(x)$ be polynomials such that $P(x) = \sum_{i=0}^{n} a_i x^i$ and $Q(x) = \sum_{k=0}^{m} b_k x^k$. Then,

$$\lim_{x \to \infty} \dfrac{P(x)}{Q(x)} = \begin{cases} \pm \infty & \deg P > \deg Q \\ \dfrac{a_n}{b_n} & \deg P = \deg Q \\ 0 & \deg P < \deg Q \end{cases}$$

Proof. If $\deg P > \deg Q$, then $n > m$, and we have

$$\lim_{x \to \infty} \frac{P(x)}{Q(x)} = \lim_{x \to \infty} \frac{a_n x^n + a_{n-1} x^{n-1} + \ldots + a_1 x + a_0}{b_m x^m + b_{m-1} x^{m-1} + \ldots + b_1 x + b_0}.$$

We divide the numerator and denominator by x^n. Then,

$$\lim_{x \to \infty} \frac{a_n x^n + a_{n-1} x^{n-1} + \ldots + a_1 x + a_0}{b_m x^m + b_{m-1} x^{m-1} + \ldots + b_1 x + b_0}$$
$$= \lim_{x \to \infty} \frac{a_n + a_{n-1} x^{-1} + \ldots + a_1 x^{1-n} + a_0 x^{-n}}{b_m x^{m-n} + b_{m-1} x^{m-n-1} + \ldots + b_1 x^{1-n} + b_0 x^{-n}}.$$

As x goes to ∞, any term of x raised to a negative power goes to 0. Therefore, the denominator goes to 0 and the numerator goes to a_n, so the limit is $\pm \infty$, where the sign would depend on the sign of a_n and whether the other terms approached 0^+ or 0^-.

If $\deg P = \deg Q$, then $n = m$. We will primarily use n. We have

$$\lim_{x \to \infty} \frac{P(x)}{Q(x)} = \lim_{x \to \infty} \frac{a_n x^n + a_{n-1} x^{n-1} + \ldots + a_1 x + a_0}{b_n x^n + b_{n-1} x^{n-1} + \ldots + b_1 x + b_0}.$$

We divide the numerator and denominator by x^n to get

$$\lim_{x \to \infty} \frac{P(x)}{Q(x)} = \lim_{x \to \infty} \frac{a_n + a_{n-1} x^{-1} + \ldots + a_1 x^{1-n} + a_0 x^{-n}}{b_n + b_{n-1} x^{-1} + \ldots + b_1 x^{1-n} + b_0 x^{-n}}.$$

All terms with x raised to a negative power approach 0 as x goes to ∞, so we are left with $\dfrac{a_n}{b_n}$ as our limit.

Lastly, if $\deg P < \deg Q$, then $n < m$. We have

$$\lim_{x \to \infty} \frac{P(x)}{Q(x)} = \lim_{x \to \infty} \frac{a_n x^n + a_{n-1} x^{n-1} + \ldots + a_1 x + a_0}{b_m x^m + b_{m-1} x^{m-1} + \ldots + b_1 x + b_0}.$$

Similar to the first case, we divide the numerator and denominator by x^m. Then,

$$\lim_{x \to \infty} \frac{a_n x^n + a_{n-1} x^{n-1} + \ldots + a_1 x + a_0}{b_m x^m + b_{m-1} x^{m-1} + \ldots + b_1 x + b_0}$$
$$= \lim_{x \to \infty} \frac{a_n x^{n-m} + a_{n-1} x^{n-m-1} + \ldots + a_1 x^{1-m} + a_0 x^{-m}}{b_m + b_{m-1} x^{-1} + \ldots + b_1 x^{1-m} + b_0 x^{-m}}.$$

As x goes to ∞, all terms in the numerator go to 0, and all terms except for b_m in the denominator go to 0, so the limit is $\dfrac{0}{b_m} = 0$. $\square$

Problem 9.6.2. Evaluate and justify the following limits:

1. $\displaystyle\lim_{x \to 3} \frac{x^2 - 7x + 12}{x^3 - 27}$

2. $\lim\limits_{x \to \infty} \sqrt{x^2 + 2x} - x$

3. $\lim\limits_{x \to -\infty} \sqrt{x^2 + 2x} - x$

Solution. 1. As we cannot directly plug in and compute, we first factor and cancel out like terms:
$\lim\limits_{x \to 3} \dfrac{x^2 - 7x + 12}{x^3 - 27} = \lim\limits_{x \to 3} \dfrac{(x-3)(x-4)}{(x-3)(x^2 + 3x + 9)} = \lim\limits_{x \to 3} \dfrac{x-4}{x^2 + 3x + 9} = \boxed{-\dfrac{1}{27}}.$

2. The radical motivates us to 'rationalize the numerator': $\lim\limits_{x \to \infty} \sqrt{x^2 + 2x} - x = \lim\limits_{x \to \infty} (\sqrt{x^2 + 2x} - x) \cdot \dfrac{\sqrt{x^2 + 2x} + x}{\sqrt{x^2 + 2x} + x} = \lim\limits_{x \to \infty} \dfrac{2x}{\sqrt{x^2 + 2x} + x}$. As we are considering x going to ∞, we assume $x > 0$ and divide the numerator and denominator by x, which means that we divide the inner content of the radical by x^2, as such: $\lim\limits_{x \to \infty} \dfrac{2x}{\sqrt{x^2 + 2x} + x} = \lim\limits_{x \to \infty} \dfrac{2}{\sqrt{1 + \frac{2}{x}} + 1} = \dfrac{2}{2} = \boxed{1}.$

3. As shown in the previous problem, $\lim\limits_{x \to -\infty} \sqrt{x^2 + 2x} - x = \lim\limits_{x \to -\infty} \dfrac{2x}{\sqrt{x^2 + 2x} + x}$. However, as we are considering x going to $-\infty$, we can safely assume $x < 0$, so $x = -\sqrt{x^2}$, suggesting that when we divide the numerator and denominator by x, we divide the inner content of the radical by x^2 then making the radical a negative term: $\lim\limits_{x \to -\infty} \dfrac{2x}{\sqrt{x^2 + 2x} + x} = \lim\limits_{x \to -\infty} \dfrac{2}{-\sqrt{1 + \frac{2}{x}} + 1}.$ As x goes to $-\infty$, $\sqrt{1 + \frac{2}{x}} \to 1^-$, so $-\sqrt{1 + \frac{2}{x}} \to -1^+$, i.e. the denominator $-\sqrt{1 + \frac{2}{x}} + 1$ approaches 0^+. The numerator stays at 2, so since the overall sign is positive, the limit is $\boxed{\infty}$. □

Problem 9.6.3. Evaluate and justify the following limits:

1. $\lim\limits_{x \to -2^+} \dfrac{x+5}{x^2 - 4}$

2. $\lim\limits_{x \to \infty} \sqrt{x+1} - \sqrt{x}$

3. $\lim\limits_{x \to \infty} \sqrt{x^2 + x} - x$

4. $\lim\limits_{x \to -\infty} \sqrt{x^2 + x} + x$

5. $\lim\limits_{x \to \infty} \dfrac{2x^2 + 3x + 1}{5x^2 - 2x + 3}$

6. $\lim\limits_{x \to -\infty} \dfrac{x^3 + x^2 + x + 1}{2x^2 - 4x + 1}$

Solution.

1. Note that we can rewrite this to $\lim\limits_{x \to -2^+} \dfrac{x+5}{(x+2)(x-2)}$. As x approaches -2 from the positive side, we see that $x+5$ will approach 3, $x-2$ will approach -4, and $x+2$ will approach 0 from the positive side, i.e. 0^+.

   Note that the signs of 3 and 0^+ are positive, but the sign of -4 is negative, therefore the overall sign of the limit is negative. We also note that 0 is in the denominator, thus we can say that the limit goes to $\boxed{-\infty}$.

2. Again, we rationalize the numerator:

$$\lim_{x \to \infty} \sqrt{x+1} - \sqrt{x} = \lim_{x \to \infty} \frac{\sqrt{x+1} - \sqrt{x}}{\sqrt{x+1} + \sqrt{x}} \cdot (\sqrt{x+1} + \sqrt{x})$$
$$= \lim_{x \to \infty} \frac{x+1-x}{\sqrt{x+1} + \sqrt{x}}$$
$$= \lim_{x \to \infty} \frac{1}{\sqrt{x+1} + \sqrt{x}}$$
$$= \boxed{0}.$$

3. Likewise,

$$\lim_{x \to \infty} \sqrt{x^2+x} - x = \lim_{x \to \infty} \frac{\sqrt{x^2+x} - x}{\sqrt{x^2+x} + x} \cdot (\sqrt{x^2+x} + x)$$
$$= \lim_{x \to \infty} \frac{x^2+x-x^2}{\sqrt{x^2+x} + x}$$
$$= \lim_{x \to \infty} \frac{x}{\sqrt{x^2+x} + x}.$$

   We then divide both the numerator and denominator by x. To deal with the radical in the denominator, note that we are considering x approaching ∞, so we can assume $x > 0$, from which it follows that $x = \sqrt{x^2}$, i.e. divide that radical by $\sqrt{x^2}$, resulting in:

$$\lim_{x \to \infty} \frac{1}{\sqrt{1 + \frac{1}{x}} + 1} = \boxed{\frac{1}{2}}.$$

4. This problem is very similar to the previous one. Again, we rationalize the numerator:

$$\lim_{x \to \infty} \sqrt{x^2+x} + x = \lim_{x \to \infty} \frac{\sqrt{x^2+x} + x}{\sqrt{x^2+x} - x} \cdot (\sqrt{x^2+x} - x)$$
$$= \lim_{x \to \infty} \frac{x^2+x-x^2}{\sqrt{x^2+x} - x}$$
$$= \lim_{x \to \infty} \frac{x}{\sqrt{x^2+x} - x}.$$

   Like before, we divide the numerator and denominator by x. However, for the radical in the denominator, we cannot simply divide by $\sqrt{x^2}$, as that would result in a denominator equal to 0. Instead, note that since we are considering x approaching $-\infty$, we assume $x < 0$, from which it follows that $x = -\sqrt{x^2}$, i.e. divide the radical by $-\sqrt{x^2}$, resulting in:

$$\lim_{x \to \infty} \frac{1}{-\sqrt{1+\frac{1}{x}}-1} = \boxed{-\frac{1}{2}}.$$

5. Divide both the numerator and denominator by x of the common highest degree of the polynomials, i.e. x^2, resulting in:

$$\lim_{x \to \infty} \frac{2+\frac{3}{x}+\frac{1}{x}\cdot\frac{1}{x}}{5-\frac{2}{x}+3\cdot\frac{1}{x}\cdot\frac{1}{x}}.$$

It then becomes obvious that all fractions with x as the denominator go to 0 as x goes to ∞, therefore we are left with $\boxed{\frac{2}{5}}$.

6. Unlike the previous exercise, the highest degree in the numerator is 3, but the highest degree in the denominator is 2, therefore we can deduce that the limit goes to either ∞ or $-\infty$. We divide the numerator and denominator by the lesser degree, i.e. x^2, to get:

$$\lim_{x \to -\infty} \frac{x+1+\frac{1}{x}+\frac{1}{x^2}}{2-\frac{4}{x}+\frac{1}{x^2}}.$$

We are left with a term x in the numerator, and since the problem asks for the limit as x goes to $-\infty$, we can conclude that the overall limit goes to $\boxed{-\infty}$. □

Exercise 9.6.4. Evaluate and justify the following limits:

1. $\lim\limits_{x \to 1} \dfrac{\sin(3x-3)}{\sin(2x-2)}$

2. $\lim\limits_{x \to -\infty} \sqrt{x^2+4x}-x$

3. $\lim\limits_{x \to \infty} x(\sqrt{x+2}-\sqrt{x})$

4. $\lim\limits_{x \to \infty} \dfrac{x^3+4x-7}{7x^2-x+1}$

Similar to Theorem 4.3.14, we have

> **Lemma 9.6.5**
> $$\lim_{x \to \infty} f(x) = \lim_{y \to 0^+} f\left(\frac{1}{y}\right).$$

Proof. Assume $\lim\limits_{x \to \infty} f(x) = L$, and consider its definition:

$$\forall \varepsilon > 0 \; \exists N \; \forall x, \; x > N \to |f(x) - L| < \varepsilon.$$

Assume $N > 0$. Then substitute $x \to \frac{1}{y}$, so we have that $x > 0 \to \frac{1}{y} > 0$, and $y > 0$. The definition becomes

$$\forall \varepsilon > 0 \ \exists N \ \forall y, \ \frac{1}{y} > N \to \left| f\left(\frac{1}{y}\right) - L \right| < \varepsilon.$$

As $N > 0$ and $\frac{1}{y} > 0$, we can take the reciprocal of $\frac{1}{y} > N$ to get $y < \frac{1}{N}$. As $\frac{1}{N}$ is some positive number, we let $\delta = \frac{1}{N}$, and it follows that

$$\forall \varepsilon > 0 \ \exists \delta > 0 \ \forall y, \ 0 < y < \delta \to \left| f\left(\frac{1}{y}\right) - L \right| < \varepsilon,$$

which is the definition of $\lim_{y \to 0^+} f\left(\frac{1}{y}\right) = L$, as desired. $\square$

Exercise 9.6.6. Evaluate and justify $\lim_{x \to \infty} x \sin\left(\frac{1}{x}\right)$. What about $\lim_{x \to \infty} x^2 \sin\left(\frac{1}{x}\right)$?

9.7 Continuity

Although we have mentioned the notion of continuity before, we formally define it here:

Definition 9.7.1. $f(x)$ is **continuous** at $x = a$ if $\lim_{x \to a} f(x) = f(a)$.

We have already proven the following results:

1. Polynomials are continuous everywhere, by Lemma 9.3.12.

2. Rational functions are continuous where they are defined, by Lemma 9.3.13.

3. Trigonometric functions are continuous where they are defined, by Theorem 9.5.4.

We have notions of different kinds of discontinuity:

Definition 9.7.2. When $f(a)$ exists and $\lim_{x \to a} f(x) \neq f(a)$, there is a **removable discontinuity** at $x = a$.

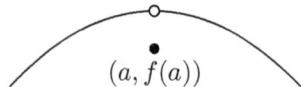

Definition 9.7.3. When $f(a)$ exists and $\lim_{x \to a} f(x)$ does not exist, there is a **essential discontinuity** at $x = a$.

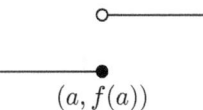

There can also be a discontinuity when $f(a)$ does not exist at all.

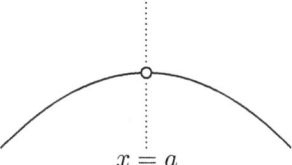

Problem 9.7.4. Is $f(x) = \dfrac{\sin x}{x}$ continuous? If not, what modifcations can we make to f such that it is continuous?

Solution. Note that $\dfrac{\sin x}{x}$ does not exist at $x = 0$, so we have a discontinuity. We can define the piecewise function

$$f(x) = \begin{cases} \dfrac{\sin x}{x} & x \neq 0 \\ 1 & x = 0 \end{cases}$$

and since $\lim\limits_{x \to 0} \dfrac{\sin x}{x} = 1$, the function is now continuous. $\square$

Theorem 9.7.5 (Continuity of Composite Functions)

If g is continuous at a and f is continuous at $g(a)$, then $f \circ g$ is continuous at a.

Proof. Given that g is continuous at a, it is true that $\lim\limits_{x \to a} g(x) = g(a)$, i.e.

$$\forall \varepsilon_1 > 0 \; \exists \delta_1 > 0 \; \forall x, \; 0 < |x - a| < \delta_1 \to |g(x) - g(a)| < \varepsilon_1.$$

We are given that f is continuous at $g(a)$, therefore $\lim\limits_{y \to g(a)} f(y) = f(g(a))$, i.e.

$$\forall \varepsilon_2 > 0 \; \exists \delta_2 > 0 \; \forall y, \; 0 < |y - g(a)| < \delta_2 \to |f(y) - f(g(a))| < \varepsilon_2.$$

Let $y = g(x)$, so the definition above can be rewritten as

$$\forall \varepsilon_2 > 0 \; \exists \delta_2 > 0 \; \forall x, \; 0 < |g(x) - g(a)| < \delta_2 \to |f(g(x)) - f(g(a))| < \varepsilon_2.$$

Our objective is to show that $0 < |x - a| < \delta_1 \to |f(g(x) - f(g(a))| < \varepsilon_2$ from the two given definitions. It suffices to let $\varepsilon_1 = \delta_2$, then it follows that $0 < |x - a| < \delta_1 \to |g(x) - g(a)| < \delta_2$. By the rewritten form of the second given definition, $0 < |g(x) - g(a)| < \delta_2 \to |f(g(x)) - f(g(a))| < \varepsilon_2$. Then, by hypothetical syllogism,

$$\forall \varepsilon_2 > 0 \; \exists \delta_1 > 0 \; \forall x, \; 0 < |x - a| < \delta_1 \to |f(g(x)) - f(g(a))| < \varepsilon_2,$$

so $\lim\limits_{x \to a} f(g(x)) = f(g(a))$, i.e. $f \circ g$ is continuous at a, as desired. $\square$

Exercise 9.7.6. Evaluate $\lim_{x \to \pi} \sin^3(7x)$.

Problem 9.7.7. Prove $f(x) = \sqrt{x}$ is continuous $\forall x > 0$.

Proof. For a given ε, let $\delta < \varepsilon\sqrt{a}$, assuming $a > 0$. Note that

$$|x - a| < \delta \longrightarrow |\sqrt{x} - \sqrt{a}| = |\sqrt{x} - \sqrt{a}| \left|\frac{\sqrt{x} + \sqrt{a}}{\sqrt{x} + \sqrt{a}}\right| = \frac{|x - a|}{\sqrt{x} + \sqrt{a}} \leq \frac{|x - a|}{\sqrt{a}} < \frac{\delta}{\sqrt{a}} < \varepsilon.$$

Therefore, $\forall \varepsilon > 0 \ \exists \delta > 0 \ \forall x, \ |x - a| < \delta \longrightarrow |\sqrt{x} - \sqrt{a}| < \varepsilon$, i.e. $\lim_{x \to a} \sqrt{x} = \sqrt{a}$. □

Exercise 9.7.8. Prove that $f(x) = \sqrt{x}$ is right-continuous at 0, i.e. $\lim_{x \to 0^+} f(x) = f(0)$.

Theorem 9.7.9

Suppose that f is continuous at $x = a$ and $f(a) > 0$. Then $\exists \delta > 0$ such that $\forall x \in (a - \delta, a + \delta)$, $f(x) > 0$.

Proof. Assuming f is continuous at $x = a$, then $\lim_{x \to a} f(x) = f(a)$, i.e.

$$\forall \varepsilon > 0 \ \exists \delta > 0 \ \forall x, \ 0 < |x - a| < \delta \to |f(x) - f(a)| < \varepsilon.$$

Now consider $\varepsilon = \frac{f(a)}{2}$, as $f(a) > 0$ implies that $\frac{f(a)}{2} > 0$, and ε can be any positive number. Then, by the definition,

$$\exists \delta > 0 \ \forall x, \ 0 < |x - a| < \delta \to |f(x) - f(a)| < \frac{f(a)}{2}.$$

We expand the absolute inequalities to get

$$\exists \delta > 0 \ \forall x, \ a - \delta < x < a + \delta \to \frac{f(a)}{2} < f(x) < \frac{3f(a)}{2},$$

and we rewrite this based on the statement of the theorem, as such:

$$\exists \delta > 0 \ \forall x \in (a - \delta, a + \delta), \ \frac{f(a)}{2} < f(x) < \frac{3f(a)}{2}.$$

We have $f(x) > \frac{f(a)}{2}$, which clearly implies that $f(x) > 0$, so we are done. □

Theorem 9.7.10

Suppose that f is continuous at $x = a$ and $f(a) < 0$. Then $\exists \delta > 0$ such that $\forall x \in (a - \delta, a + \delta)$, $f(x) < 0$.

Proof. The proof is virtually identical to that of Theorem 9.7.9. □

Problem 9.7.11. Find all values of a and b such that
$$f(x) = \begin{cases} 2x^2 - x - 7 & x \leq 1 \\ ax + b & 1 < x \leq 3 \\ x^3 & x > 3 \end{cases}$$
is continuous everywhere.

Solution. Recall that $f(x)$ is continuous at $x = a$ if $\lim_{x \to a} f(x) = f(a)$. Therefore we should be continuous at $x = 1$, i.e. $\lim_{x \to 1} f(x)$ should be defined at $f(1)$. We consider the one-sided limits separately: $\lim_{x \to 1^-} f(x) = \lim_{x \to 1^-} 2x^2 - x - 7 = -6$, therefore $\lim_{x \to 1^+} f(x) = -6$, i.e. $\lim_{x \to 1^+} ax + b = a + b = -6$.

Likewise, $\lim_{x \to 3} f(x)$ should also be defined at $f(3)$. Note that $\lim_{x \to 3^+} f(x) = \lim_{x \to 3^+} x^3 = 27$, so $\lim_{x \to 3^-} f(x) = \lim_{x \to 3^-} ax + b = 3a + b = 27$.

We now have the system of equations $a + b = -6$ and $3a + b = 27$, from which the solutions are $a = \boxed{\dfrac{33}{2}}$, $b = \boxed{-\dfrac{45}{2}}$. $\square$

Chapter 10

Derivatives

Now, we enter what lies beyond the surface of calculus. Derivatives will allow us to observe how limits can be used to help us analyze functions in greater depth than we were able to do in early algebra classes, such as finding the maximum value over an interval or graphing rational functions. There are also a variety of applied scenarios in which derivatives will prove to be immensely useful.

10.1 Introduction

Consider a function f. When, at any part, the function is increasing, we have

$$b > a \longrightarrow f(b) > f(a),$$

for two values $x = a, b$ in that part of the function. We rewrite this as

$$b - a > 0 \longrightarrow f(b) - f(a) > 0.$$

When we consider the two points $(a, f(a))$ and $(b, f(b))$, the slope of the line containing both points is also positive:

$$b - a > 0 \longrightarrow \frac{f(b) - f(a)}{b - a} > 0.$$

Likewise, we can use analogous reasoning for decreasing parts of a graph as well.

Definition 10.1.1. We call this line connecting $(a, f(a))$ and $(b, f(b))$ the **secant line**, as shown below:

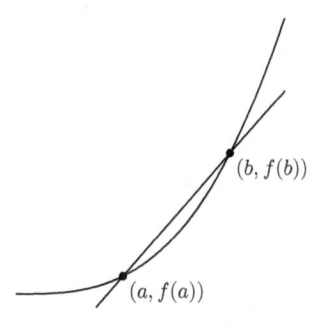

Now what happens to the slope of the secant line connecting $(a, f(a))$ and $(b, f(b))$ as b is approaching a? Observe the secant line in the figure below:

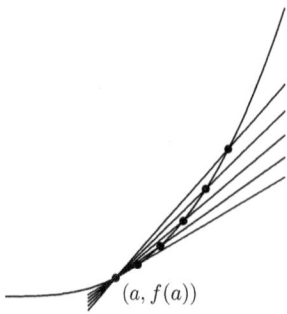

Since we are considering b approaching a, this leads us to use limits to introduce a new, important property of functions:

Definition 10.1.2. For some constant a, $\lim_{x \to a} \dfrac{f(x) - f(a)}{x - a} = f'(a)$ is called the **derivative** of $f(x)$ at $x = a$. By Lemma 9.5.3, note that

$$f'(a) = \lim_{x \to a} \frac{f(x) - f(a)}{x - a} = \lim_{h \to 0} \frac{f(a + h) - f(a)}{h},$$

which is another form of the definition of the derivative.

Definition 10.1.3. The **tangent line** of $f(x)$ at $x = a$ is the line of slope $f'(a)$ through $(a, f(a))$.

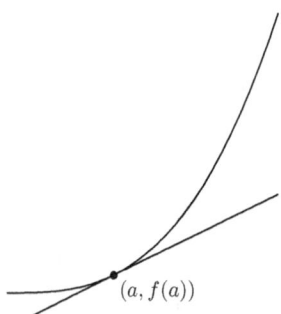

Definition 10.1.4. If $f'(a)$ exists, f is said to be **differentiable** at $x = a$.

Example 10.1.5

Let $f(x) = mx + b$ (i.e. an arbitrary linear function with slope m). For any a, prove that $f'(a) = m$.

Proof. We have

$$f'(a) = \lim_{x \to a} \frac{f(x) - f(a)}{x - a}$$

$$= \lim_{x \to a} \frac{(mx + b) - (ma + b)}{x - a}$$
$$= \lim_{x \to a} \frac{m(x - a)}{x - a}$$
$$= \lim_{x \to a} m$$
$$= m.$$

Therefore, for $f(x) = mx + b$, $f'(a) = m$. □

Problem 10.1.6. Let $f(x) = x^2$. Find $f'(2)$.

Solution. As usual, we apply the definition:

$$f'(2) = \lim_{x \to 2} \frac{f(x) - f(2)}{x - 2}$$
$$= \lim_{x \to 2} \frac{x^2 - 4}{x - 2}$$
$$= \lim_{x \to 2} \frac{(x + 2)(x - 2)}{x - 2}$$
$$= \lim_{x \to 2} x + 2$$
$$= \boxed{4}.$$

□

Exercise 10.1.7. Let $f(x) = x^3 - 3x$. Find $f'(2)$.

Exercise 10.1.8. Let $f(x) = \dfrac{1}{x}$. Find $f'(-3)$.

Exercise 10.1.9. Let $f(x) = \dfrac{2x - 5}{1 - 3x}$. Find $f'(4)$.

Exercise 10.1.10. Let $f(x) = \sqrt{x}$. Find $f'(4)$.

Problem 10.1.11. What is the equation of the tangent line of $f(x)$ at $x = a$?

Solution. The slope of the tangent line is $f'(a)$. This line must pass through the point $(a, f(a))$, so by the point-slope form of a line, the equation of the tangent line would be $y - f(a) = f'(a)(x - a)$, which rearranges to

$$y = f'(a)(x - a) + f(a).$$

□

Problem 10.1.12. Find all tangent lines of $y = x^2$ that go through $(7, 1)$.

Solution. Define $f(x) = x^2$. Consider some point $(a, f(a))$ that lies on f and has a tangent line that goes through $(7, 1)$. By Problem 10.1.11, the general equation of the tangent line would be

$$y = f'(a)(x - a) + f(a).$$

Note that $f(a) = a^2$, and $f'(a) = \lim_{x \to a} \dfrac{f(x) - f(a)}{x - a} = \lim_{x \to a} \dfrac{x^2 - a^2}{x - a} = \lim_{x \to a} \dfrac{(x - a)(x + a)}{x - a} = \lim_{x \to a} x + a = 2a$, so our tangent line is

$$y = 2a(x - a) + a^2.$$

Since our tangent line must also contain $(7, 1)$, we plug those values into the equation:
$$1 = 2a(7 - a) + a^2.$$
This rearranges to $a^2 - 14a + 1 = 0$, and the quadratic formula yields $a = 7 \pm 4\sqrt{3}$, and in fact, both are solutions to the problem. Thus, our tangent lines are
$$y = 2(7 + 4\sqrt{3})(x - (7 + 4\sqrt{3})) + 97 + 56\sqrt{3},$$
$$y = 2(7 - 4\sqrt{3})(x - (7 - 4\sqrt{3})) + 97 - 56\sqrt{3}.$$
□

> **Example 10.1.13**
> Let $f(x) = |x|$. Find $f'(7)$ and $f'(0)$.

Solution. Note that $f'(7) = \lim_{x \to 7} \dfrac{|x| - |7|}{x - 7}$. As we are considering the limit as x goes to 7, we can assume that x is positive because we essentially only care about the values of x that are close to 7. Then,
$$\lim_{x \to 7} \frac{|x| - |7|}{x - 7} = \lim_{x \to 7} \frac{x - 7}{x - 7} = \boxed{1}.$$

For $f'(0)$, we want to find $\lim_{x \to 0} \dfrac{|x|}{x}$. However, evaluating the right-hand and left-hand limits separately gives us 1 and -1 respectively, therefore $\lim_{x \to 0} \dfrac{|x|}{x}$ does not exist, and it follows that there is no tangent line at $x = 0$. In fact, if we graph $f(x) = |x|$, we see that there is a cusp (a pointed end) at $x = 0$, so we can intuitively figure out that there cannot be a tangent line at that point. □

Definition 10.1.14. For a function $f(x)$, the **derivative** of $f(x)$ is denoted as $f'(x)$ with respect to all x defined on f. As stated earlier, the limit can be written in two forms:
$$f'(x) = \lim_{z \to x} \frac{f(z) - f(x)}{z - x} = \lim_{h \to 0} \frac{f(x + h) - f(x)}{h}.$$
When evaluating derivatives using the limit definition, note that the former involves factoring, while the latter involves expanding, so choose the appropriate definition depending on the function being dealt with.

Definition 10.1.15. There are two different ways to denote the derivative of f: either $f'(x)$, which is Newton's notation, or $\dfrac{d}{dx}(f(x))$, which is Leibniz's notation. **Leibniz notation** is useful since we don't have to define the function to take its derivative. For example, we can write $\dfrac{d}{dx}(x^3)$, but not $(x^3)'$.

If $y = f(x)$, the following all mean the same thing:
$$\frac{d}{dx}(f(x)) = f'(x).$$
$$\frac{d}{dx}(y) = y' = \frac{dy}{dx}.$$

Definition 10.1.16. To **differentiate** a function is to evaluate the derivative of that function.

Example 10.1.17

Differentiate the following functions:

1. x^2

2. x^3

3. x^5

4. $x^n, \forall n \in \mathbb{Z}^+$

5. $\dfrac{3x+11}{2x-9}$

6. $\sqrt{x}$

7. $\sin x$

Solution. We may either take the limit of the given function as $z \to x$ or $h \to 0$.

1. Either method works:

$$\lim_{z \to x} \frac{f(z)-f(x)}{z-x} = \lim_{z \to x} \frac{z^2-x^2}{z-x} = \lim_{z \to x} \frac{(z-x)(z+x)}{z-x} = \lim_{z \to x} z+x = \boxed{2x}.$$

$$\lim_{h \to 0} \frac{f(x+h)-f(x)}{h} = \lim_{h \to 0} \frac{(x+h)^2-x^2}{h} = \lim_{h \to 0} \frac{x^2+2xh+h^2-x^2}{h} = \lim_{h \to 0} 2x+h = \boxed{2x}.$$

2. Factoring seems like a relatively quicker solution:

$$\lim_{z \to x} \frac{f(z)-f(x)}{z-x} = \lim_{z \to x} \frac{z^3-x^3}{z-x} = \lim_{z \to x} \frac{(z-x)(z^2+zx+x^2)}{z-x} = \lim_{z \to x} z^2+zx+x^2 = \boxed{3x^2}.$$

3. Using the helpful factorization technique $a^n - b^n = (a-b)(a^{n-1}+a^{n-2}b+\ldots+ab^{n-2}+b^{n-1})$, we can quickly deduce

$$\lim_{z \to x} \frac{f(z)-f(x)}{z-x} = \lim_{z \to x} \frac{z^5-x^5}{z-x} = \lim_{z \to x} z^4+z^3x+z^2x^2+zx^3+x^4 = \boxed{5x^4}.$$

Of course, we also have the option of expanding:

$$\lim_{h \to 0} \frac{f(x+h)-f(x)}{h} = \lim_{h \to 0} \frac{(x+h)^5-x^5}{h}$$
$$= \lim_{h \to 0} \frac{x^5+5x^4h+10x^3h^2+10x^2h^3+5xh^4+h^5-x^5}{h}$$
$$= \lim_{h \to 0} 5x^4+10x^3h+10x^2h^2+5xh^3+h^4 = \boxed{5x^4}.$$

4. From the previous examples, it seems that we have a pattern here. In fact, we can show that $\dfrac{d}{dx}(x^n) = nx^{x-1}$ using the Binomial Theorem.

$$\frac{d}{dx}(x^n) = \lim_{h \to 0} \frac{(x+h)^n - x^n}{h}$$

$$= \lim_{h \to 0} \frac{\left(\binom{n}{0}x^n + \binom{n}{1}x^{n-1}h + \ldots + \binom{n}{n-1}xh^{n-1} + \binom{n}{n}h^n\right) - x^n}{h}$$

$$= \lim_{h \to 0} \frac{\binom{n}{1}x^{n-1}h + \binom{n}{2}x^{n-2}h^2 + \ldots + \binom{n}{n-2}x^2h^{n-2} + \binom{n}{n-1}xh^{n-1} + h^n}{h}$$

$$= \lim_{h \to 0} \binom{n}{1}x^{n-1} + \binom{n}{2}x^{n-2}h + \ldots + \binom{n}{n-2}x^2h^{n-3} + \binom{n}{n-1}xh^{n-2} + h^{n-1}$$

$$= \boxed{nx^{n-1}}.$$

We can also use the fact $a^n - b^n = (a-b)(a^{n-1} + a^{n-2}b + \ldots + ab^{n-2} + b^{n-1})$ as mentioned before:

$$\frac{d}{dx}(x^n) = \lim_{z \to x} \frac{z^n - x^n}{z - x}$$

$$= \lim_{z \to x} \frac{(z-x)(z^{n-1} + z^{n-2}x + \ldots + zx^{n-2} + x^{n-1})}{z - x}$$

$$= \lim_{z \to x} z^{n-1} + z^{n-2}x + \ldots + zx^{n-2} + x^{n-1}$$

$$= x^{n-1} + x^{n-2} \cdot x + \ldots + x \cdot x^{n-2} + x^{n-1}$$

$$= \boxed{nx^{n-1}}.$$

5. It is up to your choice which method you prefer. The following uses expanding.

$$\frac{d}{dx}\left(\frac{3x+11}{2x-9}\right) = \lim_{h \to 0} \frac{\frac{3(x+h)+11}{2(x+h)-9} - \frac{3x+11}{2x-9}}{h}$$

$$= \lim_{h \to 0} \frac{\frac{3x+3h+11}{2x+2h-9} - \frac{3x+11}{2x-9}}{h}$$

$$= \lim_{h \to 0} \frac{(3x+3h+11)(2x-9) - (3x+11)(2x+2h-9)}{h(2x+2h-9)(2x-9)}$$

$$= \lim_{h \to 0} \frac{6x^2 - 27x + 6xh - 27h + 22x - 99 - 6x^2 - 6xh + 27x - 22x - 22h + 99}{h(2x+2h-9)(2x-9)}$$

$$= \lim_{h \to 0} \frac{-49h}{h(2x+2h-9)(2x-9)}$$

$$= \lim_{h \to 0} -\frac{49}{(2x+2h-9)(2x-9)}$$

$$= \boxed{-\frac{49}{(2x-9)^2}}.$$

6. A common strategy in this situation is to multiply by the radical conjugate.

$$\frac{d}{dx}\left(\sqrt{x}\right) = \lim_{h \to 0} \frac{\sqrt{x+h} - \sqrt{x}}{h}$$

$$= \lim_{h \to 0} \frac{\sqrt{x+h} - \sqrt{x}}{h} \cdot \frac{\sqrt{x+h} + \sqrt{x}}{\sqrt{x+h} + \sqrt{x}}$$

$$= \lim_{h \to 0} \frac{x+h-x}{h\left(\sqrt{x+h}+\sqrt{x}\right)}$$

$$= \lim_{h \to 0} \frac{h}{h\left(\sqrt{x+h}+\sqrt{x}\right)}$$

$$= \lim_{h \to 0} \frac{1}{\sqrt{x+h}+\sqrt{x}}$$

$$= \boxed{\frac{1}{2\sqrt{x}}}.$$

7. This is one of the more nontrivial functions to differentiate using the limit definition.

$$\frac{d}{dx}(\sin x) = \lim_{h \to 0} \frac{\sin(x+h) - \sin x}{h}$$

$$= \lim_{h \to 0} \frac{\sin x \cos h + \cos x \sin h - \sin x}{h}$$

$$= \lim_{h \to 0} \frac{\cos x \sin h - \sin x(1 - \cos h)}{h}$$

$$= \lim_{h \to 0} \frac{\cos x \sin h - \sin x \cdot \frac{\sin^2 h}{1+\cos h}}{h}$$

$$= \lim_{h \to 0} \frac{\sin h \left(\cos x - \frac{\sin x \sin h}{1+\cos h}\right)}{h}$$

$$= \lim_{h \to 0} \frac{\sin h}{h} \cdot \lim_{h \to 0} \left(\cos x - \frac{\sin x \sin h}{1+\cos h}\right)$$

$$= \lim_{h \to 0} \left(\cos x - \frac{\sin x \sin h}{1+\cos h}\right)$$

$$= \lim_{h \to 0} \cos x - \lim_{h \to 0} \left(\frac{\sin x \sin h}{1+\cos h}\right)$$

$$= \cos x - \frac{\lim_{h \to 0}(\sin x \sin h)}{\lim_{h \to 0}(1+\cos h)}$$

$$= \cos x - \frac{\sin x \cdot \lim_{h \to 0} \sin h}{1 + \lim_{h \to 0} \cos h}$$

$$= \cos x - \frac{\sin x \cdot 0}{1+1}$$

$$= \boxed{\cos x}.$$

> **Theorem 10.1.18** (Linearity of Derivatives)
> Let $h(x) = f(x) + g(x)$ and $j(x) = k \cdot f(x)$ for some $k \in \mathbb{R}$. Assume that $f(x)$ and $g(x)$ are differentiable.
>
> a) $h'(x) = f'(x) + g'(x)$.
>
> b) $j'(x) = k \cdot f'(x)$.

Proof. a) By Theorem 9.3.5,

$$\begin{aligned}
h'(x) &= \lim_{z \to x} \frac{h(z) - h(x)}{x - z} \\
&= \lim_{z \to x} \frac{f(z) + g(z) - (f(x) + g(x))}{x - z} \\
&= \lim_{z \to x} \frac{(f(z) - f(x)) + (g(z) - g(x))}{x - z} \\
&= \lim_{z \to x} \left(\frac{f(z) - f(x)}{x - z} + \frac{g(z) - g(x)}{x - z} \right) \\
&= \lim_{z \to x} \frac{f(z) - f(x)}{x - z} + \lim_{z \to x} \frac{g(z) - g(x)}{x - z} \\
&= f'(x) + g'(x).
\end{aligned}$$

b) We can always factor out constants from limits, which follows from Theorem 9.3.4 and Theorem 9.3.5:

$$\begin{aligned}
j'(x) &= \lim_{z \to x} \frac{j(z) - j(x)}{z - x} \\
&= \lim_{z \to x} \frac{k \cdot f(z) - k \cdot f(x)}{z - x} \\
&= \lim_{z \to x} \frac{k(f(z) - f(x))}{z - x} \\
&= \lim_{z \to x} k \cdot \frac{f(z) - f(x)}{z - x} \\
&= k \cdot \lim_{z \to x} \frac{f(z) - f(x)}{z - x} \\
&= k \cdot f'(x).
\end{aligned}$$
$\square$

Problem 10.1.19. Let $g(x) = f(2x)$. If $f'(x) = \alpha(x)$, what is $g'(x)$?

Solution. First, note that

$$\begin{aligned}
g'(x) &= \lim_{z \to x} \frac{g(z) - g(x)}{z - x} \\
&= \lim_{z \to x} \frac{f(2z) - f(2x)}{z - x} \\
&= 2 \cdot \lim_{z \to x} \frac{f(2z) - f(2x)}{2z - 2x}.
\end{aligned}$$

As z approaches x, $2z$ approaches $2x$, so this is equivalent to

$$2 \cdot \lim_{2z \to 2x} \frac{f(2z) - f(2x)}{2z - 2x} = \boxed{2\alpha(2x)}.$$
$\square$

Theorem 10.1.20

If $f(x)$ is differentiable at $x = a$, then it is continuous at $x = a$.

Proof. We want to show that if $\lim\limits_{x \to a} \dfrac{f(x) - f(a)}{x - a}$ exists, then $\lim\limits_{x \to a} f(x) = f(a)$, or equivalently, $\lim\limits_{x \to a} f(x) - f(a) = 0$.

We know that $\lim\limits_{x \to a} \dfrac{f(x) - f(a)}{x - a}$ and $\lim\limits_{x \to a} (x - a)$ both exist. We have that

$$\lim_{x \to a} \frac{f(x) - f(a)}{x - a} \cdot \lim_{x \to a} (x - a) = \lim_{x \to a} \frac{f(x) - f(a)}{x - a} \cdot (x - a) = \lim_{x \to a} f(x) - f(a).$$

But note that $\lim\limits_{x \to a} (x - a) = 0$, and since the RHS will be 0, the LHS, i.e. $\lim\limits_{x \to a} f(x) - f(a)$, will necessarily be 0. $\square$

Problem 10.1.21. Define the following functions:

$$f(x) = \begin{cases} x \sin\left(\dfrac{1}{x}\right) & x \neq 0 \\ 0 & x = 0 \end{cases}$$

$$g(x) = \begin{cases} x^2 \sin\left(\dfrac{1}{x}\right) & x \neq 0 \\ 0 & x = 0 \end{cases}$$

Are these functions differentiable at $x = 0$?

Solution. Consider $f(x)$ at $x = 0$. By the limit definition of a derivative, we have

$$\begin{aligned} f'(0) &= \lim_{x \to 0} \frac{f(x) - f(0)}{x - 0} \\ &= \lim_{x \to 0} \frac{x \sin(\frac{1}{x}) - 0}{x - 0} \\ &= \lim_{x \to 0} \sin\left(\frac{1}{x}\right) \\ &= \lim_{x \to 0^+} \sin\left(\frac{1}{x}\right). \end{aligned}$$

By Lemma 9.6.5, $\lim\limits_{x \to 0^+} \sin\left(\dfrac{1}{x}\right) = \lim\limits_{y \to \infty} \sin y$, and this limit does not exist, since $\sin y$ oscillates between -1 and 1. Therefore, $f'(0)$ does not exist, so f is not differentiable at $x = 0$.

Now consider $g(x)$ at $x = 0$. By the limit definition of a derivative, we have

$$g'(0) = \lim_{x \to 0} \frac{g(x) - f(0)}{x - 0}$$
$$= \lim_{x \to 0} \frac{x^2 \sin(\frac{1}{x}) - 0}{x - 0}$$
$$= \lim_{x \to 0} x \sin\left(\frac{1}{x}\right).$$

We can split this limit into right-hand and left-hand limits, then apply Squeeze Theorem on both, to determine that $\lim_{x \to 0} x \sin\left(\frac{1}{x}\right) = 0$. Thus, $g'(0) = 0$, so g is differentiable at $x = 0$. $\square$

Theorem 10.1.22 (Product Rule of Derivatives)
Assuming that the derivatives of $f(x)$ and $g(x)$ exist,

$$\frac{d}{dx}(f(x)g(x)) = f(x)g'(x) + f'(x)g(x).$$

Proof. This proof uses a similar strategy to that of Theorem 9.3.5.

$$\frac{d}{dx}(f(x)g(x)) = \lim_{z \to x} \frac{f(z)g(z) - f(x)g(x)}{z - x}$$
$$= \lim_{z \to x} \frac{f(z)g(z) - f(z)g(x) + f(z)g(x) - f(x)g(x)}{z - x}$$
$$= \lim_{z \to x} \frac{f(z)(g(z) - g(x)) + g(x)(f(z) - f(x))}{z - x}$$
$$= \lim_{z \to x} \left(\frac{f(z)(g(z) - g(x))}{z - x} + \frac{g(x)(f(z) - f(x))}{z - x} \right)$$
$$= \lim_{z \to x} f(z) \cdot \lim_{z \to x} \frac{g(z) - g(x)}{z - x} + \lim_{z \to x} \frac{f(z) - f(x)}{z - x} \cdot \lim_{z \to x} g(x)$$
$$= \lim_{z \to x} f(z) \cdot g'(x) + f'(x)g(x).$$

As we have assumed that $f(x)$ and $g(x)$ are differentiable, by Theorem 10.1.20, $\lim_{z \to x} f(z) = f(x)$, therefore

$$\frac{d}{dx}(f(x)g(x)) = f(x)g'(x) + f'(x)g(x). \quad \square$$

Theorem 10.1.23 (Quotient Rule of Derivatives)
Assuming that the derivatives of $f(x)$ and $g(x)$ exist,

$$\frac{d}{dx}\left(\frac{f(x)}{g(x)}\right) = \frac{g(x)f'(x) - f(x)g'(x)}{g(x)^2}.$$

Proof. First, we expand the fractions, then apply a similar strategy used in the previous proof.

$$\frac{d}{dx}\left(\frac{f(x)}{g(x)}\right) = \lim_{z \to x} \frac{\frac{f(z)}{g(z)} - \frac{f(x)}{g(x)}}{z - x}$$

$$= \lim_{z \to x} \frac{f(z)g(x) - f(x)g(z)}{g(x)g(z)(z - x)}$$

$$= \lim_{z \to x} \frac{f(z)g(x) - f(x)g(x) + f(x)g(x) - f(x)g(z)}{g(x)g(z)(z - x)}$$

$$= \lim_{z \to x} \frac{g(x)\left(f(z) - f(x)\right) + f(x)\left(g(x) - g(z)\right)}{g(x)g(z)(z - x)}$$

$$= \lim_{z \to x} \frac{1}{g(x)} \cdot \lim_{z \to x} \frac{1}{g(z)} \cdot \left[\lim_{z \to x} \frac{f(z) - f(x)}{z - x} \cdot \lim_{z \to x} g(x) + \lim_{z \to x} f(x) \cdot \lim_{z \to x} \frac{g(x) - g(z)}{z - x}\right].$$

By our assumptions and Theorem 10.1.20, we have

$$\frac{d}{dx}\left(\frac{f(x)}{g(x)}\right) = \frac{1}{g(x)} \cdot \frac{1}{g(x)} \cdot \left[f'(x) \cdot g(x) + f(x) \cdot -g'(x)\right]$$

$$= \frac{g(x)f'(x) - f(x)g'(x)}{g(x)^2}. \qquad \square$$

Problem 10.1.24. Evaluate the derivatives of $f(x) = x^3 \sin x$ and $f(x) = \dfrac{2x - 1}{3x + 2}$.

Solution. For the first function, we apply Theorem 10.1.22.

$$\frac{d}{dx}(x^3 \sin x) = \frac{d}{dx}(x^3) \cdot \sin x + x^3 \cdot \frac{d}{dx}(\sin x)$$

$$= 3x^2 \cdot \sin x + x^3 \cdot \cos x$$

$$= \boxed{x^2(3 \sin x + x \cos x)}.$$

For the latter, apply Theorem 10.1.23.

$$\frac{d}{dx}\left(\frac{2x - 1}{3x + 2}\right) = \frac{(3x + 2) \cdot \frac{d}{dx}(2x - 1) - (2x - 1) \cdot \frac{d}{dx}(3x + 2)}{(3x + 2)^2}$$

$$= \frac{2(3x + 2) - 3(2x - 1)}{(3x + 2)^2}$$

$$= \boxed{\frac{7}{(3x + 2)^2}}. \qquad \square$$

Problem 10.1.25. By Example 10.1.17, we have established that the derivative of $\sin x$ is $\cos x$. Using Theorem 10.1.22 and Theorem 10.1.23, find the derivatives of the rest of the trigonometric functions.

Solution. The proof of $\dfrac{d}{dx}(\cos x)$ is similar to that of $\dfrac{d}{dx}(\sin x)$.

$$\frac{d}{dx}(\cos x) = \lim_{h \to 0} \frac{\cos(x + h) - \cos x}{h}$$

$$= \lim_{h \to 0} \frac{\cos x \cos h - \sin x \sin h - \cos x}{h}$$

$$= \lim_{h \to 0} \frac{\cos x (\cos h - 1) - \sin x \sin h}{h}$$

$$= \lim_{h \to 0} \frac{\cos x \cdot -\frac{\sin^2 h}{\cos h + 1} - \sin x \sin h}{h}$$

$$= \lim_{h \to 0} \frac{-\sin h \left(\frac{\cos x \sin h}{\cos h + 1} + \sin x \right)}{h}$$

$$= \lim_{h \to 0} -\frac{\sin h}{h} \cdot \lim_{h \to 0} \left(\frac{\cos x \sin h}{\cos h + 1} + \sin x \right)$$

$$= -\lim_{h \to 0} \left(\frac{\cos x \sin h}{\cos h + 1} + \sin x \right)$$

$$= \boxed{-\sin x}.$$

Now that we have found the derivatives of sine and cosine, we can apply Theorem 10.1.23 to find $\frac{d}{dx}(\tan x)$.

$$\frac{d}{dx}(\tan x) = \frac{d}{dx}\left(\frac{\sin x}{\cos x}\right)$$

$$= \frac{\cos x \cdot \frac{d}{dx}(\sin x) - \sin x \cdot \frac{d}{dx}(\cos x)}{\cos^2 x}$$

$$= \frac{\cos^2 x + \sin^2 x}{\cos^2 x}$$

$$= \frac{1}{\cos^2 x}$$

$$= \boxed{\sec^2 x}.$$

The proof of $\frac{d}{dx}(\cot x)$ is analogous to that of $\frac{d}{dx}(\tan x)$.

$$\frac{d}{dx}(\cot x) = \frac{d}{dx}\left(\frac{\cos x}{\sin x}\right)$$

$$= \frac{\sin x \cdot \frac{d}{dx}(\cos x) - \cos x \cdot \frac{d}{dx}(\sin x)}{\sin^2 x}$$

$$= \frac{-\sin^2 x - \cos^2 x}{\sin^2 x}$$

$$= -\frac{1}{\sin^2 x}$$

$$= \boxed{-\csc^2 x}.$$

For $\frac{d}{dx}(\sec x)$, use Theorem 10.1.23 and note that the derivative of 1 is simply 0.

$$\frac{d}{dx}(\sec x) = \frac{d}{dx}\left(\frac{1}{\cos x}\right)$$

$$= \frac{\cos x \cdot \frac{d}{dx}(1) - 1 \cdot \frac{d}{dx}(\cos x)}{\cos^2 x}$$
$$= \frac{\sin x}{\cos^2 x}$$
$$= \boxed{\tan x \sec x}.$$

The proof of $\frac{d}{dx}(\csc x)$ is analogous to that of $\frac{d}{dx}(\sec x)$.

$$\frac{d}{dx}(\csc x) = \frac{d}{dx}\left(\frac{1}{\sin x}\right)$$
$$= \frac{\sin x \cdot \frac{d}{dx}(1) - 1 \cdot \frac{d}{dx}(\sin x)}{\sin^2 x}$$
$$= -\frac{\cos x}{\sin^2 x}$$
$$= \boxed{-\cot x \csc x}.$$ □

Problem 10.1.26. Prove the following results about the derivatives of function transformations.

a) $\frac{d}{dx}(f(x+k)) = f'(x+k)$.

b) $\frac{d}{dx}(f(kx)) = kf'(kx)$.

Proof. The general strategy is to substitute the transformations $x+k$ and kx with convenient variables to facilitate the manipulation of the limit definition of the derivative.

a) Let $\tilde{z} = z+k$ and $\tilde{x} = x+k$. Note that $\tilde{z} - \tilde{x} = z - x$, and that z goes to x as $\tilde{z}$ goes to $\tilde{x}$. Then,

$$\frac{d}{dx}(f(x+k)) = \lim_{z \to x} \frac{f(z+k) - f(x+k)}{z-x}$$
$$= \lim_{\tilde{z} \to \tilde{x}} \frac{f(\tilde{z}) - f(\tilde{x})}{\tilde{z} - \tilde{x}}$$
$$= f'(\tilde{x})$$
$$= f'(x+k).$$

b) Let $\tilde{z} = kz$ and $\tilde{x} = kx$. Note that z goes to x as $\tilde{z}$ goes to $\tilde{x}$. Then,

$$\frac{d}{dx}(f(kx)) = \lim_{z \to x} \frac{f(kz) - f(kx)}{z-x}$$
$$= \lim_{z \to x} \frac{f(kz) - f(kx)}{kz - kx} \cdot k$$
$$= \lim_{\tilde{z} \to \tilde{x}} \frac{f(\tilde{z}) - f(\tilde{x})}{\tilde{z} - \tilde{x}} \cdot k$$
$$= f'(\tilde{x}) \cdot k$$
$$= kf'(kx).$$ □

Remark. Keep in mind that $f'(x+k)$ and $f'(kx)$ are NOT the same as $\frac{d}{dx}(f(x+k))$ and $\frac{d}{dx}(f(kx))$.

If *something* is some function of x, then $f'(something)$ is the derivative of $f(x)$ and then plugging in $x \to something$, while $\frac{d}{dx}(f(something)) = f'(something)$ evaluated at x.

For instance, if we let $f(x) = \sin x$, then $f'(2x) = \cos 2x$ while $\frac{d}{dx}(f(2x)) = 2\cos 2x$ according to the stated theorem.

Problem 10.1.27. Using the results of Problem 10.1.26, quickly evaluate $\frac{d}{dx}(\cos x)$.

Solution. We can take advantage of the cofunction identity of sine and cosine:
$$\frac{d}{dx}(\cos x) = \frac{d}{dx}\left(\sin\left(x + \frac{\pi}{2}\right)\right) = \sin'\left(x + \frac{\pi}{2}\right) = \cos\left(x + \frac{\pi}{2}\right) = -\sin x. \qquad \square$$

Problem 10.1.28. Use the product rule twice to find $\frac{d}{dx}(f(x)g(x)h(x))$.

Solution. Initially suppose that $f(x)g(x)$ is a single function for the first application of Theorem 10.1.22, then apply the theorem again to break up $f(x)g(x)$.
$$\begin{aligned}\frac{d}{dx}(f(x)g(x)h(x)) &= f(x)g(x)\frac{d}{dx}(h(x)) + \frac{d}{dx}(f(x)g(x))h(x) \\ &= f(x)g(x)h'(x) + (f(x)g'(x) + f'(x)g(x))h(x) \\ &= f(x)g(x)h'(x) + f(x)g'(x)h(x) + f'(x)g(x)h(x). \qquad \square\end{aligned}$$

It seems that there is a pattern for the derivative of the product of an arbitrary number of functions. Here is the general statement:

Theorem 10.1.29 (Generalized Product Rule)
Consider arbitrary functions $f_1, f_2, \ldots, f_n$. Then,
$$\frac{d}{dx}\left(\prod_{k=1}^{n} f_k(x)\right) = \left(\prod_{k=1}^{n} f_i(x)\right)\left(\sum_{i=1}^{n} \frac{f'_i(x)}{f_i(x)}\right).$$

This result can be proved by mathematical induction.

Corollary 10.1.30 (General Power Rule)
$$\frac{d}{dx}(f(x)^n) = nf(x)^{n-1}f'(x).$$

Proof. We consider a special case of Theorem 10.1.29 where $f_1 = f_2 = \ldots = f_n$.
$$\frac{d}{dx}(f(x)^n) = \left(\prod_{i=1}^{n} f(x)\right)\left(\sum_{i=1}^{n} \frac{f'(x)}{f(x)}\right)$$

$$= f(x)^n \left(\frac{nf'(x)}{f(x)}\right)$$
$$= nf(x)^{n-1} f'(x). \qquad \square$$

Problem 10.1.31. Recall the result of Example 10.1.17 where it was proven that $\frac{d}{dx}(x^n) = nx^{n-1}$ for all $n \in \mathbb{Z}^+$. Demonstrate that this identity holds for all negative integers n as well.

Proof. Let $n \in \mathbb{Z}^+$. By Theorem 10.1.23, note that

$$\frac{d}{dx}(x^{-n}) = \frac{d}{dx}\left(\frac{1}{x^n}\right)$$
$$= \frac{x^n \cdot \frac{d}{dx}(1) - 1 \cdot \frac{d}{dx}(x^n)}{(x^n)^2}$$
$$= \frac{-nx^{n-1}}{x^{2n}}$$
$$= -nx^{-n-1}.$$

Let $m = -n$, such that m is a negative integer. Then we have $\frac{d}{dx}(x^m) = mx^{m-1}$, and we are done. $\square$

Clearly, for $n = 0$, $\frac{d}{dx}(x^0) = \frac{d}{dx}(1) = 0 = 0 \cdot x^{0-1}$. We have now established that $\frac{d}{dx}(x^n) = nx^{n-1}$ for all integers n. However, we can extend this rule to the rational numbers:

Problem 10.1.32. Let $n \in \mathbb{Z}^+$. Evaluate $\frac{d}{dx}\left(x^{\frac{1}{n}}\right)$.

Proof. We take advantage of the following factorization:

$$z - x = \left(z^{\frac{1}{n}}\right)^n - \left(x^{\frac{1}{n}}\right)^n$$
$$= \left(z^{\frac{1}{n}} - x^{\frac{1}{n}}\right)\left(z^{\frac{n-1}{n}} + z^{\frac{n-2}{n}} x^{\frac{1}{n}} + \ldots + z^{\frac{1}{n}} x^{\frac{n-2}{n}} + x^{\frac{n-1}{n}}\right).$$

Thus, we have

$$\frac{d}{dx}\left(x^{\frac{1}{n}}\right) = \lim_{z \to x} \frac{z^{\frac{1}{n}} - x^{\frac{1}{n}}}{z - x}$$
$$= \lim_{z \to x} \frac{z^{\frac{1}{n}} - x^{\frac{1}{n}}}{\left(z^{\frac{1}{n}} - x^{\frac{1}{n}}\right)\left(z^{\frac{n-1}{n}} + z^{\frac{n-2}{n}} x^{\frac{1}{n}} + \ldots + z^{\frac{1}{n}} x^{\frac{n-2}{n}} + x^{\frac{n-1}{n}}\right)}$$
$$= \lim_{z \to x} \frac{1}{z^{\frac{n-1}{n}} + z^{\frac{n-2}{n}} x^{\frac{1}{n}} + \ldots + z^{\frac{1}{n}} x^{\frac{n-2}{n}} + x^{\frac{n-1}{n}}}$$
$$= \frac{1}{nx^{\frac{n-1}{n}}}$$
$$= \frac{1}{n} x^{\frac{1}{n} - 1}. \qquad \square$$

Problem 10.1.33. Use Theorem 10.1.23 to find $\dfrac{d}{dx}\left(x^{-\frac{1}{n}}\right)$ for $n \in \mathbb{Z}^+$.

Proof. We take the same approach as we did for Problem 10.1.31.

$$\begin{aligned}
\frac{d}{dx}\left(x^{-\frac{1}{n}}\right) &= \frac{d}{dx}\left(\frac{1}{x^{\frac{1}{n}}}\right) \\
&= \frac{x^{\frac{1}{n}} \cdot \frac{d}{dx}(1) - 1 \cdot \frac{d}{dx}\left(x^{\frac{1}{n}}\right)}{\left(x^{\frac{1}{n}}\right)^2} \\
&= \frac{-\frac{1}{n}x^{\frac{1}{n}-1}}{x^{\frac{2}{n}}} \\
&= -\frac{1}{n}x^{-\frac{1}{n}-1}.
\end{aligned}$$
$\square$

We now have shown that $\dfrac{d}{dx}\left(x^{\frac{1}{n}}\right) = \dfrac{1}{n}x^{\frac{1}{n}-1}$ for all nonzero integers n. Finally, we deal with the general $\dfrac{p}{q}$ case for rational numbers, using results that we have discovered so far:

Theorem 10.1.34 (Power Rule).

$$\forall n \in \mathbb{Q}, \quad \frac{d}{dx}(x^n) = nx^{n-1}.$$

Proof. Using the previous result and Corollary 10.1.30, we will evaluate $\dfrac{d}{dx}\left(x^{\frac{p}{q}}\right)$ for $p, q \in \mathbb{Z}$ and $q \neq 0$.

$$\begin{aligned}
\frac{d}{dx}\left(x^{\frac{p}{q}}\right) &= \frac{d}{dx}\left(\left(x^{\frac{1}{q}}\right)^p\right) \\
&= p\left(x^{\frac{1}{q}}\right)^{p-1}\left(\frac{1}{q}x^{\frac{1}{q}-1}\right) \\
&= \frac{p}{q}\left(x^{\frac{1}{q}}\right)^{p-1}\left(x^{\frac{1}{q}-1}\right) \\
&= \frac{p}{q}x^{\frac{p}{q}-1}.
\end{aligned}$$
$\square$

Problem 10.1.35. Let $P(x)$ be the polynomial $\sum_{k=0}^{n} a_k x^k$. Find $P'(x)$.

Proof. As a direct result of Theorem 10.1.34, we have

$$\begin{aligned}
P'(x) &= \sum_{k=0}^{n} \frac{d}{dx}(a_k x^k) \\
&= \sum_{k=0}^{n} k a_k x^{k-1}.
\end{aligned}$$
$\square$

Now, notice the similarity among the following:

- $\frac{d}{dx}\left(f(x+c)\right) = f'(x+c)$.

  When we evaluate $\frac{d}{dx}\left(f(x+c)\right)$, we are actually evaluating $\frac{d}{dx}\left(f \circ g(x)\right)$, where $g(x) = x + c$.

- $\frac{d}{dx}\left(f(kx)\right) = kf'(kx)$.

  When we evaluate $\frac{d}{dx}(f(kx))$, we are actually evaluating $\frac{d}{dx}\left(f \circ g(x)\right)$, where $g(x) = kx$.

- $\frac{d}{dx}\left(f(x)^n\right) = nf(x)^{n-1}f'(x)$.

  When we evaluate $\frac{d}{dx}(f(x)^n)$, we are actually evaluating $\frac{d}{dx}\left(g \circ f(x)\right)$, where $g(x) = x^n$.

Considering the *composition* of functions will lead us into our next important property of derivatives:

Theorem 10.1.36 (Chain Rule)
Under appropriate conditions (i.e. functions are well-behaved, continuous; there are no domain or range issues, etc.),
$$\frac{d}{dx}\left(g(f(x))\right) = g'(f(x))f'(x).$$

For convenience of explanations, we will refer to f in this statement as the 'inner function' and g as the 'outside function.'

If we let $y = f(x)$ and $z = g(y)$, then it follows from Theorem 10.1.36 that
$$\frac{dz}{dx} = \frac{dz}{dy}\frac{dy}{dx}.$$

The proof of this theorem lies beyond the scope of this book.

Problem 10.1.37. Use Theorem 10.1.36 to find $\frac{d}{dx}\left(f(x^n)\right)$.

Solution. Note that the inner function is x^n, and the outside function is f. Using Theorem 10.1.36 gives us
$$\frac{d}{dx}\left(f(x^n)\right) = f'(x^n) \cdot \frac{d}{dx}\left(x^n\right) = f'(x^n) \cdot nx^{n-1}. \qquad \square$$

Exercise 10.1.38. Use Theorem 10.1.36 to demonstrate Corollary 10.1.30.

Problem 10.1.39. Let f be a function such that $f'(x) = \frac{1}{\sqrt{1-x^2}}$ for $x \in \left(-\frac{\pi}{2}, \frac{\pi}{2}\right)$. Evaluate $\frac{d}{dx}(f(\sin x))$.

Solution. By Theorem 10.1.36, we have $\frac{d}{dx}(f(\sin x)) = f'(\sin x)\frac{d}{dx}(\sin x) = f'(\sin x)\cos x$. To evaluate $f'(\sin x)$, we simply plug in $\sin x$ into the input of f', i.e. $f'(\sin x) = \frac{1}{\sqrt{1-\sin^2 x}}$. Since $x \in \left(-\frac{\pi}{2}, \frac{\pi}{2}\right)$, we have that $\sqrt{1-\sin^2 x} = \cos x$, such that $f'(\sin x) = \frac{1}{\cos x}$. Thus, $\frac{d}{dx}(f(\sin x)) = \frac{1}{\cos x} \cdot \cos x = \boxed{1}$. $\square$

Problem 10.1.40. Differentiate the following:

1. $\sin^3(x^2)$
2. $\sqrt{1+4\sin x}$
3. $\dfrac{x^2}{1+x^2}$
4. $\tan(x^3+x^2)$
5. $\sqrt[3]{\cos^4\left(\sin^5\left(x^6\right)\right)}$

Solution. You will need to be familiar with applying Theorem 10.1.36:

1. After applying Theorem 10.1.36 twice, we get $\frac{d}{dx}(\sin^3(x^2)) = 3\sin^2(x^2) \cdot \frac{d}{dx}(\sin(x^2)) = 3\sin^2(x^2) \cdot \cos(x^2) \cdot 2x = \boxed{6x\sin^2(x^2)\cos(x^2)}$.

2. Similar to the previous one, $\frac{d}{dx}(\sqrt{1+4\sin x}) = \frac{1}{2}(1+4\sin x)^{-\frac{1}{2}} \cdot \frac{d}{dx}(1+4\sin x) = \frac{1}{2}(1+4\sin x)^{-\frac{1}{2}} \cdot 4\cos x = \boxed{\dfrac{2\cos x}{\sqrt{1+4\sin x}}}$.

3. We use Theorem 10.1.23:
$$\frac{d}{dx}\left(\frac{x^2}{1+x^2}\right) = \frac{(1+x^2)\cdot\frac{d}{dx}(x^2) - x^2\cdot\frac{d}{dx}(1+x^2)}{(1+x^2)^2}$$
$$= \frac{2x(1+x^2) - 2x\cdot x^2}{(1+x^2)^2}$$
$$= \boxed{\dfrac{2x}{(1+x^2)^2}}.$$

4. By Theorem 10.1.36, $\frac{d}{dx}(\tan(x^3+x^2)) = \sec^2(x^3+x^2)\cdot\frac{d}{dx}(x^3+x^2) = \boxed{\sec^2(x^3+x^2)\cdot(3x^2+2x)}$.

5. Repeatedly apply the Theorem 10.1.36:
$$\frac{d}{dx}\left(\sqrt[3]{\cos^4\left(\sin^5\left(x^6\right)\right)}\right) = \frac{4}{3}\cos^{\frac{1}{3}}\left(\sin^5\left(x^6\right)\right)\cdot\frac{d}{dx}\left(\cos\left(\sin^5\left(x^6\right)\right)\right)$$
$$= \frac{4}{3}\cos^{\frac{1}{3}}\left(\sin^5\left(x^6\right)\right)\cdot-\sin\left(\sin^5\left(x^6\right)\right)\cdot\frac{d}{dx}\left(\sin^5\left(x^6\right)\right)$$

$$= \frac{4}{3}\cos^{\frac{1}{3}}\left(\sin^5\left(x^6\right)\right) \cdot -\sin\left(\sin^5\left(x^6\right)\right) \cdot 5\sin^4\left(x^6\right) \cdot \frac{d}{dx}\left(\sin\left(x^6\right)\right)$$

$$= \frac{4}{3}\cos^{\frac{1}{3}}\left(\sin^5\left(x^6\right)\right) \cdot -\sin\left(\sin^5\left(x^6\right)\right) \cdot 5\sin^4\left(x^6\right) \cdot \cos(x^6) \cdot 6x^5$$

$$= \boxed{-40\sin\left(\sin^5\left(x^6\right)\right)\sin^4\left(x^6\right)\cos^{\frac{1}{3}}\left(\sin^5\left(x^6\right)\right)\cos\left(x^6\right)x^5}$$

Generally, this is as far as problems involving the application of Theorem 10.1.36 go. □

Definition 10.1.41. Let $n \in \mathbb{Z}^+$. The **nth derivative** of $f(x)$ is what you get when you take the derivative of the function n times. We write this as $f^{(n)}(x)$ or repeat the $'$ symbol n times, as shown:

$$y = f(x)$$
$$y' = f'(x)$$
$$y'' = f''(x)$$
$$y''' = f'''(x)$$

and so on.

We could also use roman numerals, i.e. we would represent the fourth derivative of $f(x)$ as $f^{\text{IV}}(x)$.

Using Leibniz Notation, we can represent the second derivative of y as

$$y'' = \frac{d}{dx}(y') = \frac{d}{dx}\frac{dy}{dx} = \frac{d^2y}{dx^2}.$$

Problem 10.1.42. Let $y = x^3 + x^2 + x + 1$. Find y', y'', y''', y^{IV}, and $y^{(100)}$.

Solution.

$$y' = 3x^2 + 2x + 1$$
$$y'' = 6x + 2$$
$$y''' = 6$$
$$y^{\text{IV}} = 0$$
$$y^{(100)} = 0$$

□

Exercise 10.1.43. Let $y = x^n$. Find $y^{(n)}$.

Exercise 10.1.44. Let $y = \sin(3x)$. Find $y^{(99)}$.

Exercise 10.1.45. Find $\dfrac{d^{2017}y}{dx^{2017}}(\cos(6x))$.

Exercise 10.1.46. Find $\dfrac{d^2y}{dx^2}(f(x)g(x))$. What does the result resemble?

10.2 Implicit Differentiation

We introduce the concept with an illuminating example.

> **Example 10.2.1**
> Find the slope of the tangent line at the point $(3, 4)$ of the equation $x^2 + y^2 = 25$. What about $(4, -3)$?

Solution. This is a circle of radius 5 centered at the origin, so consider the following diagram:

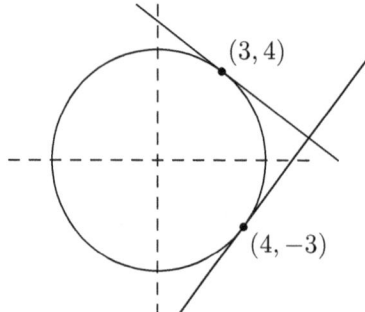

The graph of this clearly fails the vertical line test, implying that y cannot be a function of x (there exist multiple y values given one x value). Therefore, we cannot apply our usual tactics.

One approach is to consider cases separately. First, we could solve for y and get two separate equations: $y = \sqrt{25 - x^2}$ and $y = -\sqrt{25 - x^2}$, then evaluate the derivatives separately for $(3, 4)$, which lies in the top half, and $(4, -3)$ which lies in the bottom half, as shown:

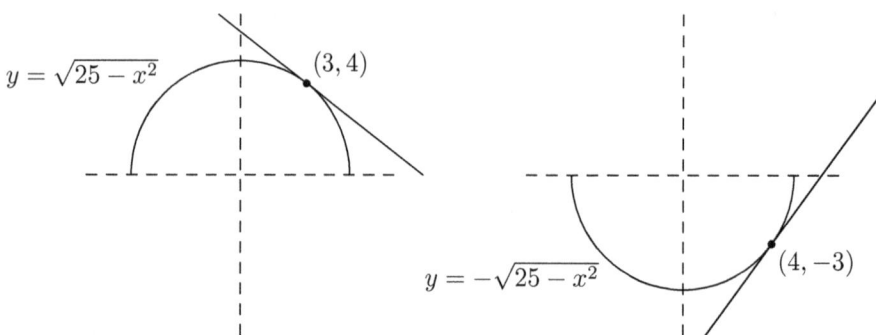

For the former, we get $y' = -\dfrac{x}{\sqrt{25 - x^2}}$, and then we plug in 3 from the point $(3, 4)$ to get the slope $-\dfrac{3}{4}$. For the latter, we get $y' = \dfrac{x}{\sqrt{25 - x^2}}$, and then we plug in 4 to get the slope $\dfrac{4}{3}$.

However, this method was inefficient and time-consuming. It is not even guaranteed that we are able to find an explicit function for y, as the example $x^2 + y^2 = 25$ was conveniently simple. In fact, we can do better.

Note that the relation $x^2 + y^2 = 25$ implies that x and y are *tied* to each other (i.e. share a relation with one another) in some way, but not in a way such that one is an *explicit* function of another. In this situation, we acknowledge that y is an **implicit function** of x, and actually be explicitly written as $y = f(x)$.

We can still find the derivative of an implicit function. As x and y have some sort of relation to each other, we let $y = f(x)$, and the following relation holds:
$$x^2 + f(x)^2 = 25.$$

As this is an identity, we note that their derivatives must also be equal:
$$\frac{d}{dx}\left(x^2 + f(x)^2\right) = \frac{d}{dx}(25).$$

Applying our various rules, we end up with $2x + 2f(x)f'(x) = 0$, i.e.
$$f'(x) = -\frac{x}{f(x)}.$$

If we plug in the point $(3, 4)$, we have that $x = 3$ and $f(3) = 4$, giving our correct answer $-\frac{3}{4}$. If we plug in the point $(4, -3)$, we have that $x = 4$ and $f(4) = -3$, giving our correct answer $\frac{4}{3}$.

To take this a step further, we don't even need to bother with substituting $y = f(x)$. Leibniz notation allows us to take the derivative of both sides of the given equation and solve for $\frac{dy}{dx}$, while treating y as some function of x. For the particular equation $x^2 + y^2 = 25$, we would do the following work:
$$x^2 + y^2 = 25$$
$$\frac{d}{dx}\left(x^2 + y^2\right) = \frac{d}{dx}(25)$$
$$\frac{d}{dx}\left(x^2\right) + \frac{d}{dx}\left(y^2\right) = 0$$
$$2x + \frac{d}{dx}\left(y^2\right) = 0.$$

How would we evaluate $\frac{d}{dx}\left(y^2\right)$? Recall that we are treating y as a function of x, therefore we use Theorem 10.1.36:
$$2x + 2y\frac{d}{dx}(y) = 0.$$

Nothing that $\frac{d}{dx}(y)$ is just $\frac{dy}{dx}$, we conclude that
$$2x + 2y\frac{dy}{dx} = 0$$
$$\frac{dy}{dx} = \boxed{-\frac{x}{y}}.$$

Now, we can simply use this formula by plugging in the appropriate values when given points like $(3, 4)$ and $(4, -3)$, and we can confirm that this formula yields the correct answers as well. □

Remark. The result from Example 10.2.1 is consistent with geometric results, i.e. the tangent line is always perpendicular to the radius at the point of intersection. Consider the following diagram:

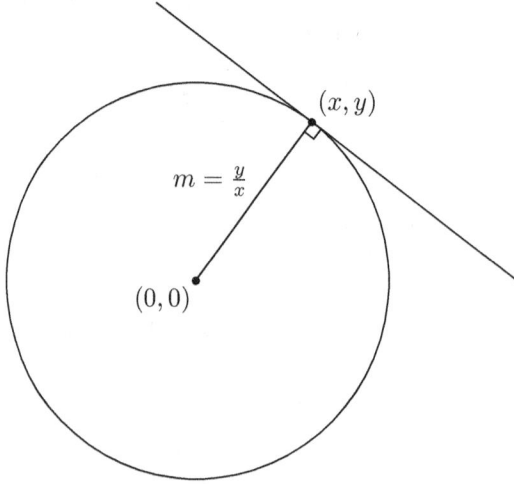

As the slope of the line connecting the radius and the point of intersection is $\frac{y}{x}$, the slope of the tangent line must be $-\frac{x}{y}$, since the tangent is perpendicular.

Problem 10.2.2. Find $\frac{dy}{dx}$ (i.e. y') for $xy^2 + x^2y^3 = 7$.

Solution. As always, we take the derivative of both sides of the equation and then simplify and solve for $\frac{dy}{dx}$. Never forget that we must treat y as a function of x, as $\frac{dy}{dx}$ means that we are evaluating the derivative of y with respect to x. Hence, we must use Theorem 10.1.36 in the process.

$$\frac{dy}{dx}(xy^2 + x^2y^3) = \frac{dy}{dx}(7)$$
$$1 \cdot y^2 + x \cdot 2y \cdot \frac{dy}{dx} + 2x \cdot y^3 + x^2 \cdot 3y^2 \cdot \frac{dy}{dx} = 0$$
$$\frac{dy}{dx} = \boxed{\frac{-y^2 - 2xy^3}{2xy + 3x^2y^2}}.$$
□

Problem 10.2.3. Find $\frac{dy}{dx}$ (i.e. y') for $x^2 + xy + y^2 = 12$.

Solution.

$$\frac{d}{dx}\left(x^2 + xy + y^2\right) = \frac{d}{dx}(12)$$
$$2x + y + x\frac{dy}{dx} + 2y\frac{dy}{dx} = 0$$
$$\frac{dy}{dx} = \boxed{-\frac{2x + y}{x + 2y}}.$$
□

Problem 10.2.4. Find all points on the oblique ellipse from Problem 10.2.3 when the tangent lines are horizontal and vertical, respectively.

Solution. When the tangent line is horizontal, $-\frac{2x+y}{x+2y} = 0$. This simplifies to $y = -2x$, and then we substitute this into the equation $x^2 + xy + y^2 = 12$ to get $x^2 - 2x^2 + 4x^2 = 12$, i.e. $x^2 = 4 \longrightarrow x = \pm 2$, and we get our respective y-values to get the points $\boxed{(2, -4)}$ and $\boxed{(-2, 4)}$.

When the tangent line is vertical, its slope is undefined. The only way $-\frac{2x+y}{x+2y}$ can be undefined is when $x + 2y = 0$, i.e. $y = -\frac{x}{2}$. We plug this into the first equation to get $x^2 - \frac{x^2}{2} + \frac{x^2}{4} = 12$, i.e. $x^2 = 16 \longrightarrow x = \pm 4$, and we solve for our respective y-values to get the points $\boxed{(4, -2)}$ and $\boxed{(-4, 2)}$. $\square$

Problem 10.2.5. Find all horizontal and vertical tangent lines on the oblique ellipse $x^2 - xy + y^2 = 7$.

Solution. First, we find $\frac{dy}{dx}$. Note that

$$\frac{dy}{dx}(x^2 - xy + y^2) = \frac{dy}{dx}(7)$$

$$2x - \left(y + x\frac{dy}{dx}\right) + 2y\frac{dy}{dx} = 0$$

$$2x - y - x\frac{dy}{dx} + 2y\frac{dy}{dx} = 0$$

$$\frac{dy}{dx} = \frac{y - 2x}{2y - x}.$$

The tangent line is horizontal when $-\frac{y-2x}{2y-x} = 0$, or $y = 2x$. We substitute this into the equation $x^2 - xy + y^2 = 7$ to get $x^2 - x(2x) + (2x)^2 = 7$, which simplifies to $x = \pm\sqrt{\frac{7}{3}}$, so our horizontal tangent lines are $y = 2\sqrt{\frac{7}{3}}$ and $y = -2\sqrt{\frac{7}{3}}$.

The tangent line is vertical when its slope is undefined. The only way $-\frac{y-2x}{2y-x}$ can be undefined is when $2y - x = 0$, i.e. $x = 2y$. We plug this into the initial equation to get $(2y)^2 - (2y)y + y^2 = 7$ and obtain $y = \pm\sqrt{\frac{7}{3}}$, so our vertical tangent lines are $x = 2\sqrt{\frac{7}{3}}$ and $x = -2\sqrt{\frac{7}{3}}$. $\square$

Problem 10.2.6. Find $\frac{dy}{dx}$ (i.e. y') for $x\sin(xy^3) + \sin^2(y) = 1$.

Solution. We repeatedly apply Theorem 10.1.36, so you should be familiar with using it.

$$\frac{d}{dx}\left(x\sin(xy^3) + \sin^2(y)\right) = \frac{d}{dx}(1)$$

$$\frac{d}{dx}(x) \cdot \sin(xy^3) + x \cdot \frac{d}{dx}\left(\sin(xy^3)\right) + 2\sin(y) \cdot \frac{d}{dx}\left(\sin(y)\right) = 0$$

$$\sin(xy^3) + x \cdot \cos(xy^3) \cdot \frac{d}{dx}\left(xy^3\right) + 2\sin(y)\cos(y)\frac{dy}{dx} = 0$$

$$\sin(xy^3) + x \cdot \cos(xy^3)\left(y^3 + x \cdot 3y^2\frac{dy}{dx}\right) + 2\sin(y)\cos(y)\frac{dy}{dx} = 0$$

$$\sin(xy^3) + xy^3\cos(xy^3) + 3x^2y^2\cos(xy^3)\frac{dy}{dx} + 2\sin(y)\cos(y)\frac{dy}{dx} = 0$$

$$(3x^2y^2\cos(xy^3) + 2\sin(y)\cos(y))\frac{dy}{dx} = -\left(\sin(xy^3) + xy^3\cos(xy^3)\right)$$

Thus, we have

$$\frac{dy}{dx} = \boxed{-\frac{\sin(xy^3) + xy^3\cos(xy^3)}{3x^2y^2\cos(xy^3) + \sin(2y)}}.$$

□

Problem 10.2.7. Find $\dfrac{dy}{dx}$ for the equation $\sin(xy) = x^2 + y^2$.

Solution.

$$\frac{d}{dx}\left(\sin(xy)\right) = \frac{d}{dx}\left(x^2 + y^2\right)$$

$$\cos(xy)\frac{d}{dx}(xy) = 2x + 2y\frac{dy}{dx}$$

$$\cos(xy)\left(y + x\frac{dy}{dx}\right) = 2x + 2y\frac{dy}{dx}$$

$$y\cos(xy) + x\cos(xy)\frac{dy}{dx} = 2x + 2y\frac{dy}{dx}$$

$$\frac{dy}{dx} = \boxed{\frac{y\cos(xy) - 2x}{2y - x\cos(xy)}}.$$

□

Exercise 10.2.8. Find $\dfrac{dy}{dx}$ for $x^3 + y^3 = 4$.

Exercise 10.2.9. Find $\dfrac{dy}{dx}$ for $y = \sin(3x + 4y)$.

Exercise 10.2.10. Find $\dfrac{dy}{dx}$ for $y = x^2y^3 + x^3y^2$.

Exercise 10.2.11. Find $\dfrac{dy}{dx}$ for $\cos^2 x + \cos^2 y = \cos(2x + 2y)$.

Exercise 10.2.12. Find $\dfrac{dy}{dx}$ for $x = \sqrt{x^2 + y^2}$.

Problem 10.2.13. Find $\dfrac{d^2y}{dx^2}$ for $x^2 + y^2 = 25$.

Solution. From Example 10.2.1, we have found that $\frac{dy}{dx} = -\frac{x}{y}$. Note that $\frac{d^2y}{dx^2} = \frac{d}{dx}\left(\frac{dy}{dx}\right)$, so $\frac{d^2y}{dx^2} = \frac{d}{dx}\left(-\frac{x}{y}\right)$. We then use Theorem 10.1.23 to get

$$\frac{d^2y}{dx^2} = \frac{y \cdot (-1) - (-x)\frac{dy}{dx}}{y^2}$$
$$= \frac{-y - \frac{x^2}{y}}{y^2}$$
$$= \frac{-x^2 - y^2}{y^3}$$
$$= -\frac{x^2 + y^2}{y^3}.$$

We are almost done! At this point, we can simply use the equation we are given, $x^2 + y^2 = 25$, and substitute in the appropriate value, to get $\boxed{\frac{d^2y}{dx^2} = -\frac{25}{y^3}}$. □

Exercise 10.2.14. Find $\frac{d^2y}{dx^2}$ for $x^2 + xy + y^2 = 1$.

10.3 Related Rates

Consider the well-known formula
$$\text{rate} = \frac{\text{distance}}{\text{time}}.$$

Depending on the problem, rate can also refer to speed or velocity.

When applying derivatives to problems about rate, we consider all measurements as functions of time, as such:

$$\underbrace{s(\overbrace{t}^{t\,=\,\text{time}})}_{\text{something you can measure}}$$

Definition 10.3.1. The **average rate of change** of s on the interval $[t_0, t_1]$ is equal to
$$\frac{s(t_1) - s(t_0)}{t_1 - t_0} = \frac{\Delta s}{\Delta t}.$$

Note that this is just the slope of the secant line connecting points $(t_0, s(t_0))$ and $(t_1, s(t_1))$.

We then consider the rate of change at the point t_0.
$$\lim_{t_1 \to t_0} \frac{s(t_1) - s(t_0)}{t_1 - t_0} = s'(t_0).$$

We will appropriately use Δs and Δt to represent the differences $s(t_1) - s(t_0)$ and $t_1 - t_0$, respectively.

Definition 10.3.2. The **instantaneous rate of change** of s at point t is equal to $s'(t)$.

$$\lim_{\Delta t \to 0} \frac{\Delta s}{\Delta t} = \frac{ds}{dt}.$$

This represents the rate of change at a single point in time, t, rather than taking the average of two points.

We now introduce the concept of related rates problems with a series of examples.

> **Example 10.3.3**
> Consider a spherical balloon which is being blown up. Its volume is changing at a constant rate, K. How does the radius of the balloon change? What about its surface area?

Solution. If the volume of the balloon is changing at a constant rate K, then

$$\frac{dV}{dt} = K.$$

We want to find the change in radius, i.e. $\frac{dr}{dt}$.

However, we keep in mind that V and r are functions of time t (always remember that measurements are functions of time!).

For a sphere, we can use the formula of a balloon, i.e.

$$V = \frac{4}{3}\pi r^3.$$

This is our main *relation* between V and r, hence 'related rates.'

We proceed with implicit differentiation; take the derivative of both sides and then use Theorem 10.1.36 on V and r as necessary:

$$\frac{d}{dt}(V) = \frac{d}{dt}\left(\frac{4}{3}\pi r^3\right)$$

$$\frac{dV}{dt} = 4\pi r^2 \frac{dr}{dt}$$

$$\frac{dr}{dt} = \boxed{\frac{K}{4\pi r^2}}.$$

Let S denote the surface area of the balloon. Then the surface area of a sphere is known to be

$$S = 4\pi r^2.$$

We implicitly differentiate to get $\frac{dS}{dt} = \frac{d}{dt}(4\pi r^2)$, which simplifies to $\frac{dS}{dt} = 8\pi r \frac{dr}{dt}$. We have already found that $\frac{dr}{dt} = \frac{K}{4\pi r^2}$, so we plug this back into the equation to get $\frac{dS}{dt} = \boxed{\frac{2K}{r}}$. □

Example 10.3.4

How fast is the top of the ladder falling down the wall when the top is at a height of 12 ft. while the bottom of the ladder is being pushed outward 6 inches per minute?

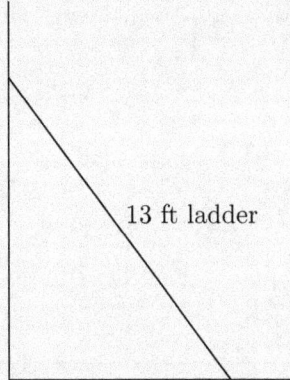

Solution. First, we draw a diagram that simplifies the problem:

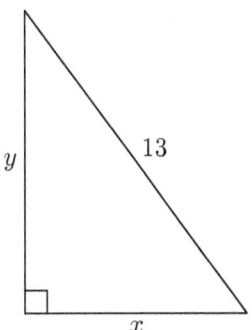

For the changing lengths, we label them with variables x and y.

As it states in the problem, the bottom of the ladder is moving outward at 6 inches per minute. We can interpret this as $\dfrac{dx}{dt} = \dfrac{1}{2}\dfrac{\text{ft.}}{\text{min.}}$.

As we want to find the rate of y falling down, we want $\dfrac{dy}{dt}$ when $y = 12$.

As we have a right triangle, we take advantage of the Pythagorean Theorem: $x^2 + y^2 = 169$. We differentiate both sides to get $\dfrac{d}{dt}\left(x^2 + y^2\right) = (169)$. Remember, we always treat x and y as functions of time, therefore we use the chain rule to get

$$2x\frac{dx}{dt} + 2y\frac{dy}{dt} = 0.$$

We plug in $\dfrac{dx}{dt} = \dfrac{1}{2}$ to get $10 \cdot \dfrac{1}{2} + 24 \cdot \dfrac{dy}{dt} = 0$, which yields $\dfrac{dy}{dt} = -\dfrac{5}{24}$. It is numerically negative, but based on the word problem, we interpret this as the ladder falling down at $\boxed{\dfrac{5 \text{ in.}}{2 \text{ min.}}}$. □

Problem 10.3.5. You are standing 500 ft. away from a tiny rocket. The rocket rises at a rate of 100 feet per second. How fast is its angle of elevation from you changing when the rocket is $500\sqrt{3}$ ft. high?

Solution. Again, we draw a simplified diagram to interpret the problem mathematically:

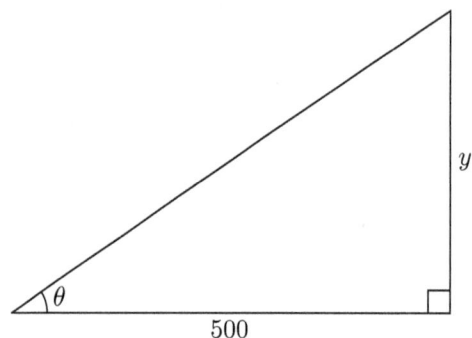

We are given that y increases 100 feet per second, i.e. $\dfrac{dy}{dt} = 100$.

We want the change in θ, which is $\dfrac{d\theta}{dt}$, when $y = 500\sqrt{3}$.

Using this right triangle relationship, we can deduce that $\tan\theta = \dfrac{y}{500}$. We differentiate this to get
$$\sec^2\theta \frac{d\theta}{dt} = \frac{1}{500}\frac{dy}{dt}.$$

Note that $y = 500\sqrt{3}$ when $\theta = \dfrac{\pi}{3}$, i.e. $\sec\theta = 2$. Substituting that and $\dfrac{dy}{dt} = 100$ into the equation, we therefore have $4\dfrac{d\theta}{dt} = \dfrac{1}{500} \cdot 100$, from which we solve to get $\dfrac{d\theta}{dt} = \dfrac{1}{20}$ radian per second, i.e. the angle of elevation is increasing at $\boxed{\dfrac{1 \text{ radian}}{20 \text{ second}}}$. □

Example 10.3.6

Consider a cone-shaped cauldron (with a radius of 50 meters and a height of 100 meters) that holds a potion. The potion leaks out at 2 cubic meters per minute. How fast is the height of the potion changing when the height of the potion in the cauldron is 80 meters?

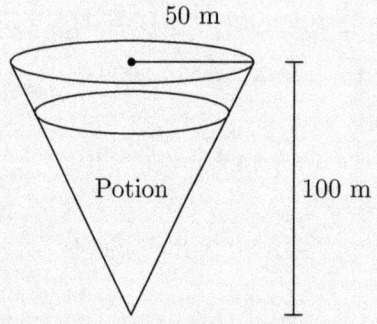

Solution. Let r and h be the radius and height of the cone with the leaking potion. We are given that $\frac{dV}{dt} = -2$. We want $\frac{dh}{dt}$ when $h = 80$.

We use the fact that the cone with the leaking potion is similar to the cone of radius 50 meters and height 100 meters. Since the radius to height ratio is $\frac{50}{100} = \frac{1}{2}$, we know that $\frac{r}{h} = \frac{1}{2}$. Furthermore, we know the volume of the cone is $V = \frac{1}{3}\pi r^2 h$.

We rearrange to get $r = \frac{h}{2}$ and substitute this into the volume formula to get $V = \frac{1}{12}\pi h^3$, then differentiate it to get

$$\frac{dV}{dt} = \frac{1}{4}\pi h^2 \frac{dh}{dt}.$$

We plug in the given $\frac{dV}{dt} = -2$ and $h = 80$ to get that $\frac{dh}{dt} = -\frac{1}{800\pi}$ meters per minute, i.e. the height is decreasing at $\boxed{\frac{1}{800\pi} \text{ meters per minute}}$. $\square$

Problem 10.3.7. Eric is walk along the path of the graph $y = x^2$, as shown:

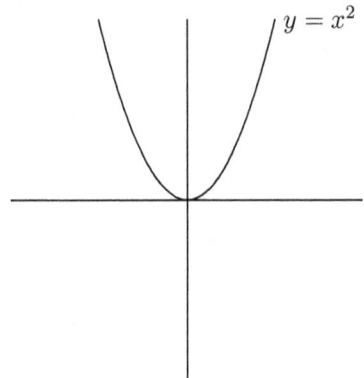

His x-coordinate increases 10 meters per second. How fast is the angle of inclination from the origin changing when his x-coordinate is 3 meters?

Solution. We let x denote Eric's x-coordinate. We are given that his x-coordinate increases 10 meters per second, which means that $\frac{dx}{dt} = 10$. We let θ be the angle of inclination from the origin. We want to find $\frac{d\theta}{dt}$ when $x = 3$.

We note that the angle of inclination from the origin is simply the angle between the line containing the point on $y = x^2$ and the origin, and the x-axis. We also have to consider x, the x-coordinate. These relationships motivate us to draw a simplified diagram, as such:

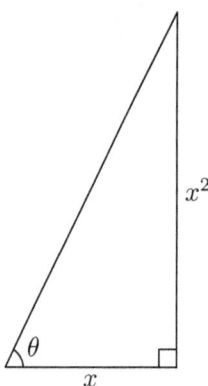

From this right triangle, it becomes apparent that $\tan\theta = x$, and this is our relation. We differentiate both sides with respect to t to get $\sec^2\theta \dfrac{d\theta}{dt} = \dfrac{dx}{dt}$.

How would we find $\sec^2\theta$? We can use the identity $\tan^2\theta + 1 = \sec^2\theta$ (which can be derived from the Pythagorean identity $\sin^2\theta + \cos^2\theta = 1$).

When $x = 3$, then $\tan\theta = 3$, therefore $\sec^2\theta = 3^2 + 1 = 10$, so we have

$$10\frac{d\theta}{dt} = 10.$$

as we are given that $\dfrac{dx}{dt} = 10$. We solve that $\dfrac{d\theta}{dt} = 1$, therefore we can conclude that the angle of inclination from the origin increases at a rate of $\boxed{1 \text{ radian per second}}$. □

Problem 10.3.8. The length of a rectangle increases by 10 cm. per hour. Its width decreases by 2 cm. per hour. When the length is 60 cm. and the width is 80 cm., determine how fast each of the following is changing:

a) Perimeter

b) Area

c) Length of diagonal

Solution. Let the length be l and width be w. The problem statement implies that $\dfrac{dw}{dt} = -2$ and $\dfrac{dl}{dt} = 10$. Let the perimeter, area, and length of diagonal be P, A, and L respectively. Therefore the problem is asking us to find $\dfrac{dP}{dt}, \dfrac{dA}{dt}$, and $\dfrac{dL}{dt}$, when $w = 80$ and $l = 60$.

a) We have our relation $P = 2(l+w)$. We differentiate both sides to get

$$\frac{dP}{dt} = \frac{d}{dt}\left(2(l+w)\right).$$

Applying the chain rule and substituting in the given information gives us

$$\frac{dP}{dt} = 2\left(\frac{dl}{dt} + \frac{dw}{dt}\right) = 2(10-2) = 16.$$

Therefore, the perimeter is increasing at a rate of $\boxed{16 \text{ cm. per hour}}$.

b) Similarly, we have that $A = lw$, and differentiating both sides and simplifying yield:

$$\begin{aligned}
\frac{dA}{dt} &= \frac{d}{dt}(lw) \\
&= \frac{dl}{dt}w + l\frac{dw}{dt} \\
&= 10 \cdot 80 + 60 \cdot -2 \\
&= 680.
\end{aligned}$$

Thus, the area increases at a rate of $\boxed{680 \text{ cm.}^2 \text{ per hour}}$.

c) We can either use the relation $L = \sqrt{l^2 + w^2}$, or $L^2 = l^2 + w^2$, then differentiate accordingly. I will focus on $L = \sqrt{l^2 + w^2}$:

$$\begin{aligned}
\frac{dL}{dt} &= \frac{d}{dt}\left(\sqrt{l^2 + w^2}\right) \\
&= \frac{1}{2\sqrt{l^2 + w^2}} \cdot \frac{d}{dt}(l^2 + w^2) \\
&= \frac{1}{2\sqrt{l^2 + w^2}} \cdot \left(2l\frac{dl}{dt} + 2w\frac{dw}{dt}\right) \\
&= \frac{1}{2\sqrt{60^2 + 80^2}} \cdot (2 \cdot 60 \cdot 10 + 2 \cdot 80 \cdot -2) \\
&= \frac{1}{200}(1200 - 320) \\
&= \frac{22}{5}.
\end{aligned}$$

The length of the diagonal increases at a rate of $\boxed{\frac{22}{5} \text{ cm. per hour}}$. $\square$

Problem 10.3.9. Observe the clock below. The minute hand is 15 cm. and the hour hand is 8 cm. How fast is the distance between the tips of the hour hand and minute hand changing at the given time?

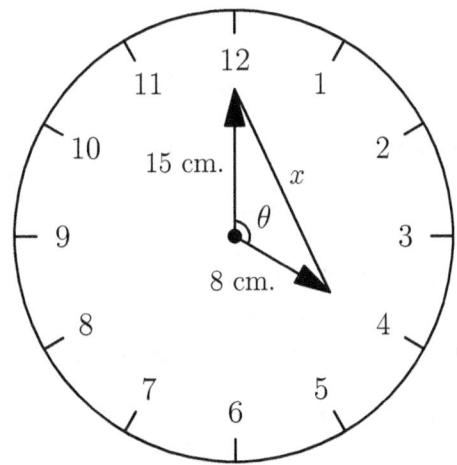

Solution. Let the distance between the tips of the hour hand and minute hand be x, and the angle between the two hands be θ. We intend to use the Law of Cosines on the triangle formed by the side lengths (the two hands of the clock) and the third side, which is x. The problem is asking us to find $\dfrac{dx}{dt}$ when $\theta = \dfrac{2\pi}{3}$, which signifies the time of 4 o'clock.

Starting off with Law of Cosines, we have:

$$x^2 = 15^2 + 8^2 - 2(15)(8)\cos\theta$$
$$= = 225 + 64 - 240\cos\theta$$
$$= 289 - 240\cos\theta.$$

Differentiate both sides to get

$$2x\frac{dx}{dt} = 240\sin\theta\frac{d\theta}{dt}.$$

When $\theta = \dfrac{2\pi}{3}$, $x = \sqrt{289 - 240\cos\left(\dfrac{2\pi}{3}\right)} = \sqrt{409}$.

Now we approach the main question: what is $\dfrac{d\theta}{dt}$? Note that the minute hand is changing at 2π radians per hour, and the hour hand is changing at $\dfrac{\pi}{6}$ radians per hour.

We then consider the context of this problem: as we are approaching 4 o'clock, the quicker minute hand is approaching the slower hour hand, and therefore θ (which is the angle between the two hands) is decreasing, so $\dfrac{d\theta}{dt} = \dfrac{\pi}{6} - 2\pi = -\dfrac{11\pi}{6}$ radians per hour.

If the time was instead 8 o'clock, $\dfrac{d\theta}{dt}$ would instead be $2\pi - \dfrac{\pi}{6} = \dfrac{11\pi}{6}$ radians per hour, as the minute hand would have to keep turning in the clockwise direction until it meets the hour hand (which will have slowly moved two-thirds of the way from the 8 to the 9 markings), and so θ would be increasing in that scenario.

Plugging in our information, we have

$$2\sqrt{409}\frac{dx}{dt} = 240 \cdot \frac{\sqrt{3}}{2} \cdot -\frac{11\pi}{6}.$$

Solving, we get $\dfrac{dx}{dt} = -\dfrac{110\pi\sqrt{3}}{\sqrt{409}}$, so our final answer would be that the distance between the tips of the hour hand and the minute hand is changing at a rate of $\boxed{-\dfrac{110\pi\sqrt{3}}{\sqrt{409}} \text{ cm. per hour}}$. □

10.4 Significance of the Derivative

First, we introduce some definitions to help us with stating the next few theorems.

Definition 10.4.1. $f(x)$ has a **local maximum** at $x = a$ if $\exists \delta > 0$ such that $\forall x \in (a - \delta, a + \delta)$, $f(x) \leq f(a)$.

Definition 10.4.2. $f(x)$ has a **local minimum** at $x = a$ if $\exists \delta > 0$ such that $\forall x \in (a - \delta, a + \delta)$, $f(x) \geq f(a)$.

Definition 10.4.3. An **extremum** refers to either a local maximum or minimum.

> **Theorem 10.4.4**
>
> If the function f has a local extremum at $x = a$, then either $f'(a) = 0$ or $f'(a)$ does not exist.

Proof. Without loss of generality, let there be a local maximum at $x = a$. The proof for the local minimum will be analogous.

Suppose $f'(a)$ exists, so we have
$$f'(a) = \lim_{x \to a} \frac{f(x) - f(a)}{x - a}.$$

This implies that $f'(a) = \lim_{x \to a^+} \frac{f(x) - f(a)}{x - a} = \lim_{x \to a^-} \frac{f(x) - f(a)}{x - a}$. We analyze the one-sided limits separately:

1. If $x \to a^+$, then $x - a > 0$ by assumption. As $x = a$ is a local maximum, $f(x) - f(a) \leq 0$ by Definition 10.4.1, therefore $\frac{f(x) - f(a)}{x - a} \leq 0$, i.e. $\lim_{x \to a^+} \frac{f(x) - f(a)}{x - a} \leq 0$.

2. If $x \to a^-$, then $x - a < 0$ by assumption. Since $f(x) - f(a) \leq 0$ by Definition 10.4.1, we conclude that $\frac{f(x) - f(a)}{x - a} \geq 0$, i.e. $\lim_{x \to a^+} \frac{f(x) - f(a)}{x - a} \geq 0$.

We have that $\lim_{x \to a^+} \frac{f(x) - f(a)}{x - a} \leq 0$ and $\lim_{x \to a^-} \frac{f(x) - f(a)}{x - a} \geq 0$, and since these one-sided limits must be equal, we necessarily have $\lim_{x \to a^+} \frac{f(x) - f(a)}{x - a} = \lim_{x \to a^-} \frac{f(x) - f(a)}{x - a} = 0$. Therefore $f'(a)$ must be 0.

If $f'(a)$ does not exist, then we have a cusp at $(a, f(a))$ which would be the local extremum. □

Definition 10.4.5. The function f has a **critical point** at $x = a$ if $f'(a) = 0$ or $f'(a)$ does not exist.

> **Theorem 10.4.6** (Extreme Value Theorem)
>
> The maximum and minimum values of a continuous function f on $[a, b]$ occur either at the end points or critical points.

The proof of this theorem lies beyond the scope of this book.

The following problems will demonstrate the usefulness of this theorem regarding minimizing and maximizing functions.

Problem 10.4.7. Maximize and minimize $f(x) = x^2 - x$ on $[-4, 4]$.

Solution. Note that $f'(x) = 2x - 1$, so the only critical point is $x = \frac{1}{2}$. Now, we examine all end points and critical points:

$$f(-4) = 20,$$
$$f\left(\frac{1}{2}\right) = -\frac{1}{4},$$
$$f(4) = 12.$$

Therefore, the maximum and minimum values of f on $[-4, 4]$ are $\boxed{20}$ and $\boxed{-\frac{1}{4}}$ respectively. $\square$

Problem 10.4.8. Maximize and minimize $f(x) = x^3 - 3x + 1$ on $[-4, 4]$.

Solution. We have $f'(x) = 3x^2 - 3$, so the critical points are $x = 1, -1$. Now, we examine all end points and critical points:

$$f(-4) = -51,$$
$$f(-1) = -1,$$
$$f(1) = 3,$$
$$f(4) = 53.$$

Therefore, the maximum and minimum values are $\boxed{53}$ and $\boxed{-51}$ respectively. $\square$

Problem 10.4.9. Maximize and minimize $f(x) = \sin 2x$ on $[0, \pi]$.

Solution. Since $f'(x) = 2\cos 2x$, the critical points are $x = \frac{\pi}{4}, \frac{3\pi}{4}$. Now, we examine all end points and critical points:

$$f(0) = 0,$$
$$f\left(\frac{\pi}{4}\right) = 1,$$
$$f\left(\frac{3\pi}{4}\right) = -1,$$
$$f(\pi) = 0.$$

Hence, the maximum and minimum values of f on $[0, \pi]$ are $\boxed{1}$ and $\boxed{-1}$ respectively. $\square$

Problem 10.4.10. Maximize and minimize $f(x) = 4x + \frac{3}{x}$ on $\left[\frac{1}{2}, 5\right]$.

Solution. After we obtain $f'(x) = 4 - \frac{3}{x^2}$, we solve for the critical points: $4 - \frac{3}{x^2} = 0 \to 4x^2 = 3$, which gives us $x = \pm\frac{\sqrt{3}}{2}$. Since we are considering the interval $\left[\frac{1}{2}, 5\right]$, we discard the negative value of x. Now, we examine all end points and critical points:

$$f\left(\frac{1}{2}\right) = 8,$$

$$f\left(\frac{\sqrt{3}}{2}\right) = 4\sqrt{3},$$

$$f(5) = \frac{103}{5}.$$

Thus, the maximum and minimum values of f on $\left[\frac{1}{2}, 5\right]$ are $\boxed{\frac{103}{5}}$ and $\boxed{4\sqrt{3}}$ respectively. $\square$

Problem 10.4.11. Squares of side length x will be cut from each corner of a 10×16 in. cardboard such that the remaining will be folded up into an open box. Find the value of x which will maximize the volume of the box.

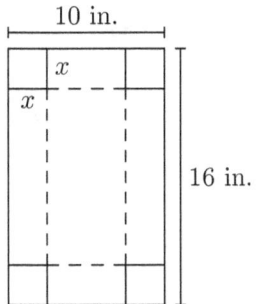

Solution. We are asked to maximize the function $V(x)$ which represents the volume of the resulting box. First, we must consider the constraints of the cardboard. Considering the 10 inch side, the side length of the squares cannot be greater than 5 inches. Therefore we must maximize $V(x)$ over the interval $[0, 5]$. We include the edge cases so we can apply Theorem 10.4.6.

The height of the box is x, and the dimensions of the base of the box would be $10 - 2x$ and $16 - 2x$, since each side is reduced by the 2 squares with side length x cut off from the corners. Therefore, $V(x) = x(16 - 2x)(10 - 2x) = 4x^3 - 52x^2 + 160x$. Then $V'(x) = 12x^2 - 104x + 160 = 4(3x - 20)(x - 2)$, so the critical points are $x = \frac{20}{3}, 2$. However, since $\frac{20}{3}$ is not in the interval $[0, 5]$, we ignore this value, so we only check $x = 0, 2, 5$, as shown:

$$V(0) = 0,$$
$$V(2) = 144,$$
$$V(5) = 0.$$

Therefore, the maximum volume would be $\boxed{144 \text{ in.}^3}$. $\square$

Problem 10.4.12. Consider the following diagram:

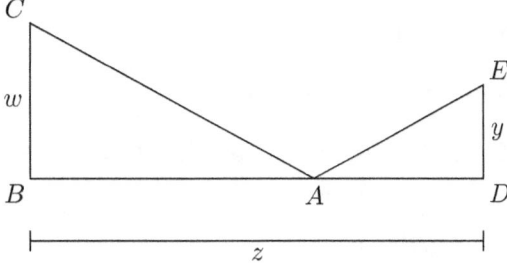

Suppose $\triangle ABC$ and $\triangle ADE$ are right triangles, with a common vertex at A. Let $BC = w$, $DE = y$, and $BD = z$. Locate A such that the sum of the hypotenuses AC and AE is minimal. Then, demonstrate that regardless of the values of w, y, z, the minimum sum of AC and AE occurs when $\angle BAC \cong \angle DAE$.

Solution. For some $x \in (0, z)$, let $BA = z - x$ and $DA = x$, as this problem would not make sense if x was equal to either of the end points (resulting in one triangle disappearing completely). By the Pythagorean Theorem, we have $AC = \sqrt{w^2 + (z-x)^2}$ and $AE = \sqrt{y^2 + x^2}$. Then consider

$$f(x) = \sqrt{y^2 + x^2} + \sqrt{w^2 + (z-x)^2},$$

which will represent the sum of the hypotenuses based on x. We wish to minimize this function over $(0, z)$. Then

$$f'(x) = \frac{x}{\sqrt{x^2 + y^2}} - \frac{z-x}{\sqrt{(z-x)^2 + w^2}}.$$

We solve for the critical point(s):

$$\frac{x}{\sqrt{x^2 + y^2}} - \frac{z-x}{\sqrt{(z-x)^2 + w^2}} = 0$$

$$\frac{x}{\sqrt{x^2 + y^2}} = \frac{z-x}{\sqrt{(z-x)^2 + w^2}}$$

$$\frac{x^2}{x^2 + y^2} = \frac{(z-x)^2}{(z-x)^2 + w^2}$$

$$\frac{x^2 + y^2}{x^2} = \frac{(z-x)^2 + w^2}{(z-x)^2}$$

$$1 + \frac{y^2}{x^2} = 1 + \frac{w^2}{(z-x)^2}$$

$$\frac{y^2}{x^2} = \frac{w^2}{(z-x)^2}$$

$$\frac{y}{x} = \frac{w}{z-x}.$$

We then solve to get $x = \dfrac{yz}{w+y}$ as a critical point. After much simplification, we get

$$f\left(\frac{yz}{w+y}\right) = \sqrt{(w+y)^2 + z^2},$$

which is our minimum sum of the hypotenuses.

In order to achieve this minimal sum, we must have $\dfrac{y}{x} = \dfrac{w}{z-x}$, as established earlier. This implies that $\dfrac{DE}{DA} = \dfrac{BC}{BA}$, so $\triangle ABC \sim \triangle ADE$. Thus, $\angle BAC \cong \angle DAE$. $\square$

Next, we introduce two very significant results.

> **Theorem 10.4.13** (Rolle's Theorem)
>
> If f is continuous on $[a, b]$ and differentiable on (a, b), and $f(a) = f(b)$, then $\exists\, a < c < b$ such that $f'(c) = 0$.

Proof. First, we will assume that f has a maximum and a minimum on $[a, b]$ in the first place. By Theorem 10.4.6, these can occur either at end points or critical points.

If either is at a critical point c where $a < c < b$, then $f'(c) = 0$ since f is differentiable on (a, b). In this case, we are done.

Otherwise, if either is at an end point, f must be constant on $[a, b]$ since $f(a) = f(b)$ and this common value would both be the maximum and the minimum. Thus, we have $f'(c) = 0\ \forall c \in (a, b)$. $\square$

Next, we introduce a well-known theorem that will also not be proved in this chapter.

> **Theorem 10.4.14** (Intermediate Value Theorem)
>
> Let $f(x)$ be continuous on $[a, b]$ and suppose $f(a) < 0 < f(b)$. Then $\exists\, a < c < b$ such that $f(c) = 0$.

Problem 10.4.15. Prove $f(x) = x^3 + x + 1$ has exactly one root.

Proof. Note that $f(-1) = -1$ and $f(0) = 1$, so by Theorem 10.4.14, $\exists\, -1 < a < 0$ such that $f(a) = 0$. Thus, there exists at least one root.

Assume there is another root b. Then $f(a) = f(b) = 0$. Clearly f is continuous and differentiable over the domain, so by Theorem 10.4.13, $\exists\, a < c < b$ such that $f'(c) = 0$. However, $f'(x) = 3x^2 + 1 > 0\ \forall x$, thus $f'(c)$ cannot be 0. We arrive at a contradiction, so a is the one and only root of $f(x)$. $\square$

> **Theorem 10.4.16** (Mean Value Theorem)
>
> If f is continuous on $[a, b]$ and differentiable on (a, b), then $\exists\, a < c < b$ such that
> $$f'(c) = \frac{f(b) - f(a)}{b - a}.$$

Proof. Consider the following function:
$$g(x) = f(x) - \frac{f(b) - f(a)}{b - a}(x - a).$$

Note that $g(a) = f(a)$, and $g(b) = f(b) - (f(b) - f(a)) = f(a)$.

As g is defined by subtracting a linear term from $f(x)$ (so all of its components are continuous and differentiable), g is also continuous on $[a, b]$ and differentiable on (a, b).

Thus, by Theorem 10.4.13, $\exists a < c < b$ such that $g'(c) = 0$, i.e.

$$f'(c) - \frac{f(b) - f(a)}{b - a} = 0,$$

which rearranges to

$$f'(c) = \frac{f(b) - f(a)}{b - a},$$

as desired. □

From this theorem, we have immediate results:

Corollary 10.4.17
If $f'(c) = 0\ \forall c$ on a certain interval, then f is constant on that interval.

Proof. Let a, b be any two points on that interval. Then by Theorem 10.4.16, $\exists a < c < b$ such that

$$f'(c) = \frac{f(b) - f(a)}{b - a} = 0.$$

Thus, $f(a) = f(b)$ for any points a, b on that interval, so f is constant on that interval. □

Corollary 10.4.18
If $f' = g'$ on an interval, then $\exists c \in \mathbb{R}$ such that $f(x) = g(x) + c$.

Proof. Let $h(x) = f(x) - g(x)$. Then $h'(x) = f'(x) - g'(x) = 0$ on an interval. By Corollary 10.4.17, h is constant on that interval, i.e. $h(x) = c$, so $f(x) - g(x) = c$, i.e. $f(x) = g(x) + c$. □

Definition 10.4.19. f is **increasing** on an interval if $\forall a, b$ on the interval, $a < b \to f(a) < f(b)$.

Definition 10.4.20. f is **decreasing** on an interval if $\forall a, b$ on the interval, $a < b \to f(a) > f(b)$.

Corollary 10.4.21
If $f' > 0$ on an interval, f is increasing on that interval. Similarly, if $f' < 0$ on an interval, f is decreasing on that interval.

Proof. For all a, b on the interval, let $a < b$ without loss of generality. By Theorem 10.4.16, $\exists a < c < b$ such that $f'(c) = \frac{f(b) - f(a)}{b - a} > 0$, so $f(b) - f(a) > 0$, i.e. $f(a) < f(b)$. Thus, $\forall a, b$ on the interval, $a < b \to f(a) < f(b)$, so f is increasing.

The proof for the latter statement is analogous. □

From Corollary 10.4.21, we can now determine which parts of a given function are increasing or decreasing, using a method called the **first derivative number line**, which will be demonstrated through the following examples.

Problem 10.4.22. Determine the intervals on which the function $f(x) = x + \dfrac{1}{x}$ is increasing and decreasing.

Solution. We find the first derivative to be $f'(x) = 1 - \dfrac{1}{x^2}$, which has critical points at -1 and 1. We use the first derivative number line, as shown below. Note that the function is undefined at $x = 0$, so we have an open circle at 0 and must consider the intervals on both sides of the open circle. Keep in mind that $x = 0$ is technically not considered a critical point, but we still include it on the first derivative number line anyway.

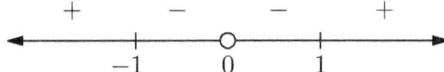

Testing values in between each of the intervals, we find that the function is increasing on $(-\infty, 1]$, decreasing on $[-1, 0)$, decreasing on $(0, 1]$, and increasing on $[1, \infty)$. □

Problem 10.4.23. Determine the intervals on which the following functions are increasing and decreasing.

1. $f(x) = 3x - 7$
2. $f(x) = x^2 - 4x + 3$
3. $f(x) = x^3 - 3x$
4. $f(x) = x^3$

Solution. We proceed with the first derivative number line:

1. Since $f'(x) = 3$, it is always positive, therefore the function is increasing on the entire domain.

2. We get $f'(x) = 2x - 4$, so we get the critical point $x = 2$. Thus, our number line is

   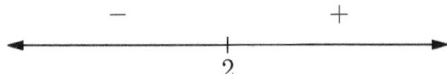

   Thus, f is decreasing on $(-\infty, 2]$ and increasing on $[2, \infty)$.

3. We evaluate $f'(x) = 3x^2 - 3$ to get the critical points $x = \pm 1$, so the number line is

   We conclude that f is increasing on $(-\infty, -1]$, decreasing on $[-1, 1]$, and increasing on $[1, \infty)$.

4. We have $f'(x) = 3x^2$, which is clearly always positive. Thus, f is increasing over the entire domain. □

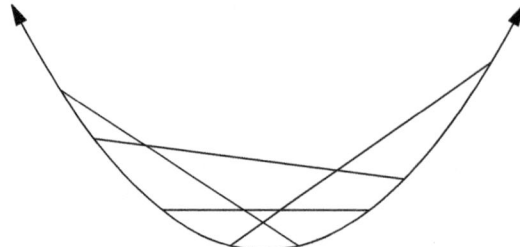

Some secant lines of a convex function

Definition 10.4.24. $f(x)$ is **convex** on an interval if $\forall a, b$ in the interval, the secant line connecting $(a, f(a))$ to $(b, f(b))$ lies above the graph on that part of the interval.

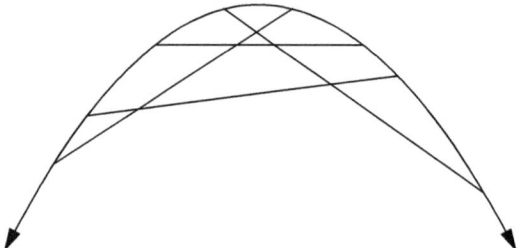

Some secant lines of a concave function

Definition 10.4.25. $f(x)$ is **concave** on an interval if $\forall a, b$ in the interval, the secant line connecting $(a, f(a))$ to $(b, f(b))$ lies below the graph on that part of the interval.

Let two arbitrary points in a convex interval be a, b, and WLOG $a < b$. Consider any point $a < x < b$.

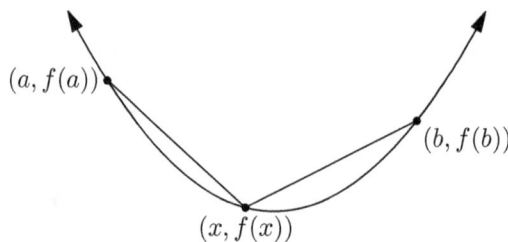

By our definition of convexity, $f(x)$ must be less than the corresponding point on the secant line connecting a and b. We can algebraically represent this as

$$\forall a < x < b, \ f(x) < \frac{f(b) - f(a)}{b - a}(x - a) + f(a),$$

where $y = \dfrac{f(b) - f(a)}{b - a}(x - a) + f(a)$ is the equation of the secant line. We can rearrange this inequality as

$$\forall a < x < b, \ \frac{f(x) - f(a)}{x - a} < \frac{f(b) - f(a)}{b - a},$$

which is another way of representing the condition for convexity.

Definition 10.4.26. For any two points a, b in a convex interval, $\forall a < x < b$, $\dfrac{f(x) - f(a)}{x - a} < \dfrac{f(b) - f(a)}{b - a}$.

Definition 10.4.27. For any two points a, b in a concave interval, $\forall a < x < b$, $\dfrac{f(x) - f(a)}{x - a} > \dfrac{f(b) - f(a)}{b - a}$.

> **Theorem 10.4.28**
> If $f'' > 0$ over an interval, then f is convex on that interval.

Proof. Let a, b be two points on the interval, and WLOG $a < b$. Let x be some point between a and b.

First, note that f' is increasing by Corollary 10.4.21. Applying Theorem 10.4.16 on the intervals (a, x) and (x, b), $\exists c, d$ such that $f'(c) = \dfrac{f(x) - f(a)}{x - a}$ and $f'(d) = \dfrac{f(b) - f(x)}{b - x}$. Since $c < d$ and f' is increasing, we have $f'(c) < f'(d)$, or $\dfrac{f(x) - f(a)}{x - a} < \dfrac{f(b) - f(x)}{b - x}$. Then, note that

$$\frac{f(x) - f(a)}{x - a} < \frac{f(b) - f(x)}{b - x}$$
$$(f(x) - f(a))(b - x) < (f(b) - f(x))(x - a)$$
$$bf(x) - xf(x) - bf(a) + xf(a) < xf(b) - af(b) - xf(x) + af(x)$$
$$bf(x) - bf(a) + xf(a) < xf(b) - af(b) + af(x)$$
$$bf(x) - bf(a) + xf(a) + af(a) < xf(b) - af(b) + af(x) + af(a)$$
$$bf(x) - bf(a) - af(x) + af(a) < xf(b) - af(b) - xf(a) + af(a)$$
$$(b - a)(f(x) - f(a)) < (x - a)(f(b) - f(a))$$
$$\frac{f(x) - f(a)}{x - a} < \frac{f(b) - f(a)}{b - a}.$$

Therefore, the interval between a and b is convex, as desired. $\square$

Exercise 10.4.29. Is the converse of Theorem 10.4.28 true? If not, what would be a counterexample?

> **Theorem 10.4.30**
> If $f'' < 0$ over an interval, then f is concave on that interval.

Proof. The proof is analogous to that of the previous theorem. $\square$

> **Theorem 10.4.31**
> If $f'' > 0$ on an interval, its tangent lines lie below the graph.

Proof. By Corollary 10.4.21, f' is increasing.

Consider a fixed point a on the interval. Then for any arbitrary x on the interval, we have two cases:

- If $x > a$, then by Theorem 10.4.16, $\exists a < b < x$ such that $f'(b) = \dfrac{f(x) - f(a)}{x - a}$. As f' is increasing, we have $f'(a) < f'(b)$, i.e. $f'(a) < \dfrac{f(x) - f(a)}{x - a}$. This rearranges to $f'(a)(x - a) + f(a) < f(x)$, which is what we wanted.

- If $x < a$, then by Theorem 10.4.16, $\exists x < b < a$ such that $f'(b) = \dfrac{f(a) - f(x)}{a - x}$. As f' is increasing, we have $f'(b) < f'(a)$, i.e. $\dfrac{f(a) - f(x)}{a - x} < f'(a)$. This rearranges to $f'(a)(x - a) + f(a) < f(x)$, the same result as before. $\square$

We now have all the tools in calculus to sketch graphs effectively. When given such a task, we consider:

1. The first derivative, which tells us whether f is increasing or decreasing on which intervals.

2. The second derivative, which gives information on the concavity (convex or concave) on which intervals.

3. Any asymptotes; consider values of x that f would be undefined in, the behavior of f as x goes to infinity or negative infinity, or other special values, etc.

4. The function's roots and y-intercept.

> **Example 10.4.32**
> Sketch $f(x) = x^3 - 3x$ and label all relevant points.

Solution. We find that $f'(x) = 3x^2 - 3$, so its critical points are ± 1, and we appropriately set up our first derivative number line and find the signs in each interval:

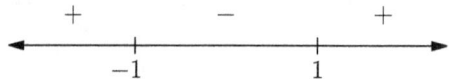

Now we know that f is increasing on $(-\infty, -1]$, decreasing on $[-1, 1]$, and increasing on $[1, \infty)$.

We take the derivative of $f'(x)$ to get that $f''(x) = 6x$. Our only possible point of inflection is 0, so we now set up our second derivative number line and find the signs:

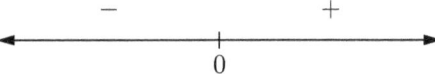

Now we know that f is concave down on $(-\infty, 0]$ and concave up on $[0, \infty)$, and that 0 is a point of inflection.

Lastly, we find the roots, which are $\pm\sqrt{3}$, and it's not hard to see that the graph passes through the origin. It can be noted that since this function is a cubic, there are no asymptotes.

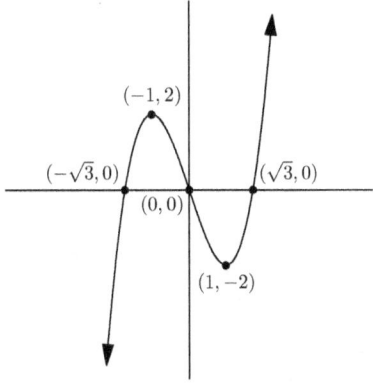

Starting from the left, we begin by sketching a sharply increasing concave curve until we reach -1.

Then, according to the first derivative number line, the function starts decreasing. Keep in mind that the shape is still concave.

Next, the concavity changes at $x = 0$, an inflection point, but the function is still decreasing.

Lastly, we finish the sketch by sharply increasing outwards while maintaining the convex shape. $\square$

Problem 10.4.33. Sketch $y = \dfrac{1}{x^2 + 1}$.

Solution. Its first derivative is $y' = \dfrac{-2x}{(x^2 + 1)^2}$, so its first derivative number line would be:

Next, we find our second derivative:

$$\begin{aligned} y'' &= \frac{-2(x^2+1)^2 + 2x \cdot 2(x^2+1) \cdot 2x}{(x^2+1)^4} \\ &= \frac{-2(x^4 + 2x^2 + 1) + 8x^2(x^2+1)}{(x^2+1)^4} \\ &= \frac{6x^4 + 4x^2 - 2}{(x^2+1)^4} \end{aligned}$$

$$= \frac{2(x^2+1)(3x^2-1)}{(x^2+1)^4}.$$

The possible points of inflection are $\pm\frac{\sqrt{3}}{3}$, and our second derivative number line would be:

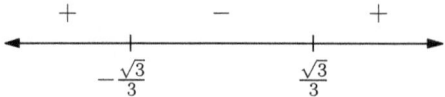

Note that $\lim_{x\to\infty}\frac{1}{x^2+1} = \lim_{x\to-\infty}\frac{1}{x^2+1} = 0$, so $y = 0$ is an asymptote as x goes to negative and positive infinity.

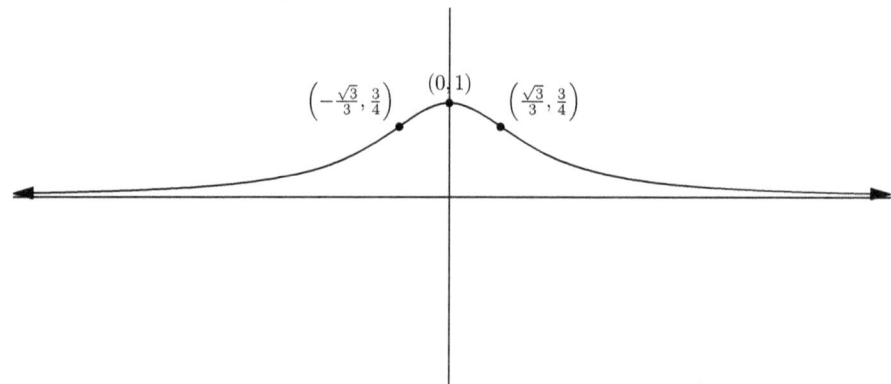

Considering all of this information, we start off our sketch with the line very close to the asymptote $y = 0$, increasing and convex.

When we hit $x = -\frac{\sqrt{3}}{3}$, we have the line become concave down, but still increasing.

When $x = 0$, the graph now is decreasing, so we continue with the line decreasing.

Lastly, when we reach $x = \frac{\sqrt{3}}{3}$, the line becomes concave up again, but continues to decrease and approach the asymptote $y = 0$ as x goes to infinity. $\square$

Exercise 10.4.34. Sketch $y = x^2 - \frac{1}{x}$.

Exercise 10.4.35. Sketch $y = \frac{x}{x^2+1}$.

Problem 10.4.36. Sketch $y = x + \sin x$.

Solution. Note that $y' = 1 + \cos x$. Since $\cos x \in [-1, 1]$, we have $1 + \cos x \geq 0$. Thus, y' is always positive except for critical points ($\ldots -\pi, \pi, 3\pi, \ldots$), indicating that y is always increasing except at the critical points, at which the tangent lines would be horizontal.

Don't be afraid to deal with infinitely many critical points, because there will probably be a recognizable pattern.

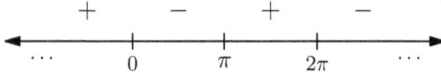

Then, we evaluate the second derivative to be $-\sin x$, so our second derivative number line would be: Notice the pattern that $+$ and $-$ are infinitely alternating. This suggests that the graph switches concavity at every multiple of π.

After considering this information, the sketch should be similar to this:

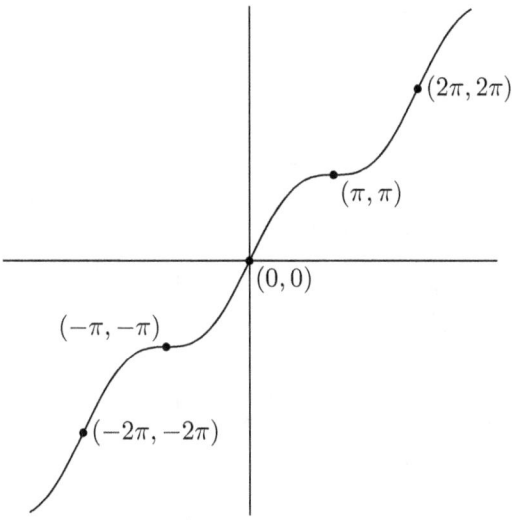

$\square$

Theorem 10.4.37
If $f'(a) = 0$ and $f''(a) > 0$ then f has a local minimum at $x = a$.

Proof. Note that

$$f''(a) = \lim_{h \to 0} \frac{f'(a+h) - f'(a)}{h}$$
$$= \lim_{h \to 0} \frac{f'(a+h)}{h},$$

and we are given that $f''(a) > 0$, so $\lim_{h \to 0} \frac{f'(a+h)}{h} > 0$. If $h > 0$, then $f'(a+h) > 0$, and if $h < 0$, then $f'(a+h) < 0$. There is no need to consider $h = 0$ since we are taking the limit. Thus, if we consider the first derivative number line, then

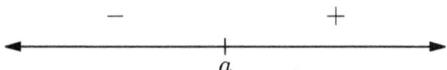

which indicates that $x = a$ is a local minimum. $\square$

Theorem 10.4.38
If $f'(a) = 0$ and $f''(a) < 0$ then f has a local maximum at $x = a$.

Proof. The proof is nearly identical to that of the previous theorem. □

10.5 Optimization

Example 10.5.1
If the radius of the sphere is 12, what is the volume of the largest cylinder that can be inscribed in the sphere?

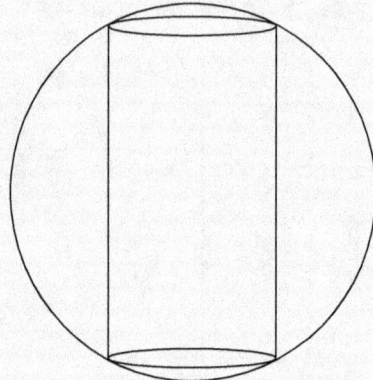

Solution. Let r, h denote the radius and height of the cylinder respectively. Notice that the diagonal of the cylinder is twice the radius of the sphere, and then we can take advantage of a right triangle relationship:

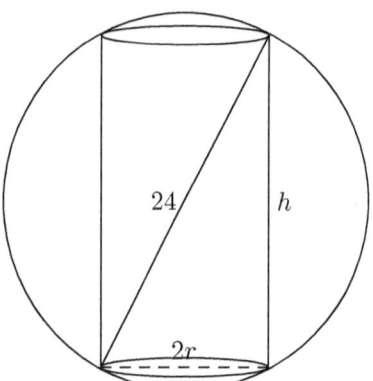

Consider the formula for the volume of a cylinder, $V = \pi r^2 h$. Since there are two variables we cannot find the maximum of this function. However, we have $h^2 + 4r^2 = 576$ from the right triangle, so we solve $r^2 = \dfrac{576 - h^2}{4}$, and substitute this back into the volume formula to get

$$V(h) = \pi \left(\frac{576 - h^2}{4} \right) h = \frac{\pi}{4}(576h - h^3).$$

We differentiate to get $V'(h) = \frac{\pi}{4}(576 - 3h^2)$, from which we get the critical point $h = 8\sqrt{3}$. Instead of going through the trouble to set up a first derivative number line, we can plug it into the second derivative. Note that $V''(h) = -\frac{3\pi}{2}h$ and thus $V''(8\sqrt{3}) < 0$. Then, by Theorem 10.4.38, $h = 8\sqrt{3}$ is a local maximum. However, since $8\sqrt{3}$ is the only critical point, it is therefore the global maximum, so the volume is minimized at $V(8\sqrt{3}) = \boxed{768\pi\sqrt{3}}$. $\square$

Problem 10.5.2. Inside a hemisphere of radius 12 is inscribed a box with a square base. What dimensions will maximize its volume?

Solution. This diagram represents the box with side length s and height h.

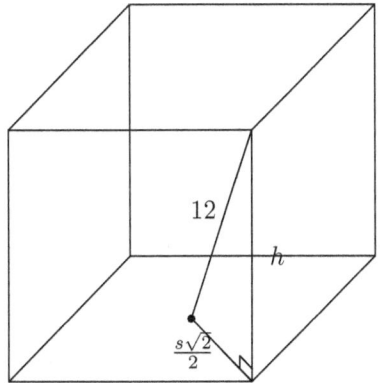

Given that it is inscribed in a hemisphere, the distance between the center of the square base (and the base of the hemisphere) and one of the four upper corners of the box must be the radius of the sphere, or 12. By properties of a square, the distance from the center of the base to one of the four lower corners must be half the diagonal of the square, or $\frac{s\sqrt{2}}{2}$.

Then, we have a right-triangle relationship and we can use the Pythagorean Theorem to relate all three sides: $h^2 + \left(\frac{s\sqrt{2}}{2}\right)^2 = 144$. This rearranges to $2h^2 + s^2 = 288$.

Given that the formula for the volume of this box is $s^2 h$, we solve the prior equation to get $s^2 = 288 - 2h^2$. Thus, we end up with $V(h) = (288 - 2h^2)h = 288h - 2h^3$.

We differentiate to get $V'(h) = -6h^2 + 288$, and the critical points are $h = \pm 4\sqrt{3}$. However, we discard $h = -4\sqrt{3}$ since length cannot be negative.

We confirm that $h = 4\sqrt{3}$ is a global maximum by substituting it into the second derivative (we have $V''(h) = -12h$, so $V''(4\sqrt{3}) < 0$). Thus, the maximum volume of the box is $V(4\sqrt{3}) = \boxed{768\sqrt{3}}$. $\square$

Problem 10.5.3. Consider a circle with a sector cut out, at angle θ. Let this resulting figure have a fixed area A. What values of r and θ will minimize the perimeter of this figure?

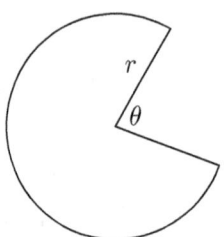

Solution. We are given that the area A is constant, so the area formula $A = \dfrac{2\pi - \theta}{2\pi} \cdot \pi r^2 = \dfrac{2\pi - \theta}{2} r^2$ establishes a relation between r and θ. Since we wish to maximize the perimeter, which is $2r + 2\pi r - r\theta$, we need to find the expression for the perimeter in terms of one variable only, so we could apply our usual optimization techniques.

Note that $A = \dfrac{2\pi - \theta}{2} r^2$ rearranges to $\theta = 2\pi - \dfrac{2A}{r^2}$. We substitute this back into the initial expression for the perimeter to get $P(r) = 2r + 2\pi r - r\left(2\pi - \dfrac{2A}{r^2}\right) = r\left(2 + \dfrac{2A}{r^2}\right) = 2r + \dfrac{2A}{r}$.

We can then evaluate $P'(r) = 2 - \dfrac{2A}{r^2}$, from which we get the critical points $r = \pm\sqrt{A}$. We discard the solution $r = -\sqrt{A}$ as length cannot be negative, so we are left with only $r = \sqrt{A}$. We get $P''(r) = \dfrac{4A}{r^3}$, so $P''(\sqrt{A}) = \dfrac{4}{\sqrt{A}} > 0$, thus we confirm that $\boxed{r = \sqrt{A}}$ and therefore $\boxed{\theta = 2\pi - 2}$ yield the minimum perimeter. $\square$

Problem 10.5.4. Show that if the point (a, b) on the parabola $y = x^2$ is the closest point to $(0, c)$ (given $c > 0$), then the line connecting (a, b) to $(0, c)$ is perpendicular to the tangent at (a, b).

Solution. The distance from (a, b) to $(0, c)$ is $\sqrt{a^2 + (c - b)^2}$. We wish to minimize this distance, but it is sufficient to minimize the expression inside the radical, as this simplifies our work tremendously when differentiating. Note that $b = a^2$, as the point lies on the parabola $y = x^2$.

Consider $D(a) = a^2 + (c - a^2)^2$, so $D'(a) = 2a + 2(c - a^2)(-2a) = 2a(1 - 2c + 2a^2)$. The critical points are $a = 0, \pm\sqrt{\dfrac{2c-1}{2}}$. However, if $c \leq \dfrac{1}{2}$, then $a = 0$ would be the only critical point.

Assume $c > \dfrac{1}{2}$. Then $D''(a) = 2 - 4c + 12a^2$, so $D''\left(\sqrt{\dfrac{2c-1}{2}}\right) = 8c - 4 > 0$, so $a = \sqrt{\dfrac{2c-1}{2}}$ is a local minimum. The same follows for $a = -\sqrt{\dfrac{2c-1}{2}}$.

Thus, the two equally closest points are $\left(\sqrt{\dfrac{2c-1}{2}}, \dfrac{2c-1}{2}\right)$ and $\left(-\sqrt{\dfrac{2c-1}{2}}, \dfrac{2c-1}{2}\right)$. The slope of the line connecting $(0, c)$ and $\left(\sqrt{\dfrac{2c-1}{2}}, \dfrac{2c-1}{2}\right)$ is $\dfrac{\frac{2c-1}{2} - c}{\sqrt{\frac{2c-1}{2}}} = -\dfrac{1}{2\sqrt{\frac{2c-1}{2}}}$.

Note that the derivative of $y = x^2$ is $y' = 2x$, so the slope of the tangent line through $\left(\sqrt{\dfrac{2c-1}{2}}, \dfrac{2c-1}{2}\right)$ is $2\sqrt{\dfrac{2c-1}{2}}$, and we confirm that these slopes are negative reciprocals of each other, so the lines are perpendicular. The same reasoning can be applied to $\left(-\sqrt{\frac{2c-1}{2}}, \frac{2c-1}{2}\right)$ as well. □

Problem 10.5.5. Maximize and minimize $a\sin x + b\cos x$ using calculus. Assume $a, b \neq 0$.

Solution. Let $f(x) = a\sin x + b\cos x$. Then $f'(x) = a\cos x - b\sin x$, so x is a critical point only when $a\cos x = b\sin x$, or $\tan x = \frac{a}{b}$. This indicates that $\sin x = \frac{a}{\sqrt{a^2+b^2}}$ and $\cos x = \frac{b}{\sqrt{a^2+b^2}}$, or $\sin x = -\frac{a}{\sqrt{a^2+b^2}}$ and $\cos x = -\frac{b}{\sqrt{a^2+b^2}}$.

When we substitute the former values into the second derivative, $f''(x) = -a\sin x - b\cos x$, we get $-a \cdot \frac{a}{\sqrt{a^2+b^2}} - b \cdot \frac{b}{\sqrt{a^2+b^2}} = \frac{-(a^2+b^2)}{\sqrt{a^2+b^2}} = -\sqrt{a^2+b^2} < 0$, so there is a local maximum at the value of x that satisfies $\sin x = \frac{a}{\sqrt{a^2+b^2}}$ and $\cos x = \frac{b}{\sqrt{a^2+b^2}}$.

However, notice that $f(x) = -f''(x)$, so we can immediately conclude that $-(-\sqrt{a^2+b^2}) = \sqrt{a^2+b^2}$ is the maximum value.

Substituting in the latter values eventually leads to the similar conclusion that $-\sqrt{a^2+b^2}$ is the minimum value. Note that in solving this problem we did not have to explicitly solve for the critical points to be able to plug them into the second derivative. □

10.6 L'Hôpital's Rule

First, we introduce a precursory theorem to aid us in proving the main formula for this section.

Theorem 10.6.1 (Cauchy Mean Value Theorem)

Suppose f, g are continuous on $[a, b]$ and differentiable on (a, b). Then $\exists\, a < x < b$ such that $(f(b) - f(a))g'(x) = (g(b) - g(a))f'(x)$, or

$$\frac{g'(x)}{f'(x)} = \frac{g(b) - g(a)}{f(b) - f(a)}.$$

Proof. Let $h(x) = (f(b) - f(a))g(x) - (g(b) - g(a))f(x)$. Note that $h(a) = (f(b) - f(a))g(a) - (g(b) - g(a))f(a) = f(b)g(a) - f(a)g(b)$, and $h(b) = (f(b) - f(a))g(b) - (g(b) - g(a))f(b) = f(b)g(a) - f(a)g(b)$, so $h(a) = h(b)$. Therefore, by Theorem 10.4.13, $\exists\, a < x < b$ such that $h'(x) = 0$, i.e. $(f(b) - f(a))g'(x) - (g(b) - g(a))f'(x) = 0$, which rearranges to our desired result. □

Theorem 10.6.2 (L'Hôpital's Rule)

Suppose $\lim\limits_{x \to a} f(x) = \lim\limits_{x \to a} g(x) = 0$ and that $\lim\limits_{x \to a} \frac{g'(x)}{f'(x)}$ exists. Then $\lim\limits_{x \to a} \frac{g(x)}{f(x)} = \lim\limits_{x \to a} \frac{g'(x)}{f'(x)}$.

Proof. Assuming that f and g are differentiable, note that they must also be continuous, by Theorem 10.1.20. Thus, $\lim_{x \to a} f(x) = \lim_{x \to a} g(x) = 0$ indicates that $f(a) = g(a) = 0$.

For some x near a, by Theorem 10.6.1, $\exists b$ between a and x such that

$$\frac{g'(b)}{f'(b)} = \frac{g(x) - g(a)}{f(x) - f(a)} = \frac{g(x)}{f(x)}.$$

Then $\lim_{x \to a} \frac{g(x)}{f(x)} = \lim_{x \to a} \frac{g'(b)}{f'(b)}$. However, note that as x approaches a, b will also approach a since b is between x and a. Thus, $\lim_{x \to a} \frac{g(x)}{f(x)} = \lim_{x \to a} \frac{g'(b)}{f'(b)} = \frac{g'(a)}{f'(a)} = \lim_{x \to a} \frac{g'(x)}{f'(x)}$, as desired. □

Problem 10.6.3. Evaluate $\lim_{x \to 2} \frac{x^2 - 3x + 2}{x^2 - 5x + 6}$ using Theorem 10.6.2.

Solution. When we plug in $x = 2$, the numerator and denominator both become 0, so we can apply Theorem 10.6.2 to get $\lim_{x \to 2} \frac{x^2 - 3x + 2}{x^2 - 5x + 6} = \lim_{x \to 2} \frac{2x - 3}{2x - 5} = \boxed{-1}$. □

Exercise 10.6.4. Evaluate $\lim_{x \to 0} \frac{\sin x}{x}$ and $\lim_{x \to 0} \frac{\sin 3x}{\sin 5x}$ using Theorem 10.6.2.

Problem 10.6.5. Evaluate $\lim_{x \to 0} \frac{1 - \cos 3x}{1 - \cos 5x}$ using Theorem 10.6.2.

Solution. First, we have $\lim_{x \to 0} \frac{1 - \cos 3x}{1 - \cos 5x} = \lim_{x \to 0} \frac{3 \sin 3x}{5 \sin 5x}$, but this still evaluates to 0 when $x = 0$ is plugged in. Therefore, we apply Theorem 10.6.2 again: $\lim_{x \to 0} \frac{3 \sin 3x}{5 \sin 5x} = \lim_{x \to 0} \frac{9 \cos 3x}{25 \cos 5x} = \boxed{\frac{9}{25}}$. □

Problem 10.6.6. Evaluate $\lim_{x \to 2} \frac{x^2 - 5x + 6}{x^2 - 4x + 4}$ using Theorem 10.6.2.

Solution. We have $\lim_{x \to 2} \frac{x^2 - 5x + 6}{x^2 - 4x + 4} = \lim_{x \to 2} \frac{2x - 5}{2x - 4}$, but this limit does not exist.

Therefore, $\lim_{x \to 2} \frac{x^2 - 5x + 6}{x^2 - 4x + 4}$ does not exist. □

Problem 10.6.7. Compute $\lim_{x \to 0} \frac{3x - \sin 3x}{x^3}$.

Solution. We repeatedly apply Theorem 10.6.2:

$$\lim_{x \to 0} \frac{3x - \sin 3x}{x^3} = \lim_{x \to 0} \frac{3 - 3\cos 3x}{3x^2}$$
$$= \lim_{x \to 0} \frac{1 - \cos 3x}{x^2}$$
$$= \lim_{x \to 0} \frac{3 \sin 3x}{2x}$$
$$= \frac{3}{2} \lim_{x \to 0} \frac{\sin 3x}{x}$$

$$= \frac{3}{2} \lim_{x \to 0} 3\cos 3x$$
$$= \boxed{\frac{9}{2}}.$$

Remark. Theorem 10.6.2 extends to $x \to \pm\infty$, $x \to a^+$, and $x \to a^-$.

Theorem 10.6.8

If $\lim_{x \to a} \frac{f'(x)}{g'(x)} = \pm\infty$, then $\lim_{x \to a} \frac{f(x)}{g(x)} = \pm\infty$. The same holds for right-hand and left-hand limits.
In other words, Theorem 10.6.2 extends to $\pm\frac{\infty}{\infty}$.

Proof. Suppose $\lim_{x \to a} f(x) = \lim_{x \to a} g(x) = \infty$. Assuming that $\lim_{x \to a} \frac{f(x)}{g(x)}$ exists, we rearrange the fraction,

$$\lim_{x \to a} \frac{f(x)}{g(x)} = \lim_{x \to a} \frac{\frac{1}{g(x)}}{\frac{1}{f(x)}},$$

and now it is appropriate to apply Theorem 10.6.2, as the numerator and denominator now go to 0. Then we differentiate,

$$\lim_{x \to a} \frac{\frac{1}{g(x)}}{\frac{1}{f(x)}} = \lim_{x \to a} \frac{-\frac{g'(x)}{g(x)^2}}{-\frac{f'(x)}{f(x)^2}} = \lim_{x \to a} \frac{f(x)}{g(x)} \cdot \frac{f(x)}{g(x)} \cdot \frac{g'(x)}{f'(x)}.$$

Thus,

$$\lim_{x \to a} \frac{f(x)}{g(x)} = \lim_{x \to a} \frac{f(x)}{g(x)} \cdot \lim_{x \to a} \frac{f(x)}{g(x)} \cdot \lim_{x \to a} \frac{g'(x)}{f'(x)},$$

so $\lim_{x \to a} \frac{f'(x)}{g'(x)} = \lim_{x \to a} \frac{f(x)}{g(x)}$, which is what we want. □

10.7 Inverses

We begin the section with a warm-up.

Problem 10.7.1. Prove that if f is increasing, then f^{-1} is increasing.

Proof. Looking back to Definition 10.4.19, $\forall a < b \to f(a) \leq f(b)$. Then the contrapositive of this implication must be true, i.e. $f(b) \leq f(a) \to b \leq a$. Let $\widetilde{b} = f(b)$ and $\widetilde{a} = f(a)$. It follows that $f^{-1}(\widetilde{b}) = b$ and $f^{-1}(\widetilde{a}) = a$, so we have $\widetilde{b} \leq \widetilde{a} \to f^{-1}(\widetilde{b}) \leq f^{-1}(\widetilde{a})$. However, note that f and f^{-1} are one-to-one (or else the inverse would not exist), so we can safely get rid of the equal signs to conclude $\widetilde{b} < \widetilde{a} \to f^{-1}(\widetilde{b}) < f^{-1}(\widetilde{a})$. Thus, f^{-1} is increasing. □

> **Theorem 10.7.2**
> Suppose f is continuous and increasing on $[a, b]$. Then f^{-1} is continuous on $[f(a), f(b)]$.

The proof, which will involve the $\varepsilon - \delta$ definition of continuity, is left to the reader.

Now it makes sense to consider the derivative of inverses. We now prove the general formula:

> **Theorem 10.7.3** (Derivative of the Inverse)
> Let f^{-1} denote the inverse function of f. Then,
> $$(f^{-1})'(x) = \frac{1}{f'(f^{-1}(x))}.$$

Proof. Assume f is continuous and one-to-one, or else it would not have an inverse. Let $f^{-1}(x) = y$, or $x = f(y)$. Note that
$$(f^{-1})'(x) = \lim_{h \to 0} \frac{f^{-1}(x+h) - f^{-1}(x)}{h}.$$
When h is small and approaches 0, $f^{-1}(x+h)$ approaches $f^{-1}(x) = y$. So, let $f^{-1}(x+h) = y + \widetilde{h}$, for some small $\widetilde{h}$. This also suggests that $x + h = f(y + \widetilde{h})$. Thus,
$$\lim_{h \to 0} \frac{f^{-1}(x+h) - f^{-1}(x)}{h} = \lim_{h \to 0} \frac{y + \widetilde{h} - y}{h}$$
$$= \lim_{h \to 0} \frac{\widetilde{h}}{x + h - x}$$
$$= \lim_{h \to 0} \frac{\widetilde{h}}{f(y + \widetilde{h}) - f(y)},$$
and note that as h goes to 0, $\widetilde{h}$ must also go to 0, as we keep in mind that $f^{-1}(x) = y$. Thus,
$$\lim_{h \to 0} \frac{\widetilde{h}}{f(y + \widetilde{h}) - f(y)} = \lim_{\widetilde{h} \to 0} \frac{\widetilde{h}}{f(y + \widetilde{h}) - f(y)} = \frac{1}{f'(y)} = \frac{1}{f'(f^{-1}(x))},$$
so $(f^{-1})'(x) = \dfrac{1}{f'(f^{-1}(x))}.$ □

Exercise 10.7.4. Use Theorem 10.1.36 to derive this formula. Why can't this method be a rigorous proof for Theorem 10.7.3?

> **Example 10.7.5**
> Find $\dfrac{d}{dx}(\sin^{-1}(x))$, $\dfrac{d}{dx}(\cos^{-1}(x))$, and $\dfrac{d}{dx}(\tan^{-1}(x))$.

Solution. We can use three methods:

1. We can directly apply the formula from Theorem 10.7.3: $\dfrac{d}{dx}(\sin^{-1}(x)) = \dfrac{1}{\cos(\sin^{-1}(x))} = \boxed{\dfrac{1}{\sqrt{1-x^2}}}$.

2. Alternatively, let $y = \cos^{-1}(x)$, so $\cos y = x$. Then, we can implicitly differentiate,
$$\frac{d}{dx}(\cos y) = \frac{d}{dx}(x) \longleftrightarrow -\sin(y)\frac{dy}{dx} = 1,$$
so $\dfrac{dy}{dx} = -\dfrac{1}{\sin y} = -\dfrac{1}{\sin(\cos^{-1}(x))} = \boxed{-\dfrac{1}{\sqrt{1-x^2}}}$.

3. Lastly, consider the identity $x = \tan(\tan^{-1}(x))$. We implicitly differentiate to get
$$\frac{d}{dx}(x) = \frac{d}{dx}(\tan(\tan^{-1}(x))) \longleftrightarrow 1 = \sec^2(\tan^{-1}(x))\frac{d}{dx}(\tan^{-1}(x)),$$
so $\dfrac{d}{dx}(\tan^{-1}(x)) = \dfrac{1}{\sec^2(\tan^{-1}(x))} = \boxed{\dfrac{1}{x^2+1}}$. $\square$

Exercise 10.7.6. Evaluate the derivatives of the rest of the inverse trigonometric functions.

Exercise 10.7.7. Use Theorem 10.7.3 to prove that $\forall n \in \mathbb{N}$, $\dfrac{d}{dx}(x^{\frac{1}{n}}) = \dfrac{1}{n}x^{\frac{1}{n}-1}$. Then, prove the general case: $\forall r \in \mathbb{Q}$, $\dfrac{d}{dx}(x^r) = rx^{r-1}$.

Exercise 10.7.8. Find $\dfrac{d}{dx}\left(\tan^{-1}\left(x^{\frac{7}{2}}\right)\right)$.

10.8 Parametric and Polar Equations

Theorem 10.8.1 (Derivative of Parametric Equations)
Assume $f(t), g(t)$ are continuous, such that
$$x = f(t),$$
$$y = g(t).$$
If $f'(t) \neq 0$, then $\dfrac{dy}{dx} = \dfrac{g'(t)}{f'(t)}$.

Proof. Since the equations $x = f(t)$, $y = g(t)$ do not necessarily define a function (there could be loops or spirals), we need to impose some restrictions. For some t_0, y is a "function" of x locally near t_0.

We can restrict the parametric equation to a certain domain and range such that it is an actual function. In this area, let $y = h(x)$, so $y = g(t) = h(x) = h(f(t))$. Then we implicitly differentiate to get
$$g'(t) = h'(f(t))f'(t) \longleftrightarrow h'(x) = \frac{g'(t)}{f'(t)},$$

which is what we wanted. □

Exercise 10.8.2. Given the parametric equations $x = \cos\theta$, $y = \sin\theta$ (what is this graph?), find $\dfrac{dy}{dx}$.

Exercise 10.8.3. Given the parametric equations $x = k(\theta - \sin\theta)$, $y = k(1 - \cos\theta)$ (where $k \in \mathbb{R}$ is some constant), find $\dfrac{dy}{dx}$.

Problem 10.8.4. How can we get the slope of $r = f(\theta)$ at some fixed $\theta = \theta_0$?

Solution. Note that $x = r\cos\theta$, $y = r\sin\theta$, so substitute $r = f(\theta)$ to get $x = f(\theta)\cos\theta$ and $y = f(\theta)\sin\theta$. Apply Theorem 10.8.1 to this, and we get

$$\frac{dy}{dx} = \frac{f'(\theta)\sin\theta + f(\theta)\cos\theta}{f'(\theta)\cos\theta - f(\theta)\sin\theta}.$$

Therefore the slope of the tangent line at $\theta = \theta_0$ is $\dfrac{f'(\theta_0)\sin\theta_0 + f(\theta_0)\cos\theta_0}{f'(\theta_0)\cos\theta_0 - f(\theta_0)\sin\theta_0}.$ □

10.9 Review

Problem 10.9.1. Consider $\triangle ABC$ where $AC = 3$, $AB = 4$, and $BC = 5$. Find the possible lengths of DE which will minimize or maximize the perimeter of $\triangle DEF$.

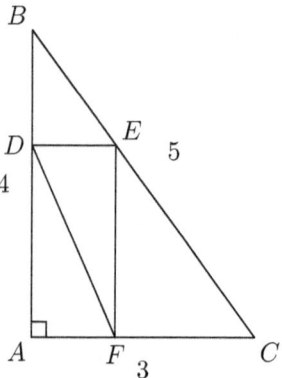

Solution. Let $DE = x$. By AA similarity, $\triangle BDE \sim \triangle BAC$, so $\dfrac{BD}{4} = \dfrac{x}{3}$, which rearranges to $BD = \dfrac{4}{3}x$. Therefore $DA = EF = 4 - \dfrac{4}{3}x$, and $DF = \sqrt{x^2 + \left(4 - \dfrac{4}{3}x\right)^2}$ by the Pythagorean Theorem. We want to optimize the perimeter, so consider the function,

$$f(x) = x + 4 - \frac{4}{3}x + \sqrt{x^2 + \left(4 - \frac{4}{3}x\right)^2}.$$

We differentiate to get

$$f'(x) = -\frac{1}{3} + \frac{\frac{25}{9}x - \frac{16}{3}}{\sqrt{\frac{25}{9}x^2 - \frac{32}{3}x + 16}},$$

and we set this equal to 0 to find the critical points, resulting in the quadratic $25x^2 - 96x + 90 = 0$. Therefore, the critical points are $x = \dfrac{48 - 3\sqrt{6}}{25}$ and $x = \dfrac{48 + 3\sqrt{6}}{25}$, and it is left to the reader to verify which yield local maximums or minimums. □

Exercise 10.9.2. Find $\dfrac{d}{dx}\left(\tan^{-1}\left(\tan^{-1}(x)\right)\right)$ and $\dfrac{d}{dx}\left(x \sin^{-1} x\right)$.

Problem 10.9.3. Let $f(x) = x^3 + x + 1$. Find $(f^{-1})'(31)$.

Solution. By Theorem 10.7.3, $(f^{-1})'(x) = \dfrac{1}{3(f^{-1}(x))^2 + 1}$. To find $(f^{-1})'(31)$, we need to find $f^{-1}(31)$ in order to use the formula. Note that 3 is the only real root that satisfies $x^3 + x + 1 = 31$, so $f^{-1}(31) = 3$, so $(f^{-1})'(31) = \dfrac{1}{3(f^{-1}(31))^2 + 1} = \dfrac{1}{3 \cdot 3^2 + 1} = \boxed{\dfrac{1}{28}}$. □

Problem 10.9.4. Find $\displaystyle\lim_{x \to \frac{\pi}{2}^-} \left(x - \dfrac{\pi}{2}\right) \tan x$, $\displaystyle\lim_{x \to 0} \dfrac{\sin^{-1} x}{\tan^{-1} x}$, and $\displaystyle\lim_{x \to 1} \dfrac{x^{100} - 1}{x^{99} - 1}$.

Solution. We apply Theorem 10.6.2.

1. For the first limit, rewrite $\tan x = \dfrac{\sin x}{\cos x}$ to get

$$\lim_{x \to \frac{\pi}{2}^-} \dfrac{\left(x - \frac{\pi}{2}\right) \sin x}{\cos x},$$

so it is now appropriate to differentiate the numerator and denominator to get

$$\lim_{x \to \frac{\pi}{2}^-} \dfrac{\sin x + (\cos x)\left(x - \frac{\pi}{2}\right)}{-\sin x} = \boxed{-1}.$$

2. Recalling that $\dfrac{d}{dx}(\sin^{-1}(x)) = \dfrac{1}{\sqrt{1 - x^2}}$ and $\dfrac{d}{dx}(\tan^{-1}(x)) = \dfrac{1}{x^2 + 1}$, we have

$$\lim_{x \to 0} \dfrac{\sin^{-1} x}{\tan^{-1} x} = \lim_{x \to 0} \dfrac{\frac{1}{\sqrt{1-x^2}}}{\frac{1}{x^2+1}} = \lim_{x \to 0} \dfrac{x^2 + 1}{\sqrt{1 - x^2}} = \boxed{1}.$$

3. Likewise,

$$\lim_{x \to 1} \dfrac{x^{100} - 1}{x^{99} - 1} = \lim_{x \to 1} \dfrac{100 x^{99}}{99 x^{98}} = \boxed{\dfrac{100}{99}}.$$

□

Problem 10.9.5. Consider a $3 - 4 - 5$ right triangle as shown.

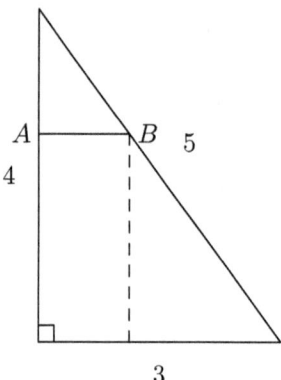

The horizontal segment $\overline{AB}$ moves downward at a rate of $\dfrac{1}{3}$ unit per year. How fast is the length AB changing when $AB = 2$ units?

Solution. Let $AB = y$, and the altitude from AB to base of side length 3 be x. We label the triangle as such:

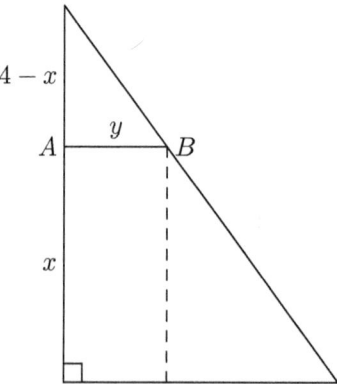

Note that the small right triangle with side lengths $4 - x$ and y is similar to the $3-4-5$ triangle by AA similarity. Thus, $\dfrac{y}{3} = \dfrac{4-x}{4}$, which rearranges to $4y + 3x = 12$.

Interpreting the problem, we are given $\dfrac{dx}{dt} = -\dfrac{1}{3}$, and we want to find $\dfrac{dy}{dt}$ when $y = 2$. We implicitly differentiate the equation above:

$$\frac{d}{dt}(4y + 3x) = \frac{d}{dt}(12) \longleftrightarrow 4\frac{dy}{dt} + 3\frac{dx}{dt} = 0,$$

and we substitute the given values to get $4\dfrac{dy}{dt} + 3\left(-\dfrac{1}{3}\right) = 0$ to get $\dfrac{dy}{dt} = \boxed{\dfrac{1}{4}}$ unit per year. Note that we did not even need to use $y = 2$, because the horizontal segment's rate of change is constant, given the relation $4y + 3x = 12$. □

Problem 10.9.6. A box with a square base and an open top has volume 1000 cubic inches. What dimensions will minimize its surface area?

Solution. Let the side length of the square base be x, and therefore the height of the box will be $\frac{1000}{x^2}$. Then the surface area can be represented by the function

$$f(x) = x^2 + 4 \cdot \frac{1000}{x},$$

and we differentiate to get $f'(x) = 2x - \frac{4000}{x^2}$, yielding the critical point $x = 10\sqrt[3]{2}$. Since $f''(x) = 2 + \frac{8000}{x^3}$, $f''(10\sqrt[3]{2}) > 0$, so $x = 10\sqrt[3]{2}$ yields the minimum surface area. Thus, the dimensions of the box will be $\boxed{10\sqrt[3]{2} \times 10\sqrt[3]{2} \times 5\sqrt[3]{2}}$. □

Problem 10.9.7. A boy flies a kite at the height of 300 feet. The wind carries the kite horizontally from the boy at a rate of 25 feet per second. How fast must he let out the string when the kite is 500 feet away from him?

Solution. We interpret the problem using a right triangle.

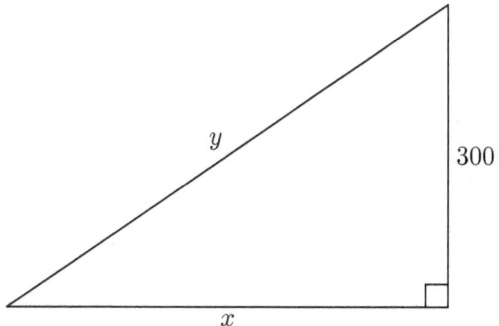

We are given $\frac{dx}{dt} = 25$, and we want to find $\frac{dy}{dt}$ when $y = 500$. By the Pythagorean Theorem, $300^2 + x^2 = y^2$, so we implicitly differentiate it to get $2x\frac{dx}{dt} = 2y\frac{dy}{dt}$. Then we substitute in values: $400 \cdot 25 = 500\frac{dy}{dt}$, i.e. $\frac{dy}{dt} = \boxed{20}$ feet per second. □

www.ingramcontent.com/pod-product-compliance
Lightning Source LLC
Chambersburg PA
CBHW081149290426
44108CB00018B/2486